Empirical Theology in Texts and Tables

Empirical Studies in Theology

Editor

Johannes A. van der Ven

VOLUME 17

Empirical Theology in Texts and Tables

Qualitative, Quantitative and Comparative Perspectives

Edited by

Leslie J. Francis
Mandy Robbins
Jeff Astley

BRILL

LEIDEN • BOSTON
2009

This book is printed on acid-free paper.

Library of Congress Cataloging-in-Publication Data

Empirical theology in texts and tables : qualitative, quantitative, and comparative perspectives / edited by Leslie J. Francis, Mandy Robbins, Jeff Astley.
   p. cm. — (Empirical studies in theology, ISSN 1389-1189 ; v. 17)
  Includes index.
  ISBN 978-90-04-16888-6 (hardback : alk. paper)
  1. Empirical theology. I. Francis, Leslie J. II. Robbins, Mandy. III. Astley, Jeff.
IV. Title. V. Series.

  BT83.53.E58 2009
  230'.046—dc22

2008045951

ISSN 1389-1189
ISBN 978 90 04 16888 6

Copyright 2009 by Koninklijke Brill NV, Leiden, The Netherlands.
Koninklijke Brill NV incorporates the imprints Brill, Hotei Publishing,
IDC Publishers, Martinus Nijhoff Publishers and VSP.

All rights reserved. No part of this publication may be reproduced, translated, stored in a retrieval system, or transmitted in any form or by any means, electronic, mechanical, photocopying, recording or otherwise, without prior written permission from the publisher.

Authorization to photocopy items for internal or personal use is granted by Koninklijke Brill NV provided that the appropriate fees are paid directly to The Copyright Clearance Center, 222 Rosewood Drive, Suite 910, Danvers, MA 01923, USA.
Fees are subject to change.

PRINTED IN THE NETHERLANDS

Dedicated to the memory of
The Right Reverend Anthony Crockett
(August 1945–June 2008)
The 80th Bishop of Bangor

CONTENTS

Preface xi
Introduction xiii

PART ONE

THEORETICAL PERSPECTIVES

Chapter One   Establishing Truth from Participation and
Distanciation in Empirical Theology 3
Jaco S. Dreyer

Chapter Two   Truth and Method in Empirical Theology 27
Hans Schilderman

Chapter Three   Religious Identity in Comparative
Research 41
Johannes A. van der Ven

Chapter Four   Epistemological Reflections on the
Connection between Ideas and Data in Empirical
Research into Religion 73
Chris A.M. Hermans

Chapter Five   Towards a Generic Model of Religious
Ritual 101
Hans Schilderman

Chapter Six   Comparative Empirical Research in Religion:
Conceptual and Operational Challenges within Empirical
Theology 127
Leslie J. Francis

viii

CONTENTS

PART TWO

QUALITATIVE PERSPECTIVES

Chapter Seven   Adolescents' Views of Denominational
Identities and of Dialogical Religious Education: An
Empirical Study from Germany 155
Friedrich Schweitzer

Chapter Eight   Ordinary Soteriology: A Qualitative Study 177
Ann Christie and Jeff Astley

Chapter Nine   Narrative Competence and the Meaning of
Life: Measuring the Quality of Life Stories in a Project on
Care for the Elderly 197
Thijs Tromp and R. Ruard Ganzevoort

Chapter Ten   The Theological Case for Christian Schools in
England and Wales: A Qualitative Perspective Listening to
Female Alumnae 217
Tania ap Siôn, Leslie J. Francis and Sylvia Baker

PART THREE

QUANTITATIVE PERSPECTIVES

Chapter Eleven   Faith or Morality? 'Theological Sediments'
Depending on the Centrality, Content, and Social Context
of Personal Religious Construct Systems 249
Stefan Huber and Constantin Klein

Chapter Twelve   Socialisation and Empirical-Theological
Models of the Trinity: A Study among Theology Students
in the United Kingdom 269
Mark J. Cartledge

Chapter Thirteen   Religious Socialisation in the Family:
A Multi-dimensional and Multi-level Perspective 291
Sabine Zehnder Grob, Christoph Morgenthaler and Christoph Käppler

CONTENTS ix

Chapter Fourteen   Apostolic Networks in Britain: Personality
and Praxis 321
William K. Kay

Chapter Fifteen   Xenophobia and Religious Pluralism: An
Empirical Study among Youth in Germany 339
Hans-Georg Ziebertz and Ulrich Riegel

Chapter Sixteen   A Church Divided by Theology and
Practice: The Case of the Admission of Children to
Communion in the Church in Wales 365
Keith Littler

List of Contributors 387

Name index 393
Subject index 401

PREFACE

This collection of essays developed from the third conference of the International Society of Empirical Research in Theology, convened during April 2006 in Bangor, North Wales. This third conference, following in the footsteps of the two earlier conferences in Nijmegen (2002) and in Bielefeld (2004), played its part in establishing the Society as a significant international forum in drawing together empirical theologians from North America and South Africa as well as from a number of European countries.

The theme of the third conference in Bangor was designed to display and to assess the strengths of empirical theology across the three domains of theoretical elaboration, qualitative methodologies and quantitative methodologies. It is the theme of the conference that has given rise to the title and to the structure of the present volume.

We are grateful to colleagues in Bangor who helped us to organise the conference and to extend a warm welcome to our visitors to Wales from other nations: Dr Robert Pope (now Head of Theology and Religious Studies) who shaped the conference with us; Professor Densil Morgan (then Head of the College of Arts and Humanities) who gave an official welcome on behalf of the University of Bangor; and the research group in the Welsh National Centre for Religious Education who ensured the smooth running and efficient oversight of the event. We also wish to record our appreciation to the British Academy for a conference grant, to Max Wood for the subject-index, and to Diane Drayson for proof reading.

A particular joy of the conference was provided by the presence and support of the Right Reverend Anthony Crockett, Bishop of Bangor, who demonstrated his support for empirical theology and his commitment for a strong alliance between the Church and the Academy. Bishop Anthony died 30 June 2008, aged 62, following a long and bravely-faced struggle with cancer. We are pleased to dedicate this volume in his memory.

Leslie J. Francis
Mandy Robbins
Jeff Astley

INTRODUCTION

Properly conceived, the work of theologians unites the agenda of the Church and of the Academy. Theologians concern themselves with talk about God and with ways in which talk about God engages with all aspects of human life and the created order. For the Church the concerns of theologians need to be connected with the religious tradition and with practical activities like ministry, liturgy, mission, service and religious education. For the Academy the concerns of theologians need to be connected with the criteria of academic objectivity, with open scrutiny and with academic activities pursued within other disciplines and faculties.

Properly conceived, theology remains an evolving and developing discipline. The subject matter of theology cannot remain static, but evolves to embrace new insights and new data emerging within the Church relevant to the understanding and discussion of God. The academic methods and tools applied to theological debate cannot remain static, but evolve to embrace new insights and new approaches emerging elsewhere within the Academy relevant to the critique, analysis and evaluation of theological materials.

It is for such reasons that over the past three decades empirical theologians have begun to take their place alongside other established members of the theology faculty within the Academy and alongside other theologians within the Church. Empirical theologians are concerned with distinctive categories of theologically-relevant data and with distinctive academic methodologies relevant to examining these data. Important landmarks in the developing and maturing self-awareness and identity of empirical theology were provided by the launch of the *Journal of Empirical Theology* (ISERT) in the late 1980s and by the inception of the International Society of Empirical Research in Theology at the beginning of the twenty-first century. Professor Johannes van der Ven was crucial to both initiatives.

In essence empirical theology is concerned with those kinds of theological data that are properly amenable to empirical investigation. While many theological notions, say those concerning an invisible and immortal transcendent deity, rightly elude empirical investigation, many other theological notions, say those concerning the relationship between

God and the created order, rightly demand empirical investigation. For example, Christian doctrines of creation pose interesting theological questions about the nature of God and about the nature of humankind that may be illuminated by empirical investigation, especially in light of the assertion that both women and men are created in the divine image.

The key insight brought by Hans van der Ven to theology is that theologians may properly progress their task by adopting perspectives and tools fashioned in the social sciences. For Van der Ven in his earlier writings it was crucial to establish that the activity was properly theological: in empirical theology theologians are encouraged to engage in an intra-disciplinary activity according to which the methods of the social sciences are appropriated within the theological academy. According to this account there is no hint of social scientists studying and scrutinising theological data from, as it were, outside the discipline itself. A somewhat different emphasis has been advanced by Leslie J. Francis who maintains that empirical theologians need to approach their activity not only in an intra-disciplinary perspective, but also in an inter-disciplinary perspective. According to this account, empirical theologians need to subject their work to scrutiny not only by other theologians, but also by other social scientists working outside the theological academy.

Against this background, the aim of the present volume is to showcase empirical theologians at work, and to do so by displaying 16 of the wide-ranging contributions offered to the conference of the International Society for Empirical Theology at Bangor University, Wales, during 2006. These 16 contributions have been organised to reflect not only the theme of that conference, but more fundamentally to highlight three key tasks by means of which the scientific capacity of empirical theology is being enhanced: theoretical perspectives, involving conceptual clarification, reflection on methodology, model building, and integration of data and theory; application of qualitative research methods to elucidate theologically relevant problems; and application of quantitative research methods to elucidate theologically relevant problems.

In the first section, on theoretical perspectives, Jaco S. Dreyer discusses establishing truth from participation and distanciation in empirical theology, and Hans Schilderman discusses further the problem of truth and method in empirical theology. Johannes A. van der Ven sets out to address two questions: what does the religious identity of individuals and communities entail, and how can this be measured? Chris Hermans provides epistemological reflections on the connection between ideas and data in empirical research in religion. Hans Schilderman argues that ritual is one of the most characteristic and manifest of religious phenomena and advances ideas regarding a generic model of religious ritual as the basis for empirical research. Leslie J. Francis discusses conceptual and operational challenges within empirical theology relevant to establishing comparative empirical research in religion.

In the second section on qualitative perspectives, Friedrich Schweitzer presents an empirical study from Germany concerning adolescents' views of denominational identities and of dialogical religious education. Ann Christie and Jeff Astley draw on Astley's notion of ordinary theology to describe and to discuss ways in which theologically-untrained adults in England express their understanding of soteriology. Thijs Tromp and R. Ruard Ganzevoort discuss findings from narrative autobiographical life-review interviews conducted among elderly participants aged eighty or over, and clarify the implicit theological dimensions of these narratives. Tania ap Siôn, Leslie J. Francis and Sylvia Baker discuss the theological case for independent Christian schools in England and Wales and set this theoretical perspective against the experiences of female alumnae from such schools.

In the third section on quantitative perspectives, Stefan Huber and Constantin Klein examine the degree to which traditional denominational doctrines influence the personal beliefs of Christians today. Mark J. Cartledge examines the impact of specific socialisation factors on certain Trinitarian beliefs among theology students training at residential theological institutions in the United Kingdom representing Ecumenical, Evangelical, Pentecostal and Adventist educational contexts. Sabine Zehnder Grob, Christoph Morgenthaler and Christoph Käppler report a multi-dimensional and multi-level perspective on religious socialisation in the family. William K. Kay examines the usefulness of personality theory in a study among church leaders within Apostolic Networks in Britain. Hans-Geog Ziebertz and Ulrich Riegel examine xenophobia and religious pluralism among young people in Germany. Keith Littler illustrates current divisions in theology and practice within the Anglican Church in Wales through a study focused on diversity of clergy views on the admission of children to communion.

PART ONE

THEORETICAL PERSPECTIVES

CHAPTER ONE

ESTABLISHING TRUTH FROM PARTICIPATION AND DISTANCIATION IN EMPIRICAL THEOLOGY

Jaco S. Dreyer

SUMMARY

This chapter discusses the methodological opposition between qualitative and quantitative research in empirical theology. It is argued, on the basis of Ricoeur's hermeneutical theory of the dialectic of participation and distanciation, that a broad hermeneutical understanding of participation and distanciation implies that all research, whether quantitative or qualitative, is characterised by both participation and distanciation. It is further argued that the dialectical tension between participation and distanciation should be maintained in all empirical research endeavours. This tension could be maintained by developing reflexivity in the threefold sense that Bourdieu uses the term: by reflecting on our own prejudices, by being part of scientific communities that help us to reflect on our prejudices, and by reflecting on our scientific practices themselves. This all forms part of learning the craft of research and developing a scientific habitus.

INTRODUCTION

The title of this chapter, *Establishing truth from participation and distanciation in empirical theology*, is certain to raise a few eyebrows. *Establishing truth?* Despite the political confidence in 'establishing truth', as evidenced by the many truth commissions that are set up in different parts of the world to establish truth with regard to human rights and other abuses, the search for truth—and even the idea of truth—has been discredited in philosophical and postmodern circles. Posel concludes in this regard: 'From a philosophical point of view, the credibility of truth has been seriously destabilised' (Posel, 2004: 3). Should we not abandon the idea of truth as an illusion?

I suggest that we do not give an affirmative answer to this question too hastily. The overriding goal of scientific inquiry is often stated as the search for 'truth' or 'truthful knowledge' (Mouton, 1996, 2001).

However, we all know that this epistemic imperative, this endless search for truthful knowledge, has proved to be an elusive ideal (Mouton, 1996). The positivist idea that we can secure truth or truthful knowledge through methodological rules (Frisby, 1976) has been discredited. This has led some to write that we should abandon the idea of truth or truthful knowledge. Heron (1996) argues, however, that it is an unnecessary mistake to abandon a concept such as truth just because it has been misappropriated and abused by positivists and others. He writes that to abandon concepts such as validity and truth is 'to sell the pass to the enemy who blocks it and controls it. Such concepts are too central to the integrity of everyday human life and discourse to be abandoned by the research community in the cause of postmodernism and poststructuralism' (Heron, 1996: 163). I agree with these authors that the concept of truth (or truthful knowledge) is a contested one, but one that can still be employed as long as we use it as a regulative ideal (Mouton, 1996), stripped of any connections with objectivism or objective facts (Heron, 1996), and always acknowledging that our efforts to establish truth, our 'truth-claims', are inseparable from the ontological, epistemological and methodological choices that we make in the research process.

The point of departure of this chapter is that the common, but mistaken, epistemological opposition between establishing truth *from participation* and *from distanciation* is related to the methodological opposition between qualitative and quantitative research. By this I mean that establishing truth from distanciation is commonly related to quantitative research, with its ideals of objectivity, control of researcher subjectivity and quantification (Dreyer, 1998). Similarly, and in opposition to quantitative research, establishing truth from participation is usually related to qualitative research, with an emphasis on the researcher's participation in the lifeworld of the participants.

Is this dualism between quantitative research, with its normative ideal of establishing truth from a distance, and qualitative research, with its normative ideal of establishing truth from participation, still relevant in empirical theology today? The methodological conflict between quantitative and qualitative research seems to have been resolved a long time ago. Van der Ven wrote more than a decade ago: 'The emphasis must be placed on the complementarity of qualitative and quantitative empirical methodology, which correspond to the participant and the observer perspectives respectively' (Van der Ven, 1993: 106; see Ziebertz, 1993). This conclusion, however, seems to be a little premature. Many researchers in the quantitative tradition still regard qualitative research as subordinate to the quantitative approach (Saludadez and Garcia, 2001), because qualitative research cannot match the precision, prediction capability and objectivity of quantitative research. On the other hand, many qualitative researchers regard quantitative research as unsuitable in the human and social sciences because of the generalisations and quantification (measurement) inherent in this approach. Although many researchers have a fairly pragmatic view of the two approaches, and regard them as complementary, some postmodern-inspired, narrative and participatory research approaches regard quantitative research with considerable disdain and even contempt. The new fashion in empirical theological research seems to be participatory research approaches. Although some would tolerate quantitative research, others say that this research, with its ideals of objectivity and the elimination of the researcher's bias, cannot be used at all. Instead, they argue for the use of qualitative research, and more specifically narrative and participatory research. In terms of the title of this chapter we can say that, for them, truth can only be established from participation, and that implies qualitative research.

The opposition between quantitative and qualitative research thus seems to be one of the enduring dualisms in social scientific, and also empirical theological, research. Bourdieu describes the persistent character of these dualisms well when he writes:

> There are antinomies…which are devoid of any meaning and have been destroyed a thousand times in the course of scientific history. But they can easily be brought back to life and—this is very important—those who revive them gain great profits from doing so. In other words, these antinomies are enormously costly to demolish because they are inscribed in social reality. Thus, the social sciences have a Sisyphean task ahead of them: they must always break, start their work of demonstration and argumentation anew, knowing that all of this work may be destroyed in a flash at any moment by being forced back into these false antinomies (Bourdieu in Bourdieu and Wacquant, 1992: 179).

In this chapter I will take up this Sisyphean task of trying to overcome the opposition between quantitative and qualitative research that has now been revived by certain protagonists of narrative and participatory research approaches. I take as a point of departure that this dualism between qualitative and quantitative research can only be demolished if we undermine the idea that they represent different methodological approaches to truth: that quantitative research implies establishing truth from distanciation and qualitative research establishing truth from participation, and that one of these is a 'better' way, or even the only way, towards truth in empirical theology. My inspiration for this task comes from Ricoeur's hermeneutical theory, and I shall first explore his views on participation and distanciation. This is followed by a reflection on some methodological implications of Ricoeur's theory. In this section I will argue that participation and distanciation form part of every research endeavour, whether we use a quantitative or a qualitative research approach. This implies that truth is established in quantitative and qualitative research from participation and distanciation. It is not, however, sufficient to conclude that truth in all empirical theological research is established from both participation and distanciation. According to Ricoeur's theory, we also have to attend to the *dialectical tension* between participation and distanciation. The methodological implications of this dialectical tension will be explored in the last section. I will argue that it is part of the craft of empirical theology to deal with the dialectical tension between participation and distanciation in all our empirical theological research endeavours.

Participation and Distanciation: A Hermeneutical Perspective[1]

How can we move beyond the dualism between qualitative and quantitative research, with its associated oppositions between insider and outsider, researcher and the researched, observer and the observed, subjectivity and objectivity, understanding and explanation, truth from participation and truth from distanciation? It is at this point that I would like to introduce the theoretical ideas of Paul Ricoeur, a master of dialectical thinking. "Where others see only dichotomies, Ricoeur sees dialectics," writes Charles E. Reagan (1996: 99). It is through the employment of his hermeneutic dialectic that Ricoeur has contributed enormously to the methodological debate in the human and social sciences (Ihde, 1995). His contribution to overcoming the epistemological dualism between understanding and explanation, and his application of the model of a text to meaningful action are two examples of his outstanding methodological contributions (Reagan, 1996).

---

[1] This section is based on an earlier article (Dreyer, 1998).

Can Ricoeur also help us to move beyond the dualism of qualitative and quantitative research as different ways of establishing truth? I would like to suggest that his views on the dialectic between participation (or belonging) and distanciation can indeed help us to do so.

In his essay, "Science and ideology", Ricoeur (1991) discusses the problematic distinction between science and ideology. He argues that a sharp and clear-cut distinction between the social sciences and ideology can only be upheld if these sciences are viewed in a positivist way. When the positivist criteria for social theory are abandoned (which he argues must be the case because they are untenable), the possibility of an epistemological break between science and ideology is lost: "We cannot play and win on two tables at once; we cannot abandon the positivist model of science to give an acceptable meaning to the idea of social theory, and at the same time take advantage of this model in order to institute an epistemological break between science and ideology" (Ricoeur, 1991: 258). Ricoeur further argues that a clear break between science and ideology presupposes a subject capable of total knowledge of ideological differences, a *Freischwebende Intelligenz* capable of evaluating ideologies from a non-evaluative and non-subjective stance. With reference to Gadamer's work, he says that this creates a dilemma that is impossible to overcome, owing to the ontological condition of pre-understanding, "the very structure of a being that is never in the sovereign position of a subject capable of distancing itself from the totality of its conditionings" (Ricoeur, 1991: 266).

Should we therefore renounce the opposition between science and ideology? In a fashion characteristic of his methodological style, Ricoeur rejects this possibility. Instead he presents us with four hermeneutical propositions (Ricoeur, 1991: 267–269; see Bien, 1995).

(1) All objectifying knowledge about ourselves in relation to society, social class, cultural tradition and history is preceded "by a relation of *belonging* upon which we can never entirely reflect" (Ricoeur, 1991: 267).
(2) Although objectifying knowledge is always preceded by a relation of belonging, it is not totally dependent on it. It renders absolute knowledge impossible, but *relative autonomy* of objectifying knowledge is still possible due to the factor of *distanciation*.[2] This distanciation that

---

[2] On the basis of Ricoeur's analysis of the hermeneutical function of distanciation (Ricoeur, 1981), in which he takes the notion of the text as the paradigm of distanciation, we can conclude that distanciation is an inherent part of communication. We can only communicate 'in and through distance,' writes Ricoeur (1981: 131). However, whereas

8   JACO S. DREYER

allows for a partial critique of ideology also implies a self-distancing, "a distanciation of the self from itself" (Ricoeur, 1991: 268). The essence of this proposition is summarised by Ricoeur (1991: 268) in the following statement: "distanciation, dialectically opposed to belonging, is the condition of possibility of the critique of ideology, not outside or against hermeneutics, but within hermeneutics."

(3) Owing to distanciation, a critique of ideology can partially free itself from the relation of belonging and can be organised in knowledge. However, this knowledge will always remain incomplete, supported by an interest, as Habermas (1971) has argued: "It is condemned to remain partial, fragmentary, insular knowledge; its *incompleteness* is hermeneutically founded in the original and unsurpassable condition that makes distanciation itself a moment of belonging" (Ricoeur, 1991: 268).

(4) A critique of ideology is necessary, but this task can never be completed: "Knowledge is always in the process of tearing itself away from ideology, but ideology always remains the grid, the code of interpretation" (Ricoeur, 1991: 269).

How do we relate this hermeneutical theory of Ricoeur to the topic of this chapter? First, I think that Ricoeur's hermeneutical perspective on participation and distanciation helps us to understand the common view that quantitative and qualitative research present us with two different routes to truth. How is this the case? I would like to argue that the dualism of 'truth-from-participation' and 'truth-from-distanciation' underlying the qualitative-quantitative research dualism is tied to the same science-ideology dialectic to which Ricoeur refers. The intention

---

Gadamer had a totally negative view of distanciation, Ricoeur (1981, 1991) is much more positive and argues that it is not something to be overcome in interpretation, but is actually the condition of understanding. A text, as codified discourse, is for Ricoeur the paradigm of distanciation, owing to the threefold autonomy that is gained by the text as against discourse. Owing to this autonomy of the text, it transcends its original context and is thus not just an extension of a dialogue. A text is decontextualised from the original discourse, and it therefore has the potential to be recontextualised by a reader (Ricoeur, 1991). The distance created by the autonomy of the text, which is also a 'temporal distance' (Ricoeur, 1991: 298), thus makes interpretation possible. This is not the end of the story, however! Ricoeur (1991: 300) says, again with reference to Gadamer, that the text has a critical power, a power to be a "critique of the real", and thus to open new worlds for the reader. This unfolding of a new world for the reader thus "implies a moment of distanciation in the relation of self to itself" and a "critique of the illusions of the subject" (Ricoeur, 1981: 144; 1991: 301). In this way "distanciation from oneself is not a fault to be combated but rather the condition of possibility of understanding oneself in front of the text," writes Ricoeur (1991: 301). Distanciation is thus not an "alienating distanciation", but a necessary detour towards the appropriation of the new worlds opened by the text (Ricoeur, 1981: 144; 1991: 301).

of both perspectives is to eliminate, or at least to reduce, ideology. From the truth-from-participation perspective the aim is to eliminate or to reduce the researcher's ideological (subjective) interpretations by stressing the importance of the interpretations of the research participants (the researched). The researcher therefore has to immerse himself or herself in the lifeworld(s) of the researched (the moment of belonging or participation) so that their voices (interpretations) are not muted by the researcher's interpretations. This implies conducting qualitative research. On the other hand, the aim of the truth-from-distanciation perspective is to eliminate or to reduce the ideological interpretations (false consciousness) of the researched and of the researcher himself or herself (the distancing and also self-distancing which is implied by distanciation). The researcher cannot, therefore, take the interpretations of the researched at face value, but has to take a critical (objectifying) stance, and this implies a moment of distanciation. Quantitative research seems to be the relevant option from this perspective.

Secondly, Ricoeur's hermeneutical theory on participation and distanciation can help us to destroy the dualism between qualitative and quantitative research, with its associated oppositions between insider and outsider, researcher and the researched, observer and the observed, subjectivity and objectivity, understanding and explanation, an insider/engaged participant perspective and an outsider/detached observer perspective, truth-from-participation and truth-from-distanciation. How? This is the task that I set myself for the rest of the chapter. I do this first by broadening the methodological meaning of participation and distanciation, and secondly by attending to the dialectical relationship between these two concepts in order to establish truth.

Participation and Distanciation in Qualitative and Quantitative Research

In this section I explore the possible methodological implications of Ricoeur's ideas on participation and distanciation. I first explore the possible meaning of these two concepts in a methodological context. Secondly, I explore quantitative research from the perspective of participation and distanciation. I will then seek to demonstrate that quantitative research, although usually associated with distanciation, cannot escape participation. More importantly, I will argue that participation in quantitative research is not something that we must strive to overcome or eliminate at all costs, but it is a necessary condition for establishing truth in quantitative research. This will be followed by an exploration of qualitative research from the perspective of participation and distanciation. I will then seek to demonstrate that qualitative research, although usually associated with participation, cannot escape distanciation. I will also argue that distanciation in qualitative research is not only unavoidable, but also an important condition for establishing truth in qualitative research.

Participation and distanciation

What could participation and distanciation possibly mean in an empirical theological research practice? I will start with *participation*. Participation, in the hermeneutical sense that Ricoeur uses it, refers to much more than the interaction between the researcher and the researched in a research context. In its broadest sense, it refers to the ontological implication of being born at a specific time and in a specific place, in a specific culture with specific traditions. It refers to our 'situatedness', our being part of a lifeworld. Drawing on the phenomenological tradition, and particularly Gadamer's work, we can say that participation refers to the fact that we all belong to a historical tradition (Ricoeur, 1981) that forms our horizons of understanding. We cannot escape from this 'belonging' to a tradition, and this shapes the prejudices with which we meet and interpret our world. A researcher is thus not someone doing research as a person from nowhere. Every researcher has his or her own history and prejudices. More concretely, we can say that every researcher comes to the research practice with a personal (including a bodily, gendered identity), social, political, cultural and economic history that forms his or her horizon of understanding.

Participation in research, however, means more than this. The researched also inescapably belong to historical traditions, to lifeworlds with their own personal, social, political, cultural and economic histories. Participation in research therefore refers to 'meeting the other' with their prejudices (Gadamer, 1993) in the research. It means that we, as researchers, enter the lifeworld(s) of the researched (Habermas, 1984). Further, it is important to point out that this immersion in the lifeworlds of the research participants does not only refer to interaction with the researched in concrete research situations. Researchers can also enter these lifeworlds through their imagination, by putting themselves in the place of the researched (Bourdieu, 1999).

Thus conceived, participation puts an enormous burden on a researcher's shoulders. It means that, as researchers, we have to seek "to honour the integrity of the phenomena we study by trying to meet religious people on their own ground and on their own terms, and by not forcing phenomena into the moulds of our own conceptual schemes" (Krüger, 1995: 89). More concretely, it implies that we have to familiarise ourselves with the social, cultural, economic and political contexts of those who participate in our research projects. Even when the researcher and the researched share the same cultural and religious milieu, this is a difficult task (Krüger, 1995). In a multicultural, multireligious context it is an even bigger challenge. Participation means that we have to immerse ourselves in the worlds of the researched by interacting with them, by learning as much as we can about them, their histories and their religious heritages, and by being sensitive towards their life experiences (Fay, 1996). Those who participate in our research projects should not be regarded as mere objects of information, but as subjects of communication (Kunneman, 1996).

Is participation limited to one aspect of the research process? I think this broad hermeneutical understanding of participation implies that researchers have to be aware that their prejudices play a role in all the aspects of research. It also means that researchers should respect the researched in the research problems that they develop, the goals and research questions that they formulate, the way in which they collect the data, the interpretations that they make and the ways in which they communicate the research results.

What could *distanciation* possibly mean in an empirical theological research practice? Just as participation should not be narrowly conceived as social interaction, we should also not limit the meaning of distanciation to a lack of involvement or a lack of interaction with the research participants in the research situation. Distanciation, from a hermeneutical perspective, refers in the first instance to an attitude or a disposition (in terms of Bourdieu's *habitus*). "Distance is a fact; placing at a distance is a methodological attitude," writes Ricoeur (1991: 281) in his discussion on hermeneutics and the critique of ideology. What does 'placing at a distance' mean in this context? It means, among other things, that the researcher cannot take the interpretations of the researched at face value, but has to take a critical (objectifying) stance. A researcher cannot be content with the descriptions and interpretations, the common sense and lay language of the researched. Sayer (1992: 39) says that science is redundant if it fails to go beyond a common-sense

12   JACO S. DREYER

understanding of the world. Bourdieu (Jenkins, 1992: 53) also points out that the research subjects' discourse takes a great deal for granted, often remains at the level of the general and reflects a 'semi-theoretical disposition' due to their desire to impress. Immediate knowledge is thus an illusion (Bourdieu, Chamboredon and Passeron, 1991). Distanciation, in a methodological perspective, means that we have to adopt a critical, reflexive stance whether we engage in quantitative or qualitative research projects. In terms of the research process, it means, for example, that researchers have to be critical towards their methodological choices (for example, the choice of a research topic or the sampling choices), the research methods they have used and the interpretations they have made (Jenkins, 1992). Distanciation also implies that researchers have to reflect critically on the metatheoretical and theoretical frameworks that implicitly or explicitly feature in their research.

Distanciation is thus first and foremost an attitude of a researcher. There are, however, also techniques of distanciation or objectification, such as the logical critique of ideas and the statistical testing of spurious self-evidences, that can be useful in moving beyond the illusion of transparency (Bourdieu, Chamboredon and Passeron, 1991). Broadly speaking, we can say that distanciation also includes all strategies of objectification, such as critical thinking, theorising, conceptualising, abstracting, comparing and contrasting. If we analyse and interpret meaning—for example by classification, comparison and counting—we are engaging in acts of distanciation. Even recording the research data is an act of distanciation.

The role of quantification and statistics as strategies of distanciation are well-known (and often abused), but there are also other important strategies of distanciation that a researcher can use. Conceptualisation and the use of theory are important strategies of distanciation in any research project. Goetz and LeCompte (1984) discuss, for example, four theorising activities that can be used in qualitative research: perception (the establishment of codes and categories); comparing, aggregating and ordering; establishing and testing of connections; and speculation. All these theorising activities can be seen as strategies of decontextualisation that facilitate distanciation.

However, the stance of a detached observer implies more than an objectivating and critical attitude towards research methods, procedures, processes and results. This attitude should also be directed to the researcher himself or herself. The researcher does not stand outside the research relationship as a transparent, rational subject (Kunneman,

1996; Dreyer, 1997), but shares the same epistemological framework as the researched. Owing to the ontological condition of pre-understanding (see above), every researcher is also a member of a lifeworld that has been intuitively mastered (Habermas, 1984). Although this lifeworld can never be fully known, researchers have to reflect critically on their own lifeworlds that they bring into the research situation. Distanciation implies that every empirical theological researcher must take a reflexive and critical stance regarding his or her cultural, economic, social and political positions. We have to ask ourselves to what extent our research incorporates the prejudices of the day (Reinharz, 1988). Bourdieu also refers to the necessity of the researcher to be self-critical, to situate himself or herself in social space, "to objectivise his position in the universe of cultural production, in this case the scientific or academic field", and constantly to guard against the 'ethnocentrism of the scientist' (in Bourdieu and Wacquant, 1992: 69). In short, we have to reflect critically on our scientific *habitus* (Bourdieu, 1988, 2004). I will return to the importance of reflexivity later.

Participation and distanciation in quantitative research

Quantitative research has always been associated with distanciation, as I mentioned in the introduction. In the positivist version of quantitative research, the main aim was to try to overcome the researcher's bias, his or her subjective involvement in the research practice. The agency of the researcher was thus denied, or where it was acknowledged, the idea was to try to minimise its impact on the research process. The use of mathematics and statistics, standardised procedures and the control of the researcher's bias all firmly established the relation between quantitative research and distanciation. It is therefore not really necessary to argue that distanciation is inherently part of quantitative research. It is, however, important to note that distanciation should not be narrowly conceived as only quantification, but should be seen more broadly, as I explained above.

The important point to make with regard to quantitative research is that participation is also an inherent part of this approach to research. Take, for example, the most extreme case of positivist research, in which the researcher tries to minimise any contact with the object of research, for example in (quasi-)experimental situations. The researcher provides the object with a stimulus, and tries to measure the outcome of a procedure. On the basis of the broad hermeneutical understanding set out above, it is clear that the researcher cannot escape from participation. He or she already participates by means of the language that is used. The researcher also does not come to the research without any prejudices, any traditions, a language, a culture or a body. He or she always has a view of the object of research, of that person's language, culture, gender and religion.

This participation of the researcher influences every aspect of the quantitative research process: the choice of a research topic, the data collection method, the sampling, the data analysis procedures and the communication of research results. Quantitative research is always done by someone, in a specific situation, with a specific background, with a specific interest in the research and the outcome of the research. This agency of the researcher will thus influence all the decisions made in the process of research.

Let us look at a few examples to illustrate the researcher's participation in quantitative research. In a research project on human rights and religion (Van der Ven, Dreyer and Pieterse, 2004) conducted by the Department of Practical Theology in cooperation with the Radboud University in Nijmegen, we decided to research the moral, religious and human rights values of the youth of South Africa in the period of transition since 1994. The choice of this theme was not done from some kind of 'neutral' position. It was done with the specific intention of trying to understand what was happening in South Africa in this dramatic period of transformation. The choice of the research programme was thus influenced by the knowledge of the importance of a specific historical situation, and the specific aim of the research was to contribute to this process of democratic change in the new South Africa.

The participation of the researchers also comes to the fore in the selection of research participants. In the study referred to above, we deliberately chose Grade 11 learners because we knew that they were the future of the country. We chose private schools with a tradition of racial integration in order to compare these schools with public schools that had no racial integration prior to 1994. The researchers' knowledge of the situation in South Africa also contributed to the construction of the questionnaire, both in terms of conceptualisation and operationalisation. We knew that certain words were too difficult for the learners to understand, and we used our knowledge of the situation with regard to political parties, the religious landscape of the country, and so on. In the data analysis, the agency of the researchers also played an important role in the statistical choices that we made (on the basis of our knowledge of the South African situation and of our theoretical knowledge as expressed in the theoretical and conceptual framework of the research). The agency of the researchers plays, of course, an important role in the interpretation of the statistical results and in the communication of the research findings. We made extensive use of our knowledge of the South African situation to relate the research results to specific burning issues in South Africa, such as the oppression of people living with HIV/Aids (Dreyer, 2002). The agency of the researchers, and also all the consultants and other people involved in the research process, contributed immensely to the research.

These examples should suffice to demonstrate that participation is an inherent part of quantitative research. More than this, however, I would like to argue that participation is not only unavoidable in quantitative research; it is actually a necessary condition for good quantitative research. In the study mentioned above, the researchers' knowledge of the political, economic, cultural and social situation in South Africa, our knowledge of the educational system in the public and private schools, our knowledge of the different religions and churches and the like contributed to the research process from beginning to end. Participation does not, however, refer only to knowledge. It also refers to the researchers' attitudes and values; to their respect for the research participants; to their commitment in this case to the establishment of democracy and a culture of human rights in the new South Africa; to their commitment to religion, and more specifically the Christian religion, and to contribute to the flourishing of human lives.

It is, of course, also possible that the biases and ideologies of the researchers could play a negative role in all the decisions made in the research process, from the construction of the research question to the communication of the results. I will return to this in the last section.

Participation and distanciation in qualitative research

Let us now turn to qualitative research. Qualitative research has always been associated with participation, with taking part in the lifeworld of the participants. The interaction with research participants in a natural setting is indicative of the importance of participation to the qualitative researcher. It is thus not necessary to elaborate on the aspect of participation in qualitative research, except to say that—as discussed above—participation should not be limited to a narrow view of participation as interaction.

The important point to make with regard to qualitative research is that distanciation in the broad hermeneutical sense is also an inherent part of this approach. As I said above, by using language, by formulating our ideas and questions and responses in a language, we are already performing the act of distanciation. Let us look at a typical qualitative research project. The choice of the research theme already implies distanciation. The interaction between the researcher and the research participant is also characterised by distanciation, for example in formulating and answering questions; in probing, in recording the data (by means of note-taking, voice recording, or video recording). In order to make sense of the research material, the researcher also has to reduce the data in some way to make it interpretable. One example of this is by coding the data. Another strategy is by comparing the different codes. In some cases the researcher in qualitative research will also make use of quantification, for example by terms such as 'more' or 'less' or by counting the frequencies of certain words, and so on. These are all strategies to assist in interpreting the data, and thus in distanciation. The researcher has to communicate his or her interpretations, and this also implies distanciation. The researcher and the research participant can disagree on the interpretation of what was said, or why it was said, or what was meant by a certain expression. These are all instances of distanciation in qualitative research. It is thus clear that qualitative research cannot escape from the act of distanciation.

These examples should suffice to demonstrate that distanciation is an integral part of qualitative research. Beyond this, however, I would like to argue that distanciation is not only unavoidable in qualitative research; it is actually a necessary condition for good qualitative research. Good qualitative research is simply not possible without strategies of objectification, such as interpreting, comparing, contrasting, coding, theorising and critical thinking (see the next section).

It is, of course, also possible that strategies of objectification, for example the use of outdated theories or a lack of critical thinking skills, could play a negative role in all the decisions made in the research process, from the construction of the research question to the communication of the results. I will return to this in the next section.

Establishing Truth from Participation and Distanciation: The Craft of Empirical Theology

In the previous section I argued, and tried to demonstrate, that a broad hermeneutical understanding of participation and distanciation implies that all research, whether quantitative or qualitative, is characterised by both participation and distanciation. We should therefore reject the common view underlying the qualitative-quantitative dualism, namely that qualitative research is characterised by participation and quantitative research by distanciation. We can also conclude, therefore, that quantitative and qualitative research approaches do not offer fundamentally different ways to truthful knowledge, to the establishing of truth. Establishing truth in empirical theology is done from both participation and distanciation, whether we conduct quantitative or qualitative research.

However, this does not mean that establishing truth will be equally successful in all research endeavours. It is not an all-or-nothing affair. In this section I would like to reflect on an important condition for establishing truth from participation and distanciation, namely that the dialectical tension between participation and distanciation should be maintained in the research process. First, I look at the importance of maintaining the dialectical tension between participation and distanciation in quantitative and qualitative research. Secondly, I briefly discuss some ways in which the tension between participation and distanciation can be maintained.

The dialectical tension between participation and distanciation in quantitative and qualitative research

Why do we need both participation and distanciation for establishing truth? In this context it is helpful to recall that Ricoeur relates the dialectical tension between participation and distanciation to the tension between science and ideology. Because there is no clear epistemological break between science and ideology, the search for truth is a task that can never be completed. It is always a fallible process. My interpretation is that the dialectical tension between participation and distanciation is necessary to ensure that knowledge stays within the realm of science and does not become ideological. To put it somewhat simplistically: participation needs the correction of distanciation, and distanciation needs the correction of participation.

Here I would like to add another aspect from Ricoeur's theory, namely the tension between ideology and utopia. I would like to interpret the dialectical relation between participation and distanciation from the dialectical relation between ideology and utopia (Dreyer, 2004). To the extent that the tension collapses and participation takes precedence over distanciation, the knowledge produced runs the risk of being ideological, that is, it tends to conform to the status quo and continue the illusions of immediate knowledge. As a consequence, the validity or plausibility of the 'truth-claims' of the research will suffer. However, it is not only the validity or plausibility of qualitative research that will suffer if the aspect of distanciation is not well attended to. This is equally true for quantitative research, for example by using the wrong criteria for a factor analysis, or by poor scale construction, or by poor conceptualisation and poor operationalisation. Whether this is due to ignorance (through a lack of training, lack of ability, etc.) or not, the validity or plausibility of the truth-claims of the research will suffer if we do not pay sufficient attention to distanciation, whether it is quantitative or qualitative research.

On the other hand, to the extent that distanciation takes precedence over participation, the knowledge produced runs the risk of being utopian, that is, it tends towards escapism and loses its connection with the lifeworld of the research participants. Again we can conclude that the validity or plausibility of the truth-claims of the research will suffer. However, a lack of participation is not only a danger for quantitative research. The validity or plausibility of the truth-claims of qualitative research, with its emphasis on interaction with the researched and on taking the lifeworld of the researched seriously, can also suffer from a lack of participation in the broad, hermeneutical sense. For example, if a male researcher with a gender bias conducts interviews with women, but does not reflect on his gender bias, if this is a kind of blind spot for him, the quality of the research could suffer as a result. The point is that, whether we conduct quantitative or qualitative research, if we do not pay sufficient attention to participation, the validity or plausibility of the truth-claims of the research will suffer.

Does this imply that there are no differences between quantitative and qualitative research? I do not think so. One way to look at the differences between quantitative and qualitative research is to use a metaphor from optics. We use different instruments for different tasks. Both are reliable, work on magnification, etc., but they differ in the objects of the research. A telescope is used to see what is not visible to the eye because it is too far away, what is distant, for example the moon or the stars (high level of abstraction). A microscope, on the other hand, is also used to study things that are not visible to the naked human eye, but these things are incredibly small. Although they are both instruments of science, they are used for different purposes because the object of study differs. In a similar way, we can say that some aspects, for example the interaction between learners in a group or a sports team, can be better studied through a qualitative approach (by means of observation and interviews for example) than through a quantitative approach. However, the prevalence of HIV/Aids can be studied better by means of large-scale epidemiological studies that use a quantitative approach. The main point in this chapter is that there is no methodological 'royal road' to truth. Qualitative and quantitative research approaches have different strengths and weaknesses, but they share the same epistemological challenges and limitations (Bryman, 1988).

Although participation and distanciation form part of both quantitative and qualitative research, I think that quantitative and qualitative research approaches do indeed differ in terms of the challenges to maintain the tension between participation and distanciation, because of their different strengths and weaknesses. Without going into much detail, we can say that the strength of quantitative research lies in the direction of distanciation, and that of qualitative research in the direction of participation.

In order to maintain the dialectical tension between participation and distanciation, quantitative researchers thus have to pay particular attention to the aspect of participation. How can this be done? I think there are numerous ways in which quantitative researchers can strengthen the moment of participation in their research: for example, by immersing themselves in the lifeworlds of the researched in the first (exploratory phase) of their research, by testing their ideas and interpretations with the researched, by involving other people (colleagues and other experts), by interacting with the research participants and by studying the research contexts.

Qualitative researchers, on the other hand, have to pay particular attention to the aspect of distanciation. How can this be done? Again, I think there are numerous ways in which qualitative researchers can strengthen the act of distanciation in their research: for example, by making explicit use of concepts and theories, by using techniques for data analysis (for example coding in grounded-theory research), by making explicit the choices that they make and the reasons for these choices, and by using techniques for data display. The challenge for both quantitative and qualitative research approaches is to maintain the tension between participation and distanciation. We can say that the quality of the research, and thus also the validity or plausibility of the truth-claims of the research, depends on the extent to which researchers succeed in maintaining the tension between participation and distanciation in quantitative and qualitative research.

Maintaining the dialectical tension between participation and distanciation in empirical theology

It should now be clear that it is important that we maintain the dialectical tension between participation and distanciation in both quantitative and qualitative research. How can we ensure that this tension is maintained in the research situation? Here I would like to make use of some of the theoretical ideas of the French anthropologist and sociologist, Pierre Bourdieu.

What can we learn from Bourdieu with regard to the above problematic? On the basis of Bourdieu's theory I would say the key notion here is reflexivity. The idea of reflexivity is, of course, not a new one. Many researchers, especially those working from a postmodern, narrative approach, place considerable emphasis on the importance of reflexivity in research. Bourdieu's conception of reflexivity is, however, quite interesting as it is deeply rooted in his empirical research experience, and not only based on philosophical speculation (Bourdieu, 1990, 2000, 2004; Bourdieu and Wacquant, 1992).

In order to explain Bourdieu's views on reflexivity I start with the well-known triad of concepts in his theory of practice, namely habitus, field and capital. These three concepts developed over the years through his empirical research in Algeria and later his research in France. The idea is not to try and explain these concepts in detail, but to look briefly at how Bourdieu has used them in relation to the scientific field.

I start with the idea of a *scientific habitus*. The concept of habitus is probably the most distinctive notion of Bourdieu's theory. In brief, the concept of habitus refers to the dispositions that actors acquire through socialisation and experience and that influence their actions. Bourdieu refers to this as structured dispositions. The important idea is that a habitus is the stock of dispositions from which we act, but this habitus is also something that can change. It is thus not deterministic in any sense, and Bourdieu has stressed that the concept is meant as a bridge between subjectivity and objectivity. What does a scientific habitus mean? With reference to Bourdieu's work, we can say that a scientific habitus is the sum total of the dispositions from which a researcher conducts his or her research. One of these dispositions that a researcher should acquire is the ability to reflect on his or her influence on the research. It means that as researchers we need to reflect on our social origin, cultural background, research skills, and so on. Bourdieu adds here that this reflexivity of the researcher should not be the kind of psychological navel-gazing so characteristic of some (postmodern) research approaches, in which researchers endlessly reflect on themselves. This last form of reflexivity is the one most commonly stressed in all sorts of methodological textbooks. What Bourdieu adds is that this should become part of the researcher's habitus. Furthermore, it is not something that can be acquired at once, but is a lifelong learning process. In the context of this chapter, we can say that a scientific habitus also refers to the researcher's lifelong learning, of acquiring expertise with regard to participation (for example gaining intercultural experiences, becoming more gender sensitive, and so on) and distanciation (acquiring new statistical techniques, expanding theoretical frameworks, sharpening critical skills, and so forth).

The second concept is that of the field, in this case the *scientific field*. Bourdieu refers to the differentiation of the scientific field as one of the major achievements of the modern period. One of the characteristics of the scientific field is that research is conducted not only by an individual researcher, but actually by a community of researchers. Reflexivity in this context refers to the fact that the researcher, despite all efforts towards reflexivity, can never be totally transparent. This is also what Ricoeur says about the epistemic subject: one gets to know oneself through another, and this also applies to the researcher as the subject of research. Researchers thus have to use the critical instruments of science against one another in order to enhance reflexivity, and to contribute to maintaining the tension between participation and distanciation.

The third concept is that of *symbolic capital*. Bourdieu says that researchers are positioned in the scientific field, and this is where his concept of capital comes in. Every researcher has his or her own symbolic capital, and this also plays a role in the way in which science is done. This brings power issues within the scientific field to the fore. Research as part of the scientific field is not conducted from a neutral position, but is always related to the researcher's standing within the field, the discipline to which he or she belongs, the intellectual tradition to which he or she belongs, the research group in which he or she takes part, and so on. Reflexivity is thus required by all in the scientific field. All researchers have a responsibility to help one another to maintain the tension between participation and distanciation, to make fellow researchers aware of their ideological positions and utopian strivings. "In short, we must create conditions such that the worst, the meanest, and the most mediocre participant is compelled to behave in accordance with the norms of scientificity in currency at the time" (Bourdieu in Bourdieu and Wacquant, 1992: 178).

The above ideas are not new. Many researchers and philosophers of science have stressed the importance of reflexivity, both as part of the researcher's reflection on his or her research, and as part of research as a social activity. Bourdieu, however, adds another, very important dimension to reflexivity. He says that researchers have to reflect not only on themselves, as individuals, or as a community of researchers. Researchers also have to reflect on the scientific field itself, and more specifically on the intellectualist bias that is so typical of this field.

Why? Bourdieu gives an interesting account of the development of the scholastic fallacy, as he also terms it. The scientific field gradually developed into an independent field of modern societies. This field, according to Bourdieu, is characterised by a sort of leisurely existence removed from the hardship of the economic sphere. This leisurely existence of scholarship is in sharp contrast with the daily struggles of many people who face economic hardship and who struggle to survive. The danger is that intellectuals come to regard themselves as superior to those outside the academic world, and that they tend to project their way of thinking about practice onto the practices themselves. As researchers we therefore have to "question the privilege of a knowing 'subject'" (Bourdieu, 2000: 119). Bourdieu explains that the logic of practice (practical knowledge) is often different from our scientific knowledge, and we have to be alert to this important difference. This is another example in which, if the researchers are not also critical of the scientific endeavour itself, research can lose its connection with the lifeworld of those whom we research. Our research can thus become utopian in the sense of escapism—of little or no relevance to those outside the academic sphere.

How can we overcome the epistemological dualism between truth established from distanciation or participation, and the resultant methodological dualism between quantitative and qualitative research? By maintaining the tension between participation and distanciation. How can we maintain this tension? By developing a reflexivity in the threefold sense that Bourdieu uses the term: by reflecting on our own prejudices, by being part of scientific communities that help us to reflect on our prejudices, and lastly by reflecting on our scientific practices themselves. All this forms part of learning the craft of research and of developing a scientific habitus (Bourdieu, 2004).

Conclusion

Is the search for truth or truthful knowledge in empirical theology an illusion? Or perhaps an ideology? I would say 'Yes' to these questions if we let go of the tension between participation and distanciation in our efforts to establish truth in empirical theology. Truth cannot be established from a distance, from a neutral or objectivist stance. This view was discredited a long time ago as an illusion. Without participation, without acknowledging our research participants and ourselves as embodied human beings in interaction with one another and our worlds, our prejudices, in both qualitative and quantitative empirical theological research, the search for truth in empirical theology will be an illusion. However, neither can truth be established only from participating in the lifeworlds of our research participants (or co-researchers as some prefer). The illusion of the epistemological privilege of the observer in positivistic approaches should not be replaced by another illusion, namely that of the epistemological privilege of the participant. Without distanciation, critical thinking, theorisation, conceptualisation, abstraction, classification, comparison and contrast, the search for truth, regardless of whether we use quantitative or qualitative research approaches, will only tend to reproduce our illusions. More than this, though, we have to be vigilant, through our reflexivity as individual researchers but also as part of research communities, to maintain the dialectical tension between participation and distanciation, in the broad hermeneutical sense that I explained above, in our qualitative and quantitative empirical theological research endeavours. Establishing truth in empirical theology, whether we conduct qualitative or quantitative research, can only be done from both participation and distanciation, in a never-ending process of learning and developing the craft of doing empirical theology.

24 JACO S. DREYER

REFERENCES

Bien, J. (1995), Ricoeur as social philosopher, in L.E. Hahn (ed.), *The Philosophy of Paul Ricoeur*, pp. 287–305, Chicago, Illinois, Open Court.

Bourdieu, P. (1988), *Homo Academicus* (tr. by P. Collier), Cambridge, Polity Press.

——. (1990), *In Other Words: essays towards a reflexive sociology*, Stanford, California, Stanford University Press.

——. (1999), *The Weight of the World: social suffering in contemporary society*, London, Polity.

——. (2000), *Pascalian Meditations* (tr. by R. Nice), Stanford, California, Stanford University Press.

——. (2004), *Science of Science and Reflexivity* (tr. by R. Nice), Chicago, Illinois, University of Chicago Press.

Bourdieu, P. and Wacquant, L.J.D. (1992), *An Invitation to Reflexive Sociology*, Cambridge, Polity Press.

Bourdieu, P., Chamboredon, J.-C. and Passeron, J.-C. (1991), *The Craft of Sociology: epistemological preliminaries*, (ed. by B. Krais and tr. by R. Nice), Berlin, De Gruyter.

Bryman, A. (1988), *Quantity and Quality in Social Research*, London, Routledge.

Dreyer, J.S. (1997), Praktiese teologie, refleksiewe verwetenskapliking en die verhouding tussen wetenskaplike kennis en praktiese handelinge, *Praktiese teologie in Suid-Afrika*, 12 (1), 13–30.

——. (1998), The researcher: engaged participant or detached observer? A reflection on the methodological implications of the dialectics of belonging and distanciation for empirical research in practical theology, *Journal of Empirical Theology*, 11(2), 5–22.

——. (2002), Justice for the oppressed: the HIV/AIDS challenge, in J.S. Dreyer and J.A. van der Ven (eds.), *Divine Justice: human justice*, pp. 85–112, Pretoria, Research Institute for Theology and Religious Studies.

——. (2004), Theological normativity: ideology or utopia? Reflections on the possible contribution of empirical research, in J.A. van der Ven and M. Scherer-Rath (eds.), *Normativity and Empirical Research in Theology*, pp. 3–16, Leiden, Brill.

Fay, B. (1996), *Contemporary Philosophy of Social Science: a multicultural approach*, Oxford, Blackwell.

Frisby, D. (1976), Introduction to the English translation, in T.W. Adorno, *The Positivist Dispute in German Sociology* (tr. by G. Ady and D. Frisby), pp. ix–xliv, London, Heinemann.

Gadamer, H.-G. (1993), *Truth and Method* (2nd rev. edition) (rev. tr. by J. Weinsheimer and D.G. Marshall), London, Sheed and Ward.

Goetz, J.P. and LeCompte, M.D. (1984), *Ethnography and Qualitative Design in Educational Research*, New York, Academic Press.

Habermas, J. (1971), *Knowledge and Human Interests* (tr. by J.J. Shapiro), Boston, Massachusetts, Beacon Press.

——. (1984), *The Theory of Communicative Action*, volume 1 (tr. by T. McCarthy), Boston, Massachusetts, Beacon Press.

Heron, J. (1996), *Co-operative Inquiry: research into the human condition*, London, Sage.

Ihde, D. (1995), Paul Ricoeur's place in the hermeneutic tradition, in L.E. Hahn (ed.), *The Philosophy of Paul Ricoeur*, pp. 59–70, Chicago, Illinois, Open Court.

Jenkins, R. (1992), *Pierre Bourdieu*, London, Routledge.

Krüger, J.S. (1995), *Along Edges*, Pretoria, University of South Africa.

Kunneman, H. (1996), *Van theemutscultuur naar walkman-ego: contouren van postmoderne individualiteit*, Amsterdam, Boom.

Mouton, J. (1996), *Understanding Social Research*, Pretoria, Van Schaik.

——. (2001), *How to Succeed in your Master's and Doctoral Studies: a South African guide and resource book*, Pretoria, Van Schaik.

Posel, D. (2004), Truth? The view from South Africa's Truth and Reconciliation Commission, in *KEYWORDS: Truth*, pp. 1–25, Cape Town, Double Storey.

Reagan, C.E. (1996), *Paul Ricoeur: his life and his work*, Chicago, Illinois, University of Chicago Press.

Reinharz, S. (1988), Feminist distrust: problems of context and content in sociological work, in D.N. Berg and K.K. Smith, *The Self in Social Inquiry: researching methods*, pp. 153–172, Newbury Park, California, Sage.

Ricoeur, P. (1981), *Hermeneutics and the Human Sciences: essays on language, action and interpretation* (ed. and tr. by J.B. Thompson), Cambridge, Cambridge University Press.

———. (1991), *From Text to Action: essays in hermeneutics II* (tr. by K. Blamey and J.B. Thompson), London, Athlone Press.

Saludadez, J.A. and Garcia, P.G. (2001), Seeing our quantitative counterparts: construction of qualitative research in a roundtable discussion, *Forum Qualitative Sozialforschung: Qualitative Social Research* 2, 1. [Online journal available at: http://qualitative-research.net/fqs/fqs-eng.htm]

Sayer, A. (1992), *Method in Social Science: a realist approach* (second edition), London, Routledge.

van der Ven, J.A. (1993), *Practical Theology: an empirical approach*, Kampen, Kok Pharos.

van der Ven, J.A., Dreyer, J.S. and Pieterse, H.J.C. (2004), *Is There a God of Human Rights? The complex relationship between human rights and religion: a South African case*, Leiden, Brill.

Ziebertz, H.-G. (1993), Komplementarität von Forschungsmethoden, in J.A. van der Ven and H.-G. Ziebertz (Hrsg.), *Paradigmenentwicklung in der praktischen Theologie*, pp. 225–260, Kampen/Weinheim, Kok/Deutscher Studien Verlag.

CHAPTER TWO

TRUTH AND METHOD IN EMPIRICAL THEOLOGY

Hans Schilderman

SUMMARY

In the previous chapter Jaco Dreyer explores the extent to which the long-standing antithesis of qualitative versus quantitative research can be overcome by way of the hermeneutic notion of establishing truth. To answer this question Dreyer takes Ricoeur's dialectics of participation and distancing as his point of departure in a scholarly reflection on philosophical and methodological points of view. In his conclusion Dreyer arrives at a balanced view of the necessity to do justice to both qualitative and quantitative approaches, which, in their dialectic interaction, contribute to the process of establishing truth.

This commentary on Dreyer's argument seeks to clarify some epistemological and methodological issues relating to the notion of establishing truth in Ricoeur's hermeneutics. I take Dreyer's discussion as a starting point for the inquiry: can hermeneutics indeed solve methodological issues pertaining to quantitative and qualitative research? I elaborate on this by distinguishing between meaning and knowledge, and call for valid criteria to demarcate scientific and non-scientific claims. I proceed to cast some doubt on methodological efforts to arrive at 'truth' itself, be it from an empirical or a hermeneutic perspective. Knowledge claims can be raised and criticised scientifically if they are based on clear methodological procedures that permit us to target meaning as a concept open to empirical research. I conclude with some proposals for methodological innovation in empirical theology that link a hermeneutic approach to priorities in empirical research.

STATING THE PROBLEM

In the previous chapter Dreyer advocates that quantitative and qualitative research methods should be complementary—at any rate not incommensurable—approaches. But does the discussion of empirical method in fact fit seamlessly into Ricoeurian hermeneutics? One can reformulate and in a sense reconcile the two methodological views by means of a dialectics of participation (understanding) and distancing (explaining). In so doing, however, one must realise that the epistemological discussion of method cannot be ignored, as it represents a specific 'configuration' whose own claims have to be assessed as well. The key question of how to ascertain truth by methodological means is critical, in that our social reality is not only an object but also a condition, aim and, inescapably, a bias in research. Social or religious facts never display a natural objectivity but need to be understood in terms of context, time and social opportunity. Recognition of that fact means that we remain tied to histories, communities and cultures, whose concerns we cannot escape. Thus, to quote an insight of Max Weber, the issue of truth and method displays an elective affinity (*Wahlverwantschaft*) between ideas and interests.

The debate on qualitative and quantitative methods in the social sciences reflects different views of the relationship between truth and interest. Quantitative research studies the characteristics of phenomena based on iterative data collection and comparison, using figures that permit replicated measurements aimed at the construction and validation of general theories. It reconstructs reality in the form of models that allow hypotheses to explain as great a variety of that reality's characteristics as possible with a minimum of interrelated concepts. Qualitative research systematically collects and analyses empirical data as well, but is more interested in the interpretive processes embedded in the social phenomena under investigation. It tries to understand reality from a heuristic perspective as the best possible position to reconstruct intrinsic, more 'subjective' and process-oriented characteristics of social phenomena. In this participatory approach the interests motivating the research are decisive for its procedures to establish the truth of knowledge.

Though one could easily argue that the choice of either qualitative or quantitative methods is based on pragmatic goals, the fact is that methods tend to reflect ideological positions, especially when connected with truth claims and the concomitant standards, such as objectivity, parsimony, informativeness, replicability, efficiency and validity. Such controversies were common in German sociological literature during the 1950s and 1960s, when critical rationalism and dialectical theory thrashed out the logical conditions for scientific method (Adorno and Popper, 1976). In empirical theology there have been similar debates (Van der Ven and Ziebertz, 1993). However high the academic stakes when it comes to these regulative ideas of establishing truth, one has to keep a keen eye on the implied social processes as well. There is no cynicism in the observation that, apart from differences in argumentation, there is a clear distinction between the corresponding academic cultures, each of which promotes its own interest within relatively closed communities, styles and traditions.

These interests of quantitative and qualitative research display an elective affinity with the ideas of distancing and participation in hermeneutic philosophy. Hermeneutics is generally considered a paradigm for interpreting texts. Since Gadamer's *Wahrheit und Methode* hermeneutics can no longer be understood as merely a technique, method or theory; it is the experience of thought itself in the activity of interpreting texts. One of Ricoeur's contributions to modern hermeneutics that Dreyer highlights is the integration of hermeneutic textual analysis with interpretation of action. Texts have an autonomy of their own that distances readers from their own subjectivity, transposing them to another reality that is depicted in the text and allows for new interpretations. This 'de-contextualisation' is a necessary condition for 're-contextualisation' to occur, whereupon the newly grasped meaning is reintegrated with the lifeworld, the meaningful context in which the reader belongs. Here she puts the text into action in the sense that she participates by translating the meaning of the text into dialogue. The linguistic potential of the text (*langue*) is put into action (*parole*).

Thus there is a dialectics of participation and distancing implied in the action of establishing truth by appropriating meaning. The idea of dialectics ensures that we attribute meaning while simultaneously being affected by it (Ricoeur, 1991). In this dialectics Ricoeur recognises the insights offered by the 'masters of suspicion'. One needs to be critically aware that 'truths' are indeed '*established*': our knowledge is intrinsically linked with ideologies and utopias that are equally reflected in the imaginative abilities of our minds, ingrained in our histories and embedded in our communities. According to this view, we cannot but understand scientific research in terms of intelligible actions, in which we simultaneously explore and establish the reality we live in (Ricoeur, 1974). In this academic praxis, distancing relates to the process of objectifying in quantitative research, whereas participation looks at the context from which this process evolves and to which it returns, similar to the practice of qualitative research traditions. Hence both are necessary to establish truth. With this emphasis Ricoeur provides a critical link between *erklärende* and *verstehende* scientific disciplines.

30 HANS SCHILDERMAN

Having summarised the problem, I now raise some issues that reopen the methodological debate on empirical research. Dreyer's attempt to demolish the idea that quantitative and qualitative methods represent different ways to truth raises some questions.

MEANING AND KNOWLEDGE

One wonders to what extent the discourse on meaning, as the formal object to address the question of truth from a hermeneutic perspective, precludes discussion of a scientific notion of understanding truth, namely knowledge. Meaning introduces a discourse of interpretation, and focuses on intentional acts of signifying our reality. It takes the discussion of establishing truth, understood as the production of knowledge, into the realm of semiosis, that is, the production of meaning. The argument here sees meaning as the more primordial, generic concept, already present before we embark on issues of scientific research and therefore better suited to address ideological threats that we may not discern if we limit our discussion to the assessment of knowledge only. These threats require critique that the interpretive dialectics of participation and distancing facilitates. An account of meaning in the establishment of truth would offer that. The introduction of hermeneutics indeed allows us to reflect philosophically on interpretive processes, but it may sidestep scientific discussion of epistemology, which is the theory of knowledge (acquisition) as a basic characteristic of justified belief. In fact, Ricoeur illustrates this in the way he integrates Frege's notions of sense and reference in his hermeneutic programme.

Sense and *reference*, Frege's well-known concepts, mark the beginning of the 'linguistic turn', being the recognition of the constructive qualities of language by human scientists. Language is not simply an instrument that unambiguously conveys propositions referring to external objects, but constitutes reality itself and thus illustrates that knowledge follows the logic of language. Frege draws a logical distinction from this observation. The 'sense' (*Sinn*) of a proper noun or sentence applies to the intention, meaning or connotation: it pertains to anything that can be subsumed under that heading (intension). In other words, sense is the mode of presenting the referent that expresses its cognitive significance. 'Reference' (*Bedeutung*), on the other hand, applies to the denotation, that is, the object that a proper name refers to and that defines the class of phenomena to which it points (extension). It applies to the 'what' that was displayed by the 'how' of meaning (Mendelsohn, 2005: 27–40). The aim of Frege's distinction lies in his criticism of Mill's view that proper names only refer and have no meaning beyond that. Frege's criticism is shared by Ricoeur, and Dreyer follows in his footsteps. Indeed, we cannot abstain from meaning when referring to reality. However, one has to realise that in this hermeneutic endeavour we transpose the notion of meaning from reference to structure, from denoting phenomena to the inner world of a text.

Ricoeur applies Frege's distinction of sense and reference in his hermeneutic analysis by distinguishing four interrelated phases of a 'hermeneutic arc' (Schwartz, 1983). In the first phase the relationship between author and text is clarified in an attempt to bridge the socio-cultural distance between past and present. The act of writing has distanced us from the text as we are trying to make sense of it, and thus we engage in a process of re-appropriation. In the second phase of the hermeneutic arc the rule-governed structure of a text is analysed. In doing so one distances oneself from the self-referential meaning of the text, and this is where hermeneutics already benefits from science, especially its semiotic theory. In a third phase the referential function comes into it, in the sense that discourse is directed to something beyond itself. Though a (historical) text is somewhat opaque when it comes to ostensive meaning, one cannot deny the existence of an objective world beyond the author's subjectivity. The fourth and final phase focuses on the relationship between the world to which the text refers and the reader who tries to appropriate its meaning for the world he lives in. In this hermeneutic arc distancing primarily entails recognition of the otherness of the text, whereas appropriation (or participation) implies the process of self-examination as we interpret its meaning.

In Ricoeur's analysis one looks in vain for explicit socio-scientific accounts of the referential function, at least to the extent that they rely on empirical analysis of actions instead of texts.[1] It is the interpreting, constructing subject that is centre stage, not without methodological

---

[1] This is not a criticism of this part of Ricoeur's analysis. His concern is primarily to avoid the kind of epistemological dichotomisation of understanding and explaining resulting from Gadamer's disregard of questions regarding the establishment of knowledge, and Habermas' confusion of the problem of social understanding in communication with the problem of understanding per se. It is doubtful, however, whether Ricoeur's attempt to reconcile participatory and distanced meaning can avoid a subjective stance and simultaneously encompass a more broadly scientific account of meaning. See Robinson, 1995.

suspicion nor without critical recognition of the otherness of meaning as disclosure of the world. The epistemological significance of the referential function for the discussion of scientific method, however, remains largely unclear.[2] Thus my question reads: is the dialectic relationship of participation (interpretation) and distancing (explaining) scientifically relevant?

DEMARCATION

The answer to the question should be negative in the absence of criteria to distinguish science from non-science. Who is actually participating or distancing, and why, where, when and how? I find that in hermeneutic thought there is often a discrepancy between the focal role assigned to the interpreter on the one hand and her sheer anonymity on the other. On the whole we seem to assume that it is we who interpret, that is I—who, it turns out, just happens to be a scholar or philosopher. Scientists, however, make far more specific claims about the reality under scrutiny than non-scientists. This requires us to define demarcation criteria, clear standards to draw lines between science and non-science. Though modern epistemologists doubt if such demarcation criteria are at all feasible, the problem as such needs to be identified (Gieryn, 1999).

The question of demarcation criteria obviously arose in the nineteenth-century academic debate between science and religion. It gained considerable public prominence after Darwin's *Origin of Species* (1859) highlighted the explanatory power of natural selection theories *vis-à-vis* traditional religious doctrines of creation. However, it was American scientists such as White (1898) and Draper (1910) who translated the science-religion debate into epistemological terms and positioned it in historical analyses. In subsequent decades the mainstream debate increasingly dropped the polemics with religion and focused on purely epistemological issues. Weber dealt with the problem of demarcation in his methodology of ideal types as a way for scientists to avoid identifying their personal values with those of their academic study object. Many others discussed the issue as well. Thus the sociologist Merton (1942)

---

[2] One can question the extent to which the process of distancing can be considered a methodological tool. Ricoeur (1973) himself apparently refutes that, since he understands distancing as constitutive for the written text.

identified guiding principles that distinguish between shared scientific property (communalism), independence of personal identity markers (universalism), academic selflessness (disinterestedness), and rigid scrutiny (organised scepticism).[3] However, it was Popper who established a by now widely accepted demarcation criterion. It draws a sharp methodological inference from Merton's last guiding principle. In view of the logical asymmetry between verifying and falsifying claims, Popper introduces the notion of corroboration, according to which those hypotheses or theories that withstand rigorous testing are rightfully entitled to the adjective 'scientific', since they are more informative, explanatory and parsimonious and have far greater potential for growth.

However, those who accept Popper's falsification principle for demarcating scientific from non-scientific knowledge pay a price in the hermeneutic realm of meaning.[4] The emphasis on immunisation, criticism and falsification that appears to lie at the heart of scientific progress does not necessarily stand up to conventional strategies that focus on meaning construction from our narrative past. At any rate one can question whether meaning is not discarded after all in rigid refutations of conjectures that do not match harsh empirical reality.

VERISIMILITUDE

Does a demarcation between scientific and non-scientific claims also offer authoritative methods to come 'closer to the truth'? If there is a dialectics of participation and distancing, what is the trade-off between the two in an approximation of truth?

In the critical rationalist approach the notion of verisimilitude was coined by Karl Popper (2002), who maintains that his falsification

---

[3] Merton (1942) developed these CUDOS in his sociology of science. Interestingly, Merton attracted attention with his doctoral thesis ("Science, technology and society in 17-century England") that offers a sequel to Max Weber's proposition about the affiliation of Protestant ethics with the rise of capitalism. In the so-called Merton thesis he suggests an elective affinity between Protestant pietism and early experimental science in 17th and 18th century England and Germany, in which scientific progress could be fuelled by religious motives such as that of disclosing a God-given world.

[4] One must remember that Popper's criticism was both epistemological, in rejecting the positivist claims of *Wiener Kreis* empiricists, and socio-political, in criticising the ideologies he had in mind when writing his *The Open Society and its Enemies* in 1939. According to him knowledge acquisition is best understood by analogy with problem solving, in which consequences of beliefs are tested by a method of trial and error (Popper, 1999).

process results in scientific growth to the extent that theories are corroborated under pressure of critical tests, and are therefore legitimately entitled to claim greater truth. The notion of verisimilitude ensures that knowledge growth keeps up with the truth of its propositions without resorting to inductive reasoning. Thus, a theory—as tested in the empirical cycle—is truer inasmuch as it is able to predict more true and fewer untrue (falsified) consequences. However, there is no criterion of truth other than methodological scepticism. It validates a better methodological fit between theory and empirical facts, but does not answer referential truth questions. Thus one cannot refute claims that reality exists beyond our perception and methodological tests.[5] Even if we apply intra- and intertheoretical criteria to resolve the issue, Popper fails to close the logical gap between statements of empirical fact and truth claims.

In the hermeneutic paradigm, the notion of verisimilitude is explicitly relevant to the spatial metaphors of participation and distancing. Ricoeur, who understands the dialectics of appropriation (participation in Dreyer's terms) and distancing as the "final figure which the dialectic of explanation and understanding must assume", links appropriation with play (Ricoeur, 1991: 87). Appropriation is '*Aneignung*': actualised meaning transferred from author, text and reader to the dialogical event in which it is interpreted. Play here serves as the heuristic fiction in which participants are 'metamorphosed in the true', thereby realising mimesis in its proper sense, namely as a transformation according to the truth. Though Ricoeur acknowledges that actors may fall prey to illusions, he simultaneously argues that hermeneutic appropriation as an act of self-presentation—in contrast with the quest for absolute knowledge—is the only proper means to deal with interpretive conflicts.

This Ricoeurian view does not tell us, however, by what criteria we can determine how 'metamorphosed in the true' we actually are. One implicit criterion to assess meaning is probably that our interpretations need to be true to life. In the humanities one indeed finds notions of verisimilitude in scholarly works on literature and theatre, where

---

[5] Popper (1979a, 1979b) discusses this in his three-worlds theory, which allows him to discard the essentialist view of reality that characterises Cartesian dualism (his interactive view of World 1 as that of physical objects and World 2 as mental frame of reference), while maintaining the objectivity of mental and cultural objects (World 3) in the sense that they can be falsified in scientific theories. For a recent discussion, see Ter Hark (2004).

characters' enactments are assessed according to norms of literary canon, form and authenticity. Here establishing truth does not require a statement about reality independent of the observer, as it does in the epistemological view, but demands agreement from the observer in the sense of suspension of disbelief in exchange for belief that an enacted truth offers a compelling image of real life. Claims of composition supersede those of representation. However, this again begs some serious questions. The truth may be convincingly enacted, but however profound the performance, it may fall prey to vicissitudes such as disagreements about canon, disturbances of plot, discontinuities in form, and divergent audience opinion. Arbitrariness may rule when truth can be established and demolished depending on the appreciation or disappointment of its interpreters.

The apparent failure to answer the question of verisimilitude raises the question whether notions of distancing and participation are not better understood as skills, competencies to deal with knowledge claims, rather than as judgements to prove propositional claims to truth. If so, what would be the methodological consequences?

Induction and Deduction

My answer to this question introduces two complementary lines of reasoning. One is to relate participation and distancing to inductive and deductive research procedures respectively. The other is to understand meaning obtained according to these procedures as a concept of belief that is susceptible to empirical research.

Dreyer relates participation and distancing to qualitative and quantitative research respectively. Surprisingly, he omits the favoured epistemological priorities of these research types, namely inductive and deductive techniques. In inductive research procedures, advocated by qualitative researchers, one looks for patterns that allow for tentative hypotheses and general rules that match observations by comparing corresponding characteristics of personal or socio-cultural phenomena. Inductive reasoning generalises from observation of cases to (rules for) the class of these cases. This open, verification-oriented procedure of proving claims implies that given premises can yield many conclusions. In deductive research procedures, advocated by quantitative researchers, one applies general rules to specific cases following the logic of condition and effect, in which rules explain empirical phenomena with claims to generic validity for classes of cases. This procedure is characterised by trial and error that aims to develop knowledge by means of falsifying theoretical claims in an attempt to broaden the empirical range of phenomena explained.

One cannot simply equate distancing and participation with induction and deduction, but one can ask how the assumed hermeneutic dialectics of the first two notions fits the epistemological claims of the respective researchers. Here it should be noted that the empirical research cycle contains a phase difference between induction and deduction. Empirical research procedures first require induction, which—taken in a broad sense—is an inspirational, exploratory, empathic and tentative technique characterised by freedom of design and conceptualisation but with the explicit aim of hypothesis building. The next step is deduction, which requires the derivation of clear-cut predictions about the empirical reality based on the hypothetical and theoretical assumptions from the inductive phase, resulting in operational definitions and their corresponding variables that cohere in the nomothetic structure of a theory. My point here is not to dichotomise induction and deduction as competing strategies for knowledge production, but to highlight their conditional relationship in a cyclic, iterative research procedure. Knowledge is the product of a sequential acquisition process: first induction, then deduction.[6] Put negatively, the relationship between induction and deduction is *not* dialectical. Methodologically, dialectics is a procedure to handle truth claims by formulating them as hypotheses with implicit, contending propositions. Dialectics is an art of rational argumentation that clarifies and reformulates propositions and counter propositions, up to a point where contradictions are counterbalanced in new propositional claims that no longer suffer from the fuzziness of previous formulations of the problem. Thus the Ricoeurian approach of counterbalancing participation and distancing fails to appreciate the sequential relationship of inductive and deductive approaches to arrive at epistemological truth-claims.

Exchanging a dialectic approach for a sequential one has an important implication. If meaning is studied by means of both inductive and

---

[6] In his classic handbook on methodology, De Groot (1969) takes the empirical cycle as the scientific version of basic experiential cycles of reasoning, of which the creative and hermeneutic cycles are analogous manifestations, as he clarifies with reference to Bahle's *Prinzip der schöpferische Gestaltung* and Jaspers' *Hermeneutische Zirkel des Verstehens*.

deductive procedures, this has consequences for the notion of meaning itself. The academic endeavour requires us to aim for theoretically informed knowledge about meaning: its experiential conditions, the referred interpretive object and affective and volitive valence, its behavioural and socio-cultural characteristics and cognitive clarificatory effort. One empirically suitable concept for studying meaning is that of belief. The dynamic or process characteristics of meaning can be researched by way of the empirical cycle. Meaning can be conceptualised and operationalised as belief to pass the induction and deduction phases of the empirical cycle. Following the continuous loop of the cycle, meaning can be understood as socio-culturally dependent, temporal and inescapably related to interests.

This cyclic loop of meaning through the empirical cycle can be seen as a process of belief-update, in which an agent acknowledges changed meaning by taking new pieces of information into account and adapting referents from the past to current ones. Notions of belief-update and belief-revision feature in socio-scientific theories, for instance those of attitudinal change. Belief-update crops up in philosophical discourse as well. For instance, in modern epistemology the so-called belief-revision theory seeks to describe and explain processes of 'defeasible reasoning', in which premises of arguments are true whereas the conclusions are clearly false. Rooted in Aristotelian dialectics, it resurfaced in discussions of artificial intelligence to explain anomalies in logical programming.

Moving from the cyclic to the iterative characteristics of research, one can deal with this process in terms of belief consequences. The idea is not merely to update belief but also to revise it. Belief-revision may assume various forms, such as integration of new sets of belief (belief-merger), removal of beliefs (contraction of belief), addition of beliefs without checking for consistency (expansion of belief), addition with such a check (strict belief-revision), or restoration of beliefs (consolidation of belief). Thus exchanging a dialectical for a sequential process of addressing meaning allows us to draw inferences for empirical research.

INNOVATION

My proposal to relate meaning to knowledge claims is pertinent to developing the craft of empirical theology that Dreyer has in mind. What would be innovative directions of empirical research? I answer that question by indicating three opportunities for empirical research into meaning. To this end I apply a distinction made by the Nijmegen sociologist Ultee (2003), who distinguishes between multi-moment, multi-actor, and multi-context perspectives in empirical research.[7]

First, we can study socio-religious reality from a multi-moment perspective. This is usually understood to refer to longitudinal or quasi-experimental research designs that indeed imply measurements at different points in time. However, the multi-moment perspective focuses on the subjective or socio-cultural meaning of these different points in time. This perspective pertains to empirical research into respondents' interpretations of the socio-religious reality in which they are immersed biographically or historically at different times. A respondent can look back on her life plot, on the generational chain in which she is a link, or on the history of which she is part. Instead of such retrospection a multi-moment focus may also imply a prospective look: what is my destiny in life, what will my children do, what course will history take? This type of research follows respondents through certain temporal episodes and charts the updated or revised meanings they attribute to these. This research focus avoids the pitfall of prevailing attitudinal research that assumes stable cognitive attitudinal markers only. Especially in times of rapid social change, like that affecting religion today, this type of research may gain status.

Secondly, multi-actor research aims to study the tissue of socio-religious realities in the immediate lifeworld of individuals. This lifeworld actually represents a multi-layered network of actors who take account of their position in the network, their access to resources and various aims of action. A multi-level approach studies the lifeworld cohesion of interconnected levels: the micro level of intimate interaction, the meso level of group interactions, and the macro level of interactions with state institutions. Research is not limited to any one of these levels but explicitly studies their interactive links in the lifeworld. Here, too, established research can be criticised for not addressing the patterns of meaning implied in the participatory character of reality in terms of level-specific differences in role, status and authority underlying people's communication. In empirical research we lack insight, not only into

---

[7] Ultee himself does not apply his methodological programme either hermeneutically or specifically to religion, but merely looks for an innovative sociology in which social reality remains the object of study but with reference to quantifiable social characteristics.

the characteristics of respondents' interpretation within each level, but also into conflict and synergism between these interactive levels. Again, this type of research is relevant to theological questions. Thus one can study the differentiation of spiritual lifestyles according to the ongoing process of individualisation, the highly complex interaction of private and public life, and shifting evaluations of the church-state relationship.

Thirdly, a multi-context approach is necessary to account for the diverse cultural, national and religious settings in which interpretive processes arise. Comparative religion already uses such an approach, but a purely comparative stance does not pursue exactly the same aim as a multi-context approach. Here research focuses on interpretive variables such as the conditions, subject matter and objectives of the process of meaning-giving in each context. Thus the really relevant questions concern the varieties of religious interpretations that prevail or become lost in particular eras and in different cultural environments. A cardinal question in religious research concerns the interpretation of religion's adaptation to its socio-cultural context: to what extent do religious interpretations predict successful or abortive processes of social accommodation and assimilation? How do these processes give rise to belief-update or belief-revision? Such questions are crucial for empirical insight into religious change.

The aforementioned research options offer good opportunities to apply the hermeneutic principles of participation and distancing in empirical theological research.

REFERENCES

Adorno, T.W. and Popper, K. (1976), *The Positivist Dispute in German Sociology*, London, Heinemann.
Darwin, C. (1859), *On the Origin of Species by Means of Natural Selection: or the preservation of favoured races in the struggle for life*, London, John Murray.
de Groot, A.D. (1969), *Methodology: foundations of inference and research in the behavioural sciences*, The Hague, Mouton.
Draper, J.W. (1910), *History of the Conflict Between Religion and Science*, London, Kegan Paul.
Gieryn, T.F. (1999), *Cultural Boundaries of Science: credibility on the line*, Chicago, Illinois, Chicago University Press.
Mendelsohn, L. (2005), *The Philosophy of Gottlob Frege*, Cambridge, Cambridge University Press.
Merton, R.K. (1942), *The Sociology of Science: theoretical and empirical investigations*, Chicago, Illinois, Chicago University Press.

40 HANS SCHILDERMAN

Popper, K. (1979a), Three worlds: the Tanner lectures on human values, *Michigan Quarterly*, 18(1), 1–23.
——. (1979b), *Objective Knowledge: an evolutionary approach*, Oxford, Clarendon Press.
——. (1999), *All Life is Problem Solving*, London, Routledge.
——. (2002), *Conjectures and Refutations: the growth of scientific knowledge*, London, Routledge.
Ricoeur, P. (1973), The hermeneutic function of distancing, *Philosophy Today*, 17, 129–141.
——. (1974), Hegel Aujourd'hui, *Etudes théologiques et religieuses*, 49, 353, quoted by J. van den Hengel, P. O'Grady and P. Rigby (1989), Cognitive linguistic psychology and hermeneutics, *Man and World*, 22(1), 43–70.
——. (1991), Appropriation, in M. Valdés (ed.), *A Ricoeur Reader: reflection and imagination*, pp. 86–98, New York, Harvester Wheatsheaf.
——. (1991), *From Texts to Action: essays in hermeneutics*, *II* (tr. By K. Blamey and J.B. Thompson), London, Athlone Press.
Robinson, G.D. (1995), Paul Ricoeur and the hermeneutics of suspicion: a brief overview and critique, *Premise*, II (8), 12.
Schwartz, S. (1983), Hermeneutics and the productive imagination: Paul Ricoeur in the 1970s, *The Journal of Religion*, 63(3), 290–300.
ter Hark, M. (2004), *Popper, Otto Selz, and the Rise of Evolutionary Epistemology*, Cambridge, Cambridge University Press.
Ultee, W. (2003), *Sociologie: vragen, uitspraken, bevindingen*, Groningen, Nijhoff.
van der Ven, J.A. and Zieberts, H.-G. (1993), Relevanz der Paradigmendiskussion für die praktische Theologie, in J.A. van der Ven and H.-G. Zieberts, *Paradigmentwicklung in der praktischen Theologie*, pp. 7–17, Kampen, Kok, Weinheim, Deutscher Studien Verlag.
White, A.D. (1898), *A History of the Warfare of Science with Theology in Christendom*, New York, Appleton.

CHAPTER THREE

RELIGIOUS IDENTITY IN COMPARATIVE RESEARCH

Johannes A. van der Ven

Summary

This chapter seeks to answer two questions: what does the religious identity of individuals and communities entail, and how can we research it? The concept of religious identity entails two terms: religion and identity. In this chapter religion refers to individuals and communities dealing with the dialectical relation between autonomy and contingency, especially in existentially meaningful situations and experiences, in the perspective of transcendence. Identity refers to the dialectic relation between 'same' and 'other' (Aristotle 1054a30–1059a14). 'Same' in religious identity is expressed in permanence in time, and 'other' in the relation between identity and alterity. Finally, I analyse the relation in comparative research on religious identity between, on the one hand, two methods, qualitative and quantitative, and, on the other hand, two perspectives, insider and outsider.

Introduction

The novel *Snow* by Nobel Prize winner Orhan Pamuk is set in the city of Kars in a remote corner of north-eastern Anatolia, which has been dominated alternately by Greeks, Turks, Kurds, Armenians, Georgians and Russians. In our own day it has seen a struggle between Islamists and Kemalists, and between activists, traitors, profiteers, fellow travellers and victims. At the end the writer, who plans to record all these intricacies in a book, is told by the receptionist of the hotel of the same name, Snow: "If you write a book set in Kars and put me in it, I'd like to tell your readers not to believe anything you say about me, anything you say about any of us. No one could understand us from so far away" (2005: 435). The quotation epitomises the no less complex task facing a scientific researcher who tries to compare the religious identities of individuals and communities 'from so far away'.

42 JOHANNES A. VAN DER VEN

IDENTITY: PERMANENCE IN TIME

In this section I discuss the following themes in identity as permanence in time. The first is that permanence of identity in time can be described in terms of the dialectic between sameness and self, which differ in structure. Even though identity may appear to be homogeneous, it is characterised by multiplicity and hybridity and may comprise any number of aspects. Like all forms of identity, religious identity is marked by the dialectic of ascription and achievement. But is achieved identity a free choice based on personal intentionality, or is it imposed by extraneous structural factors? And finally, is that choice mediated by religious representations (ideological identity), religious rites (ritual identity), religious institutions (institutional identity) or by some or all of these?

Sameness and self

A hallmark of identity, whether individual or communal, is that it remains the same over time. It survives the 'ravages of time'. But the fact that it is not affected by time does not make it an invariable constant. Because of temporal change identity undergoes necessary transformation, evidenced by individual human development. That does not imply that it changes its form while the essence remains untouched. Such essentialism should make way for the following argument. Just as individuals or communities used to relate to historical circumstances in a given era (T1), so they relate, analogously, to current historical circumstances (T2). Thus permanence of identity lies in continuity of relations to time, for example, T1 and T2.

This entails an important insight. Identity does not precede time, it is not above or buried in the depths of time, but is embodied in time. It is not a reified process independent of its carriers, be they individuals or communities. It is actualised in the interaction between these carriers and the surrounding culture in time. It is grounded in the way individuals and communities, in interaction with culture, see themselves as 'the same' in varying circumstances throughout history up to the present. That determines its hermeneutic character (cf. Van der Ven, 2005: 120–123).

That tells us something about the past and the present, but what about the future? Permanence in the past and the present can be reconstructed hermeneutically after the event. But reconstructing future permanence in retrospect is a contradiction in terms. It negates the very nature of future time. Future permanence cannot be reconstructed hermeneutically; it can only be expressed, attested, proclaimed hermeneutically as a promise. One can only promise that one will be 'the same' in the future—that one will remain loyal, engaged, committed (Ricoeur, 1992: 115–125). In so doing one promises to keep one's word and puts oneself under a certain obligation to do what one says. Stating that one will keep one's promise entails a risk, for who can foretell the future, who foresees the long- and short-term consequences of one's own and other people's actions? The other party can only look to the trustworthiness of the person making the promise. The only 'guarantee' offered is that person's reliability. The underside is betrayal: the suspicion of a trap can always rear its head; any promise can be broken (Ricoeur, 2005: 127–134). This applies to the collective self as much as to individual selves. The permanence of a community's future identity, too, resides in a promise, whose sole basis is trustworthiness and reliability: a promise to keep the social contract, the rule of law, within that community, or to adhere to contractual treaties between communities. The essential difference between groups of animals and those of human beings refers to the fact that the latter are able to make and keep promises (Cassirer, 1932).

Needless to say, such future-oriented identity is also enacted in a continuity of relations. Just as individuals and communities related to the historical circumstances of a bygone era (T1) and relate to present circumstances in terms of their current self-understanding (T2), so they promise to relate to the unknown historical circumstances that will befall them in the future (T3). The basis of permanence in time is hermeneutic self-understanding, for the past and the present in the mode of reconstruction, for the future in the mode of promise.

Multiplicity and hybridity

While identity does imply permanence, it does not mean oneness. From Aristotelian dialectics we have to distinguish on the one hand between sameness and self and on the other between one and many. In other words, individuals and communities have not just one but several identities. Thus apart from religious identity they have a social, an economic, a political and a cultural identity. People are not just members (or non-members) of religious communities, but also have—probably stronger—ties with their partners, parents, children, siblings, friends (social identity), teachers, pupils, colleagues, bosses and underlings (professional identity), adherents or members of political parties (political identity), and active or passive practitioners of folk or classical art (cultural identity). In other words, the dialectic between sameness and self is not enacted only in the area where ultimate questions about autonomy and contingence are symbolised and ritualised in a transcendent perspective (religious identity). It also functions in areas pertaining to primary relations and the lifeworld (social identity), careers (professional identity), the exercise of political power (political identity), and the symbolisation of all these domains (cultural identity). People perceive their identity not merely in terms of religious sameness and self, but also of social, economic, political and cultural sameness and self. This is expressed in taking responsibility and fulfilling duties (Sen, 2006). It does not concern self-evident undertakings but life plans entailing long- and short-term goals, in which desirability and feasibility rival each other, as do means and resources that are scarce and have to be distributed equitably (Rawls, 1971: 399–433). It is important because it gives their history 'life coherence', to which they attest in their 'narrative coherence' (Ricoeur, 2000: 484, n. 41).

But that does not mean that these identities necessarily constitute an integral whole. Euphoric speculations can easily lead one to talk of a 'polyphonic identity'. Usually there is a hybrid combination of diverse identities without any optimal harmony between them. Clinical psychology records phenomena such as dissociation, levelling and elimination of areas of identity, as well as a double bind when two or more areas conflict (Hermans, 1974: 239–276). Max Weber realised long ago that religious identity can conflict with economic identity because of the opposing principles of religion (solidarity) and economics (competition); with political identity because of the differing power claims of revelation and democracy; with sexual identity because of different notions about sexual experience and orientation; or with intellectual identity because of the conflicting demands of academic freedom versus a *sacrificum intellectus* (cf. Weber, 1978: 542–571). There are three possible ways out of this kind of conflictual, hybrid identity construct (Hirschman, 1970): tolerating cognitive dissonance if one does not want to give up any of the identity areas (loyalty), critically championing changes in one of these areas (voice), or deciding to quit (exit).

Ascription and achievement

Against the background of such multiple identities one could ask to what extent they are ascribed or achieved. The question also pertains to religious identity. It is often said that one is born into a particular religious community because one's parents (and other relatives) belong to it, or conversely that one is not born into a religious community because one's parents are not members. This argument from kinship can be further explicated in terms of the helplessness and need for security of (young) children, their emotional dependence on, and the emotional influence of, the family, which include internalisation of family values and identification mechanisms. That would explain religious ascription in terms of religious kinship relations.

In non-Western countries religious ascription cannot be underestimated, but even there phenomena are emerging that are typical of religious identity in Western countries: a decline in religious ascription and growing religious (or nonreligious) achievement at an increasingly early age. Religious choice can be differentiated into acceptance or rejection of one or more religious representations, rituals and/or forms of participation in a religious institution, including total rejection of the latter (believing without belonging). People may also opt for multiple religious belonging, and not only in Africa, where some groups take part in African traditional rituals as well as those of Christian churches and Islamic mosques (Van der Ven, Dreyer and Pieterse, 2004: 350–355; Anthony, 2003), or Japan, where Shinto rituals are performed at the beginning of life, Buddhist rituals at the end of life and Christian rituals for marriage (Valkenberg, 2006: 130), but also in Western countries where Christian and Zen rituals are sometimes combined. In other words, religious identity in itself is complex, quite apart from its interaction with social and cultural identities.

A choice based on reflective achievement offers a better chance of tolerance of other religions than a choice based on convention. This is because in weighing one's options one discovers similarities as well as differences, and because differences between religions are often much smaller than those within religions. Another reason is that one considers not just the pros and cons of one's own religion but also those of other religions. In addition such a choice is an ongoing, dynamic process, which means that tolerance is constantly nurtured. During the Renaissance that was not considered an evil, since faith in God and differences between religions were seen as manifestations of the

46 JOHANNES A. VAN DER VEN

relation between the one and the many (e.g. by Pico della Mirandola) and truth about God as the totality of viewpoints about God (e.g. by Nicholas of Cusa) (Coskun, 2006: 62–63).

In the so-called Radical Enlightenment, however, many Christian denominations regarded tolerance as an evil, because it threatened the absolute, universal and 'exclusive' truth-claims of these churches. Tolerance might trigger a reflective choice process, leading to a liberal interpretation of the Trinity and Christology, which in its turn could foster deism, agnosticism and atheism. These fears were rife, not only in the Christian world but also in Judaism and Islam. There, too, reflective religion was considered hazardous (Israel, 2006: 97). This makes the relation between ascription and achievement a less innocuous issue than it seems at first glance. Does the heavier emphasis on religious achievement that characterises present-day, mainly Western, culture indeed result in a sliding scale of tolerance, religious liberalism, deism, agnosticism and atheism?

Intentionality and structure

What I have said about deliberative reflection in religious choice could create the impression that it is entirely an outcome of the individual or community's own intentions. That is by no means true. There are two dimensions to religious choice: one's own intention and structural factors. The latter comprises factors that surpass the individual or community and influence them from supra-cyclical economic, political, judicial, social and cultural trends

Thus the principle of the separation of Church and state, so intrinsic to the democratic state, influences attitudes towards religious representations, rituals and institutions. It makes quite a difference whether that principle is interpreted from a cooperative, an accommodative or a laicist angle (Durham, 1996). A cooperative interpretation sees state and Church as two independent entities, but with the state subsidising the Church by way of funding its clergy and schools, maintaining its buildings and/or withholding church tax. An accommodative interpretation does not allow for such subsidies. Instead the Church is viewed as part of the national culture and conditions are created for preserving it by recognising the religious calendar and granting financial exemptions. A laicist interpretation erects a wall of separation between state and Church and the latter is cordoned off to prevent it from playing any role in the public domain.

RELIGIOUS IDENTITY IN COMPARATIVE RESEARCH 47

There is also reverse influencing of society by religious identity in the form of religious influence on certain economic factors, such as the elective affinity (*Wahlverwandschaft*) between Calvinism and capitalism (Weber), or the traditional role division between males and females discussed in this volume by Leslie Francis. Religion moreover influences civil society, for instance through charitable, diaconal and voluntary work, mutual solidarity, integration and cohesion, and the impact of religious culture on the legal culture, and hence on legislative, administrative and judicial decisions. In short, the interaction between religion and society is characterised by antecedent and consequential relations. Society influences religion (antecedent relations), while religion influences society (consequential relations), which in its turn feeds back into the antecedent relations. This results in a dynamic, ongoing spiral process, which can be frozen at any point and subjected to research. The process does not have a linear upward or downward movement, for from which angle would it be seen as moving either upward or downward? According to a one-sided secularisation hypothesis the growing influence of society on religion could be regarded as an upward movement, but critics of that hypothesis would view it the other way round. It seems more likely that the process is curvilinear. At all events, the relative strength of antecedent and/or consequential relations can only be determined by careful empirical research into religious representations (about God, Jesus, Muhammad, creation, salvation), religious rituals (weekly and annual, as well as rites of passage) and religious institutions (monocratic, democratic, congregationalist). One also has to allow for the possibility that relations can be positive, negative, ambivalent, or non-existent.

At a theoretical level one might ask whether intentionality and structural causes are not mutually exclusive. The answer is negative, because there is no such thing as total intentionality or total causality, at least not in the human sciences. Total intentionality would mean that everything people do is a product of their own initiative without any influence from the contributions of earlier generations, including the institutions they shaped. That is inconceivable, since human beings are woven into synchronic and diachronic networks and the institutions embodying these. People do take the initiative, but it is their initiative *in* the world, not the initiative *of* the world. In other words, it is never more than an intervention (Kant, 1965: 410ff). But total causality does not exist either. If it did, the primary experience of 'mine-ness' would be an illusion, for instance that the actions I perform are *my* actions, the body I have and am is *my* body, the memory storing my knowledge is *my* memory, the thoughts I think are *my* thoughts, and the imagination I use to plan my future is *my* imagination designing *my* future (Ricoeur, 1992: 104–112). These experiences cannot be reduced to *qualia* (the quality of 'mine-ness'), explicable exclusively in terms of our physiological hardware, in this case the brain (Den Boer, 2004: 68–69). That would be to negate the structural interaction between body and mind, as well as the interaction between mind and culture, in which the manifold symbolisations of 'mine-ness' are accumulated in love, art, morality, religion and science. In fact, it would reduce human life to its material substratum.

Religious representations, rituals and institutions

I have now distinguished between different substantial aspects of religion: religious representations, rituals and institutions. They may be regarded as three possible carriers of religious identity, namely ideological, ritual and institutional identity. After all, some individuals and communities experience their religious identity as primarily ideological, others as mainly ritual and yet others as institutional. But is this trichotomy correct? There are other possible classifications, such as those of Glock (1962) and Stark and Glock (1968). They discern five substantial aspects, of which the first two are an ideological aspect (belief), corresponding to what I call religious representations, and a ritualistic aspect. Their other three aspects are an experiential aspect (feeling), an intellectual aspect (knowledge) and a consequential aspect denoting the influence of religion in daily life (effects). It is noteworthy that these classifications do not include the aspect of religious institutions, even though notions about the essential characteristics of such institutions, as well as their structure and function, could determine the religious identity of individuals and communities.

In empirical research there seems to be some uncertainty about the adequacy of the classifications. Glock and Stark eventually removed the consequential aspect from their list, since it refers to a consequence rather than a component of religion. In some empirical studies three of the remaining four aspects—the ideological, ritualistic and experiential aspects—appear to cluster together, the ideological aspect being the dominant one. Other studies yield two dimensions, one comprising the ideological plus the experiential aspect, the other comprising the ritualistic aspect. In yet other research the aspects appear to form a single factor, the ideological aspect again being dominant. This raises a question: is religion in fact controlled by the acceptance of religious truths, the ideological aspect, or is the measuring instrument such that the other aspects are heavily tinctured by the ideological aspect and are therefore not properly differentiated? The polemical question has been asked whether Glock and Stark's list does not constitute a sacred artifact (Felling, Peters and Schreuder, 1987: 40). Certainly the last word has not been said, even though the literature tends to treat Glock and Stark's list as axiomatic, despite the fact that it really calls for critical study and conceptual reflection (Wulff, 1991: 208–219). The crucial question is: does the crux of religion lie in religious representations (ideological aspect), or in a combination of religious representations and rituals, as Pals (1996: 270, 282–283) concludes from his study of the literature. If we focus on religious identity the question reads: does religious identity primarily comprise an ideological identity (religious representations) and/or a ritual identity?

In contemporary cognitive science of religion Glock and Stark's list has been superseded by the dichotomy that Pals found in the literature. He sees religion as comprising mainly religious representations and religious rituals, without devoting any substantial attention to my third aspect, that of religious institutions. But quite apart from that, the view that religion consists of religious representations and religious rituals tells us very little unless the relation between these two aspects is clarified, for that relation is the real issue when we look for the core of religion and religious identity.

Although the cognitive science of religion does recognise the relation of religious representations to religious rituals, it barely looks at the converse relation of religious rituals to religious representations.

Let me first deal with the relation of religious representations to religious rituals. It is usually assumed—and basically I would agree—that religious rituals inculcate religious representations in memory, thus enhancing their emotional saliency, promoting their interiorisation and reinforcing personal identification with them.

But the cognitive science of religion also speculates on the functioning of religious representations in ritual in a more specific way. It is assumed that participants in rituals have notions about the acts God performs during such celebrations. These can be divided into two categories: representations of direct divine acts and representations of indirect divine acts. An example of a representation of direct divine acts is the Catholic mass. After all, it is said, in the minds of Catholics God

50   JOHANNES A. VAN DER VEN

intervenes directly and accomplishes a transubstantiation of bread and wine into the body and blood of Jesus. An instance of a representation of indirect divine acts is the baptismal rite. In the minds of participants, according to this view, God intervenes indirectly, for the direct actor in this ritual is the ordained priest: he is the one who baptises, not God. In this view the baptismal act is traceable to the ordination act by an ordained bishop, whose legitimacy in turn derives from the acts of the apostles, whose legitimacy derives from Jesus' acts, whose legitimacy stems from God's sending of Jesus, his son. The message, then, is: in transubstantiation God acts directly, in baptism God acts indirectly (Lawson and McCauley, 1990; Boyer, 2001: 258ff; McCauley and Lawson, 2002; Vial, 2006).

My objection concerns the conceptual shakiness of this speculation, arising from the distinction made between the two sacraments, baptism and the eucharist. After all, in both instances the ritual act is performed by an ordained priest in communication with the religious community: in that respect there is no difference between them. But that is not all. The question is how to interpret the relation between the human act of the priest and the community on the one hand and the divine act on the other. The answer is not to assume indirect divine action in baptism and direct action in the eucharist. In both instances God's active presence is both direct and indirect. The solution lies in replacing the causal, mechanistic operation that is said to characterise the indirect divine act in baptism, including the purely instrumental chain of causes and effects, with a dialectic relation between divine act and human act. This dialectic entails that God acts not only *via* the acts of the officiating priest and community (indirectly), but also *in* those acts (directly). In both baptism and the eucharist God acts both *via* (indirectly) and *in* human acts (directly). As Schillebeeckx (1973) puts it, God's activity is that of mediated immediacy, in which 'mediated' refers to the 'via' in indirect acts and 'immediacy' refers to the 'in' in direct acts. One could see it as a typical example of Catholic sacramentology, deriving from deeper conceptions of creation and grace (Schoonenberg, 1971). These are applicable in our instance, since it concerns the Catholic eucharist.

But the relation between religious representations and rituals should not be seen only in terms of the former relating to the latter, but also, as noted already, the other way round. According to Catholic sacramentology that relation could be described as follows. People's religious experience during ritual celebrations is translated into the symbolic language of religious representations that have crystallised in many age-old religious traditions. The rituals activate memory and open up the archives of these traditions, thus broadening and deepening people's experience of the celebrations and rendering it fruitful for the non-ritual side of their lives. This is the relevance of the adage that the cognitive patterns of religious representations derive from experiential patterns underlying participation in liturgy: ritual patterns are the source of representational patterns.[1]

This leads me to posit that the relation between religious representations and rituals should be approached not only from the point of view of religious studies generally, but more particularly by way of research into concrete ritual practices in concrete religions and denominations. It will be then seen, I hypothesise, that religious institutions with their diversity of representations and rituals play a decisive role. Against this background I propose to distinguish between three substantial aspects: religious representations, rituals and institutions.

IDENTITY AND ALTERITY

However important the identity of individuals and communities in terms of permanence in time, it cannot be isolated from other individuals and communities. To explain this point I first explore the reciprocity of the identity of self and other. Then I outline a critical condition for that reciprocity: taking the other's perspective. Finally I relate the five themes examined in the first section to the identity of the other—both an individual and a collective other.

Self and other

The dialectic between the identity of self and other can be understood with reference to a reconstruction by Honneth (1994) of the young Hegel's concept of recognition (*Anerkennung*) in his *Jenaer Schriften*, augmented by notes from Ricoeur (2005). Honneth describes three models illustrating the reciprocity of the identities of self and other: love, respect and esteem. Violations of reciprocity correspond with these models.

---

[1] This translates into its empirical meaning the adage *lex orandi lex credendi*—which in Augustine's work, especially since the controversy with semi-Palagianism about the *initium fidei* and the *initium boni*, already had a normative connotation (liturgy *should* determine faith).

The first model is family love. Here one already sees that the development of identity is marked by a polarity between active striving to earn recognition and passive striving to be recognised. Both poles are actualised in the security, trust, care and love offered by the family. They are expressed in a striving to lose oneself in the other and separate oneself from the other, the need for attachment and detachment, the longing to be together and to be alone, the desire to be present and absent. This dialectic gives rise to identity. But there are also violations of this twofold striving: nonrecognition or misrecognition rather than recognition, humiliation rather than care. That happens when a child is ensnared in a symbiotic relationship (Jacoby, 1990), treated from an attitude of dubious love (Van den Berg, 1958) or abandoned to its fate. In these instances it feels misunderstood, either sucked in or declared nonexistent.

The second model is respect (*Achtung*) in a democratic state. Again mutual recognition is crucial. In fact, the rule of law is based on it, as is evident in the social contract that citizens have with one another in a reconstructive rather than a genetic, historical sense. The legal system, especially human rights, is based on the notion that every citizen deserves to be recognised on the basis of her intrinsic human dignity. That is why everybody is equal before the law and has equal freedom. Violations of this principle assume two forms. One is discrimination on the grounds of attributes like gender, sexual orientation, race, colour, language, culture or religion, which violates the dignity of individuals and communities alike and drives them to all kinds of struggle—economic, political, cultural and religious (Margalit, 1999). The underclass rebel against the way the upper classes are recognised, whereas they themselves, who are seen as second rate people, *Untermenschen*, are not (Honneth, 2003; Fraser and Honneth, 2003). Following Hegel and Rousseau, who strongly influenced Hegel in this regard, one might say: "The struggle for recognition can find only one satisfactory solution, and that is a regime of reciprocal recognition among equals" (Taylor, 1994: 50). The other violation of the principle of equal freedom is crime, which infringes mutual recognition, the bedrock of the legal system. It is a breach of the social contract, to which the state's only proper response is coercion. The accent is not on the alienation of property but on the person who is injured, wounded by the crime—"my honour, not the thing" (Ricoeur, 2005: 184). For that reason the penalty transcends vengeance in pursuit of justice, for the aim is to restore "my injured self [as] recognized" (Ricoeur, 2005: 184).

The third model is social esteem. Ideally society should be structured so that every person enjoys the social esteem he merits by virtue of his contribution to the good life from diverse social positions in the various sectors, with due regard to differences in responsibilities, burdens and contributions. But this presupposes a homogeneous community with homogeneous values, norms and criteria for measuring each person's contribution. Such a society does not exist (at any rate, no longer exists), marked as it is by axiological diversity. Appraisals within and between sectors differ, the very functions performed in these are assessed differently. This has implications for mutual recognition in society. When individuals and groups disagree, the only solution is to agree on the requisite assessment through reasoned legitimation. If the parties fail to reach agreement, and agreeing to disagree does not resolve the deadlock, it needs something other than discourse ethics in Habermas' sense, namely a culture of readiness to compromise. Such a culture not only accords with the present state of society, as is evident in the empirical study by Boltanski and Thévenot (2006). It is also the only way to express the human dignity of the parties to the conflict (Ricoeur, 2005: 206).

The relevance of these three models to religious identity is easy to see. In the first model, that of love and care in a religious home, the child's religious identity flourishes, whereas neglect and lovelessness stunts the growth not just of its identity in general but also of its religious identity. In the second model democratic principles such as freedom of conscience and religion are basic to the development of individuals' and communities' religious identity. It grows from their experience of respect and recognition on an equal footing with other—religious and nonreligious—individuals and communities. This is inimical to both religious privilege and religious discrimination. The third model, in which social esteem is based on reasoned legitimation and mutual readiness to compromise, also applies to religious individuals and communities. Inasmuch as these learn to give up their absolute claims and participate in consultation and negotiation with due regard to the principle of give and take, they will get the social esteem they are entitled to—a form of recognition that is essential for their identity.

Taking the other's perspective

Development of mutual recognition hinges on an ability to take the other's perspective. That raises two questions. First, who *is* the other and what does the relation between self and other entail? Secondly, is it really possible to take the other's perspective?

There are several answers to the first question: who is the other? The answers can be subsumed under the concepts of anteriority, posteriority, exteriority, interiority and superiority. Anteriority means that the phenomenon of the self is preceded by that of the other and is constituted by it. Levinas says that the pleas 'do not kill me', 'do me justice', 'love me' that the other addresses to the self constitute the self when it responds to them. In posteriority the phenomenon of self is followed by that of the other, as in Husserl's phenomenology, and understanding of the other is preceded and influenced by self-understanding. In exteriority, as in Sartre's thinking, the other threatens the self, because by looking at the self from outside the other freezes, objectifies and reifies the self. In interiority, as conceptualised by Buber, constitution of self and other lies in the depth of the interpersonal relationship: in their encounter they become I and Thou (Theunissen, 1965). Postmodernism has added a fifth approach. It sees the other as an enigma. The other does not belong to the category of *différence* but represents a separate, irreducible category, *différance*—certainly for Derrida, who deconstructs the other into 'unnameable not-being' (De Vries, 1999). That puts the other on a level that transcends, in an absolute sense, the level at which the self knows itself and its world, and thus is superior to self. But it does not end there, for the self is likewise an irreducible category, *différance*: the self is always 'another' to himself. To complicate matters further, what does this twofold superiority of other and self imply for the one who is studying the other? She studies 'another' that enigmatically eludes her, at the same time eluding herself as 'another'. And who is the 'real other' in such a study—the one who is studied or the one studying the other and penetrating the latter's world as 'another' (Smith, 2004: 260)?

It is not easy to choose between these approaches. From a strong conceptualist perspective they are contradictory and contrasting. From the perspective of weak conceptualism they do not refer to the relation between self and other as such, but to varying aspects of that relationship in varying circumstances: sometimes the other emerges as anterior, sometimes as posterior, sometimes as exterior, sometimes as interior, sometimes as superior, sometimes as equally superior.

Weak conceptualism brings me to the second question: is it at all possible to take the other's perspective? Here a brief reference to psychological research into the development of empathy is helpful (Hoffmann,

1993; Van der Ven, 1998: 313–315). In the five developmental phases different aspects feature in differing circumstances. In phase one the infant develops automatic, non-voluntary responses such as crying, to stimuli (like crying) received from others (infants, adults). No distinction is made between self and other at this stage (global empathy). In phase two, when the infant is about a year old, it is capable of realising that the person in distress is someone else, not the self, but that person's inner state is as yet unknown to the infant, who assumes it to be the same as its own (egocentric empathy). In phase three, at about two or three years, the child develops empathy for the distinctiveness of the other's feelings and knows that they differ from its own (altruistic empathy). Phase four, in late childhood, sees the development of an empathy with the other's feelings that transcends the situation here and now, and the child shows understanding for the other's life conditions and history, even for those of an entire group. This empathy can develop into a feeling of compassion, accompanied by a desire to help the other because the child feels sorry for him. Thus it is not (only) a matter of assuaging the sorrow of the child who empathises with the other, but (also) of alleviating the other's need (sympathy). In phase five causal attribution processes emerge, in which the child looks for the causes of the other's feelings of distress. If she concludes that the other is to blame for these feelings, empathy may decline and even cease. If she concludes that it is attributable to causes beyond the other's control, moral feelings may develop, such as empathic anger, a sense of injustice, guilt, be it guilt because of inaction or guilt by association.

More generally, as development progresses, the self forms a theory of mind, that is, a set of notions in its own mind about what goes on in others' minds—in other words, what experiences, emotions, beliefs, arguments, conclusions, plans and the like are operating in the other's mind. But research has shown that the theory of mind is not a solid, massive constant but comprises numerous, varying aspects. I mention three: proximity, motivation and levels of understanding. First, understanding other people depends on how well people know each other, although some are better at understanding others and some people are easier to understand. Here proximity is a factor. Reading others' minds depends on the size of the group to which the other belongs, from the most intimate to the most tenuous, entailing groups of 5, 12, 150, 500 up to 2000 individuals (Dunbar, 1998: 187). The second aspect concerns the strength of the motivation to understand the other. Thus research indicates that couples who have been together for brief lengths of time show more mutual empathy than couples who have been together for lengthy periods, probably because they are more motivated to understand one another. Paradoxically, often the 'radically other' is the proximate rather than the remote other (Smith, 2004: 253). The third aspect concerns levels of understanding. The first level is the ability to read the other's mind separately from one's own. The second is to read the other's mind inasmuch as the other has certain ideas or wishes relating to the self and the self perceives these. The third level is to read the other's mind, including her ideas and wishes relating to oneself, so as to anticipate these by either accepting or rejecting them, or by simulating acceptance while actually rejecting them. The latter is a much researched form of (conscious or unconscious) deception, which is why the theory of mind has been called 'Machiavellian intelligence' (Givón, 2005).

Remarkably, the theory of mind, on which taking the other's perspective is based, plays a minor role in religious literature. Religious individuals and communities have a lot to say about dialogue with the other, either religious or interreligious, but often that is overshadowed and dominated by their own vision and mission. This is justified by arguing that one cannot have dialogue without introducing one's own views and that dialogue complements mission (Chia, 2003: 188) or even serves the purpose of mission (Bosch, 1991: 483–489). But how should the dialogue be conducted when all the partners take their own convictions as absolute and absolutely unique? Or, as John Locke put it, when "every church is orthodox to itself"? Can it mean anything other than that the other's religion, and not only one's own religion, deserves recognition, respect and esteem? The Ratzingerian document *Dominus Jesus* (2000) contradicts this, for it professes respect for the other as a person but not for the other's religion (i.e. his or her religious representations, rituals, institutions). Is it surprising if adherents of other religions react suspiciously when Christians invite them to interreligious dialogue, since they, the Christians, have the concept of mission in mind, focusing on conversion and church growth (Thangaraj, 1999; Hasselmann, 2001: 31)? What chance has the other's religious identity got of being recognised if we "demand that they can and should shed the narratives and practices they take to be necessary to their lives"? (Asad, 2003: 75).

The other's identity

The ability to take the other's perspective implies reading the other's life through the other's eyes. This could involve all five of the themes mentioned above. The first is the hermeneutic dialectic of sameness and self in the course of time, which does not only apply to the identity of the self, but also to that of the other. Continuity of relations means that the self is absorbed in the way the other understood herself in various periods and still understands herself as 'the same'. This 'hermeneutics of the other' also applies to the other's self-understanding as remaining 'the same' in the future and attesting it in a promise of loyalty, which is made both individually and collectively.

The second theme is the multiplicity and hybridity of identity. Particularly in a time like our own, in which religion appears on the global stage, there is a risk that the collective and individual identity of the other will be seen as an exclusively religious identity. History has shown that even when religion is foremost, identity is still determined by other factors as well. Churchill—not a conventionally religious man—interpreted the war with Nazi Germany in terms of a clash of civilisations, claiming that the survival of Christian civilisation was at stake. This was not dominated by the desire to maintain a Christian identity but by the will to save Western economic, political and social identity from collapse. Only if it is clear that this latter identity can be preserved for future generations, "men will still say, 'This was their finest hour'", as Churchill put it (Burleigh, 2006: 214–215).

The third theme concerns the dialectic between achieved and ascribed religious identity. By and large identity in Western cultures is characterised by personal, reflective decisions more than in non-Western cultures, where authority, tradition, community and convention are more influential. Taking the other's perspective is impaired when encounters with non-Western individuals and groups are dominated by the researcher's expectation that notions about individual self-determination are wholeheartedly shared by non-Western people. He should observe the limits of research ethics (Mentzel *et al.*, 1995).

The fourth theme is even more complex. It concerns the extent to which religious choices are indeed based on personal considerations, or are unconsciously based on the influence of pre-existing institutional structures. This presents the researcher with the ethical dilemma of deciding whether to stick to the other's insider notions, in which she sees her identity as self-chosen, or whether to expose that self-chosen identity in terms of 'false consciousness' from an outsider perspective. This is a common problem in research into religious sects, whose members make much of the 'new life' which, from their insider perspective, they claim to have chosen without seeing through the pious jiggery-pokery of religious control, manipulation and indoctrination. The same phenomenon is observable in established religions, inasmuch as unbridled power and deprivation of mental freedom feature there as well. The problem looms large when human rights like freedom of conscience, religion, expression, association and assembly are curtailed, and adherents of religion magnanimously take it for granted. It has to be resolved on the basis of human dignity by prudently complementing an insider perspective with an outsider perspective, but without declaring the latter superior to the former as some scholars tend to do (McCutcheon, 2006)—for that, too, would undermine the required freedom.

The fifth and last theme is the substantial aspects of the other's religious identity, individual and collective, that need to be taken into account: the religious representations, rituals and institutions. More particularly: to what extent are these representations, rituals and institutions really characteristic, distinctive, even unique features of the religion concerned, when compared with other religions? What is meant by characteristic, distinctive, unique? People often refer to a canon of texts on which their 'unique' beliefs and 'characteristic' practices are based. But that does not solve the problem, for there are different kinds of canonical texts: normative texts that are binding, such as creeds; social texts that provide a shared vocabulary at the time and create social identity; and exemplary texts that serve as religious paradigms. Besides, the traditions that grew from these texts are equally diverse, as are their authoritative pronouncements on conflicting interpretations of texts. The need for 'uniqueness' is understandable, since it draws a line between orthodox and heterodox groups, between that religion and other religions, and also impedes religious mobility in the form of 'conversion' from that religion to another. Yet the emphasis on uniqueness makes one lose sight of similarities and mutual influencing between religions. Again we face the dilemma of insider perspective and outsider perspective, for religious overlapping is only discernible from an outsider perspective. Here, too, the solution lies in complementary use of both perspectives. In so doing one should not lose sight of the necessary dialectic in such complementation, for anything taken from other religions is interpreted in terms of the self-understanding of one's own religion and is assimilated discursively into that tradition. Only by

Figure 3.1: Relation between methods and perspectives

	Qualitative method	Quantitative method
Insider perspective	1	2
Outsider perspective	3	4

deciphering this discursive tradition can we trace the nature of another religion (Satlow, 2006).

RELIGIOUS IDENTITY IN QUALITATIVE AND QUANTITATIVE COMPARATIVE RESEARCH

What we have said so far could give rise to the misconception that the best approach to comparative research into religious identity is the qualitative method, because it does more justice to the insider perspective and quantitative methods merely serve to complement the outsider perspective. But the distinction between qualitative and quantitative methods is not the same as that between insider perspective and outsider perspective. That is to say, both a qualitative method in respect of non-numerical, mainly verbal data and a quantitative method in respect of numerical data offer scope for the use of both the insider and the outsider perspective, as is evident in figure 3.1: cells 1 and 4 are as relevant as cells 2 and 3.

The relevance of all four cells also applies to comparative cross-cultural research, which, like cross-sectional research, makes use of both qualitative and quantitative methods. Both types of research seek to trace and analyse similarities and differences. In cross-sectional research one examines similarities and differences in the relation between two or more variables among two or more culturally homogeneous groups in a given population. In cross-cultural research one examines similarities and differences in the relation between two or more variables among two or more culturally heterogeneous populations or two or more different ethnic groups in the same country. In other words, cross-cultural research can employ both qualitative and quantitative methods, and both methods can be used from an insider and an outsider perspective.[2]

---

[2] This is counter to Ragin's view (1994: 77–154) that qualitative, quantitative and comparative research are respectively aimed at commonalities, covariation and diversity.

60 JOHANNES A. VAN DER VEN

To substantiate this view I deal with the interaction between theory and data in both methods; the level of abstraction in theory formation; synchronicity and diachronicity; individuals, groups and contexts; and cultural and linguistic equivalence.

Interaction between theory and data

All scientific research proceeds from a problem, as we know from the theory of science since Dewey in the first half of the twentieth century (Dewey, 1986; Van der Ven, 1993: 124–128). The problem could stem from contradictions between theory and data, between different data or between different theories. In order to get a grip on the problem the researcher analyses it in order to break it up into several questions. This activity of analysing the problem consists of two dimensions: one is basing the analysis on theoretical insights, the other is to conduct the analysis in such a way that an answer to the problem emerges from the data to be collected. Hence at the very outset of the study there is an inchoate interaction between data and theory. As a general rule, there can be no theory without data and no data without theory. Naturally this calls for qualification, for there is enough speculative theory in which data are sorely lacking. But theory without data is inconceivable if that theory is to make reliable, valid reference to the relevant domain in the empirical world. Conversely, there are plenty of descriptions of so-called facts, such as anecdotes, stories and journalistic reports, in which theory is lacking. It does not make these descriptions trivial, but they only acquire the connotation of data when they are presented in an organised fashion and qualify for analysis and interpretation.

The idea that all research is characterised by an interaction between data and theory is sometimes overlooked in debates on the relation between qualitative and quantitative methods. The qualitative researcher is assumed to be interested mainly or exclusively in data, undirected by theory, and only arrives at relevant insights on the basis of these data. The quantitative researcher is assumed to be interested only in her own theory, which she imposes on the data by manipulating control and/or independent variables, or reconceptualising the key concepts to confirm her theory-generated hypotheses (Ragin, 1989: 67). Of course, these are caricatures, but I have been around the scientific world long enough to know that such assumptions hold sway when controversies reach boiling point. The false assumption is that the less theory you have, the better for the insider perspective, and the more theory you have, the better for the outsider perspective.

But scientific insight does not happen without interaction between data and theory, an observation first made explicit by August Comte. In quantitative and qualitative research alike there is theory formation both before and after data collection. Let me explain in more detail.

In qualitative research prior theory formation can assume various forms: a system of categories in terms of which the data are approached, as in basic content analysis; an open series of categories as in the template method; a conceptual framework as in the researcher's map of territory; or an open questionnaire as in ethnographic content analysis. Without this theory formation one fumbles in the dark when deciding which data to research and what aspects of these data are relevant. Theory formation after the data have been collected is no less important in qualitative research. It comprises several steps: systematic data description; selection and reduction of data through classification; construction of typologies, for instance by crossing two categories from one class with those of another class; pattern construction (Pleijter, 2006). In research into religious identity, for example, it may turn out that religious burial rites deal more in transcendent God images than religious birth rituals, which are characterised by immanent-transcendent or simply immanent God images.

In quantitative research prior theory formation consists in a structure of concepts, resulting in a conceptual model. Here the rule is parsimony: the fewer the concepts and the more they are conceptually interrelated, the better. The concepts are rendered observable and measurable by operationalising them with a view to data collection. The data collection is followed by subsequent theory formation. This takes the form of systematic data description; reduction of data through, for example, factor analysis—applying the criterion of interpretability, which is not possible without theoretical scrutiny (Kim and Mueller, 1984); empirical exploration or testing of the conceptual model; considering the empirical reliability and validity of the model; and possibly suggestions for modifying the model. In this way one could explore the question why it is that more people in the United States of America than in Europe define their identity in religious terms, which could disclose differences in regard to the welfare state and/or religious mobility caused by religious competition (Verweij, 1998).

So the difference between qualitative and quantitative research does not lie in mutually exclusive attention given to data or theory. The emphasis on data or theory may differ, but that applies as much to projects within qualitative and quantitative research as between

62 JOHANNES A. VAN DER VEN

qualitative and quantitative research. Moreover, the notion that qualitative research is more amenable to an insider perspective *because* it puts greater emphasis on data, and that quantitative research is more amenable to an outsider perspective *because* of its greater emphasis on theory conflicts with (methodo-) logical thought.

Level of abstraction in theory formation

Even if there is consensus that research stands or falls by the interaction between data and theory, the difference between qualitative and quantitative methods is still sought in different levels of abstraction. The level is said to be lower in the first case than in the second. It is associated with the notion that the lower the level of abstraction the better for the insider perspective, and the higher that level the better for the outsider perspective. But is that true?

The focus can be narrowed down to an element that is a precondition for any theory formation at whatever level of abstraction: classification. Classification occurs in both the insider and the outsider perspective. By way of example we can look at the images religious leaders in the Catholic Church have of themselves, such as priest, father, friend, spiritual leader, helper, prophet, mother, guide, therapist, sister, brother. In his quantitative survey research, Schilderman (2005: 190–199) interprets these images with the help of concepts from these religious leaders' insider perspective. He does so rightly and convincingly, because they function as these leaders' self-images. Some of these images (father, mother, brother, sister, friend) are undeniably concepts at a low level of abstraction. But since these concepts are used analogously, I would add that one can legitimately ask what they mean to both the religious leaders themselves and to members of their religious institutions. Does the concept 'friend' refer, both for leaders and for members, to one or more of the forms of friendship identified by Aristotle—mutual profit, recreational pleasure and mutual intimacy? Does the concept of kinship, from which father/mother and brother/sister derive, colour their relationship by way of sharing life, sacrificial love and kin altruism (versus reciprocal altruism)? Asking these simple questions, which is necessary for getting further analytical insight into the meaning of these images, immediately raises the level of abstraction. In addition, from an outsider perspective, one has to ask what these images mean in the framework of the typically hierarchic structure of religious institutions. More particularly, how do these images of kinship and friendship relate to the typology of authority in terms of charismatic, traditional, legal and professional authority (Weber, 1980)? What do they mean in a traditional, legalistic, professional institution such as the Catholic Church, where research has shown this typology applies (Sonnberger, 1996)? Both kinds of concepts—kinship-related and authority-related—are necessary. When it comes to their level of abstraction they might be seen as equal.

The idea that religious people proceeding from an insider perspective use only concrete concepts or concepts at a low level of abstraction is illusory. What does one make of a home-made, so to speak, centrifugal classification of Christian denominations by members of the Catholic Church, in which the first on the list is considered closest and the last on the list the most distant (Eastern Christianity, Anglicanism, Lutheranism, Calvinism and the Free Churches)? The question is what this classification is based on. Explicating the reasons why Eastern Christian identity is considered closer to that of the Catholic Church than that of the Protestant Churches will necessarily entail a high level of abstraction. And what about the taxonomic classification of the relation with other religions by members of various Christian denominations, when they define their religious identity in terms of exclusivism, inclusivism, pluralistic inclusivism, inclusive pluralism (Dupuis, 1999) or pure pluralism (Hick, 1989)? To expound this classification one needs an explicit theology of religion on a rather high level of abstraction (Valkenberg, 2006: 97–98). At all events, differences in level of abstraction are not essentially linked with the difference between insider and outsider perspectives. Both have low and high levels of abstraction.

Even if the levels of abstraction of the insider and the outsider perspective are not essentially different, is it not better to keep the level of abstraction as low as possible in studies of religion and religious identity? Isn't there a danger that by raising that level the focus will be on similarities between individuals and groups rather than on differences? Does it not obscure the uniqueness of the religious identity of certain individuals and groups in comparison with others? I don't think so. An optical metaphor may be helpful. When one constructs more abstract concepts, one's eye may travel upward from below and downward from above. When looking upward from below, that is, from concrete phenomena to a more overarching category, one notices the similarities. If one looks down from that category to the concrete phenomena, the differences become apparent. The rule is probably—I say 'probably', because empirical study of classification is still in its

64   JOHANNES A. VAN DER VEN

infancy—that raising the level of abstraction and looking down from that level at concrete phenomena increases the chance of identifying differences (Medin and Waxman, 2002). This parallels Aristotle's insight that the genus concept, in terms of which two or more phenomena are regarded as a species, highlights difference: "A genus is what is predicated in what a thing is of a number of things exhibiting differences in kind" (Aristotle, 102a31–32).

Diachronicity and synchronicity

One objection to quantitative methods is that they focus on population attributes here and now without regard to their history. Their focus is synchronic. From the aforementioned hermeneutic point of view that religious identity is actualised in past, present and future, this is a serious objection. If the so-called analogy of relations in time and the promise for the future play no role, it would curtail an essential dimension of that identity.

Qualitative methods, on the other hand, offer ample scope for the diachronicity of religious identity. The moment one starts a dialogue with religious individuals and communities it almost automatically activates their religious memory and everything stored in it since early childhood. It offers unique access to the religious archive in which individuals and communities preserve their representations and experience, their codes and scripts from one generation to the next. Interviewing individuals and groups from different generations reveals the historical layers in that archive (Hervieu-Léger, 1993). In the process of interviewing them one can also ask them how they relate to the future, not only in regard to their hopes and desires but also to their commitment and engagement—in effect their promises.

It would be facile, however, to claim that quantitative methods offer no scope for diachronicity. The so-called multi-moment approach could be used more often than has been the case hitherto. In this approach respondents may be asked retrospectively about such matters as the following: family history (including relations with partner(s), parents and children and relocations); school career; professional career; roles as voluntary workers and members of associations; history of their dealings with colleagues, and relations with bosses. In conjunction with this, one can also look into issues with a more direct bearing on religious identity: history of their interpretation of religious representations and participation in religious rituals; history of their membership of religious communities and institutions; history of their orientations to ethical issues like abortion, euthanasia and same-sex marriage (Ultee, 2004). The multi-moment approach breaks through the supposedly essential difference between qualitative and quantitative methods in connection with diachronicity and synchronicity. It also severs the supposedly exclusive link of the former with an insider perspective and the latter with an outsider perspective.

Individuals, interactions and contexts

Another respect in which qualitative and quantitative methods are said to differ is that the former allows for the unrepeatable uniqueness of the individual, whereas the latter views her merely as a specimen from a particular category. Another alleged difference is that qualitative methods view individuals in their interactions with other individuals and communities, whereas quantitative methods ignore these interactions. A third difference is that the former is said to place individuals in their broad context, while the latter disregards context and treats individuals like atomised monads and communities like islands in an otherwise empty ocean.

These assumptions exaggerate the differences. In the case of individuals, qualitative methods do enable us to highlight their uniqueness, but when analysing qualitative data we still have to look for categories that will accommodate similar individual traits, which once again obscures their uniqueness. Quantitative methods, on the other hand, may include not just closed questions but also open questions, thus affording scope for personal experience and representations; but here, too, these are slotted into categories during analysis. In the case of interactions with other individuals and communities it is just as easy to exaggerate the differences. When researching these interactions respondents may be questioned about their relations with parents, partner(s), children, sibling and friends (e.g. friends for profit, recreation and/or personal concern) (Eisinga *et al.*, 2002). The same applies to their relations with groups and communities (e.g. in the economic, political, social, cultural and religious spheres). As for context, official administrative data on suburb, municipality, province and country[3] can be incorporated into the study,

---

[3] Examples of attributes of countries include GDP, level of democracy and social welfare, as used by S. Ruiter and N.D. de Graaf (2006) in hierarchic logistic regression models in a multi-level analysis.

and in regard to the specifically religious context there are often survey and/or ecclesiastic data on membership, participation and voluntary activities available from different denominations and religions.

This refutes the notion that qualitative methods are actor-oriented and quantitative methods purely variable-oriented (Ragin, 1991: 34–68). As noted already, quantitative methods are enriched not only by a multi-moment approach, but also by a multi-actor and a multi-context approach (Ultee, 2004). Given such a three dimensional approach (multi-moment, multi-actor, multi-context) there are no essential differences between the two methods on this score. The exclusive link between qualitative methods and an insider perspective on the one hand, and quantitative methods and an outsider perspective on the other, is also severed.

Cultural and linguistic equivalence

Comparative research rightly concerns itself with the problem of cultural and linguistic equivalence. The problem is differentiated into construct equivalence, method equivalence and item equivalence (Van de Vijver and Leung, 1997: 7–26). Construct equivalence concerns the question of defining the concepts under investigation in a manner that corresponds with their purport in the relevant populations. That does not always happen, as when the identical definition of religious honour and shame is used among both West European and Asian populations. Does this represent an essential difference between qualitative and quantitative methods? In both methods researchers, whether from an insider or an outsider perspective, have to use techniques that reduce the danger of cultural construct bias in their open questions to informants and the closed questions submitted to them.

An example of a quantitative technique is the factor analysis in three steps used by Hermans (2004) and by Anthony, Hermans and Sterkens (2005) in their study of Christian, Islamic and Hindu students in India. First, they conducted a factor analysis of the combined items scores of all three populations, which resulted in an adequately interpretable factor pattern. Next, they conducted a factor analysis of the individual items scores of each population separately. Third, having removed items in the second step that appeared to deviate from the factor pattern discovered in the first step, they conducted a factor analysis of the combined scores of all populations on the remaining items. This procedure not only yielded a general pattern of items for the three populations in the third step, but also a differential pattern for each population in the second step, which might be seen as indicative of the 'otherness' of each. Thus, in the third step all three populations appeared to refer to the idea of *commonality pluralism*, expressed as follows: "different religions reveal different aspects of the same ultimate truth". In the second step the Hindu population alone appeared to refer to the idea of a *universal religion*, expressed as follows: "the similarities among the religions are a basis for building up a universal religion" (Hermans, 2004: 32–33; Anthony, Hermans and Sterkens, 2005: 170).

The second form of equivalence, that of method, pertains to the problem as to whether, in questioning informants, sufficient allowance is made for differences in, for example, social desirability, response styles (e.g. extremity scoring and acquiescence), stimulus familiarity and interviewer/tester effects. This problem, too, arises in both qualitative and quantitative methods. In both instances researchers should use techniques to reduce the risk of method bias, as these can be found in respective handbooks.

Finally, item equivalence requires that the questions in both qualitative and quantitative studies represent an accurate cultural and linguistic operationalisation of the concept under investigation. Here the method used by Leslie Francis and his co-workers in the study reported in this volume is commendable. They developed specific religiosity scales for Judaism, Christianity, Islam and Hinduism (Sahin and Francis, 2002; Francis, Robbins, Bhanot and Santosh, 2003; Francis and Katz, 2007). They did not use the application technique (i.e. implementing the same instrument among different populations), but opted for the adaptation and assembly technique, which enabled them to achieve a sort of indigenisation that contributed to the appropriateness of the instrument for each specific religion (Van de Vijver and Leung, 1997: 36–37). In addition they used the translation/back-translation procedure, which may entail a risk of setting too much store by literal translations (Van de Vijver and Leung, 1997: 39), but may also be seen as a first step in the TRAPD procedure, which implies translation, review, adjudication, pretesting and documentation (Harkness, Van de Vijver and Mohler, 2003: 38–43). Again there is no essential difference between the qualitative and quantitative methods, since both need special techniques to reduce item bias.

68   JOHANNES A. VAN DER VEN

CONCLUSION

The message of this chapter is twofold. The first is that comparative research into religious identity falls short if we content ourselves with answers to one or a few questions by two or more populations. It is a complex task, since it is structured by a hermeneutic dialectic between two dimensions: identity as permanence in time and the relation between identity and alterity. The second message is that the research should cut across certain traditional dichotomies, such as those between qualitative and quantitative methods and between an insider and an outsider perspective.

REFERENCES

Anthony, F.-V. (2003), Churches of African Origin: forging religio-cultural identity of a third kind, *Kritu Jyoti*, 19(1), 61–90.

Anthony, F.-V., Hermans, C. and Sterkens, C. (2005), Interpreting religious pluralism: comparative research among Christian, Muslim and Hindu students in Tamil Nadu, India, *Journal of Empirical Theology*, 18(2), 154–186.

Asad, T. (2003), *Formations of the Secular: Christianity, Islam, modernity*, Stanford, California, Stanford University Press.

Barnes, J. (1984) (ed.), *The Complete Works of Aristotle: the revised Oxford translation*, Princeton, New Jersey, Princeton University Press.

Bhanot, S. and Santosh, R. (2001), *The Hindu Youth Research Project 2001*, Oxford, Oxford Centre for Hindu Studies.

Boltanski, L. and Thévenot, L. (2006), *On Justification. Economies of Worth*, Princeton, New Jersey, Princeton University Press.

Bosch, D. (1991), *Transforming Mission: paradigm shifts in theology of mission*, New York, Orbis.

Boyer, P. (2001), *Religion Explained*, New York, Basic Books.

Burleigh, M. (2006), *Sacred Causes: religion and politics from the European dictators to Al Quaeda*, New York, Harper.

Cassirer, E. (1932), Vom Wesen und Werden des Naturrechts, Zeitschrift für Rechtsphilosophie, *Lehre und Praxis*, 6(1), 1–27.

Chia, E. (2003), *Towards a Theology of Dialogue*, Unpublished Dissertation, Radboud University, Nijmegen.

Coskun, D. (2006), *Law as Symbolic Form: Ernst Cassirer and the anthropocentric view of law*, Unpublished Dissertation, Radboud University, Nijmegen.

de Vries, H. (1999), *Philosophy and the Turn to Religion*, Baltimore, Maryland, John Hopkins University Press.

den Boer, J. (2004), *Neurofilosofie: hersenen, bewustzijn, vrije wil*, Amsterdam, Boom.

Dewey, J. (1986), *The Theory of Inquiry: the later works*, volume 12, Carbondale, Illinois, Southern Illinois University Press.

Dunbar, R. (1998), The social brain hypothesis, *Evolutionary Anthropology*, 6, 178–190.

Dupuis, J. (1999), The truth will make you free, *Louvain Studies*, 24, 211–263.

Durham, W. (1996), Perspectives on religious liberty, in van der Vyver, J. and J. Witte (eds.), *Religious Human Rights in Global Perspective, Legal Perspectives*, pp. 1–44, The Hague, Nijhoff.

RELIGIOUS IDENTITY IN COMPARATIVE RESEARCH 69

Eisinga, R., Coenders, M., Felling, A., Grotenhuis, M.K., Oomens, S. and Scheepers, P.L.H. (2002), *Religion in Dutch Society: 2000*, Amsterdam, Steinmetz Archive.

Felling, A., Peters, J. and Schreuder, O. (1987), *Religion im Vergleich*, Frankfurt, Lang.

Francis, L.J. and Katz, Y.J., (2007), Measuring attitude toward Judaism: the internal consistency reliability of the Katz-Francis Scale of Attitude toward Judaism, *Mental Health, Religion and Culture*, 10, 309–324.

Francis, L.J., Robbins, M., Bhanot, S. and Santosh, R. (2003), Mental health and religion among Hindu young people, in S. Bhanot and R. Stantosh (eds.), *The Hindu Youth Project 2001*, pp. 52–59, Oxford, Oxford Centre for Hindu Studies.

Fraser, N. and Honneth, A. (2003), *Umverteilung oder Anerkennung? Eine politisch-philosophische Kontroverse*, (tr. by Wolfgang Burckhardt), Frankfurt, Suhrkamp.

Givón, T. (2005), *Context as Other Minds: the pragmatics of sociality, cognition and communication*, Amsterdam, Philadelphia, John Benjamin.

Glock C. (1962), On the study of religious commitments, *Religious Education*, 57(4), S98–S110.

Harkness, J., van de Vijver, F.J.R. and Mohler, P.P. (2003), *Cross-Cultural Survey Methods*, Hoboken, Wiley.

Hasselmann, C. (2001), De wereldethiek-verklaring van Chicago 1993, *Concilium*, 37(4), 24–37.

Hermans, C. (2004), *Empirische theologie vanuit praktische rationaliteit in religieuze praktijken: epistemologische reflecties op de ontwikkeling van een academische discipline*, Inaugurele rede, Radboud Universiteit, Nijmegen.

Hermans, H. (1974), *Waardengebieden en hun ontwikkeling*, Amsterdam, Swets and Zeitlinger.

Hervieu-Léger, D. (1993), *La religion pour mémoire*, Paris, Cerf.

Hick, J. (1989), *An Interpretation of Religions: human responses to the transcendent*, New Haven, Connecticut, Yale University Press.

Hirschman, A. (1970), *Exit, Voice, and Loyalty*, Cambridge, Massachusetts, Harvard University Press.

Hoffman M.L. (1993), Empathy, social cognition, and moral education, in A. Garrod (ed.), *Approaches to Moral Development: new research and emerging themes*, pp. 157–179, New York, Teachers College Press.

Honneth, A. (1994), *Kampf um Anerkennung: zur moralischen Grammatik sozialer Konflikte*, Frankfurt, Suhrkamp.

———. (2003), *Unsichtbarkeit; Stationen einer Theorie der Intersubjektivität*, Frankfurt, Suhrkamp.

Israel, J. (2006), *Enlightenment Contested*, Oxford, Oxford University Press.

Jacoby, M. (1990), *Individuation and Narcissism: the psychology of the self in Jung and Kohut*, London, Routledge.

Kant, I. (1965), *The Critique of Pure Reason*, New York, St. Martin's Press.

Kim, J. and Mueller, C. (1984), *Factor Analysis, Statistical Methods and Practical Issues*, Beverly Hills, California, Sage.

Lawson, E. and McCauley, R. (1990), *Rethinking Religion: connecting culture and religion*, Cambridge, Cambridge University Press.

Margalit, A. (1999), *The Decent Society*, Cambridge, Massachusetts, Harvard University Press.

McCauley, R. and Lawson E. (2002), *Bringing Ritual to Mind: psychological foundations of cultural forms*, Cambridge, Cambridge University Press.

McCutcheon, R. (2006), "It's a lie. There's no truth in it! It's a sin!": On the limits of the humanistic study of religion and the costs of saving others from themselves, *Journal of the American Academy of Religion*, 74(3), 720–750.

Medin, D. and Waxman, S. (2002), Conceptual organization, in W. Bechtel and G. Graham (eds.), *A Companion to Cognitive Science*, pp. 167–175, Oxford, Blackwell.

70 JOHANNES A. VAN DER VEN

Mentzel, M. *et al.* (1995) (eds.), *Ethische vragen bij sociaal-wetenschappelijk onderzoek*, Assen, Van Gorcum.

Pals, D. (1996), *Seven Theories of Religion*, New York, Oxford University Press.

Pamuk, O. (2005), *Snow*, London, Faber and Faber.

Pleijter, A. (2006), Typen en Logica van Kwalitatieve Inhoudsanalyse in de Communi-catiewetenschap, Unpublished dissertation, Radboud, University Nijmegen.

Ragin, Ch. (1989), *The Comparative Method: moving beyond qualitative and quantitative stategies*, Berkeley, California, University of California Press.

——. (1991), *Issues and Alternatives in Comparative Social Research*, Leiden, Brill.

——. (1994), *Constructing Social Research: the unity and diversity of method*, Thousand Oaks, California, Pine Forge Press.

Rawls, J. (1971), *A Theory of Justice*, Cambridge, Massachusetts, Harvard University Press.

Ricoeur, P. (1992), *Oneself as another*, Chicago, Illinois, Chicago University Press.

——. (2000), *La mémoire, l'histoire, l'oubli*, Paris, Seuil.

——. (2005), *The Course of Recognition*, Cambridge, Massachusetts, Harvard University Press.

Ruiter, S. and de Graaf, N.D. (2006), National context, religiosity and volunteering: results from 53 countries, *American Sociological Review*, 71, 191–210.

Sahin, A. and Francis, L.J. (2002), Assessing attitude toward Islam among Muslim adolescents: the psychometric properties of the Sahin-Francis scale, *Muslim Education Quarterly*, 19, 35–47.

Satlow, M. (2006), Defining Judaism: accounting for "religions" in the study of religion, *Journal of the American Academy of Religion*, 74(4), 837–860.

Scheepers, P., Gijsberts, M. and Hello, E. (2002), Religiosity and prejudice against ethnic minorities in Europe: cross-national tests on a controversial relationship, *Review of Religious Research*, 43(3), 242–265.

Schilderman, H. (2005), *Religion as a Profession*, Leiden, Brill.

Schillebeeckx, E. (1973), *Stilte gevuld met parabels, politiek of mystiek?* Brugge, Emmaus/Desclée, De Brouwer.

Schoonenberg, P. (1971), *The Christ: a study of the God-man relationship in the whole of creation and in Jesus Christ*, New York, Herder and Herder.

Smith, J. (2004), *Relating Religion: essays in the study of religion*, Chicago, Illinois, The University of Chicago Press.

Sonnberger, K.I. (1996), *Die Leitung der Pfarrgemeinde: eine empirisch-theologische Studie unter niederländischen und deutschen Katholiken*, Kampen/Weinheim, Kok/Deutscher Studien-verlag.

Stark, R. and Glock, C. (1968), *American Piety: the nature of religious commitment*, Berkeley, California, University of California Press.

Taylor, C. (1994), The politics of recognition, in C. Taylor and A. Gutmann (eds.), *Multiculturalism: examining the politics of recognition*, pp. 25–74, Princeton, New Jersey, Princeton University Press.

Thangaraj, M. (1999), Evangelism sans proselytism, in J. Witte and R. Martin (eds.), *Sharing the Book*, pp. 335–352, New York, Orbis.

Theunissen, M. (1965), *Der Andere: Studien zur Sozialontologie der Gegenwart*, Berlin, De Gruyter.

Ultee, W.C. (2004), De Nijmeegse sociologie de laatste tien jaar en nu. <homepage Ultee>

Valkenberg, P. (2006), *Sharing Lights On the Way to God: Muslim-Christian dialogue and theology in the context of Abrahamic Partnership*, Amsterdam/New York, Rodopi.

van de Vijver, F. and Leung, K. (1997), *Methods and Data Analysis for Cross-Cultural Research*, London, Sage.

van den Berg, J. (1958), *Dubieuze liefde in de omgang met het kind*, Nijkerk, Callenbach.

van der Ven, J.A. (1993), The qualitative inhaltsanalyse, in J.A. van der Ven and H.-G. Ziebertz (eds.), *Paradigmenentwicklung in der praktische Theologie*, pp. 113–164, Deutscher Studien Verlag, Weinheim.

———. (1998), *Formation of the Moral Self*, Grand Rapids, Michigan, Eerdmans.

———. (2005), An empirical or a normative approach to practical-theological research? A false dilemma, in J.A. van der Ven and M. Scherer-Rath (eds.), *Normativity and Empirical Research in Theology*, pp. 101–136, Leiden/Boston, Brill.

van der Ven, J.A., Dreyer, J.S., and Pieterse H.J.C. (2004), *Is There a God of Human Rights?* Leiden, Brill.

Verweij, J. (1998), *Secularisering tussen feit en fictie: een internationaal vergelijkend onderzoek naar determinanten van religieuze betrokkenheid*, Tilburg, Tilburg University.

Vial, Th. (2006), How does the cognitive science of religion stack up as a big theory à la Hume? *Method and Theory in the Study of Religion*, 18(4), 351–371.

Weber, M. (1978), *Gesammelte Aufsätze zur Religionssoziologie*, Tübingen, Mohr.

———. (1980), *Wirtschaft und Gesellschaft: Grundriss der verstehenden Soziologie*, Tübingen, Mohr.

Wulff, D. (1991), *Psychology of Religion*, New York, Wiley.

CHAPTER FOUR

EPISTEMOLOGICAL REFLECTIONS ON THE CONNECTION BETWEEN IDEAS AND DATA IN EMPIRICAL RESEARCH INTO RELIGION

Chris A.M. Hermans

SUMMARY

The logic of science coincides, according to Popper, with a logical account of the method of empirical science. This thesis is disputed by other philosophers of science, such as Norwood Russell Hanson. The discovery of theories in science is characterised by the logic of abduction or retroduction. This logic of abduction is integrated by Ragin in a unitary model of empirical science. Ragin gives abductive reasoning a place next to deductive and inductive reasoning in the process of connecting ideas to reality. On the basis of this unitary model, three types of empirical research in theology can be distinguished: quantitative, qualitative and comparative. At the end of the chapter, two fundamental objections to this unitary model are raised. First, does truth not disappear in a model which puts abductive reasoning at the heart of the connection between ideas and reality? The second question is related to the specific topic of research on religion. Is the kernel of religion, namely the existence and activity of God, not reduced to human processes?

INTRODUCTION

Science looks for knowledge about reality. The core problem in this chapter is: how do we obtain scientific knowledge about religion through empirical research?

Empirical research connects ideas with data. The ideas are part of a theory, for example, the rational choice theory of Stark and Bainbridge (1985) or the ritual form hypothesis of Lawson and McCauley (1990). Data are presented as evidence of theoretical ideas, and ideas are seen as explanations of data. But is a connection between ideas and data, between theory and reality justified? The validity of this connection calls for epistemological reflection. Epistemology—that is, the theory of knowledge—considers how different kinds of knowledge come into being, what justifies a particular piece of knowledge, and which criteria are used to substantiate its truth (Audi, 2003). Epistemology is more than the logic of science. In his analysis of science and scientific progress Kitcher looks at the whole complexity of scientific praxis. This includes not only the logic of scientific discovery, but also its authority, power and status, the semantics in a field of scientific research, the relevance of research questions, the underlying framework of scientific texts, acknowledgment of certain research methodologies, and various research instruments (Kitcher, 1993: 74). In this chapter I restrict myself to the logic of the connection between ideas and data with a view to building and testing scientific theories.

I start with Popper's notion that the logic of science amounts to a logical account of the method of empirical science (Popper, 1959). I will defend the thesis that the discovery of scientific theories is not covered by the principles guiding the method of empirical inquiry, as Kuhn (1996) claimed in the debate with Popper. Kuhn's point lost out because he failed to work out a logic of scientific theorising. In the second section I consider some characteristics of this logic with reference to the work of Norwood Russell Hanson (1958, 1965). One characteristic is abductive or retroductive inference, which Hanson took over from Charles S. Peirce. Next I integrate abductive reasoning with a unitary model of empirical science developed by Ragin. Ragin gives abductive reasoning a place alongside deductive and inductive reasoning in the process of connecting ideas with reality. Within this unitary model I then outline three types of empirical research: quantitative, qualitative and comparative.

The model is very promising as a way of integrating different types of empirical research aimed at building and testing scientific theories. I raise two fundamental questions about such a model. First, does truth not disappear in a model that puts abductive reasoning at the heart of the connection between ideas and reality? I will argue that this need not happen, provided there is a correspondence between the logic of the mind and the logic of reality. The second question relates to the specific research topic, namely religious experiences that refer to a transcendent agent. Are scientific theories of religion that try to ground religion in reality, more specifically in human nature, necessarily reductive? Is the kernel of religion, namely the existence and activity of God, not reduced to human processes?

Is Something Missing from 'the Logic of Scientific Discovery'?

My first question is whether a logic of science is indeed "a logical account of the method of empirical science", as Karl Popper puts it in his classic *The Logic of Scientific Discovery* (1959: 17). Is the problem of theory building covered by the guiding principles of empirical scientific methodology? I start my argument with some of Popper's core concepts, because it was the reaction to Popper by scholars like Kuhn and Feyerabend that raised awareness of an aspect not covered by his theory, namely a logic of theoretical discovery.

Popper's *The Logic of Scientific Discovery* (1959) greatly influenced the modern (dominant) notion of empirical science. He maintains that scientific growth is accomplished through critical negation and refutation of existing theories rather than attempts to find positive, certain evidence. This idea helped Popper to solve a problem faced by empirical sciences formulated by Hume. Hume advocated an inductive, justificatory logic of science, which required observed data to be verified. On the basis of finite observations scientists construct universal propositions (laws). Hume's problem was that laws could not be verified by means of inductive empirical inference. Hence the ultimate ground for the truth of scientific theories is a habit of mind that constitutes the order of things—"because of 'custom or habit'; that is because we are conditioned, by repetitions and by the mechanism of the association of ideas" (Popper, 2002: 4). Scientific reasoning was the mental habit of associating and connecting sensory elements. The truth of scientific theories depends ultimately on the (psycho)logic of the mind, not on the logic of reality.

This leaves the scientist with a serious problem in that they themselves, the subjects, play a crucial role in grounding the truth of scientific theories. One can say that Karl Popper's major concern in the philosophy and method of science was to remove the subject of the scientist (Bertilson, 1978: 6). Science is built on the logic of falsification, in which reality gets a chance to refute predictions based on our theoretical understanding of it: let reality decide on the truth of our propositions, not the psychology of the researcher. Popper made a radical distinction between the contexts of discovery and justification. The processes of conceiving new ideas are the concern of psychology, not of logic (Popper, 1959: 26–27). Justification occurs by way of scientific inquiry. The methodological rules of inquiry, which serve as falsifying test criteria, can be agreed upon by all scientists. Based on scientific theories, hypotheses about reality are formulated. If these hypotheses are not empirically falsified, the theory is corroborated. Scientists can deduce new hypotheses from existing theories and expand a theory to previously unresearched fields. The more hypotheses are formulated and tested in different situations, the stronger or more robust the theory. But a theory will never be verified. A high degree of corroboration only tells us something about its past performance, "but it says nothing whatsoever about future performance, or about the 'reliability' of a theory" (Popper, 2002: 18).

Popper undoubtedly made a major contribution to the theory of scientific thinking and methodology, especially in his stress on the logic of falsification and on methodological rules of scientific inquiry. The discussion in philosophy of science after the *Logic of Scientific Discovery* (1959) was not so much about the correctness of his claims, but whether his theory included everything that could be said about scientific discovery. Does Popper afford insight into the growth of science and the mechanisms that guide it? Scholars like Kuhn and Feyerabend challenged Popper's account of the mechanisms of scientific growth. How are new theories conceived? Can Popper explain the discontinuity between scientific theories—what Kuhn calls scientific revolutions? I don't think Popper's theory of critical rationality explains the production of new scientific theories.

According to Bertilson (1978), what Kuhn and others tried to do was to understand the ways and mechanisms of building new scientific theories. The history of science records innovations like the laws of planetary motion of Johannes Kepler (1571–1630) that cannot be traced back to existing scientific theories. How does one explain such epistemological breaks in the history of science? Kuhn's attempt at an explanation failed to underpin its intrinsic rational claims, as Bertilson (1978) shows. His incommensurability thesis, according to which scientific paradigms are seen as monadic languages, begged the major question of the discovery of new theories. Popper rightly avers that Kuhn offers no alternative to the principle of falsification (Popper, 1983: xxxi). But that principle and the theory of critical rationality do not account for the act of conceiving scientific theories. What is the actual reasoning that scientists apply to produce some hypothesis about reality? What distinguishes good reasons from bad reasons for suggesting a hypothesis in the first place? Are there rational criteria of good reasoning while groping for the unprecedented (Hanson, 1965: 42)?

To flesh out this abstract argument I refer to two current discussions in the social sciences that have had an enormous impact on theories about religion. 'Mainline' theory and research in the psychology of personality completely omit religiosity or spirituality as a separate sphere of human functioning. Religion is studied as a function of some psychological process such as coping (Pargement, 1997). There is nothing wrong with these empirical studies, but they rest on theoretical assumptions that religion or spirituality is not intrinsic to human well-being. But why should religiosity or spirituality not be an independent sphere of human flourishing? Some scholars have developed personality theories in which spirituality is defined as a form of self-transcendence that is necessary for human well-being (see Cloninger, 2004; Emmons, 1999). What good reasons could there be for including religion or spirituality as a sphere of human psychological functioning in itself? Are those reasons purely psychological, because the researcher is a believer? Or could there be a logic behind the act of conceiving theories?

Some Characteristics of a Logic of Conceiving Theories

Is there a logic of the discovery of scientific theories? Or should we settle for a psychology and sociology of scientific discovery? I favour the first position and base my argument on ideas developed by Norwood Russell Hanson (1925–1967). Hanson was born in the USA and studied and lectured at Cambridge (UK) before returning to the USA in 1957. He worked at Indiana University and, since 1963, at Yale. His best known work is *Patterns of Discovery* (1958). He has written many articles on the logic of discovery. In 1965 he published a chapter in a book on Charles S. Peirce entitled "Notes toward a logic of discovery". It incorporates many of his ideas published in earlier articles. My account is based on this publication, which appeared just two years before his death in 1967.

Hanson was a philosopher of science whose ideas were picked up by Kuhn in his famous book, *The Structure of Scientific Revolutions* (1962). But unlike Kuhn, Hanson tried to reconstruct the logic of discovery of theories (assuming that there is one). I will first give a summary of this logic and then elaborate on it.

In a logic of discovery—
C proceeds retroductively, *from an anomaly* to,
B the delineation of a *kind* of explanatory H which
A fits into an organised *pattern* of concepts (Hanson, 1965: 50).

Before explaining the sequence (C-B-A), let me make a preliminary remark. Hanson warns that a logic of discovery is different from the reconstruction of the logic of finished research reports (Hanson, 1965: 45). The latter helps us understand the arguments in scientific journal articles (Hanson, 1958: 71), but it must not be mistaken for a logic of discovery. In a hypothetical-deductive account of science, a scientist is sometimes pictured as having a "ready-made theory (replete with established hypotheses) and a vast store of initial conditions in hand—deductively generating testable observation statements from these" (Hanson, 1965: 53). This H-D account is appropriate for testing a hypothesis based on an existing scientific theory. Arguing from initial conditions (A, B, C) and a hypothesis (H) deduced from some scientific theory, certain observation statements in social reality (D_1, D_2, D_3) are predicted. The scientist does not know whether these observations are 'out there' in reality. The observations (D_1, D_2, D_3) are 'out there' for him to discover—to find out facts which either fit the predictions or not. The discovery that concerns us here is that of new scientific theories. Is there a logic of discovery of scientific theory?

The logic of discovery starts with an anomaly, or what Peirce calls a real doubt. For Peirce 'the irritation of doubt causes a struggle to attain a state of belief' (Peirce, 1992: 114). The grounds for doubt are surprising facts in reality which are not explained by existing theories. The scientist is puzzled, perplexed, even confused because of something that struck her in reality. The starting point is an observed anomaly. In his *Patterns of Discovery* (1958) Hanson takes great pains to reconstruct how Johannes Kepler arrived at his theory of the elliptic orbit of the planet Mars. Kepler started with Tycho's observations of Mars (also see Peirce's analysis in CP, vol. 1: 65–74). These data rule out the possibility that Mars has a circular orbit. In the theoretical framework of astronomy at that time that was anomalous, because all planets were understood to orbit in perfect circles (Hanson, 1958: 74). Kepler started with anomalous facts and reasoned from these data to formulate hypotheses and theories, not the other way round (Hanson, 1958: 88). This type of reasoning towards an explanation that is not theoretically given is called retroductive inference or abduction. Hanson draws heavily

EPISTEMOLOGICAL REFLECTIONS

on Peirce to understand this kind of reasoning, which is typical of the logic of discovery. Abduction is reasoning towards an explanation or 'reasoning backwards'. "An *abduction* is a method of forming a general prediction without any positive assurance that it will succeed either in the special case or usually" (Peirce CP, vol. 2: 270). Abduction is the process of forming an explanatory hypothesis (H) and the premises (A, B, C) that go with it. It starts with an anomalous fact (D_1), or a set of anomalous facts (D_1, D_2, D_3), such as Tycho's observations. These facts are anomalous in the framework of existing theory. Something asks for explanation that is not covered by this theory. The scientist, Kepler, does not make wild guesses trying to explain the anomalous facts. He is looking for reasons to explain them. As Peirce (CP, vol. 5: 188) puts it: "It must be remembered that abduction, although it is very little hampered by logical rules, nevertheless is logical inference, asserting its conclusion only problematically or conjecturally, it is true, but nevertheless having a perfectly definite logical form." Hence abductive or retroductive reasoning is a form of reasoning, not just wild guesses. "If one would ask an investigator why he does not try this or that wild theory, he will say 'It does not seem reasonable'" (Peirce CP, vol. 5: 173). The reasons sought for are a premise cluster (A, B, C) plus some hypothesis (H) which explains the anomaly (Hanson, 1965: 60). Remember, none of this is given to the researcher. Kepler did not know what he was looking for, but made a conjecture in the form of a hypothesis (H) that could explain the observed facts. "The form of inference, therefore, is this: The surprising fact, C, is observed. But if A were true, C would be a matter of course. Hence, there is reason to suspect that A is true" (Peirce CP, vol. 5: 189). The reason for accepting H is that it explains the anomalous facts (i.e. makes them non-anomalous). Kepler did not prove that his theory of the orbit of Mars was true by making new observations. He also did not make new predictions based on his hypothesis. His greatness was that he retroduced an explanation (H) which, if taken to be true, would account for the anomalous facts (Hanson, 1958: 89).

In addition to a specific type of reasoning (abduction), Hanson mentions a second characteristic of a logic of discovery. "Retroductive inference terminates *not* in the advancing of a single, specific and detailed H, but rather in the delineation of what *type* of H is most plausibly to be considered as worthy of further serious attention" (Hanson, 1965: 64). There could be more than one plausible hypothesis: "A shocking anomaly becomes somewhat less disturbing when one has puzzled out what *kind* of hypothesis could explain this" (Hanson, 1965: 64). For example, the *ritual form hypothesis* of Lawson and McCauley (1990) and McCauley and Lawson (2002) is based on two principles which together offer an explanation of the experience of God (what they call 'some culturally postulated superhuman agent') in rituals. According to Lawson and McCauley, two principles determine the form of a ritual. Its effect can be seen as a logically necessary outcome of its form (Rappaport, 1999: 138). Both principles relate to the manner in which the 'superhuman' agent is involved in the ritual. What clues to the operation of a transcendent actor does the form of the ritual offer? The authors use the term 'CPS agent', which stands for 'culturally postulated superhuman agent'. This could be God, but also angels, ancestors, etc. We prefer the term 'CPC agents' or 'transcendent agents'. These agents are considered to be non-natural causes which affect the life of an individual, a community or nature. What two principles determine the form of rituals?

The first principle pertains to the primary manifestation of a transcendent agent in the structure of the ritual activity. This agent can operate either through the people performing the ritual, or through some other element (e.g. a sacred object like a rosary or a sacred place like the cave at Lourdes). This is known as the principle of superhuman agency (PSA), "which connection with the CPS-agents in the representation of a religious ritual constitutes the initial entry, i.e. the entry with the 'most direct connection' with the ritual at hand" (McCauley and Lawson, 2002: 27). Rituals seek to make people experience God's activity. That is why the role of the ritual element closest to the CPC agent determines the form of the ritual. It could be either the ritual actor (priest, shaman, pandit), who acts as an intermediary between the participants and God (CPC agent), or some other ritual element such as the holy water that a person takes home from church or some place of pilgrimage.

The second principle relates to that which serves as a primary manifestation of the CPC agent in the structure of a ritual. Ultimately there is always a CPC agent operative in a ritual, but some rituals build on other rituals that are considered necessary for the operation of the CPC agent. The CPC agent has her primary manifestation in these underlying rituals, where she is 'immediately' present. The longer the chain of rituals to get to the 'immediate' presence of a CPC agent, the less important a ritual is in a religious system. A ritual that puts the believer in direct contact with God is more important than

EPISTEMOLOGICAL REFLECTIONS   81

a ritual that does not. This is known as the principle of superhuman immediacy (PSI).

The third characteristic of a logic of discovery is that the anomalous fact x is placed in an intelligible pattern of ideas. "Discovery is thus characterised as the drawing of an aspect of x, such that x is at last seen as part of a more comprehensive and comprehensible pattern" (Hanson, 1965: 48). Hanson distinguishes pattern statements from detail statements. "Perceiving the pattern in phenomena is central to their being explicable as a matter of course" (Hanson, 1965: 48): that is, observed phenomena (D_1, D_2, D_3) can be explained on the basis of a premise cluster (A, B, C) plus some hypothesis (H). Suppose we see a picture of something which could be a bird but also an antelope (see Hanson, 1958: 87). And suppose we make the conjecture that it is a bird. One can count the lines in the picture and state that the bird has four feathers. This is an observable statement and can be falsified. "The statement that the figure is of a bird, however, is not falsifiable in the same sense. Its negation does not represent the same conceptual possibility, for it concerns not an observational detail but the very pattern which makes those details intelligible" (Hanson, 1958: 87). Theories provide patterns, in which data appear as explained by certain hypotheses. Observation statements (D_1, D_2, D_3) only make sense in a conceptual pattern. To deny an observation statement has consequences for the conceptual pattern in which the observations make sense. But denial of a pattern statement is epistemologically completely different. A pattern of ideas is the framework in which (empirical) facts appear to be intelligible. The aim of discovery is to find an intelligible pattern of ideas. The formulation of this pattern (e.g. Kepler's theory of the Martian orbit) is not deduced from accepted scientific theories, nor inductively concluded from observed facts. This intelligible pattern of ideas is the result of a conjecture or abductive reasoning (see above). This intelligible pattern of ideas provides us with grounds in scientific inquiry. Finding an intelligible pattern of ideas is the aim of a logic of discovery.

CONNECTING IDEAS WITH DATA: A UNITARY MODEL

What is scientific inquiry into human religious experiences or the religious practices of persons and groups? In simple terms: empirical inquiry is the connection of data with ideas, or the process through

82   CHRIS A.M. HERMANS

which data come to be understood as evidence of ideas. A researcher records believers' statements about their belief in God or some transcendent reality and interprets this as theism (or some other type of belief in God). Different types of reasoning are applied to the connection between data and ideas. The distinction between qualitative and quantitative research derives from the distinction between different types of reasoning. Quantitative research draws on hypothetical-deductive reasoning, and qualitative research is based on inductive reasoning about the connection between data and ideas. This distinction is found in most handbooks on socio-scientific methodology (see De Groot, 1966; Miles and Huberman, 1994).

The question is whether this 'standard' picture is not simplistic. Where does abductive reasoning fit into it? On the basis of a model developed by Charles Ragin (1994a), I argue that (1) socio-scientific research entails threefold reasoning, (2) there is no deduction without an element of induction and vice versa, and (3) retroduction or abduction is the link between analytic frames and images or sensitising concepts. Ragin's model claims to unify different research traditions (or socio-scientific methodologies) into just one model. This makes it especially interesting for my line of argument in this section. Ragin based his model on some of Hanson's philosophical ideas described in the previous section (Ragin, 1994: 47). He is one of the few modern socio-scientific methodologists who has given retroduction or abduction a place in the process of relating ideas to data.

According to Ragin, a simple model of socio-scientific research depicts it as the connection of ideas with data (see figure 4.1). Ideas are abstract and general, while data are concrete and specific. The 'distance' between ideas and data is bridged by intermediate structures, which Ragin calls analytic frames and images. At the top of the model are ideas, such as the secularisation theory of Bruce (2002), the rational choice theory of religion (Stark and Bainbridge, 1985), or the ritual form hypothesis of Lawson and McCauley (1990) and McCauley and Lawson (2002).

In empirical research we never test a whole theory but formulate some hypotheses about the problem that we are studying. It is hypotheses that we put to the test, not a whole theory. The more hypotheses are formulated and tested, the more a theory is corroborated empirically (Popper, 2002). The totality of hypotheses and their constituent concepts is what Ragin calls an analytic frame. "An analytic frame

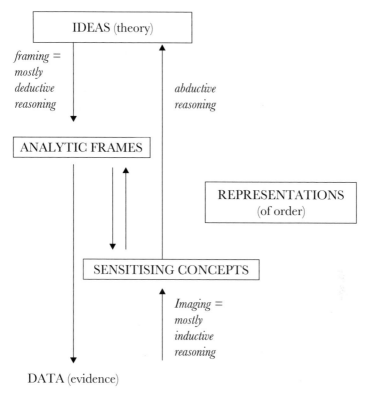

Figure 4.1: Model of connection between ideas and data in empirical research (based on Ragin, 1994a)

defines a category of phenomena... and provides conceptual tools for differentiating phenomena in the category" (Ragin, 1994: 61). Put differently: analytic frames classify and characterise religious phenomena. Classification entails framing phenomena by case (Ragin, 1994: 63). The research is aimed at answering the question: "What is this—the phenomenon being studied—a case of?" For example, a prayer service is framed as an instance of a specific ritual form involving special ritual instruments and patients, and a eucharist as an instance of a ritual involving special ritual agents (see McCauley and Lawson, 2002). A case (e.g. a specific prayer service or eucharist) is framed as an instance of a more general category. When we use concepts to characterise cases, they frame cases by aspect. Framing by aspect indicates how the cases in a category vary (Ragin, 1994: 64). For example, even numbered rituals vary with regard to the number of enabling rituals invoking the immediate, active presence of God or some transcendent reality. The type of reasoning that proceeds from ideas (e.g. ritual form hypothesis) to an analytic framework is deductive. "Generally, a hypothesis involves the deduction of a specific proposition or expectation from a general theoretical argument or perspective" (Ragin, 1994: 14).

At the bottom of the empirical research model are data, seen as evidence of some argument that makes sense of the data. Anything in the world could be data, that is information about reality. But the researcher selects data and puts them together, making connections between elements that at first glance seem unrelated. This synthesis of separate elements in a coherent whole characterises inductive reasoning in socio-scientific research (Ragin, 1994: 56). Ragin (Ragin, 1994: 67) calls the result of the synthesis of evidence an image or sensitising concept. I use the latter term, because it has a broader basis in socio-scientific methodology. The term 'sensitising concept' was coined by Herbert Blumer in 1954 in reaction to the aridity of social theory that was far removed from social reality. A sensitising concept remains close to the meanings that participants in a religious practice attach to the world. A sensitising concept is a second order concept rather than a repetition of the believer's first order discourse. It is already one step removed from the data but adopts—as much as is warranted—the perspective of the persons being studied. "A sensitizing concept is a starting point in thinking about a class of data of which the social researcher has no definite idea and provides an initial guide to her research" (Van den Hoonaard, 1997: 2). The researcher keeps her feet in the data (i.e. religious experiences and practices), while trying to find categories that can organise them. Sensitising concepts can be closer to or more distant from experience, but they are always connected with the meaning attached to some experience or practice by the participants. Blumer formulated five steps to define and test sensitising concepts: (1) deriving concepts from the participants' perspective; (2) exploration; (3) inspection; (4) relating to other social contexts; and (5) organising the same family of terms (see Van den Hoonaard, 1997: 37–47). Many of these methodological rules are to be found in modern qualitative methodologies, such as grounded theory (Glaser and Strauss, 1967; also see later developments in Glaser, 1992; Strauss and Corbin, 1998).

Ragin calls the process of formulating sensitising concepts *imaging*: the researcher abstracts from a real to an idealised case of which the real case is an instance. A pure or ideal case is never equivalent to a real case. If we study the Bible reading of some religious group (e.g. some Pentecostal group in the inner city of Amsterdam) and interpret

EPISTEMOLOGICAL REFLECTIONS
85

it as a Pentecostal religious experience, we need to conceptualise what we understand by a Pentecostal religious experience. The characteristics of that experience are not present in their pure form in the specific case of this Amsterdam group. But sensitising concepts are not so far removed from the meanings attached to the group's Bible reading as to be completely abstract from the participants' perspective.

According to Ragin (1994: 74), the process of constructing sensitising concepts (or *imaging*) complements the process of deriving analytic frames from theory (or *framing*). The essence of scientific inquiry into social reality (e.g. religious experiences and individual and group practices) is the connection between ideas and data, which is not direct but is mediated by analytic frames and sensitising concepts. When a researcher works top-down from a theory of religion or ritual he deduces hypotheses (H) and a cluster of premises (A, B, C) stating the conditions under which some observations in reality can be made. The reasoning towards an analytic frame is mainly deductive, but should not be restricted to that. There needs to be some pre-understanding of the social reality that is being researched. Framing without understanding based on some knowledge of the reality under investigation is impossible. Put differently, *framing* presupposes *Verstehen*. In the scientific research model of connecting ideas with data this is indicated by a dotted arrow between analytic frames and ideas (see figure 4.1). When the researcher works bottom-up from data seen as evidence for a sensitising concept the reasoning process is mainly inductive, but not exclusively so. Inductive reasoning implies that concepts emerge from data (see e.g. Strauss and Corbin, 1998: 137). However, in formulating sensitising concepts researchers draw on relevant scientific knowledge of reality. "It is difficult to form an image from evidence without first using some sort of initial frame to highlight or define relevant evidence" (Ragin, 1994: 72). The process of imaging is mostly, but not only, inductive.

At the heart of Ragin's model is the interplay or 'dialogue' between analytic frames and sensitising concepts, which is characterised by abduction or retroduction. Following Hanson's analysis, abductive reasoning has three attributes.

First, abduction is a form of backward reasoning. The only 'givens' of which the researcher can be sure are observed phenomena (D_1, D_2, D_3). The claims of scientific theory are, however, general, in that phenomena are 'explained' in terms of some general statement or regularity in reality. For Peirce this claim is a form of contrafactual reasoning. "Contrafactual reasoning allows an antecedent (belief-premiss) itself not empirically ascertainable and it infers a consequent which may or

86 CHRIS A.M. HERMANS

may not be observable" (Bertilson, 1978: 108). Contrafactual reasoning has the following structure: "*x* being the fact, then *y* would be as well". Only the consequent (*y*) is observed, not the antecedent (*x*). General statements (laws) say what would be the case if tested infinitely by the research community. These statements never lose their 'would be' character (Bertilson, 1978: 109). Only crude empiricism would assert the absolute truth of some general theory describing reality as it is. Epistemologically this implies that the problem of validity is never settled once and for all. The 'fit' between ideas and data, between analytic frames and sensitising concepts, can always be contested.

Second, abduction is reasoning towards the *type* of analytic frame (H) that can most plausibly be considered worthy of further serious attention. Only hypotheses (or explorative research expectations) based on a well-defined analytic frame can be empirically tested (i.e. falsified), but we should never forget that a hypothesis is 'chosen' from a particular type of analytic frame. For example, if a researcher formulates a research hypothesis on the basis of the *ritual form hypothesis* (Lawson and McCauley, 1990), she could have used a different frame such as the *ritual frequency hypothesis* (Whitehouse, 1995; 2000). Both theories rely heavily on the new cognitive science of religion. The type of hypothesis formulated on the basis of this theory differs from hypotheses formulated on the basis of ritual theories in cultural anthropology (e.g. Smith, 1987). In the *ritual form hypothesis*, experiences of ritual participants are put in the perspective of their structure of thinking and ensuing ritual competences. Smith views ritual from a phenomenological perspective of the category of the sacred, focusing on the construction of ritual environments.[1] Researchers always choose a certain type of analytic frame. The process of reasoning involved in this choice is neither deductive nor inductive, but abductive.

Third, abductive reasoning 'explains' facts by fitting them into a pattern of ideas. In research reports and journal articles researchers try to falsify hypotheses. The explanation is grounded in a pattern of ideas plus hypotheses, and the two together form a theory. As stated above, observational statements can be falsified. When this happens it affects the robustness of a theory. But the pattern itself is essentially different

---

[1] The focus of the cognitive science of religion is not on rituals as symbolic actions. "Evolution does not create specific behaviours; it creates mental organisation that makes people behave in particular ways" (Boyer, 2001: 268). How does the human mind function to permit rituals to operate in the manner they manifestly do?

from the expectations formulated in research hypotheses. The pattern does not rest on observations, but makes the facts intelligible. Denial of a pattern is epistemologically of a different order from denial of an observation. The pattern is the 'why' of the explanation offered by, for example, the ritual form hypothesis. This 'why' can never be grounded in deductive or inductive reasoning. "The problem of some philosophers of science is that they are inclined to regard physical theory either as an inductive compound on the one hand, or as a kind of deductive system at the other" (Hanson, 1958: 88).

Let me summarise my argument in this section. (1) Connecting ideas with data entails a threefold reasoning process: deductive, inductive and abductive reasoning. (2) Formulating an analytic framework (i.e. a premise cluster A, B, C and some hypothesis H) based on theory involves mostly deductive reasoning, whereas formulating sensitising concepts to synthesise data meaningfully calls mainly for inductive reasoning. Ragin calls the first process framing, the second imaging. Framing is mostly deductive, but not without an inductive element. Imaging is mostly inductive, but not without a deductive element. (3) At the heart of the connection between ideas and data is abductive reasoning. Deductive reasoning can never cross the gap between analytic framework and sensitising concepts; inductive reasoning can never make the leap from sensitising concepts to analytic frames. The 'fit' between analytic frames and sensitising concepts is a conjecture about a pattern of ideas that offers a representation of reality. This pattern is never found through empirical research, whether the reasoning is upward (inductive) or downward (deductive).

Different Types of Empirical Research into Religion

The unitary model of empirical research into religion (section 3) enables us to describe different types of research. Following this model, we presuppose that there is no fundamental or essential difference between these types of research. All types of empirical research into religion in the social sciences (including empirical theology, sociology, psychology, cultural anthropology) should be covered by this model. Types of research connect ideas with data in different ways (especially the role of analytic frames in research), but they do not violate the epistemological premises of the unitary model. I confine myself to a brief definition of the different types of research and some methodological requirements. Ragin (1994) distinguishes between three types of research:

- quantitative research to study covariances;
- qualitative research to study commonalities;
- comparative research to study diversity.

At the end of this section I refer to two other types of research pertinent to the scientific study of religion, namely critical normative and foundational studies, which I link up with the foregoing unitary research model. However, these types of scientific studies are not in themselves empirical in the sense that they connect ideas with data. They represent reflections (either normative or foundational) *about* this connection but do not develop and test theories *derived from* empirical research into religion.

The first type of research—quantitative research—works with a more or less elaborated analytic frame that remains more or less the same throughout the study. This approach is classic in so-called hypothetical-deductive scientific work (see discussion above). Analytic frames comprise a cluster of premises (A, B, C) and one or more hypotheses (H_1, H_2). For example, given a ritual in which (A) a special ritual agent (priest, imam, pandit) mediates (B) the presence of God (or some superhuman agent), which presence is manifested (C) here and now in the ritual process, participants in this ritual will have a strong awareness of God (H_1) and strong emotions (H_2). Analytic frames are easily translated into phenomena (D_1, D_2, D_3) that can be observed if the predictions formulated in the hypothesis are correct. The observations made in social reality stay within the boundaries of the analytic framework. Put differently, there is a fit between data matrix and analytic frame. Quantitative research can be either descriptive or explanatory (Verschuren, 1999; Segers, 2002). In both types of research one looks for connections between variables (i.e. personal characteristics such as experiences of God's presence and strength of emotions). The difference between descriptive and explanatory research is that the latter implies causality. Some (independent) variable, such as the form of the ritual, *causes* another (dependent) variable, such as experience of God. Causality is determined on the basis of the correlation between dependent and independent variables. Descriptive research describes (the strength of) the association between variables without looking for causality. The method of correlation or covariation is common to both

EPISTEMOLOGICAL REFLECTIONS

types of quantitative research (Ragin, 1994: 145). Patterns of covariation provide important clues about the causal relationship between characteristics of research elements.

It favours generality and parsimony.
It uses generic units such as individuals, families, states, cities, and countries.
It can be used to assess broad relationship across countless cases.
It condenses evidence to simple coefficients, using mathematical procedures.
It can be used to test broad theoretical arguments and to make projections about the future (Ragin, 1994: 153).

The second type of research—qualitative research—does not start with a fixed analytic frame. Researchers do not know what the investigated case is 'a case of' (Ragin, 1994: 75). All qualitative research starts from phenomena which are arranged or synthesised in some meaningful way, resulting in sensitising concepts (Ragin, 1994: 87–88). Sensitising concepts can be more or less close to the first order discourse of people's religious experience or practices (also see Van den Hoonaard, 1997: 33). Qualitative research traditions differ with regard to the possibility of abstracting from first order discourse. In ethnomethodology there are strong adversaries of decontextualisation of concepts from data (Ten Have, 2004: 21–23). The crux of the debate is whether there is a need to generalise in scientific research. In his unitary model, Ragin takes the position that science is essentially a reasoned process of classification (framing by case) and characterisation (framing by aspect) of phenomena. Analytic frames may be very vague at the start of a research project. But one cannot eliminate the role of analytic frames and theories that generalise from concrete phenomena and clarify what it is 'a case of'. Here I want to cite Peirce's reflection on explanation. In his view, explanation never refers to isolated facts but always to the connection between facts and other facts (Peirce CP, vol. 7: 200). A simple, isolated fact is taken for granted. The demand for an explanation arises when there is a puzzling nexus of facts. Why is this so? What is it a case of? Explanation is searching for commonalities or uniformities.

Uniformities are precisely the sort of facts that need to be accounted for. That a pitched coin should sometimes turn up heads and sometimes tails calls for no particular explanation; but if it shows heads every time, we wish to know how this result has been brought about. Law is *par excellence* the thing that wants a reason (Peirce CP, vol. 6: 12).

Ragin stresses that in qualitative research one does not know in advance which commonalities between cases exist in order to classify the object of research. The technique of systematic examination of relevant similarities in order to develop sensitising concepts is called analytic induction (Ragin, 1994: 93). Glaser and Strauss (1967) call this the constant comparative method. Comparison between cases helps researchers to establish similarities and differences. This research strategy enables them to challenge the sensitising concepts they are developing.

Ragin (1994: 103) summarises the main characteristics of qualitative research as follows:

- Qualitative methods are holistic, meaning that aspects of cases are viewed in the context of the whole case.
- Qualitative methods are used to uncover essential features of a case and then illuminate key relationships among these features.
- A qualitative researcher will argue that his or her cases *exemplify* one or more key theoretical processes or categories.
- Finally, as qualitative research progresses, there is a reciprocal clarification of the underlying character of the phenomena under investigation and the theoretical concepts that they are believed to exemplify.

Ragin's third type of empirical research is comparative research. In the unitary model of empirical research this type uses an analytic frame which is neither fixed (as in quantitative research) nor fluid (as in qualitative research). Ragin (1994: 105) sees the focus of comparative research as the study of diversity, in which "the category of phenomena that the investigator is studying is usually specified at the outset, and the goal of the investigation is to explain the diversity in a particular set of cases". In comparative research investigators start out with a specific analytic frame, but unlike quantitative researchers they leave the initial frame open for revision. On the basis of her analytic frame, the researcher has a clear idea about the cases she wants to study and what features are of interest (i.e. which variables to include in the research). But unlike quantitative researchers, they are open to different configurations of characteristics (variables) of the cases, which can explain differences in outcomes.

> Thus, in research that emphasises diversity the focus is on the similarities in a category of cases with the same outcome (for example, countries

EPISTEMOLOGICAL REFLECTIONS 91

> with riots) that (1) distinguish that category from other categories (countries with other forms of austerity protest) and (2) explain the outcome manifested in that category (Ragin, 1994: 106).

Lawson and McCauley (1990), for example, distinguish between two types of ritual: odd-numbered and even-numbered. Comparative research could be aimed at understanding what differences between cases of each type might be relevant to its effect on ritual participants. In contrast to qualitative research, comparative researchers concentrate on understanding diversity within categories. "The main difference is that in qualitative research the emphasis is on clarifying a category and enriching its representation, whereas in comparative research the emphasis is on using contrasts between cases to further the researcher's understanding of their diversity" (Ragin, 1994: 115). Comparative researchers take categories from an analytic framework, but at the same time keep a keen eye on differences between cases within categories. An example of comparative research into religion is the study of Hindu, Muslim and Christian students in Tamil Nadu (India) (Anthony, Hermans and Sterkens, 2005). In the data analysis (see Anthony, Hermans and Sterkens, 2005: section 3.4) we establish comparable categories and look for differences between cases (i.e. religious groups) in each category. Ragin would favour a combination of quantitative and qualitative research, in which the qualitative part focuses on establishing differences between cases. In this research project we could only collect quantitative data (survey design). However, as our data analysis illustrates, quantitative data, too, serve to establish both comparable categories and differences between cases within these.

In addition to the three types of empirical research, the study of religion should include normative and foundational studies. I refer specifically to normative reflections on the patterns of ideas suggested by scientific theories. Theories never lose their 'would-be' relation to reality. "The form of inference, therefore, is this: The surprising fact, C, is observed. But if A were true, C would be a matter of course. Hence, there is reason to suspect that A is true" (Peirce CP, vol. 5: 189). We quoted this above in our analysis of a logic of conceiving theories. A perennial question in scientific inquiry is: "Why are some hypotheses more correct than others assuming there to be a multitude of hypothetic possibilities to cover 'anomalous cases'?" (Bertilson, 1978: 184). This question cannot be resolved by testing hypotheses empirically (see above), but calls for reflection on the pattern of ideas used in the research. "What inquiry presents as general may indeed be a disguise for an individual and ideological social order" (Bertilson, 1978: 133). Hence we need critical normative reflections on the implicit assumptions of theories of religion from different positions: feminist (Gross, 2005), anti-colonialist, black, Latino/Latina, African, etc. We have claimed that there is a logic in the act of conceiving theories. If so, it is possible to criticise their normative claims.

Continuity Between a Logic of the Mind and a Logic of Reality

Can we claim that there is in fact a scientific connection between ideas and reality? Is this truth claim not invalidated if we put abductive reasoning at the heart of the connection between ideas and data? Should we not abandon any notion of truth when it comes to reality? In my view we do not have to, if we assume continuity between a logic of the mind and a logic of reality. According to Peirce (1998) we have to suppose that the same process of semiosis works in our minds and in reality. Semiosis is a model for the process leading to a general rule. How do we know if the rule is true? Here I invoke another idea of Peirce's, namely the connection between notions of truth, reality and the community of inquiry.

Science aims at explaining reality by means of general rules. Total irregularities do not call for explanation, since we are not surprised by them. Facts of a general or orderly nature call for explanation (Boersema, 2003). Two opposing positions (nominalism and realism) have to be rejected, since both rest on a dichotomy between mind and reality. Nominalists accept a subjective account of truth, claiming that we attach labels to observed regularities in empirical reality. If a community of interpreters agree with an argument, it is valid. This boils down to the idea that knowledge is a social construct. Realists, on the other hand, posit an objective truth. A universal principle or law is true "not because it happens to fit the data before us, but because it is an adequate representation of a real force in nature" (Parker, 1998: 191). Despite their opposition, nominalism and realism share one basic presupposition, namely a dichotomy between reality and mental conceptions. The problem with nominalism is that it cannot explain the existence of laws or general rules. The nominalist maintains that they are just individual 'labels' for events, both current and future. But this does not explain how a general rule can predict future events. "If the prediction has a tendency to be fulfilled, it must be that future events have a tendency to conform to a general rule" (Peirce CP, vol. 1: 26). Realism, on the other hand, fails to explain general rules. If reality is conceived of as a static order external to the operation of the mind, one cannot explain how general rules governing reality can be known. General rules are not incognisable (Peirce)—causes residing in reality but something in people's minds.

As soon as we introduce a dichotomy between reality and mind, the problem of bridging this gap arises. However, both reality and mind incline towards order. Peirce calls this process semiosis. A sign is any-thing which is interpreted (De Pater and Swiggers, 2000: 126). Without signs we could not understand ourselves, others or the world. "A sign, or *representamen*, is something which stands to somebody for something in some respect or quality" (Peirce CP, vol. 2: 228). According to Peirce, the same semiotic process operates in reality as in the mind interpret-ing that reality. Reality is in an evolutionary process similar to semiosis. In the logic of events in reality there is a movement towards 'order'. This logic is too complex to be explained by mechanistic models, in which events unfold according to limited laws that are given in advance. Semiosis is a general model for development towards a general rule. This process towards order or generality is the ground for the continuity between the logic of the mind and the logic in reality.

> It is certain that the only hope of retroductive reasoning ever reaching the truth is that there may be some natural tendency toward an agreement between the ideas which suggest themselves to the human mind and those which are concerned in the laws of nature (Peirce CP, vol. 1: 81).

But how do we know that this order is true? We might accept the truth of some claim about reality which is not true at all. Has abductive reasoning in the unitary model of science made us aware that the con-nection between ideas and data is a conjecture (although not without reasons)? For Peirce truth and reality are related concepts. On the one hand truth refers to cognitions about the real. If not, there is no escape in relativism or, as Peirce puts it, "the vagaries of me and you" (Peirce CP, vol. 5: 311). On the other hand truth is what is destined in the long run to be agreed upon by the community of investigators (Potter, 1996: 109). The real is what a community in the long run affirms and reaffirms. It is not necessary for us already to know the truth about reality, only that we know it in the long run. Peirce rejects the idea that there can be reality which is incognisable. A proposition whose falsity can never be established contains no error, for how would it be possible to establish that error? That is why Peirce sees reality and truth as two connected, even convertible terms. But truth and reality suppose the notion of a community "without definite limits, and capable of a definite increase of knowledge" (Peirce CP, vol. 5: 311). The truth about reality presupposes a state of complete information. There is truth in what we know about reality here and now, but truth to the limits of absolute knowledge can only be reached in the future through ongoing investigation. What we know about reality can always be falsified by further investigation. We cannot claim absolute knowledge, all knowledge we have is fallible. Truth is what can stand the test of falsification in the long run. Therefore Peirce states that "the existence of thought now depends on what is to be hereafter; so that it has only a potential existence, dependent on the future thought of the community" (Peirce CP, vol. 5: 316). Whether this future completeness can ever be reached cannot be claimed absolutely. To quote Peirce (CP, vol. 5: 357):

> [T]his very assumption involves itself a transcendent and supreme interest, and therefore from its very nature is not susceptible to any support from reasons. This infinite hope which we all have (for even the atheist will constantly betray his calm expectation that what is Best will come about) is something so august and momentous, that all reasoning in reference to it is a trifling impertinence.

We can only hope to reach truth in the long run in a community of inquiry without limits. This hope is not something beyond the act of knowing, but we need to see it as immanent in every such act. For Peirce there will never be sufficient or necessary reasons for or against that hope. Infinite hope belongs to the domain of practical matters and is not a theoretical conundrum for the sciences. Hope belongs to the category of voluntary acts and the admirable ideal (*summum bonum*) on which one wants to act (Peirce CP, vol. 5: 130). This makes hope ultimately a practical matter, which can only be 'captured' in the act of knowing (interpretation) and acting in accordance with the rules formulated in this interpretation.

A Nonreductive, Naturalist View of Religion

Are scientific theories about religion which ground religion in reality, more specifically in human nature, necessarily reductive? Is the kernel of religion, namely the existence and activity of God, not reduced to human experiential processes? Should we not leave naturalist theories to the social sciences and religious studies, and construct theological theories about religious experience? I will argue that there is no contradiction if a naturalist theory of religion is non-reductive. This type of theory is theologically legitimate from a transcendence-in-immanence perspective. A non-reductive naturalist theory equips theology for interdisciplinary debate and comparative research. In this debate theologians are needed because of their inside knowledge of the semantics of Christian practices.

First, naturalist theories regard religion as a natural human category, not as a supernatural category. The latter is characterised as 'theological': that is, as belief in the supernatural. Theology is about something 'over there' in contrast with 'over here' (Chesnik, 2002). Naturalism restricts the study of religion to what can be researched in natural categories, in the sense of things experienced by people. It finds its grounds in the canon of criteria for good academic research. One criterion is the need to restrict research to what is observable. It is impossible to test statements about a reality 'over there'. How would one decide whether a proposition about that reality is false or true? Scientific knowledge is fallible. All knowledge is constructed by human beings and can never escape the human condition, which implies that it could be proven wrong. Understood thus, naturalism has always been typical of social sciences that study religion and religious studies.

The question is whether naturalism is compatible with theology. Yes, it is—but not every form of naturalism and not every type of theology. Theology can be understood as a science about God (*theologia*), but also as a science about the human experience of God's manifestation in individual lives, society, history and nature (*oikonomia*) (Beinert, 1985). Catholic theology after the anthropological turn has adopted the second perspective on the subject of theology. Theology reflects on the way people experience God in rituals such as the eucharist or a rite of absolution. This form of theology can be compatible with naturalism without falling into the trap of (neo-)Pelagianism.

There are two types of naturalism: a reductive and a nonreductive type. Reductive naturalism wants to restrict the study of religion in general, and rituals in particular, to observable reality. For example, if people pray and state that they feel freed from anxiety, then the meaning of their prayer is deliverance from anxiety. Whether or not a person has experienced this effect can be tested empirically. The theory is reductive because is reduces religion to 'natural causes' and neglects the insider perspective of the religious person, who refers to some non-natural cause (e.g. God). Non-reductive naturalism wants to acknowledge the way religious persons experience a situation as caused by God. Religious experiences (like prayer) differ from other experiences precisely because they assume some non-natural cause. This cause is not studied independently of human action but as God acting through human activity. Religious practices and experiences have a characteristic that distinguishes them from other practices and experiences. They cannot be reduced to psychological, neurological, sociological or whatever origins. A social scientist recognised for his non-reductive naturalist view of religion is William James (Chesnik, 2002). For James religious experience is part of nature. In experience (as a natural category) religious people feel themselves connected with some non-natural cause which orders existence. The objective truth of religion to which an empirical psychologist can assent is a continuation of our natural life, not an addition to it.

Secondly, we want to stress that a nonreductive naturalist theory of religious rituals equips liturgical science for interdisciplinary debate (especially with ritual studies) and comparative research. A nonreductive naturalist theory opens up common ground for liturgical science to enter the debate on rituals and ritual activities with other sciences, in particular the social sciences and ritual studies (Grimes, 2000). It is also one of the best theories for comparative research into Christian rituals and those of other religions. Cognitive theories like the *ritual form hypothesis* appear particularly promising, because they identify mental structures which act as transhistorical and crosscultural constraints on ritual competence (Martin, 2000: 54). Participation in this interdisciplinary debate is important for liturgical studies, not only with a view to its own theory building but also to secure its place in the university. To be recognised as an academic discipline liturgical studies must take part in the public debate in the university. In order to be able to participate in this public debate about religious rituals in general, and Christian rituals in particular, it must speak a conceptual language that makes it an academic partner for other disciplines. A nonreductive naturalist theory of ritual competence meets this requirement.

Thirdly, is a nonreductive naturalist view of religion theologically justified? Can Christianity be regarded as 'a religion', to be studied alongside other religions? Can the Christian liturgy be studied from the perspective of religious rituals? Some theologians fear that common experiential features of religion will become the norm for Christianity. Thus a human category becomes a straitjacket for the Christian tradition's speech about God. Christianity cannot be regarded as simply 'a religion'; it is a *sui generis* category. God, known above all in the life and death of Jesus Christ, is Totally Other, not to be slotted into what is defined as religion in human categories (Schüssler-Fiorenza, 2000: 10–12). The dilemma seems to be that Christianity is either a *sui generis* concept (incommensurable with all other phenomena), or it loses its distinctiveness from the rest of personal and societal life. The dilemma is false, however, because it introduces a dichotomy between transcendence and immanence. Once this dichotomy has been introduced, it can never be bridged. But the theological model of incarnation opposes such a gap. Human beings are themselves by virtue of 'being from God' (Houtepen, 1998). Incarnation refers to human participation in God, which is seen as a gift of divine grace. The antithesis of divine and human actions is false. In the act of faith the initiative is reversed: God takes over, leading human beings into In/finite time and space, which is God. Finitude is not infinitude, but it is open to it.

Hence we opt for a theological model of transcendence-in-immanence. There are traces and signs of a transcendent reality in our immanent reality. On the one hand we should avoid making Christian religion an isolated category; on the other hand we should avoid reducing it to the phenomena in personal and social life.

REFERENCES

Anthony, F.-V., Hermans, C.A.M. and Sterkens, C. (2005), Interpreting religious pluralism: comparative research among Christian, Muslim and Hindu students in Tamil Nadu, India, *Journal of Empirical Theology*, 18(2), 151–186.

Audi, R. (2003), *Epistemology: a contemporary introduction to the theory of knowledge*, New York, Routledge.

Arendt, H. (1978), *The Life of the Mind: willing*, London, Secker and Warburg.

Barret, J.L. and Lawson, E.T. (2001), Ritual intuitions: cognitive contributions to judgments of ritual efficacy, *Journal of Cognition and Culture*, 1(2), 183–201.

Beinert, W. (1985), *Dogmatik studieren: Einführung in dogmatische denkens und arbeiten*, Regensburg, Pustet.

Bertilson, M. (1978), *A Social Reconstruction of Science Theory: Peirce's theory of inquiry, and beyond*, Lund, Dissertation Lund University.

Blumer, H. (1954), What is wrong with social theory? *American Sociological Review*, 19, 3–10.

Boersema, D. (2003), Peirce on Explanation, Paper read at annual conference of the Society for the Advancement of American Philosophy.

Boyer, P. (2001), *Religion Explained: the human instincts that fashion gods, spirits and ancestors*, London, Heineman.

98 CHRIS A.M. HERMANS

Bruce, S. (2002), *God is Dead: secularisation in the West*, Oxford, Blackwell.

——. (1999), *Choice and Religion: a critique of rational choice theory*, Oxford, Oxford University Press.

Chesnik, C. (2002), Our subject 'over there': scrutinizing the distance between religion and its study, in L.E. Cady and D. Brown (eds.), *Religious Studies, Theology and the University: conflicting maps, changing terrain*, pp. 45–64, Albany, New York, State University of New York Press.

Cloninger, C.R. (2004), *Feeling Good: the science of well-being*, New York, Oxford University Press.

de Groot, A.D. (1966), *Methodologie: grondslagen van onderzoek en denken in de gedragsweten-schappen*, Gravenhage, Mouton.

de Pater, W. and Swiggers, P. (2000), *Taal en teken: een historisch systematische inleiding in de taalfilosofie*, Leuven, Leuven University Press.

Emmons, R.A. (1999), *The Psychology of Ultimate Concerns: motivation and spirituality in personality*, New York, Guilford Press.

Glaser, B. and Strauss, A. (1967), *Discovery of Grounded Theory*, Chicago, Illinios, Aldine.

——. (1992), *Basics of Grounded Theory Analysis: emergence versus forcing*, Mill Valley, California, Sociology Press.

Grimes, R.L. (2000), *Deeply into the Bone: re-inventing rites of passage*, Berkeley, California, University of California Press.

Gross, R.M. (2005), A Response, in R. Gothoni (ed.), *How to do Comparative Religion? Three ways, many goals*, pp. 187–119, Berlin, De Gruyter.

Hanson, N.R. (1958), *Patterns of Discovery: an inquiry into the conceptual foundation of science*, Cambridge, Cambridge University Press.

——. (1965), Notes toward a logic of discovery, in R.J. Bernstein (ed.), *Perspectives on Peirce*, pp. 42–65, Westport, Connecticut, Greenwood Press.

Houtepen, A. (1998), 'Op zoek naar de levende God': Edward Schillebeeckx en de Godsvraag in de huidige westerse cultuur, *Tijdschrift voor theologie*, 38(3), 256–279.

Kitcher, P. (1993), *The Advancement of Science: science without legend, objectivity without illusions*, Oxford, Oxford University Press.

Kuhn, T.S. (1996), *The Structure of Scientific Revolutions*, Chicago, Illinois, University of Chicago Press.

Lawson, E.T. and McCauley, R.N. (1990), *Rethinking Religion: connecting cognition and culture*, Cambridge, Cambridge University Press.

Martin, L.H. (2000), Comparison, in W. Braun and R.T. McCutcheon (eds.), *Guide to the Study of Religion*, pp. 45–56, London, Cassell.

Malley, B. and Barret, J. (2003), Can ritual form be predicted from religious belief? A test of the Lawson-McCauley hypotheses, *Journal of Ritual Studies*, 17(2), 1–14.

McCauley, R.N. (2001), Ritual, memory, and emotion: comparing two cognitive hypotheses, in J. Andresen (ed.), *Religion in Mind: cognitive perspectives on religious belief, ritual, and experience*, pp. 115–140, Cambridge, Cambridge University Press.

McCauley, R.N. and Lawson, E.T. (2002), *Bringing Ritual to Mind: psychological foundation of cultural forms*, Cambridge, Cambridge University Press.

Miles, B.M. and Huberman, A.M. (1994), *Qualitative Data Analysis: an expanded sourcebook*, Thousand Oaks, California, Pine Forge Press.

Pargement, K.I. (1997), *The Psychology of Religion and Coping: theory, research, practice*, New York, Guilford Press.

Parker, K.A. (1998). *The continuity of Peirce's thought*, Nashville, Tennessee, Vanderbilt University Press.

Peirce, C.S. (1992), *The Essential Peirce, volume 1 (1867–1893)*, Bloomington, Indiana, Indiana University Press.

——. (1998), *The Essential Peirce, volume 2 (1893–1913)*, Bloomington, Indiana, Indiana University Press.

EPISTEMOLOGICAL REFLECTIONS 99

———. (1935–1966), *Collected Papers of Charles Sanders Peirce*, (edited by C. Hartshorne, P. Weiss and A.W. Burks), Cambridge, Massachusetts, Harvard University Press [abbreviated to CP].

Popper, K. (1959), *The Logic of Scientific Discovery*, London, Routledge.

———. (1963), *Conjectures and Refutations: the growth of scientific knowledge*, London, Routledge.

———. (1983), *Realism and the Aim of Science: from the postscript to the logic of scientific discovery*, London, Routledge.

———. (2002), *The Logic of Scientific Discovery*, London, Routledge.

Potter, V.G. (1996), *Peirce's Philosophical Perspectives*, New York, Fordham University Press.

Pyysiäinen, I. (2003), Buddhism, religion, and the concept of 'God', *Numen*, 50, 147–71.

Ragin, Ch. (1987), *The Comparative Method: moving beyond qualitative and quantitative strategies*, Berkeley, California, University of California Press.

———. (1994), *Constructing Social Research: the unity and diversity of method*, Thousand Oaks, California, Pine Forge Press.

———. (1994), *Fuzzy Set Social Sciences*, Chicago, Illinois, University of Chicago Press.

Rappaport, R.A. (1999), *Ritual and Religion in the Making of Humanity*, Cambridge, Cambridge University Press.

Schüssler Fiorenza, F. (2000), Religions: a contested site in theology and the study of religion, *Harvard Theological Review*, 93(1), 7–34.

Segers, J. (2002), *Methoden voor de sociale wetenschappen*, Assen, Van Gorcum.

Stark, R. and Bainbridge, W.S. (1985), *The Future of Religion: secularisation, revival and cult formation*, Berkeley, California, University of California Press.

Smith, M.M. (1987), *To Take Place: toward theory in ritual*, Chicago, Illinois, University of Chicago Press.

Strauss, A. and Corbin, J. (1998), *Basics of Qualitative Research: techniques and procedures for developing grounded theory*, London, Sage.

ten Have, P. (2004), *Understanding Qualitative Research and Ethnomethodology*, London, Sage.

van de Vijver, F. and Leung, K. (1997), *Methods and Data Analysis for Cross-Cultural Research*, Thousand Oaks, California, Pine Forge Press.

van den Hoonaard, W.C. (1997), *Working with Sensitizing Concepts: analytical field research* (Qualitative research methods series, 41), Thousand Oaks, California, Pine Forge Press.

Verschuren, D. (1999), *Designing a Research Project*, Utrecht, Lemma.

Wester, F. (1991), *Strategieën voor kwalitatief onderzoek*, Muiderberg, Coutinho.

Wester, F. and Peters, V. (2004), *Kwalitatieve analyse: uitgangspunten en procedures*, Bussum, Coutinho.

Whitehouse, H. (1995), *Inside the Cult: religious innovation and transmission in Papua New Guinea*, Oxford, Clarendon Press.

———. (2000), *Arguments and Icons: divergent modes of religiosity*, Oxford, Oxford University Press.

CHAPTER FIVE

TOWARDS A GENERIC MODEL OF RELIGIOUS RITUAL

Hans Schilderman

SUMMARY

In this chapter I first identify, somewhat synoptically, three mainstream approaches in the empirical study of ritual. Secondly, I show how some elements of these approaches can be incorporated into a simple theoretical model that provides a generic framework for subsequent elaboration. Thirdly, I illustrate that aim by focusing on one aspect of the model, namely ritualising as a specific activity.

INTRODUCTION

Ritual is one of the most characteristic and manifest of religious phenomena. As the dedicated location of divine worship it lies at the heart of a religion's identity. This is where its confession is unambiguously demonstrated in the public domain. Ritual is the very practice of a religion. The fact that ritual participation seems to be affected by the secularisation process, albeit primarily in Western European countries, has raised questions about the relation between religion and ritual. Is ritual a necessary condition for religion? Are the characteristics of ritual within a religion similar to those outside it? Does ritual necessarily imply the religious attributes of belonging and believing? The fact that I phrase these questions in rather formal, abstract terms assumes a further question. While one may easily agree that denominational frames of reference for religious ritual, like Catholic liturgy as a theological discipline, are appropriate to clarify and legitimise prevailing ritual codes and traditions, are they also suitable to conceptualise and explain the characteristics of religious ritual in a broader, theoretical context? After extensively studying ritual from the confessional perspective of Dutch Roman Catholic ministry (Schilderman and Felling, 2003; Schilderman, 2005), I grew interested in the foundational aspects of religious ritual. I have dealt with these questions elsewhere from a conceptual (2007a) and an epistemological (2007b) perspective.

Here I broaden my project by examining the socio-scientific field of religious ritual with a view to constructing an analytical model of religious ritual that can be used in empirical research. More specifically, I hope to determine to what extent ritual can be regarded as a necessary dimension of religion; and, if so, how it relates to believing and belonging as other, more or less obvious dimensions of religion. In so doing I will avoid a classical approach that merely studies religious ritual in terms of confessional problems in church history and systematic theology, which as a rule do not really strive for an analytical clarification of the empirical characteristics of worship. Hence I do not posit a normative theological problem. Although I find normative theological questions and issues crucially important for analysing worship, I will look into that aspect in another publication. I focus here on socio-scientific theories that allow us to analyse, explain and compare the formal, 'secular' characteristics of ritual in religions. Ultimately my aim is to provide a simple model of religious ritual that can be used for conceptual design in empirical research.

Socio-Scientific Approaches

The history of the social sciences presents several paradigms for studying ritual as a religious practice. If one opts for an action theory paradigm as an analytical frame of reference, a basic, primordial question is whether ritual makes any sense apart from its physical manifestation. Some scholars maintain that ritual has no meaning at all: it is a self-contained practice performed purely for its own sake. Thus Staal argues that ritual has no meaning beyond its self-evident practice. It is a 'mindless', purely self-referential execution of a prescribed action sequence. According to him, theoretical problems arise only to the extent that external goals or functions of ritual come to be assumed that disregard the fact that ritual may be performed without any beliefs on the part of the participants (Staal, 1979; 1984). This view, however, blurs the distinction between behaviour and action. Weber defines action as behaviour associated with personal meaning (Weber, 1976: 1). According to this Weberian assumption, ritual would lose its action characteristics as soon as its behavioural characteristics are regarded as coinciding with its meaning. Even if one could establish that primitives do not perceive their rituals as significant for their social and cultural identity, one would have a hard time proving that modern worshippers do not attribute any meaning while participating in religious rituals. More important, however, is the understatement inherent in the argument that rejecting the external significance of ritual would render any further theorising redundant.

Mainstream scholars of ritual maintain that ritual has meaning quite apart from its immediate expression. Here one can distinguish between three schools of thought that discriminate theoretically in their view of the meaning of ritual in its social and religious settings. These differences reflect alternative theories of religious ritual that need to be clarified prior to conceptual and empirical research. The three basic theories in the empirical study of the meaning of religious ritual are functionalism, structuralism and interactionism.

Functionalism

One broad approach in socio-scientific study of the meaning in religious rituals is functionalism. It emphasises—as Bigelow (1998) cites Malinowski (1926)—"the principle that in every type of civilisation, every custom, material object, idea and belief fulfils some vital function, has some task to accomplish, represents an indispensable part within a working whole". The functionalist paradigm studies ritual in its organic interaction with, or adaptation to, several other phenomena that together form a whole. The whole is usually the culture, which locates ritual in an inherited pattern of meanings that it transmits, develops and renews. Here social reality is understood as analogous to an organism, in which every part has to fulfil a particular function that is vital to the organism's well-being. The meaning of ritual can be equated with the function it fulfils. Functionalists among the classic anthropologists include Evans-Pritchard, Radcliff-Brown, Boas, Benedict, Mead and Sapir.

In the French functionalist tradition, Durkheim and Mauss are the principal authors who highlight ritual as fulfilling a fundamental social function. In Durkheim's definition ritual is closely connected with the believing and belonging dimensions of religion. In his study of totems in primitive aboriginal societies Durkheim maintains that society is represented by sacred objects (Durkheim, 1912, vol. 1: 50). In fact, God and society are one and the same; Durkheim refers to totems uniting God and the clan (Durkheim, 1912: 108). The sacred object is a—to be believed—symbol of the social reality of belonging. This close relation between believing and belonging is embodied in ritualising. In ritual acts the sacred object symbolising the divine is experienced as a collective force that is objectified and imposed on the participants. By handling the sacred objects with ritual reverence, society is experienced as a social and moral order. Mauss, Durkheim's colleague and nephew, contributed to a peculiar aspect of Durkheim's view of religious ritual, namely its character as a gift. Basic actions of giving, receiving and repaying strengthen the moral bond between persons and restore—at least in archaic societies—societal solidarity (Mauss, 1954: 37–41). In the sacrificial gift, people recognise their own existence as a gift that needs to be reciprocated. In fulfilling this sacrificial obligation they are slotted into the primordial structure of their group. The sacrificial gift erases distinctions of individual and social identity (Hubert and Mauss, 1964). Thus the crucial point is not that society is the source of the sacred, but that the sacred conceals this origin in order to create and maintain the social dynamics of obligatory exchange—the very heartbeat of society—as expressed in the religious practice of revering objects that represent the sacred. This turns the reciprocal character of the gift into a debt obligation relationship between gods and humans, thus providing a basic motive for ritual (Godelier, 1999: 171–199).

In the Anglo-Saxon world different strands of functionalism were in evidence in the early twentieth century. Malinowski—generally considered the founder of social anthropology—represents a bio-logically oriented functionalist approach, maintaining that ritual, and especially magic, attempt to control the contingencies pertaining to need satisfaction and the cultural or moral responses to these needs.[1] Malinowski's view of ritual is clarified by his theory of culture. Needs, says Malinowski (1960), represent the substratum of a culture; they account for its functioning. In his view each social institution offers codes and resources that address specific needs. These needs can be explored by studying the different norms for action applied in cultural practices. Social institutions are artefacts of organised behaviour that represent these norms and prompt the concomitant practices. Ritual is a language that expresses and reinforces a social charter of the norms

---

[1] One has to keep in mind that ritual is a generic category that not only includes control, as in magic, but may also satisfy other needs such as social inclusion and affection. This follows from an application of Schütz's theory of needs, which distinguishes between an active and a passive side to the needs of social inclusion (interest versus acceptance), control (leadership versus guidance) and affection (liking versus closeness) (Schütz, 1960).

TOWARDS A GENERIC MODEL OF RELIGIOUS RITUAL 105

and practices reflected in myth. In his actual fieldwork, Malinowski initially attributed a quite modest role to rites. He observed that whereas rites are usually simple, the formulas accompanying them are fairly complex. Rites merely transfer the formula to an object, as Malinowksi clarified in his study of spells in Trobriand magic (1932: 403–408). In other studies, Malinowksi (1970: 316–326) attributes more significance to rites as basic referential actions to translate linguistic representations from and into their respective contexts.[2]

Ritual fulfils needs at three levels. First, it functions as a direct response to basic needs in terms of role behaviour that typifies the normative significance of these needs. Secondly, ritual can be seen as a response to instrumental needs, in which case it serves as a means of social control. Thirdly, ritual can be viewed in its moral or religious dimension, where it functions in fact as a final legitimation in the face of life's contingencies. Thus ritual is a cultural institution through and through, although ultimately based on organismic needs.

Structuralism

The structuralist approach focuses on the structures through which a culture mediates meaning. This meaning is constructed by cultural practices such as rituals that act as signification systems. Structuralists interpret and analyse the social reality of ritual by differentiating elements in terms of oppositions and contrasts, and by ordering these into hierarchical structure, which are assumed to be universal principles that organise social reality. Since the structures are thought to offer a grammar and syntax for signification, scientific method can uncover their meaning. Structuralism usually does not aim at meticulous clarification of empirical phenomena, but assumes generic structures that allow for reconstruction of ritual meaning in different times and settings. Structures can be considered the *tertium comparationis* to establish commonalities between different actions or things. Though metaphors

---

[2] In his review of Ogden and Richards' seminal *The Meaning of Meaning*, Malinowski highlights the ritual usage of words as one of the primitive modes of realising the meaning of spoken words by giving them emotional emphasis, phrasing them in technical terms, and including strong imperatives and expressions of hope, success and achievement. Thus ritual is a referential mechanism that highlights the context or situation, in terms of which all language can (and should) be understood as a (quasi-magical) mode of action.

and similes commonly achieve this, the symbolic structures in cultures or in consciousness may also clarify implied meaning. In the social sciences structuralism was represented—among others—by such different scholars as Lévi-Strauss and Piaget who, according to Gardner (1981), may be considered its architects.

Lévi-Strauss is widely considered to be the father of structuralism in the social sciences. He applied De Saussure's linguistic theory to anthropological and ethnological research. By studying cultures in terms of interrelated signs, Lévi-Strauss developed a method to perform analyses and operations on these signs and their alleged structures, which he subsequently checked against empirical reports of field observations. He advanced the idea of the 'savage mind' (*la pensée sauvage*), in which ritual interacts with myth in a shared practice to deal with seemingly insoluble existential problems. According to Lévi-Strauss, myth is the mind's reflection of behavioural codes relating to such problems. Myth renders the problems intelligible in narrative and reflects them as shared orientations. Rites put these codes into action and turn them into an experiential reality. Thus ritual links the creative origin of a culture as depicted in myth to contemporary times by means of imitation: the disjoined, mythical past is brought to life through the conjoined past that unites the living and the dead by perpetuating ritual structures from generation to generation (Lévi-Strauss, 1974: 236). Lévi-Strauss takes a middle position between the view that myth is a foundational projection of a rite and the notion of ritual as dramatised myth. According to him these positions underestimate the dialectics within ritual on the one hand, and between ritual and myth on the other. Instead he understands ritual as a dynamic interplay of elements of any one rite corresponding to any one myth, according to some key that structures the interplay and that should be studied to determine the implicit beliefs and practices in various cultural interactions (Lévi-Strauss, 1963: 232–241; 1973: 60–67, 238–255).

Though they were friends, citing each other's scholarly works, Piaget is a very different kind of structuralist from Lévi-Strauss. He does not deal with ritual at great length: his relevant observations pertain to his studies of children's cognitive development, observable, for instance (at about the age of three), in daily rituals centring on eating, dressing and sleeping and an insistence on proper form, or in symbolic play in which roles and actions have to be performed in strictly codified ways. Piaget himself only occasionally refers to religious aspects of ritual in a derivative form, for instance when discussing Lévi-Strauss' view of totemism as a social construct necessary for cognitive development (Piaget, 1971: 106–119).

On a more fundamental level, however, Piaget's notion of action as the main substratum of the mind and his idea of intelligence as operating by way of internalised action chains are relevant to the study of ritual. In determining the stages of cognitive development, Piaget observed characteristic mergers of mental and environmental states in fallacies such as animism (attributing a living soul to inanimate objects and natural phenomena), realism (confusing mental states and external objects), and artificialism (ascribing purpose to artefacts). Curiously, Piaget's views on activity as the main factor in cognitive development have seldom been applied to the analysis of religious ritual.[3] However, an important inference that can be made from Piaget's structuralism is the basic notion of reconstructive action, in which symbolic representation of objects from the outside world is the basic incentive for cognitive development. This makes it possible to understand ritual in its structuralist analogy to language: it not merely acts as a reference (e.g. to myth) but is a formative skill as well (enhancing religious cognitive development). Initial impetuses for such an approach can be observed in neo-structuralist studies of religious ritual, such as the biogenetic, neuro-scientific and cognitivist approaches to ritual that, though not explicitly building on Piagetian theory, focus on phylogenetic and ontogenetic aspects of ritual (D'Aquili, Laughlin and McManus, 1979; McCauley and Lawson, 2002).

Interactionism

The interactionist approach focuses on the processes in which meaning is culturally constructed. The emphasis here is on the interaction processes in which persons assign meaning while addressing basic existential questions and issues. It can be considered a reaction against both a functionalist approach that underestimates the relatively autonomous character and diversity of meaning-giving, and a structuralist approach that tends to withdraw from the actual events and performances in which meaning is expressed and generated. Thus what counts is not the implicit function that meaning fulfils nor the internal structures that

---

[3] Other authors of the cognitive developmental school, such as Kohlberg (1984) and even Fowler (1981: 244–245), pay little or no attention to ritual when identifying stages of moral or religious development.

facilitate it, but the outward, explicit interactions that display their own intelligibility in performative and receptive actions. The interactionist approach can be said to derive from the pragmatic tradition of symbolic interactionism, although its actual stance is somewhat different. In fact, one can distinguish between two varieties that developed into schools with different emphases that call for attention. The two schools share some dissatisfaction with the functionalist and structuralist approaches, though they also refer to them and build on some of their insights. The first school is interpretive interactionism, which is associated with Geertz. The second school can be labelled performative interactionism and is linked to Goffman and representatives of the ritual studies approach (Turner, Schechner and Grimes).

Interpretive interactionism propounds the idea that culture should be studied by interpreting the actual expressions of meaning in symbols observable in the interactions of that culture. To illustrate the significance of symbols Geertz employs the metaphor of the human being as a spider in a web. Humans act to interpret their surroundings as webs of significance. In so doing they—like spiders spinning their webs—maintain and develop the meaning that culture entails. According to Geertz, anthropologists should not study meaning in its implicit functions or characteristic structures but in the way symbols signify a culture in the overt actions of its members. Religion represents the core of a culture: it synthesises a people's ethos and worldview. Geertz (1993: 90) defines religion in this notion of culture as "a system of symbols which acts to establish powerful, pervasive, and long-lasting moods and motivations in men by formulating conceptions of a general order of existence and clothing these conceptions with such an aura of factuality that the moods and motivations seem uniquely realistic". Ritual is 'consecrated behaviour' in that it symbolically fuses ethos and worldview. The world experienced and the world envisaged are forged together in a basic act of imagination. This placing of proximate acts in ultimate contexts distinguishes the 'real' from the 'really real'. Thus religion integrates a human being's lived life ethos by summing up quality of life, moral and aesthetic styles, and comprehensive insights. In this way a religion evokes the ultimate significance of a culture's life ethos as expressed in its ideal moral, aesthetic, emotional and intellectual models.

Another school is performative interactionism, represented by Goffman and the ritual studies approach. Performative interactionism highlights the significance of meaning as an act demonstrated before an audience. This implies that symbolic interaction is not only an

TOWARDS A GENERIC MODEL OF RELIGIOUS RITUAL 109

event to be reconstructed for its meaning, but also part and parcel of action itself in every conceivable way—a process that is intended, instigated, enacted, displayed, received, valued, etc. Goffman (1959: 28–29, 51–59) introduced the term 'dramaturgical action' to label the type of interaction that infuses an event with meaning based on the expressive force of persuasion. In that sense Goffman (1969: 136–137) speaks of degrees of action, which turn its seriousness or realness into a measure of dramaturgical success. Drama indeed offers a remarkable coordination of beliefs based on the realness of the actor's intentions, the corresponding image of these in the intentions of his public, and the conviction of adequate transference. Dramatic interaction is not limited to theatre but occurs in real life as well: competitions, ceremonies, trainings, demonstrations, therapies and, last but not least, rites. Goffman (1974) is a master at capturing the subtleties of ordinary interaction ritual, demonstrating how we stake out and demarcate the experiences that make up our lives and compartmentalise them, in public ('front stage') performances and in private ('backstage') rehearsals of these performances. Thus Goffman (1997: 114) regards ritual, more or less in line with Durkheim but without any religious connotation, as the basic metaphor of social life. He defines it as "a perfunctory, conventionalised act through which an individual portrays his respect and regard for some object of ultimate value to that object of ultimate value or to its stand-in". Goffman usually understands this in the sense of observing proprieties. Here an agent explicitly expresses her social status and adjusts to the social structure of a community. In doing so each agent becomes an object of ritual care. Goffman describes this as a delicate social process of 'face work'. One sincerely expresses one's intentions to a public, but simultaneously takes care not to lose face in that expression. In social interaction an individual shows authentic respect for other agents, each according to his own social status. Here ritual guides the traffic rules of social life.

This role of performative interactions in everyday life has also been studied by academic scholars of ritual. Turner, Schechner and Grimes can be said to have developed Goffman's performative interactionism by highlighting the significance of the interplay of drama and play for everyday life. Turner (1969) maintains that dramatic performance ritually re-appropriates the ancient dynamics of social structures that enable people to deal with the significant concerns of daily life. 'Social drama' offers an opportunity to manage conflicting loyalties in a culture arising from membership of different reference groups ('star groups').

Ritual is the explicit performance of that drama. It is 'serious play' in which onlookers have an opportunity to both identify and distance themselves. This in turn makes it possible for real life social drama to develop (Turner, 1982). According to Turner, ritual is "a stereotyped sequence of activities involving gestures, words and objects performed in a sequestered place, and designed to influence preternatural entities or forces on behalf of the actors' goals and interests" (Turner, 1972: 183). Schechner (1977) works out a performance theory, in which he compares the implicit rhetorical structure in social drama with the social processes in staged performances. Ritual and theatre demonstrate some interplay in this coordination of social drama and staged performance. However, while theatre is associated with pleasure in entertainment, ritual is oriented to efficacy (Schechner, 2003: 112–169) . Grimes, who coined the term 'ritual studies' in several foundational investigations, sees ritualising as a reconstructive and deconstructive process in following and changing ritual codes. He can be considered a founder of ritual studies in that he discerned ritual as a generic category of action. Thus Grimes (1995: 40–57) distinguishes between different modes of ritual sensibility, in which types of ritual are categorised in terms of socio-cultural frames of reference: dominant mood that is appealed to, linguistic claim ('voice'), type of activity and motivation. Grimes remains very much aware of the subtleties of ritual interaction. In his framework ritualising may be seen as biographical and narrative variation of cultural traditions of ritual. Grimes' approach is somewhat contrary to the common perception of ritual as formal, traditional, invariant, rule-governed and sacrally symbolised performance (Bell, 1997: 139–155). His challenging views reflect the significance of ritualising as a performative but informal activity aimed at creative reconstruction ('performance') of existing schemes by current participants ('re-invented ritual') (Grimes, 2000).

Conceptual Model

The foregoing theories may exemplify various paradigms of meaning in ritual, but they are not necessarily commensurable in a generic theory of religious ritual. However, the overview suggests ingredients for an argued choice that takes into account some basic insights of established theories. Thus we proceed rather eclectically and, for the sake of building a theory, select those notions on which most of the aforementioned authors would probably agree. The framework is generic in the sense that it is abstract, simple and basic, which has an obvious advantage for classifying various detailed research questions and studies under an umbrella heading.

A basic structure

Looking back on the theories of ritual studies, some basic questions arise. I mention three. One concerns the pretension of a basic model for religious rituals. What is the aim of such a model? What does it stand for? What should it clarify? A second question relates to the choice of concepts in the model. What are the necessary and sufficient conditions for the model? What basic concepts need definition? What basic variables have to be taken into account? A third question is theoretical. What is the relationship between the concepts? Are the research questions properly argued and do they have sufficient capacity to generate knowledge? Can hypotheses be formulated and corroborated? Answering these three questions can help to develop a basic model of religious ritual.

First, what would be the aim of such a basic model? Functionalism obviously looks for preconditions and aims of ritual action. Determining ritual functions tells us when and how religious ritual emerges, and when and how it reaches a destination of some kind. Ritual is 'relative to sacred things', as Durkheim puts it. It has an origin that is considered crucial, not so much for ritual itself as for its eventual instrumental significance. For Malinowksi this origin is located in needs and the values that protect them. Needs, while fundamentally biological, are present in institutions and culture as well. Put differently, needs and values instigate or initiate ritual, while the participants' actions gear these needs and values to some end, the realisation of which is its function. Thus we say that ritual is not a stand-alone event: it is part of an overarching socio-cultural process insofar as it is assumed to accord with the function of that process. Consequently ritual should be assigned a middle position in any model: it has both causes and effects.

From a functionalist perspective the clarification of conditions (ritual), means and ends thus represents a basic aim. Structuralism, on the other hand, seeks to reconstruct the logical structures and principles that underlie ritual behaviour. It accounts for the referential structures from which ritual encodes and decodes meaning. These structures shed light on the basics of linguistic, gestural and cognitive expression of meaning in behavioural processes that—ontogenetically or phylo-genetically—also account for cultural and mental development. Thus structuralism explains how ritual recognises and selects meaning from the socio-cultural stock of knowledge. It clarifies both the working of Lévi-Strauss' 'savage mind' as a basic structure to account for individu-als' necessary identification with their culture, and their decentring (Piaget) in the adaptation process that explains the development of intelligence. Whatever one may think of the value and commensurability of these structuralist theories, they attempt to answer 'how' questions about ritual and thus evoke the notion of competence. What qualifies as an element of religious ritual is not a matter of performance but of competence.[4] The approach relates to the grammar of language (myth) and action (ritual), and the skills needed to comprehend them. What are the rules of ritual expression of the various forms of religious meaning, and are they adequately understood? A generic model cannot ignore this basic issue. Thus another aim of a model would be to offer insight into different religious forms of meaning and the skills needed for their ritual decoding and encoding.

Interactionist approaches, on the other hand, are performance oriented. They assume that interactions determine the actual form of ritual as it is experienced in events. Meaning is bestowed on ritual participants, but the latter also gear it to their objectives. In so doing they get entangled in the meanings that emerge from their own interac-tions. When clarifying meaning we can never disregard our practical involvement in it. Thus a model of ritual has to take into account the participants' perspectives in terms of their intentions, expressions and interpretations of the meaning that they attribute to ritual. In other words, meaning is a category of difference: it varies not only in its distinct forms but also among different types or groups of agents, who cherish or reject these forms of meaning in the divergent socio-cultural and historical interpretations that these meanings engender. Whatever conceptions of belonging, believing and ritualising are included in a

---

[4] Linguists like Chomsky and Sebeok make a sharp distinction between competence, being the ability to comprehend meaning (i.e. what a speaker, or agent for that matter, already knows based on the grammatical structure or organisation of language), and performance, which provides the evidence for investigating competence in the sense of its actual demonstration by a subject. Blurring this distinction obscures insight into the development of meaning.

theoretical framework, ritual research must clarify the varieties of its religious expressions.

Consideration of these basic approaches in the study of ritual yields six requirements of a basic ritual model. A basic model: (a) should specify the aims of ritual (functionalist argument) (b) relative to the context in which it functions (interactionist argument); (c) should offer empirically-based explanations of ritual (functionalist argument) (d) in terms of the structures of meaning that it conveys (structuralist argument) (e) with due regard to varieties of coding skills (structuralist argument); and, finally, (f) should deal with the actual characteristics of ritual as experienced by participants (interactionist argument).

Secondly, what are the basic concepts to be used in constructing a generic model? In our discussion of the three paradigms we gathered strong support for distinguishing the aforementioned three dimensions of religious ritual (Schilderman, 2007b: 22–28). However abstract they may be, these dimensions can act as generic headings for the basic issues reflected by the different approaches. Ritualising, believing and belonging are notions found in all the paradigms that we reviewed. Ritualising is the activity that makes the sacred object the focus of the group whose identity it symbolises (Durkheim). According to Malinowski, ritualising is an activity to safeguard the pursuit of socially sanctioned and institutionally integrated need satisfaction. To Lévi-Strauss, ritual codifies the origins of mind and clarifies the believed destiny of a group vis-à-vis life's contingencies. In Piaget's view, we actually think in terms of action sequences, which we ritualise to balance the requirements of our believed identity and of our social life. The subtle studies of Goffman and the ritual studies school focus on the codification of our everyday performances that display our ingrained beliefs about who we are. According to Geertz, religious ritual presents envisaged realities as objects of experience and thus realises and communicates beliefs that are crucial for a culture's identity. One way or another ritualising, belonging and believing seem to be vital ingredients of a theory of religious ritual.

Thirdly, what is the relation between these notions of ritualising, believing and belonging? If ritual is indeed an intermediary concept, as we assume on functionalist grounds, we are left with questions about antecedence and consequence. First, the antecedents: how do we explain ritual? Is there any cause for ritual to occur, to be developed, performed, maintained, to change, or to end? Such questions put ritual in a socio-cultural and historic context. According to action theory, they have to be phrased in terms of social causes of ritual action by highlighting the dispositions of the actors involved in or affected by the ritual practice. Since these dispositions are considered antecedents of action, we regard them as orientations in the broad sense of the word: needs, values, appraisals, attitudes or evaluations relevant to ritual, which thus may act as incentives, motives or legitimations for its practice. Secondly, the consequences: what are the effects of ritual? The question may be redundant if one looks only at the intrinsic value and meaning of ritual and rejects its implicit or explicit utility. But recognition of its intrinsic significance does not exclude it actually having effects, whether overt or hidden, that need to be described and explained in the nomenclature of concurring or competing theories. A basic distinction in this regard is whether or not consequences are made ritually explicit: are ritual aims intended; are they ritualised; are they observed, or not noticed at all and only to be reconstructed on the basis of research outcomes; are they considered crucial or regarded as accessories? These questions, too, can be researched in terms of various theories and by means of various research methods.

The three sets of questions can be incorporated into a generic model. In this formal model ritual acts (performance, 'ritualising') are envisaged as both a dependent and an independent variable (see Figure 5.1). As a dependent variable, ritual can be explained by the orientations (conditions A) that are ritually expressed ('embodied', 'enacted', 'performed'). In that case, whatever orientations a model includes can be considered independent variables that predict variations of the experienced ritual, which then features as a criterion or dependent variable. However, ritual can also be considered an independent variable when one explores its function. In that case, ritual outcomes depend on ritual variations: ritualising acts as a predictor of ritual outcomes. That brings us to another point. In the investigation one may observe relevant ritual characteristics beyond the ritualising act itself, which will influence the explanation of ritual effects (conditions B). Hence we include another set of conditions pertaining to ritual setting characteristics in the broad sense, which can be expected to exert an influence one way or another.[5]

---

[5] In this scheme 'conditions B' are depicted as a *moderator variable* in that they influence (i.e. enhance or reduce) the direction and/or strength of the effect of the predictors on the criterion variable. Depending on one's theory, one can also treat conditions B as an *intervening* or *mediating variable*, that is, a construct expected to transmit the effect of an independent to a dependent variable and that is included for the sole aim of

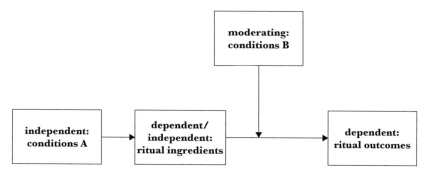

Figure 5.1: A generic model

That gives us a basic structure which, while still formal, integrates our basic research questions. Though it does not mean that all questions have to be answered in one research project, it permits the inclusion of different research questions, be it at the level of ritual research projects or programmes.

A basic theory

Now that we have a basic structure for ritual research we may turn to a theory that conceptualises the basic variables. Although our structure is based on various theories, our model seeks to accommodate some of the generic insights discussed above. To this end we use five propositions derived from these insights.

The first proposition is that ritual is need-driven and value-oriented. A need is a state of mind that experiences a lack of something deemed necessary. A value qualifies this need: it protects its significance and orients its satisfaction. Ritual is considered instrumental in expressing these values and satisfying the underlying needs. This functionalist view was applied by Malinowksi in his own way. His conception of needs as a basic category to explain ritual has to be worked out in new directions for several reasons. First, since needs are a theoretical notion in the social sciences, need assessment theories have to be consulted. A basic tenet here is that needs have to be defined in terms of

---

interpreting this effect. Finally, one can see conditions B as a *conditional variable*, in the sense of a variable that acts as a condition for the model as a whole. It thus represents a proposition according to which different premises of the same model can be researched and eventually compared.

116   HANS SCHILDERMAN

an experienced gap between real and ideal conditions that vary on a scale for different persons. Needs do not only vary personally but also in their socio-cultural significance. They are marked by various values, which are cherished by different stakeholders in a community and define the ideal conditions that needs seek to satisfy. These values have to be taken into account: they influence the direction of needs, whereas needs themselves are outcome-oriented and, in principle, must be satisfiable (Reviere, Berkowitz, Carter and Ferguson, 1996: 3–8). Secondly, one has to acknowledge that Malinowski's view of needs and values operates in an anthropological theory of primitive cultures that differs crucially from modern contexts. For instance, the fundamental importance he assigns biological needs may indeed reflect the priorities of everyday life in primitive cultures, but these needs are more incidental in modern cultures, which are less exposed to contingencies relating to biological need satisfaction. The ideal conditions in modern contexts are governed by other values, mainly those of autonomy and social justice as major issues in the economic and political frameworks of needs in modern societies (Doyal and Cough, 1991). Thus one should expect ritual to meet other needs and express other values in different contexts. Thirdly, though Malinowski pays attention to religious needs at the highest levels of need satisfaction, they seem to be defined primarily in terms of their legitimising function and thus pertain more to the orienting function of values than to needs. Hence the location and characteristics of religious needs have to be defined, not only their location in some taxonomy of needs but also their specific characteristics, with due regard to the values signifying the ideal situations for which the needs strive. Since values qualify the ideal situations envisaged by needs, one should define both needs and values in an overarching value system that not only ranks specific values, but also explains their pursuit in experienced needs.

A second proposition concerns the characteristics of ritualising. The term 'ritualising' indicates the behavioural acts that ritual entails. The value system, that is, the shared sets of needs and values, is enacted by solemnly centring behaviour on a religious object. The common term '(ritual) observance' pinpoints this aspect: ritual is an act of paying attention and due deference to some principle of action, in which the essential character of needs and values is reflected and publicly demonstrated in gestures, words and handling of religious objects. Ritual expresses explicit care that typifies an action as ritual. It makes sacred objects the focus of attention in ceremonial acts that convey awe and respect. Ritual is a public act, which means that it explicitly

TOWARDS A GENERIC MODEL OF RELIGIOUS RITUAL 117

or implicitly involves an audience—not necessarily coinciding with the actual ritual participants—and shared needs and values symbolised by the sacred object. The notion of ritual as 'careful' action usually entails some sort of formalism, conforming to more or less traditional rules embedded in a prevailing ritual system. However, ritual does not merely reconstruct meanings represented in the ritual system. The use of the term 'ritualising', rather than 'rite' or 'ritual', emphasises that a ritual's meaning is not exhausted by simply complying with prescribed rules of action, practising ingrained habits or following cultural customs. Put differently, ritual has to be described in terms of a dynamics of formalism and non-formalism (Schilderman, 2007a: 98–102). This is necessary in order to respect situational requirements and take note of the interests that ritual participants promote and pursue. Another important factor is their interactive display of personal identity. If this dynamics is not accounted for, ritual would be understood as an empty shell without the focus and energy generation that are highlighted in Durkheimian theories. Ritual would merely represent and conserve codes of action, culminating in repetitive gestures. It would lack the formative effort to balance personal needs and values in the face of environmental requirements and opportunities. Ritual does not merely point to a (sacred) object but also shapes and moulds the way this object is conceived of and actually transforms the participant. This view acknowledges the structuralist notion that ritual is not passive imitation but an effort to reconstruct one's identity. It is a moral and religious exercise, as it questions one's conscience: it puts ritual participants to the test in their dealing with religious objects. It also confirms another perspective that we considered, namely performative interactionism. On the basis of Grimes' insights, one can say that ritual is inventive in that it develops from atypical contexts requiring participants' active imagination, which is then displayed in performances that have to be studied in their own right.

A third proposition pertains to the ritual system. This system is assumed to fulfil two crucial functions: it offers a reference and facilitates competence. First, the ritual system is referential. It provides consultancy by systematically reflecting the meanings underlying ritual enactment. It is the basic framework comprehending the different signs, texts, codes and metaphors in ritual, the unity of which is safeguarded by myth. Myth is the narrative structure that binds the forms of meaning together in a time perspective and 'plot', conveying a sense of origin and destiny. It fuses these forms of meaning into a narrative structure, so they can be memorised and handed down to future generations. Thus myth allows the 'performance' of meaning in adaptation to specific contexts. Secondly, a ritual system facilitates ritual competence in terms of both skill and authority or jurisdiction to perform it. This competence is ratified by ritual canon that specifies which rites are valid or, to be more precise, which forms of meaning have exclusive priority for group performance at given times and places. A canon not only selects and discriminates; it also qualifies and authorises the conditions of ritual actions. A canon lays down rules of action and interpretation and assigns certain social positions the role of handling the religious objects and interpreting them in the proper ritual action sequences.

The two aspects of the ritual system—the reference aspect relating to myth and the competence aspect relating to canon—make it possible to decode and encode behaviour in a form of meaning that is typical for ritualising. We call this system of reference and competence the ritual system (conditions B in the basic structure). Why is it important to include it? First, inclusion of a ritual system acknowledges that reference and competence in ritual may vary. The reference aspect in primitive and indigenous ritual is likely to differ from modern ritual systems, which is one reason to include these formal aspects of the ritual system. The competence aspect permits a judgement of the actual ritualising: is it proper or improper, authorised or unauthorised, skilful or unskilful? In short, we explore the ritual system to determine if and how ritualising is functional or dysfunctional in terms of actual effects as measured against the ritual's own frame of reference and competence. Thus the system relates to the actual effects of ritual in terms of 'make-belong' and 'make-belief', aspects which we now have to consider.

A fourth proposition pertains to belonging. Ritual is an act of 'make-belong' for the participants. For functionalist theorists this may be one step ahead of Durkheim's own theory, which stresses the primordial significance of totem or emblem for group identity inherent in the sacred object, even before effects of ritual are established. Actually, however, it prevents a circular argument, in which the proof ('God equals clan') is already assumed in the sacred object (the totem) that ritually identifies the group. The risk of blurring cause and effect can be avoided by conceptualising the activities of ritualising, belonging and believing separately and defining their relationship in hypotheses. Hence a sense of belonging as observed in activities should be distinguished from ritualising itself. Since most, if not all, of the aforementioned authors would agree in some way about the social effects of ritual in terms of group cohesion and collective identity, we conceptualise belonging in distinct terms. We differentiate between belonging as expressed trust, group membership and social participation, and actual ritual activity. In explaining belonging as an effect of ritualising we allow for the orienting and socialising influence of the ritual system. Thus ritualising transforms ritual participants into a collectivity, whose identity is decoded and encoded with reference to the forms of meaning in the ritual system. From the basic structure we deduce that ritualising codifies these forms of meaning in terms of the needs and values that are significant to the ritual participants. Thus needs and values that characterise individual deprivations and preferences come to be experienced as collective orientations via ritual. To some extent the gap between the actual and ideal situation is closed by expressing a common origin and destiny. The contingencies arising from needs are sensed as a natural condition on the one hand, and on the other hand as controllable to some extent by the forces of interpersonal effort and group cohesion. The experienced needs and practised values are shared in the ritual act and thus contribute to a sense of belonging.

The fifth and last proposition concerns believing. Ritualising is an act of make-belief. The religious effects are phrased, though not explicitly in these terms, by Geertz. In our model, assigning an 'aura of factuality' to conceptions of a 'general order of existence' by means of ritual is the reference aspect of the ritual system that facilitates belief. The origin and destiny narrated in myth gain belief status in ritual, giving rise to the experience that core needs are satisfied and ultimate values are attained, or at least attainable.[6] The contingencies associated with need satisfaction acquire a design character: they are understood as having a purpose and as leading—through the effort of ritual participants or via supernatural agencies—to a shared destiny that fulfils the needs. Values are understood in terms of ultimate realities to be enjoyed in particular moments of ritual participation. Beliefs reflect values and needs as real commodities existing in the outside world: they are believed to be true and are experienced as real.

---

[6] Though Geertz's moods and motivations show clear semantic and conceptual parallels with needs and values, in our model there is a slightly different theoretical assumption. Geertz uses these affective dispositions as results of the symbolic system, while in our model they are its conditions, which of course does not exclude actual reinforcing and socialising effects.

120 HANS SCHILDERMAN

Why is this thought to be an effect of ritual? For an answer we need to consider all the assumptions so far. The religious object that is the focus of ritualising is the object of belief: it concentrates the participants' efforts on shared symbols of ultimate significance. From that we make at least three important inferences. The first is that a symbol 'stands for' needs and values, hence it may not be identified with these dispositions. It has a credal character that ultimately defines the core of religion. However, it only acquires that meaning insofar as it maintains a viable, and indeed universal, correspondence to ultimate needs and values. The second inference relates to the experience of (sacred) symbols as an act of imagination. That is why we speak of 'believing' rather than 'belief'. This act of imagination entails forming a mental concept that is not mediated by the senses and whose meaning does not rely on actual correspondence to blunt reality. A third inference relates to the ritual system, in which myth serves to interpret the ritual occasion as meaningful if—and only if—the religious object offers a focal channel for the make-belief that needs and values represent experiential realities. Thus the myth does not represent the object of belief; it acts as a modelling device to interpret the experience of the sacred object as an act of imagination or transformation. This is where the exercise character of ritual counts, and where both the ritual participants' abilities and the officiants' competence come into it.

When we now fit these five theoretical assumptions into the basic structure we can finally present our basic theoretical model. We assume that needs and values explain ritual varieties. Ritual is said to express these values in ultimate terms and compensate for the needs that are craved for. The effects are twofold. One is a sense of belonging, since in ritual the sacred symbol expresses the needs and values of a group, which thus can be trusted and used to achieve social cohesion. The other effect is believing, an act of imagination in which the values are experienced as real commodities and ultimate needs can be fulfilled. To attain these effects, the ritual system must be checked: its forms of meaning must be acknowledged in a way that relates them to myth, and must be applied properly and skilfully by meeting the canonical requirements of ritual conduct. We can depict the interrelations of our assumptions by substituting them in the basic structure from the previous section (see Figure 5.2). This gives us a simple, abstract view of our research object. The basic concepts can be elaborated in subsequent research.

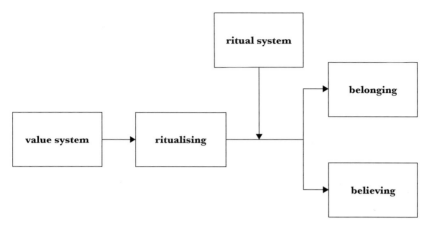

Figure 5.2: The theoretical ritual model

Ritualising Conceptualised

According to our model, ritualising is one aspect of an overarching theory of ritual that also includes causes, aims and conditions. The key concept, nevertheless, is specifically ritualising. I define it as a process in which values are ritualised in behaviour. It is the formal expression of these values in ways that predispose the individual to shared and (religiously) prescribed forms of action (devotion), in which the values gain reality (are believed). Again one can describe this process in numerous ways, involving choices of concepts, theories and hypotheses that are far more specific and detailed than our simple model suggests. By means of an example I give a brief theoretical description of one particular concept in the basic model: ritualising.

Ritual, especially in its religious forms and expressions, implies some sort of identification with values in a way which allows and stimulates the imaginative processes that lead participants to believe that these values are uniquely real. Religious ritual encodes this reality with the help of a system of religious forms of meaning. These are a set of stimuli for fictional processes on the part of the participant.[7] According to recent studies in cognitive psychology, this can be understood as an appraisal process in which a trade-off is made between involvement

---

[7] Here 'fiction' merely puts the focus on an act of imagination which establishes an affective relationship with the represented entities; it does not denote dissimulation or include falsification of epistemological or ontological claims.

(approaching) and distance (avoidance). The process entails three sequential steps involving cognitive functions: perception, experience and behaviour. This threefold appraisal structure has been conceptualised and operationalised in cognitive psychology by Konijn and Hoorn in their so-called PEFIC model, and has been tested empirically in research into appreciation of fictional characters in play, television, computer simulation and politics (Hoorn and Konijn, 2003; Konijn and Hoorn, 2005). I follow these authors by applying their argumentation to our basic model.

First, there is the perception process in which characteristics of the ritual situation are decoded into terms that identify the ritual stimuli according to available models. The ritual situation is scrutinised for models that facilitate cognitive and emotional recognition guided by religious interpretive codes. These models may vary in experienced interaction, for instance with regard to their imagery (iconicity), character (personality) or presence (transcendence/immanence). In religious ritual they are usually coded according to the traditions and conventions of a particular religion. Here one may assume that the ritual system— which we included in our basic model on structuralist grounds—offers models in its reference aspect (myth) and competence aspect (canon). In terms of cognitive theory these models are judged according to various norms: their 'ethics' (are they good or bad?), their 'aesthetics' (are they beautiful or ugly?) and their 'epistemic' qualities (are they realistic or unrealistic?). This perception is usually a natural and straightforward process of recognition, interpretation and assessment.

Secondly, the perceived ritual situation or event is experienced, that is measured against the personal concerns of the ritual participant. This is where—in our sketch of the basic model—the value system (needs and values) comes into play. To allow the needs and values to become a significant fictional reality or not a comparative process is initiated: a ritual experience in which personal and socio-cultural concerns and ritual models are compared, following the assessments in the perceptual process. In the comparison the first question concerns relevance: does it touch on my personal concerns or not? In addition a comparison of valence is made: does it arouse feelings of attraction or repulsion? Finally, the comparative process entails the question of correspondence: is the model similar or dissimilar to my identity? The ritual experience hinges on the answers to these questions and ultimately determines whether and to what extent the concerns are shared and believed.

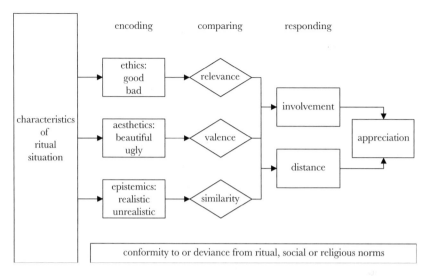

Figure 5.3: Threefold appraisal structure of ritualising

Thirdly, the results of the experience are translated into behaviour that demonstrates the actual appraisal in overt (social) terms. Basically, then, ritualising can be seen as encoding the concerns in terms of overt behaviour, usually following the codes of the ritual system that—again according to our basic model—helps to turn the relevant concerns into overt behaviour. The fact that this is usually done before a more or less committed audience typifies the encoding process not only as one of personal behaviour, but as a practice in which actions are recognised demonstrations of one's belonging and convey the belief character of the ritually expressed concerns. There is no reason, however, to assume that this involves an immediate process of full identification. Ritual enactment is best understood as an interplay of both involvement and distance that are activated simultaneously. Thus the ritual performance is a response that involves a trade-off between social and religious inclusion and exclusion—a result of the comparative process in the ongoing ritual participation. The actual response is one that evolves in the course of the ritual and results in ritual appreciation.

This concise example of a cognitive psychological theory applied to the concept of ritualising suggests that my basic model may help us to explore new directions in the study of religious ritual based on the theoretical and empirical work of some classic precursors in the social sciences. I hope that it contributes to the interdisciplinary discourse in ritual studies.

REFERENCES

Bell, C. (1997), *Ritual: perspectives and dimensions*, Oxford, Oxford University Press.

Bigelow, J. (1998), *Functionalism in the social sciences*, in *Routledge Encyclopedia of Philosophy*, volume 3, pp. 813–819, London, Routledge.

D'Aquili, E., Laughlin, C. and McManus, J. (eds.) (1979), *The Spectrum of Ritual: a biogenetic structural analysis*, New York, Columbia University Press.

Doyal, L. and Gough, I. (1991), *A Theory of Human Need*, London, Macmillan.

Durkheim, E. (1912), *Les formes élémentaires de la vie religieuse*, Paris, Alcan.

Fowler, J.W. (1981), *Stages of Faith: the psychology of human development and the quest for meaning*, San Francisco, California, Harper and Row.

Gardner, H. (1981), *The Quest for Mind: Piaget, Lévi-Strauss, and the structuralist movement*, Chicago, Illinois, University of Chicago Press.

Geertz, C. (1993), *The Interpretation of Cultures: selected essays*, New York, Fontana Press.

Godelier, M. (1999), *The Enigma of the Gift*, Chicago, Illinois, University of Chicago Press.

Goffman, E. (1959), *The Presentation of Self in Everyday Life*, New York, Doubleday.

——. (1969), *Where the Action is: three essays*, London, Penguin.

——. (1974), *Frame Analysis: an essay on the organization of experience*, Cambridge, Massachusetts, Harvard University Press.

——. (1997), Social Life as ritual, in C. Lemert and A. Branaman (eds.), *The Goffman Reader*, pp. 109–127, Oxford, Blackwell.

Grimes, R. (1995), *Beginnings in Ritual Studies*, Columbia, South Carolina, University of South Carolina.

——. (2000), *Deeply into the Bone: re-inventing rites of passage*, Berkeley, California, University of California Press.

Hoorn, J.F. and Konijn, E.A. (2003), Perceiving and experiencing fictional characters: an integrative account, *Japanese Psychological Research*, 45(4), 250–268.

Hubert, H. and Mauss, M. (1964), *Sacrifice: its nature and function*, London, Cohen and West.

Kohlberg, L. (1984), *The Psychology of Moral Development: the nature and validity of moral stages*, San Francisco, California, Harper and Row.

Konijn, E.A. and Hoorn, J.F. (2005), Some like it bad: testing a model for perceiving and experiencing fictional characters, *Media Psychology*, 7(2), 107–144.

Lévi-Strauss, C. (1974), *The Savage Mind*, London, Weidenfeld and Nicolson.

——. (1963), *Structural Anthropology* (volume 1), New York, Basic.

——. (1973), *Structural Anthropology* (volume 2), Middlesex, Penguin.

Malinowski, B. (1926), Anthropology, in *Encyclopaedia Britannica* (thirteenth edition), London, Encyclopaedia Britannica.

——. (1932), *Argonauts of the Western Pacific: an account of native enterprise and adventure in the archipelagos of Melanesian New Guinea*, London, Routledge.

——. (1960), *A Scientific Theory of Culture and Other Essays*, Oxford, Oxford University Press.

——. (1970), The problem of meaning in primitive language, in C.K. Ogden and I.A. Richards (eds.), *The Meaning of Meaning: a study of the influence of language upon thought and of the science of symbolism*, pp. 96–336, New York, Harcourt Brace Jovanovich.

Mauss, M. (1954), *The Gift: forms and functions of exchange in archaic societies*, London, Cohen and West.

McCauley, R.N. and Lawson, E.T. (2002), *Bringing Ritual to Mind: psychological foundations of cultural forms*, Cambridge, Cambridge University Press.

Piaget, J. (1971), *Structuralism*, London, Routledge and Kegan Paul.

Reviere, R., Berkowitz, S., Carter, C. and Ferguson, C. (eds.) (1996), *Needs Assessment: a creative and practical guide for social scientists*, Washington, DC, Taylor and Francis.

TOWARDS A GENERIC MODEL OF RELIGIOUS RITUAL

Schechner, R. (1977), *Essays on Performance Theory: 1970–1976*, New York, Drama Book Specialists.
——. (2003), *Performance Theory*, London, Routledge.
Schilderman, J.B.A.M. and Felling, A.J.A. (2003), Sacramental incentives in pastoral ministry, *International Journal of Practical Theology*, 7(2), 211–237.
Schilderman, H. (2005), *Religion as a Profession*, Brill, Leiden.
——. (2007a), Ritual praxis: defining rites from an action perspective, in H. Streib (ed.), *Religion Inside and Outside Traditional Institutions: empirical studies in theology 15*, pp. 125–145, Leiden, Brill.
——. (2007b), Liturgical studies from a ritual studies perspective, in H. Schilderman (ed.), *Discourse in Ritual Studies: empirical studies in theology 14*, pp. 3–34, Leiden, Brill.
Schütz, A. (1960), *Der sinnhafte Aufbau der sozialen Welt: eine Einleitung in die verstehende Soziologie*, Wien, Springer-Verlag.
Staal, F. (1979), The meaninglessness of ritual, *Numen*, 26, 2–22.
——. (1984), The search for meaning: mathematics, music, and ritual, *American Journal of Semiotics*, 2, 1–57.
Turner, V. (1969), *The Ritual Process: structure and anti-structure*, Chicago, Illinois, Aldine.
——. (1972), Symbols in African ritual, *Science*, 16(179), 1100–1105.
——. (1982), *From Ritual to Theatre: the human seriousness of play*, New York, Performing Arts Journal.
Weber, M. (1976), *Wirtschaft und Gesellschaft: Grundriss der verstehenden Soziologie*, Tübingen, Mohr, Paul Siebeck Verlag.

CHAPTER SIX

COMPARATIVE EMPIRICAL RESEARCH IN RELIGION: CONCEPTUAL AND OPERATIONAL CHALLENGES WITHIN EMPIRICAL THEOLOGY

Leslie J. Francis

SUMMARY

The aims of this chapter are to expose and to evaluate the attempt of one specific tradition of empirical theology to establish a basis for comparative empirical research in religion. This tradition is strongly rooted in an empirical social science approach to the measurement of individual differences in religiosity. The argument will proceed in six steps. The first step begins by formulating a research question intelligible within an individual differences approach to social science enquiry. The second step is shaped by a social scientific analysis of the dimensions of religion and argues for the primacy of one dimension as the basis for comparative empirical research in religion. The third step examines the usefulness of this dimension of religion for comparative empirical research within an English speaking Christian context across denominational divides. The fourth step broadens the discussion to embrace comparative empirical research within Christian contexts across linguistic divides. The fifth step broadens the discussion further to embrace comparative empirical research across religious traditions, illustrated by Hinduism, Islam and Judaism. The sixth step illustrates three examples of this research approach within the individual differences tradition applied in practice.

RESEARCH QUESTION

The way in which comparative empirical research is conducted is shaped fundamentally by the research tradition within which the research problem or research question is formulated. The tradition in empirical theology discussed in this chapter has been informed by and influenced by an individual differences approach within empirically-based psychology. The individual differences approach in psychology is grounded on certain core assumptions including: the view that human behaviour is not entirely random but patterned in discernible ways; the view that there are certain readily discernible factors which are core to

128   LESLIE J. FRANCIS

organising and predicting individual differences (say, for example, sex); the view that deeper, more covert factors, can be accessed and measured by appropriately tailored psychometric instruments (say, for example, personality differences of extraversion and introversion).

While the individual differences approach adopted by this approach to empirical theology has been informed by an individual differences approach shaped by social sciences (and hence not dependent on any one specific theological tradition), this approach has also been supported by an individual differences approach within Christian theology. The individual differences approach within Christian theology is rooted in a doctrine of creation (inspired by Genesis 1:27) in which the God of the Christian tradition is conceived as embracing differences. This is the God who creates individual differences in the form of male and female, both created in the image of God. This individual differences approach to the doctrine of creation recognises that the God who intends such rich diversity as sex differences appears also to intend individual differences grounded in such diversity as ethnicity and, say, personality.

Given a grounding in an individual differences approach, the fundamental research question concerns ways in which there is empirical evidence for religion being associated with a variety of individual differences central to human personal and social functioning. The research question is of key importance in the religious domain to those who are custodians of religious traditions, and in the secular domain to those who are concerned with the stability of the social order and with the well-being of individuals. Put another way, religious leaders may have a responsibility to know about the consequences of their religious traditions on the lives of people. Secular leaders may have a responsibility to know about the positive contributions (and negative consequences) of religious traditions on the common good, the social and spiritual capital, and general infrastructure of society.

Dimensions of Religion

Religion is clearly a complex phenomenon. The established tools of social science and the established tools of theology bring very different insights to the analysis and critique of this phenomenon. The present approach to empirical theology has been informed by and is influenced by a social scientific analysis of the dimensions of religiosity as relevant to an individual differences approach. One apparently crude,

COMPARATIVE EMPIRICAL RESEARCH IN RELIGION 129

but deceptively powerful, social sciences model of individual differences in religiosity distinguishes between the dimensions of affiliation, belief, practice, and attitude. Each of these dimensions is of theological significance and of social significance.

Religious affiliation is a measure of belonging and of self-identification with a religious tradition. This is the level of information which it is acceptable to assemble as part of a public census. For social scientists, religious affiliation is conceptualised as an aspect of individual identity, alongside, say, factors like sex and ethnicity. Religious affiliation does not function as a secure predictor of other dimensions like religious belief and religious practice, but nonetheless it remains of key interest to empirical theologians and to social scientists. For empirical theologians it is important to consider the theological significance of claiming affiliation without adopting the practice or belief systems of a religious tradition. For social scientists it is important to recognise the empirical evidence for the enduring power of religious affiliation (in the absence of practice and belief) to predict individual differences of considerable social significance. While social scientists may find it acceptable to group broad faith traditions (as demonstrated by inclusion of the broad category 'Christian' within the 2001 census in England and Wales), empirical theologians may be much more aware of the implications of theological differences within the Christian tradition.

Religious belief is a measure of the cognitive component of religion. The ways in which religious belief is conceptualised and measured may vary considerably between theological and social scientific traditions. Individual differences in religious belief may be expressed very differently by the theologically naïve and the theologically trained and sophisticated. Early attempts by social scientists to conceptualise and to measure Christian belief tended to imagine that conservative belief defined the recognised norm. Such conceptualisation worked well to characterise those who scored high on such instruments as conservative Christian believers. It remained more problematic, however, to characterise low scorers on such instruments, where potential confusion exists between atheists, agnostics and liberal believers. A further confusion arises when the content of belief is confused with the manner in which belief is held. Conservative belief does not equate with dogmatic belief. Empirical theologians may be much more aware of the theological complexity involved in defining and calibrating the dimensions of Christian belief.

130 LESLIE J. FRANCIS

Religious practice is a measure of the behavioural component of religion. Again the ways in which religious practice is conceptualised and measured may vary considerably between theological and social scientific traditions. Distinctions, too, need to be made between the observance of public practice (say, church attendance) and the observance of private practice (say, personal prayer). Early attempts by social scientists to assess the psychological correlates of prayer concentrated primarily on assessing the frequency of prayer without differentiation among the different types or forms of prayers. Empirical theologians may be much more aware of the complexity and theological differences of prayer within the Christian tradition.

Attitude toward religion is a measure of the affective component of religion. A very long tradition in social psychology has developed considerable conceptual and methodological sophistication in defining and operationalising the attitudinal dimension of religion. This domain is concerned with how individuals feel (negatively and positively) toward religion. Early attempts by social scientists to provide measures of attitude toward religion may have been distracted by over-emphasis on the outward and more visible aspects of the Christian tradition. Empirical theologians may be more aware of the inward and more spiritually salient aspects of the Christian tradition. The following sections argue why it is that this attitudinal dimension provides the best foundation for comparative empirical research in religion.

English-Speaking Christian Contexts

The first step in establishing comparative empirical research in religion is that of conceptualising the research problem in a social context shaped primarily by one religious tradition and by one language. The empirical example was provided by the social and historical situation of England dominated by one language and one religious tradition, Christianity. It is in this context that the Francis Scale of Attitude toward Christianity was originally formulated and tested as an appropriate tool for establishing comparative empirical research in religion. In this context the measurement of attitude carried a number of important advantages over the measurement of affiliation, belief or practice.

First, although affiliation has been shown to be of conceptual and empirical value within both theology and social sciences, there are significant limitations for this construct within the individual differences approach. On the one hand, the level of measurement achieved is only that of discrete categories. Individuals are located either within one category or another. On the other hand, affiliation categories take on significantly different meanings within different denominational groups. While nominalism is high, say, among Anglicans; in another group, say among Baptists, nominalism is low.

Second, although practice may be easy to conceptualise and to measure on ordinal or (possibly) interval scales, the actual meaning of practice may vary according to a range of constraints. For example, an irreligious young person may attend church because of family pressures, while a highly religious elderly person may stay away from church because of health-related problems. Moreover, practice may convey different significances within different denominational environments.

Third, although belief may be open to clear conceptualisation and (in some senses) refined measurement on (probably) interval scales, the formulation of indices of religious belief are conceptually complex (both theologically and psychologically). It is this formulation of measures of belief which may distinguish one denominational group from another, the theologically educated from the theologically naïve, and so on. While such issues are of central importance to certain fields of theological enquiry, they may simply provide distraction to the broader individual differences approach concerned with comparative research dealing with the personal and social correlates of religion.

As a deep-seated underlying construct concerned with affective response (favourably toward or negatively against) religion, a well developed attitude scale is able to calibrate individual differences in religiosity across age groups and across denominational divides. The Francis Scale of Attitude toward Christianity has been shown to function in a consistent and reliable manner across the United Kingdom (in England, Northern Ireland, Scotland and Wales), across the denominations (with separate studies among Catholics and Protestants), and across the age range (from the age of eight years to late adult life).

The first step concerned with extending this research tradition outside the United Kingdom involved testing the stability and psychometric properties of the Francis Scale of Attitude toward Christianity within other English-speaking cultures. A family of studies has now reported on the satisfactory use of the instrument in, for example, Australia, Canada, Kenya, Nigeria, Republic of Ireland, South Africa and the United States of America.

132 LESLIE J. FRANCIS

The horizons for comparative empirical research in religion have been enlarged against the background of a common religious heritage and a common shared language.

CHRISTIAN CONTEXTS ACROSS LINGUISTIC DIVIDES

The second step in establishing comparative empirical research in religion is that of conceptualising the research problem in a social context still shaped primarily by one religious tradition, but fragmented by diversity of language. Having examined the functioning of the Francis Scale of Attitude toward Christianity within a number of English-speaking contexts, the next generation of studies began to explore the performance of the instrument in translation.

The advantages and difficulties of translating psychometric instruments across languages are now well discussed in the literature. It is recognised, for example, how the change of a single word within a psychometric instrument in one language may change the pattern of responding to that one item and consequently disturb the pattern of correlations between the items. Translation of a whole instrument may prove to be so much more disruptive.

The first general principle in translating psychometric instruments is the conceptual task of ensuring that the concepts expressed in one language are adequately expressed in another language. This is much more complex than simply offering a word-for-word translation, although it may be relatively straightforward if the original instrument is itself expressed simply and in a clear manner. The process of translation is then followed by back-translation into the original language. Discrepancies between the original wording and the back-translation draw attention to potential problems with the translation.

The second general principle in translating psychometric instruments is the empirical task of examining whether the instrument displays comparable psychometric properties in the translated form to those established in the original form. Factor analyses and reliability analyses are able to examine whether the individual items perform in similar ways in translation. A family of studies has now reported on the satisfactory psychometric properties of the Francis Scale of Attitude toward Christianity translated into, for example, Arabic (Munayer, 2000), Chinese (Francis, Lewis and Ng, 2002), Dutch (Francis and

Hermans, 2000), French (Lewis and Francis, 2003), German (Francis, Ziebertz and Lewis, 2002), Greek (Youtika, Joseph and Diduca, 1999), Norwegian (Francis and Enger, 2002), Portuguese (Ferreira and Neto, 2002), Spanish (Campo-Arias, Oviedo, Dtaz and Cogollo, 2006), Swedish (Eek, 2001) and Welsh (Evans and Francis, 1996).

The horizons for comparative research in religion have been enlarged against the background of a common religious heritage and an instrument that has the capability of operationalising the construct of attitude toward Christianity in a variety of languages.

Research Across Religious Traditions

The third step in establishing comparative empirical research in religion is that of conceptualising the research problem in social contexts shaped by different religious traditions. Having established the usefulness of the attitudinal dimension within the individual differences approach to investigating the personal and social correlates of religiosity within a Christian context, an international group of scholars have begun to examine the potential for developing parallel instruments shaped within other religious contexts, namely (in chronological order of development), Islam, Judaism and Hinduism.

The core characteristics of the Francis Scale of Attitude toward Christianity are that it focuses on the affective response to the Christian tradition, that it identifies five key visible aspects of this tradition equally intelligible to children, adolescents and adults (God, Jesus, Bible, prayer and Church), and that the construct is operationalised through 24 Likert-type items arranged for scoring on a five-point scale: agree strongly, agree, not certain, disagree, and disagree strongly. The translation of this construct into other religious traditions involved proper theological awareness of the subtlety, complexity and diversity within these traditions.

The first of these instruments to be published was the Sahin-Francis Scale of Attitude toward Islam (Sahin and Francis, 2002). The items of the Francis Scale of Attitude toward Christianity were carefully scrutinised and debated by several Muslim scholars of Islam until agreement was reached on 23 Islam-related items which mapped closely onto the area assessed by the parent instrument. The psychometric properties of the instrument were assessed on 381 Muslim adolescents in England and 1,199 Muslim adolescents in Kuwait.

134   LESLIE J. FRANCIS

The second of these instruments was the Katz-Francis Scale of Attitude toward Judaism (Francis and Katz, 2007). A similar process involving Jewish scholars of Judaism reached agreement on 24 Judaism-related items which mapped closely onto the area assessed by the parent instrument. The psychometric properties of the instrument were assessed on 618 Hebrew-speaking undergraduate students attending Bar-Ilan University.

The third of these instruments was the Santosh-Francis Scale of Attitude toward Hinduism (Francis, Santosh, Robbins and Vij, in press). A similar process involving Hindu scholars of Hinduism reached agreement on 19 Hinduism-related items which mapped closely onto the area assessed by the parent instrument. The psychometric properties of the instrument were assessed on 330 young Hindus in England, and 100 Hindus in India.

The horizons for comparative research in religion have been enlarged against the background of a common understanding of the affective dimension of religion now operationalised within the framework of four major religious traditions: Christianity, Hinduism, Islam and Judaism.

Research Applications

The overall research question, set within an individual differences approach, was to establish comparative empirical research capable of assessing the extent to which religion is associated (positively or negatively) with a variety of factors central to human personal and social functioning. In this context a wide variety of constructs and hypotheses have now been organised alongside the family of affective measures of religion, beginning with attitude toward Christianity and more recently extended to other faith traditions. The practical application of the research can be tested against three specific examples, concerned with the relationship between religion and mental health, the relationship between religion and well-being (positive psychology), and the relationship between sex differences and religion.

These three specific and quite different research questions are displayed as examples of comparative empirical research in religion. Each of these research questions arises from a problem which is shaped by theological enquiry and which is of direct relevance to the agenda of practical, pastoral and moral theologians. Each of these research

COMPARATIVE EMPIRICAL RESEARCH IN RELIGION

questions is also relevant to a large body of research shaped within the traditions of the social sciences.

RELIGION AND MENTAL HEALTH

Practical, pastoral and moral theology has held a long-standing interest in mental health-related issues and in the provision of mental health-related care. In so far as research in the social sciences tradition also has taken mental health-related issues seriously, there may be good reason for dialogue between the perspectives of the two disciplines.

On a broader front, the psychology of religion has advanced two very different theoretical positions regarding the relationship between Christianity and mental health. One position has taken the negative view that Christianity is associated with lower levels of mental health, while the other position has taken the positive view that Christianity is associated with higher levels of mental health (see, for example, Batson, Schoenrade and Ventis, 1993). The negative view is exemplified, for example, in the classic writings of Freud, who sees the Judaic-Christian tradition as capturing the human psyche in a state of infantile immaturity, leading to psychological vulnerability and neuroses (Freud, 1950; Vine, 1978). The opposite psychological view is exemplified, for example, in the classical writings of Gordon Allport, who sees the religious images of the Judaic-Christian tradition as providing powerful developmental tools promoting and leading to psychological health (Jung, 1938; Allport, 1950).

The empirical literature on the relationship between religion and mental health is also divided between some studies which report a positive association, some studies which report a negative association, and some studies which fail to find association in either direction (Koenig, McCullough and Larson, 2001). Such disparate findings suggest that the two constructs of religion and of mental health need careful definition before the problem concerning their relationship can be properly defined and operationalised.

One particularly attractive way of defining and operationalising the construct of mental health is provided by Eysenck's dimensional model of personality (Eysenck and Eysenck, 1985). Eysenck's dimensional model of personality, as operationalised through the Eysenck Personality Scales (Eysenck and Eysenck, 1991), maintains that abnormal personality is not discrete from, but continuous with normal personality. Accordingly neurotic disorders lie at one extreme of a dimension of normal personality, ranging from emotional stability, through emotional lability, to neurotic disorder. Similarly, psychotic disorders lie at one extreme of another dimension of normal personality, ranging from tendermindedness, through toughmindedness, to psychotic disorder. Therefore it is possible to define and operationalise the dimensions of neuroticism and psychoticism so that they appear to be orthogonal and independent of each other. Eysenck's dimensional model of personality adds a third orthogonal dimension which is not in itself concerned with psychological disorder. The third dimension ranges from introversion, through ambiversion, to extraversion.

A series of studies conducted in England over the past 25 years has mapped the relationship between attitude toward Christianity (as assessed by the Francis Scale of Attitude toward Christianity) and mental health (as assessed by the Eysenckian personality measures). Two main conclusions emerged from this series of studies.

The first conclusion concerns the relationship between attitude toward Christianity and neuroticism scores. Eysenck and Eysenck (1975) defined high scorers on the neuroticism scale as being anxious, worrying, moody, and frequently depressed individuals who are likely to sleep badly and to suffer from various psychosomatic disorders. They are seen as overly emotional, reacting too strongly to all sorts of stimuli, and finding it difficult to get back on an even keel after emotionally arousing experiences. Strong reactions interfere with their proper adjustment, making them react in irrational, sometimes rigid ways. Highly neurotic individuals are worriers whose main characteristic is a constant preoccupation with things that might go wrong, and a strong anxiety reaction to these thoughts. After controlling for the expected sex differences, according to which females score more highly than males on both indices of religiosity (Argyle and Beit-Hallahmi, 1975) and neuroticism (Jorm, 1987), reported analyses demonstrate no significant relationship between neuroticism scores and a positive attitude toward Christianity (Francis, Pearson, Carter and Kay, 1981a; Francis, Pearson and Kay, 1983a; Francis and Pearson, 1991).

The second conclusion concerns the relationship between attitude toward Christianity and psychoticism scores. Eysenck and Eysenck (1976) define high scorers on the psychoticism scale as being cold, impersonal, hostile, lacking in sympathy, unfriendly, untrustful, odd, unemotional, unhelpful, lacking in insight, and strange, with paranoid

COMPARATIVE EMPIRICAL RESEARCH IN RELIGION

ideas that people are against them. Eysenck and Eysenck (1976) also use the following descriptors: egocentric, self-centered, impersonal, lacking in empathy, solitary, troublesome, cruel, glacial, inhumane, insensitive, sensation-seeking, aggressive, foolhardy, making fools of others, and liking odd and unusual things. Eysenck and Eysenck (1975) maintained that emotions such as empathy and guilt are characteristically absent in people who score high on measures of psychoticism. Repeated analyses demonstrate a significant negative relationship between psychoticism scores and a positive attitude toward Christianity (Kay, 1981; Francis and Pearson, 1985a; Francis, 1992). This finding lends support to the theory that Christianity is associated with higher levels of mental health and contradicts the theory that Christianity is associated with lower levels of mental health.

A subsidiary conclusion also emerged from this series of studies, but this conclusion provides no further indication of the relationship between Christianity and psychological health. The subsidiary conclusion concerns extraversion. Originally Eysenck defined high scorers on the extraversion scale as sociable, outgoing, impulsive, carefree, and optimistic. This definition clearly combines the two notions of sociability and impulsivity (Eysenck and Eysenck, 1963). While both of these two components appear to have been well represented in the earlier editions of the extraversion scale, the more recent editions have been largely purified of impulsivity, which now relates more closely to psychoticism (Rocklin and Revelle, 1981). While according to the earlier operationalisations of extraversion, introverts emerge as holding a more positive attitude toward Christianity, according to the later operationalisations repeated analyses demonstrate no significant relationship between extraversion scores and attitude toward Christianity (Francis, Pearson, Carter and Kay, 1981b; Francis, Pearson and Kay, 1983b; Francis and Pearson, 1985b; Williams, Robbins and Francis, 2005).

The consensus of these focused analyses is given further support by studies conducted among other samples of school pupils in the United Kingdom, using the Francis Scale of Attitude toward Christianity, including 8- to 11-year-olds (Robbins, Francis and Gibbs, 1995), 11-year-olds (Francis, Lankshear and Pearson, 1989), 12- to 16-year-olds (Francis and Montgomery, 1992), 15- to 16-year-olds (Francis and Pearson, 1988) and 16- to 18-year-olds (Wilcox and Francis, 1997; Francis and Fearn, 1999). The findings have also been replicated among secondary school pupils in Germany (Francis and Kwiran, 1999).

138 LESLIE J. FRANCIS

Another set of studies has employed the Francis Scale of Attitude toward Christianity alongside the Eysenck measures of personality among students and adults, including studies in the United Kingdom (Francis, 1991, 1992, 1993, 1999; Francis and Bennett, 1992; Carter, Kay and Francis, 1996; Bourke and Francis, 2000; Shuter-Dyson, 2000), Australia and Canada (Francis, Lewis, Brown, Philipchalk and Lester, 1995), Northern Ireland (Lewis and Joseph, 1994; Lewis, 1999, 2000, 2001), Republic of Ireland (Maltby, 1997; Maltby and Lewis, 1997), the USA (Lewis and Maltby, 1995; Roman and Lester, 1999), France (Lewis and Francis, 2000), Greece (Youtika, Joseph and Diduca, 1999), Hong Kong (Francis, Lewis and Ng, 2003), and South Africa (Francis and Kerr, 2003). Once again, the basic pattern was confirmed that attitude toward Christianity was negatively correlated with psychoticism, but unrelated to either extraversion or neuroticism. Moreover, more recent studies have reported similar results using the Katz-Francis Scale of Attitude toward Judaism (Francis, Katz, Yablon and Robbins, 2004) and the Santosh-Francis Scale of Attitude toward Hinduism (Francis, Robbins, Santosh and Bhanot, 2008).

Being purely cross-sectional correlational studies, the data currently available are not able to adjudicate on the direction of causality in the relationship reported. Eysenck's psychologically-driven theory would argue for the priority of personality in shaping these relationships, seeing individual differences in personality to be biologically based. According to this account individuals who record low scores on the psychoticism scale would be more drawn to the Christian tradition. Such a view is consistent with Eysenck's notion regarding the relationship between low psychoticism and greater conditioning into tenderminded social attitudes and the general location of religiosity within the domain of tenderminded social attitudes (Eysenck, 1975, 1976). On the other hand, such a psychologically-driven theory may be hard-pressed to explain the lack of relationship between neuroticism scores and religion, since the psychological mechanism posited here suggests that religion provides an attractive escape for neurotic anxieties.

An alternative theologically-driven theory would argue for the priority of religious experience in shaping the relationship between personality, mental health and religion, seeing religion as essentially transformative of individual differences. According to this account, individuals who record high scores on the scale of attitude toward Christianity would be challenged by their faith to transform and reject those qualities listed by Eysenck as characterising the high scorer on the psychoticism

COMPARATIVE EMPIRICAL RESEARCH IN RELIGION

scale: egocentric, self-centred, impersonal, lacking in empathy, solitary, troublesome, cruel, glacial, inhumane, insensitive, sensation-seeking, aggressive and foolhardy (Eysenck and Eysenck, 1976). On the other hand, such theologically-driven theory may be more hard-pressed to account for the lack of association between attitude toward Christianity and neuroticism. Throughout the Gospel tradition the Christian faith consistently proclaims the twin messages of 'Fear not' and 'Peace be with you', from the angelic annunciation preceding the Lucan birth narrative to the Johannine post-resurrection appearances. According to such theory the Christian disciple should be less troubled by those qualities listed by Eysenck as characterising the high scorer on the neuroticism scale: anxious, worrying, moody, frequently depressed, poor sleepers, suffering from various psychosomatic disorders, and overly emotional (Eysenck and Eysenck, 1975).

Religion and Well-Being

Practical, pastoral and moral theology has also held a long-standing interest in the life-enhancing consequences of religious faith, belief and practice. Many strands within the scriptures, for example, hold out enticing promises of life in all its fullness, happiness, joy and blessedness for those who put their trust in the Lord, walk in the paths of righteousness, or embrace the fruit of the Holy Spirit. In so far as research in the social science tradition also takes aspects of positive psychology seriously, there may be good reason for dialogue between the perspectives of the two disciplines.

Once again, the empirical literature on the relationship between religion and positive psychology is divided between some studies which report a positive association, some studies which report a negative association, and some studies which fail to find association in either direction. Taking the notion of happiness as a key indicator within positive psychology, Francis, Jones and Wilcox (2000) undertook a thorough review of the available literature, and concluded that a major problem with integrating and interpreting the findings was posed by the wide variety of ways in which the construct of happiness was defined and assessed.

Evaluating these empirical studies, Francis, Jones and Wilcox (2000) argue that future studies need to agree on a more robust form of measurement. One particularly attractive way of defining and operationalising

140   LESLIE J. FRANCIS

the construct of happiness is provided by the Oxford Happiness Inventory developed by Argyle, Martin and Crossland (1989) on the basis of a thorough theoretical discussion of the nature of happiness. Drawing on earlier analysis, Argyle and Crossland (1987) suggest that happiness can be measured by taking into account three empirical indicators: the frequency and degree of positive affect or joy; the average level of satisfaction over a period; and the absence of negative feelings, such as depression and anxiety. The test constructors report for this 29-item scale an internal reliability of 0.90 and a seven week test-retest reliability of 0.78. Validity was established against happiness ratings by friends and by correlations with measures of positive affect, negative affect and life satisfaction. A series of studies employing the Oxford Happiness Inventory in a range of different ways has confirmed the basic reliability and validity of the instrument and begun to map the correlates of this operational definition of happiness. For example, Hills and Argyle (1998a) found that happiness was positively correlated with intensity of musical experience. Hills and Argyle (1998b) found that happiness was positively correlated with participation in sports. Chan and Joseph (2000) found that happiness was correlated positively with self-actualisation, self-esteem, likelihood of affiliation, community feeling, and self-acceptance.

The Francis Scale of Attitude toward Christianity has now been employed in a series of studies alongside the Oxford Happiness Inventory. The first study, reported by Robbins and Francis (1996), was conducted among 360 undergraduates in the United Kingdom. The second study, reported by Francis and Lester (1997), replicated the original study in a different cultural context among 212 undergraduates in the United States of America. The third study, reported by French and Joseph (1999), was conducted among 101 undergraduate students in the United Kingdom. The fourth study, reported by Francis, Jones, and Wilcox (2000), employed three separate samples drawn from the United Kingdom: 994 secondary school pupils during the final year of compulsory schooling, 456 first-year undergraduate students, and 496 members of a branch of the University of the Third Age, a relatively informal education network for senior citizens. The fifth study, reported by Francis and Robbins (2000), was conducted among 295 participants attending a variety of workshops and courses on the psychology of religion, ranging in age from late teens to late seventies. The sixth study, reported by Francis, Robbins, and White (2003) was conducted among 89 students in Wales. All eight samples employed in these six studies demonstrated a significant positive correlation between happiness and attitude toward Christianity, after controlling for the possible contaminating influence of personality. On the other hand, no significant relationship was found between attitude toward Christianity and happiness among a sample of 331 students in Germany reported by Francis, Ziebertz, and Lewis (2003).

In order to establish the extent to which the correlates of the attitudinal dimensions of religiosity established within a Christian or post-Christian context by means of the Francis Scale of Attitude toward Christianity held true within a context shaped by Judaism, Francis and Katz (2002) administered the Katz-Francis Scale of Attitude toward Judaism, alongside the Hebrew translation of the Oxford Happiness Inventory and the Hebrew translation of the short form of the Revised Eysenck Personality Questionnaire, to a sample of 298 female Hebrew-speaking undergraduate students. In a second study, Francis, Katz, Yablon and Robbins (2004) administered the same set of instruments to a sample of 203 male Hebrew-speaking undergraduate students. The data from both studies confirmed a small but statistically significant positive association between attitude toward Judaism and happiness.

Further research is now needed to build on the present findings in two ways. First, the present conclusions regarding the relationship between attitude toward Judaism and happiness rest on two studies, both conducted among undergraduates in a religious university. Replication studies are needed among other age groups and in other sectors of society in Israel. Second, the present tradition of research, concerned with the attitudinal dimension of religion alongside the Oxford Happiness Inventory, begun in a Christian context and more recently extended to a Jewish context, requires further extension within the context of other major faith traditions. Opportunities for doing this are provided by the Sahin-Francis Scale of Attitude toward Islam and the Santosh-Francis Scale of Attitude toward Hinduism.

RELIGION AND SEX DIFFERENCES

Practical, pastoral and moral theology has held a long-standing interest in a number of issues concerned with the differences between men and women. Grounded in different emphases within the doctrine of creation, and on different views regarding the interpretation of scriptural texts, debates continue on such issues as the appropriate role of women

142   LESLIE J. FRANCIS

within Christian leadership. Yet one of the most pressing problems facing practical theologians and the Christian churches in many parts of the Western world concerns the failure of congregations to attract and to retain men. Callum Brown's (2001) analysis of the demise of Christianity in Britain draws heavily on the notion of the feminisation of the churches. In so far as research in the social sciences tradition also has taken seriously the problem of explaining the connection between the Christian faith and being female, there may be good reason for dialogue between empirical theology and the perspectives developed by social scientists on this issue.

According to Argyle and Beit-Hallahmi (1975) the conclusion that women are more religious than men is one of the best attested findings in the psychology of religion. More recent reviews generally confirm this finding, often in the non-Christian world as well as in the Christian world (Stark, 2002), although some studies like Loewenthal, MacLeod and Cinnirella (2001) caution against unguarded generalisation beyond the Christian and post-Christian contexts. The real major source of controversy, however, is not concerned with establishing the *empirical* grounds for the observation that women are more religious than men (especially in the Christian and post-Christian contexts), but with establishing a satisfactory *theoretical* basis to provide an adequate account of the reasons for the observed differences.

Sociologically-grounded theories have attempted to account for the well-established gender differences in religiosity in terms of the different experiences of males and females in society. Such theories can be broadly divided into two categories: gender role socialisation theories, and structural location theories. Gender role socialisation theories begin not from individual differences in the psychological experiences of males and females but from the differences in their social experiences. Mol (1985), for example, provides a classic description of gender role socialisation theories when he argues that:

> males of all classes in modern western society are socialised into thinking and believing that drive and aggressiveness are positive orientations. They learn to cope with conflict and play it often as an institutional game. Specific goals are primary and conflict resolution secondary.

By contrast, the socialisation of females is said to emphasise conflict resolution, submission, gentleness, nurturance, and other expressive values that are congruent with religious emphases.

COMPARATIVE EMPIRICAL RESEARCH IN RELIGION 143

Structural location theories also begin from a sociological rather than a psychological basis. There are two main forms of structural location theory advanced to account for greater religiosity among women. The first form emphasises the child rearing role for women. For example, Moberg (1962) argues that the family-centred role of women encourages dependence on personal influences and that religion, which deals with personality, is therefore more appreciated by women than by men. The second form emphasises the different place of women in the workforce. One strand of this argument is a development of the classic secularisation thesis, as illustrated by Lenski (1953) and Luckman (1967). According to this argument, religious involvement declines with participation in the modern secular world. Since women are less likely to be fully a part of the ongoing secular world, at least in terms of outside-the-home employment, they are also likely to be less secularised than men.

Reviewing the relevance of both groups of theories towards the end of the twentieth century, Francis (1997) concluded that their plausibility was beginning to wear thin. He argued that the strength of gender role socialisation theories to account for gender differences in religiosity was being eroded by societal trends which may encourage treating boys and girls in similar ways. Similarly, he argued that the strength of structural location theories to account for gender differences in religiosity was being eroded by social trends which may encourage providing similar opportunities for men and for women.

Psychologically-grounded theories have attempted to account for the well-established gender differences in religiosity in terms of the different personality profiles of men and women. In a pioneering study, Thompson (1991) challenged existing explanations for sex differences in religiosity, based on structural location theories or differential socialisation theories, by arguing that religiosity should be affected more by gender orientation than by being female or male. According to this account, being religious is a consonant experience for *people* with a feminine orientation, and men as well as women can have a feminine orientation. This leads Thompson to the view that the observed sex differences in religiosity is not a real function of sex *per se*, but can be explained by the different proportions of women and men with a feminine worldview.

The notions of feminine and masculine orientations as personality constructs are developed, for example, by Bem (1981) in the refinement

144 LESLIE J. FRANCIS

of the Bem Sex Role Inventory. According to this conceptualisation, masculinity and femininity are not bipolar descriptions of a unidimensional construct, but two orthogonal personality dimensions. Empirically, the Bem Sex Role Inventory demonstrates considerable variations in both femininity and masculinity among both men and women. Although the very measurement of gender orientation is not without significant criticism (Maznah and Choo, 1986; Schenk and Heinisch, 1986; Archer, 1989), the usefulness of the theory to account for a wide range of individual differences remains widely supported in the literature.

Thompson proceeded to argue that, if being religious is a gender type attribute characterising women's lives in general, then multivariate analyses which control for the personality dimensions of masculinity and femininity should reveal that being female continues to have a significant effect on predicting religiosity. However, if being religious is a function of gender orientation, then multivariate analyses which control for the personality dimensions of masculinity and femininity should result in no additional variance explained by being female. Thompson's empirical analysis, using data from 358 undergraduate students in New England, who completed the Bem Sex Role Inventory together with five measures of religiosity, provided clear support for the view that being religious is a function of gender orientation.

Thompson's (1991) pioneering study in the United States of America was replicated by three studies in the United Kingdom. In the first of these studies, Francis and Wilcox (1996) explored Thompson's hypotheses, using data from 159 students in Wales who completed the Bem Sex Role Inventory together with the Francis Scale of Attitude toward Christianity. Like Thompson's original analysis, this study demonstrated that the significant relationship between religiosity and being female disappeared after controlling for individual differences in masculinity and femininity. In the second of these studies, Francis and Wilcox (1998) administered the Bem Sex Role Inventory together with the Francis Scale of Attitude toward Christianity to two samples of adolescents. The first sample comprised 340 males and 347 females between the ages of 13 and 15 years. The second sample comprised 59 males and 233 females between the ages of 16 and 18 years. Multiple regression analysis indicated that among the older group individual differences in gender orientation explained all the variance in attitude toward Christianity between males and females. Among the younger age group, sex still explained additional variance in attitude toward Christianity after taking gender orientation into account. In the third of these studies, Francis (2005) administered the same two instruments to a sample of 496 older men and women in England, mainly in their sixties and seventies. These data demonstrate that femininity scores are the main predictor of individual differences in religiosity (as assessed by attitude toward Christianity) and that after femininity scores have been taken into account neither masculinity scores nor biological sex provide any additional predictive power in respect of religiosity (as assessed by attitude toward Christianity).

Three main conclusions emerge from analyses conducted on these data sets. First, gender orientation has been shown to provide significant prediction of individual differences in religiosity. Second, femininity has generally emerged as a much stronger predictor than masculinity of individual differences in religiosity. Third, with the exception of the study among 13- to 15-year-olds, biological sex has not functioned as a predictor of individual differences in religiosity after gender orientation has been taken into account.

At one level these findings appear clear and unambiguous. If psychologically-grounded theories regarding the nature and the assessment of gender role orientation are able to account for differences in religiosity not only between the sexes but also within the sexes, sociologically-grounded theories designed to account for differences between the sexes in religiosity become redundant and need to be recognised as dealing with only part of the observed problem, ignoring the issue of differences within the sexes in religiosity.

At another level, however, these findings may seem simply to have reformulated the problem rather than provided an answer to it. In its reformulated form the problem now concerns why it should be the case that psychological femininity is so clearly associated with religiosity. The solution to this problem depends upon establishing the *level* of psychological data being accessed by measures of femininity and masculinity. One account proposes that these measures merely access surface traits which are themselves a consequence more of nurture than of nature. This is the view taken, for example, by Stark (2002:501) who argues that "the most compelling results in favour of the socialisation explanation involved the use of a masculinity-femininity scale (*sic*)". This interpretation, however, is questioned by the research underpinning the alternative account.

This alternative account proposes that these measures of masculinity and femininity access deeper dimensions of personality which are themselves largely shaped by nature and are determinative of a wide range of individual differences. This view is supported, for example, by Eysenck's dimensional model of personality which conceives masculinity—femininity as comprising one of the seven constituent components of psychoticism (Eysenck, Barrett, Wilson and Jackson, 1992) and which conceives the personality dimension of psychoticism as biologically based (Eysenck and Eysenck, 1976). This biological basis accounts both for the different levels of psychoticism recorded between the sexes and for the wide variation of levels of psychoticism recorded within the sexes. Moreover, studies like Francis and Wilcox (1999) confirm the correlation between Eysenck's measure of psychoticism and the Bem Sex Role Inventory's measures of masculinity and femininity. According to this account, being religious is consistent not so much with being female as with a distinctive personality profile characterised by low psychoticism scores in general and by high femininity scores in particular.

This conclusion concurs with the consensus derived from a considerable body of research concerning the relationship between personality and religion conducted between the publication of Argyle and Beit-Hallahmi's (1975) classic review in *The Social Psychology of Religion* and Beit-Hallahmi and Argyle's (1997) revised view in *The Psychology of Religious Behaviour, Belief and Experience*. In the first book they concluded that there was no consistent evidence for a relationship between personality and religion. In the second book they concluded that the most secure research evidence regarding the relationship between personality and religion pointed to a consistent negative association between psychoticism scores and religiosity scores.

The established association between low psychoticism scores, high femininity scores and high religiosity scores is explained by Eysenck's broader theory of social learning. According to this theory, sexual and aggressive impulses are conditioned into tenderminded social attitudes, and the qualities associated both with femininity and with religiosity belong to this domain of tenderminded social attitudes (Eysenck, 1975, 1976). At the same time individuals who are high on psychoticism are more resistant to conditioning into tenderminded social attitudes (Francis, 1992). This conclusion is also consistent with the research traditions which link rejection of religiosity with high levels of risk taking (Miller and Hoffmann, 1995; Miller and Stark, 2002), and with criminality (Stark, 2002). Not only are risk taking and impulsivity established components of psychoticism (Eysenck and Eysenck, 1976), but psychoticism has been shown to be a key predictor of the criminal personality (Eysenck, 1977). Here, then, is a simple and elegant

COMPARATIVE EMPIRICAL RESEARCH IN RELIGION 147

biologically-based theory that accounts not only for the observation that women are more religious than men, but also for the observation that both men and women who record high scores on psychological femininity are more religious than men and women who record low scores on psychological femininity.

Further research is now needed to build on these foundations in three main ways. First, the present findings, grounded in a Christian understanding of religiosity, remain limited to the United Kingdom and the United States of America. Wider replication in other Christian or post-Christian countries would help to test the generalisability of the findings. Second, this model of research grounded in a Christian understanding of religiosity could be extended to embrace other major religious traditions, in particular drawing on the Katz-Francis Scale of Attitude toward Judaism, the Sahin-Francis Scale of Attitude toward Islam, and the Santosh-Francis Scale of Attitude toward Hinduism. Third, the present findings are all based on the model of gender role orientation proposed by Bem (1981). Given the somewhat dated conceptualisations of masculinity and femininity operationalised by this instrument it would be helpful to develop new studies utilising other operationalisations of these key (and controversial) constructs.

For practical, pastoral and moral theologians these conclusions carry significant implications for the ways in which the Church can respond to one of the major practical challenges of the twenty-first century, the evangelisation of men. Once the problem has been reconceptualised in terms of personality differences rather than in terms of sex differences, the plausibility and likely effectiveness of specific pastoral strategies can be evaluated in a very different light.

CONCLUSION

In an early paper entitled 'Measurement reapplied', Francis (1978) outlined an ambition of what could be achieved if a number of researchers (who were literate both in theology and in the social sciences) agreed on employing a common attitudinal measure of religiosity across a wide range of studies. Dr William K. Kay, Dr Marian Carter and Paul Pearson were the first three colleagues to accept that invitation and a number have followed in their footsteps, including Professor Yaacov Katz in the Jewish tradition, Dr Abdullah Sahin in the Islamic tradition, and Romila Santosh in the Hindu tradition. In recent years a particularly

148   LESLIE J. FRANCIS

significant contribution has been made by the research groups in the
University of Ulster at Magee College led by Dr Christopher Lewis.
All told over 250 dissertations, articles and chapters have employed
this family of attitudinal measures to form a secure foundation for
comparative empirical research in religion.

The present chapter has attempted to review the attempt of one specific tradition of empirical theology to establish a basis for comparative
empirical research in religion. The main conclusions from this review
are: that a great deal has been achieved in the English-speaking Christian and post-Christian world; that significant inroads have been made
to extend the research into non-English-speaking parts of the Christian
and post-Christian world; and that the task of extending the research
to the non-Christian world has only just begun. Nonetheless, a number
of studies are currently underway using the Islamic, Jewish and Hindu
measures, while experimental work is currently shaping new instruments
appropriate for use among Buddhists, Sikhs and Pagans.

REFERENCES

Allport, G.W. (1950), *The Individual and his Religion*, New York, Macmillan.
Archer, J. (1989), The relationship between gender-role measures: a review, *British Journal of Social Psychology*, 28, 173–184.
Argyle, M. and Beit-Hallahmi, B. (1975), *The Social Psychology of Religion*, London, Routledge and Kegan Paul.
Argyle, M. and Crossland, J. (1987), Dimensions of positive emotions, *British Journal of Social Psychology*, 26, 127–137.
Argyle, M., Martin, M. and Crossland, J. (1989), Happiness as a function of person-ality and social encounters, in J.P. Forgas and J.M. Innes (eds.), *Recent Advances in Social Psychology: an international perspective*, pp. 189–203, Amsterdam, North Holland, Elsevier Science Publishers.
Batson, C.D., Schoenrade, P. and Ventis, W.L. (1993), *Religion and the Individual: a social-psychological perspective*, Oxford, Oxford University Press.
Beit-Hallahmi, B. and Argyle, M. (1997), *The Psychology of Religious Belief and Experience*, London, Routledge.
Bem, S.L. (1981), *Bem Sex Role Inventory: professional manual*, Palo Alto, California, Con-sulting Psychologists Press.
Bourke, R. and Francis, L.J. (2000), Personality and religion among music students, *Pastoral Psychology*, 48, 437–444.
Brown, C.G. (2001), *The Death of Christian Britain*, London, Routledge.
Campo-Arias, A., Oviedo, H.C., Dtaz, C.F. and Cogollo, Z. (2006), Internal consistency of a Spanish translation of the Francis Scale of Attitude toward Christianity short form, *Psychological Reports*, 99, 1008–1010.
Carter, M., Kay, W.K. and Francis, L.J. (1996), Personality and attitude toward Chris-tianity among committed adult Christians, *Personality and Individual Differences*, 20, 265–266.

COMPARATIVE EMPIRICAL RESEARCH IN RELIGION   149

Chan, R. and Joseph, S. (2000), Dimensions of personality, domains of aspiration, and subjective well-being, *Personality and Individual Differences*, 28, 347–354.

Eek, J. (2001), *Religious Facilitation through Intense Liturgical Participation: a quasi-experimental study of Swedish pilgrims to Taizé*, Lund, University of Lund Studies in Psychology of Religion.

Evans, T.E. and Francis, L.J. (1996), Measuring attitude toward Christianity through the medium of Welsh, in L.J. Francis, W.K. Kay and W.S. Campbell (eds.), *Research in Religious Education*, pp. 279–293, Leominster, Gracewing.

Eysenck, H.J. (1975), The structure of social attitudes, *British Journal of Social and Clinical Psychology*, 14, 323–331.

——. (1976), Structure of social attitudes, *Psychological Reports*, 39, 463–466.

——. (1977), *Crime and Personality* (3rd edition), St Albans, Paladin.

Eysenck, H.J., Barrett, P., Wilson, G. and Jackson, C. (1992), Primary trait measurement of the 21 components of the PEN system, *European Journal of Psychological Assessment*, 8, 109–117.

Eysenck, H.J. and Eysenck, M.W. (1985), *Personality and Individual Differences: a natural science approach*, New York, Plenum Press.

Eysenck, H.J. and Eysenck S.B.G. (1975), *Manual of the Eysenck Personality Questionnaire (adult and junior)*, London, Hodder and Stoughton.

——. (1976), *Psychoticism as a Dimension of Personality*, London, Hodder and Stoughton.

——. (1991), *Manual of the Eysenck Personality Scales*, London, Hodder and Stoughton.

Eysenck, S.B.G. and Eysenck, H.J. (1963), On the dual nature of extraversion, *British Journal of Social and Clinical Psychology*, 2, 46–55.

Ferreira, A.V. and Neto, F. (2002), Psychometric properties of the Francis Scale of Attitude toward Christianity among Portugese university students, *Psychological Reports*, 91, 995–998.

Francis, L.J. (1978), Measurement reapplied: research into the child's attitude towards religion, *British Journal of Religious Education*, 1, 45–51.

——. (1991), Personality and attitude towards religion among adult churchgoers in England, *Psychological Reports*, 69, 791–794.

——. (1992), Is psychoticism really the dimension of personality fundamental to religiosity? *Personality and Individual Differences*, 13, 645–652.

——. (1993), Personality and religion among college students in the UK, *Personality and Individual Differences*, 14, 619–622.

——. (1997), The psychology of gender differences in religion: a review of empirical research, *Religion*, 27, 81–97.

——. (1999), Personality and attitude toward Christianity among undergraduates, *Journal of Research on Christian Education*, 8, 179–195.

——. (2005), Gender role orientation and attitude toward Christianity: a study among older men and women in the United Kingdom, *Journal of Psychology and Theology*, 33, 179–186.

Francis, L.J. and Bennett, G.A. (1992), Personality and religion among female drug misusers, *Drug and Alcohol Dependence*, 30, 27–31.

Francis, L.J. and Enger, T. (2002), The Norwegian translation of the Francis Scale of Attitude toward Christianity, *Scandinavian Journal of Psychology*, 43, 363–367.

Francis, L.J. and Fearn, M. (1999), Religion and personality: a study among A-level students, *Transpersonal Psychology Review*, 3 (2), 26–30.

Francis, L.J. and Hermans, C.A.M. (2000), Internal consistency reliability and construct validity of the Dutch translation of the Francis scale of Attitude toward Christianity among adolescents, *Psychological Reports*, 86, 301–307.

Francis, L.J., Jones, S.H. and Wilcox, C. (2000), Religiosity and happiness: during adolescence, young adulthood and later life, *Journal of Psychology and Christianity*, 19, 245–257.

Francis, L.J. and Katz, Y.J. (2002), Religiosity and happiness: a study among Israeli female undergraduates, *Research in the Social Scientific Study of Religion*, 13, 75–86.

———. (2007), Measuring attitude toward Judaism: the internal consistency reliability of the Katz-Francis Scale of Attitude toward Judaism, *Mental Health, Religion and Culture*, 10, 309–324.

Francis, L.J., Katz, Y.J., Yablon, Y. and Robbins, M. (2004), Religiosity, personality and happiness: a study among Israeli male undergraduates, *Journal of Happiness Studies*, 5, 315–333.

Francis, L.J. and Kerr, S. (2003), Personality and religion among secondary school pupils in South Africa in the early 1990s, *Religion and Theology: a journal of contemporary religious discourse*, 10, 224–236.

Francis, L.J. and Kwiran, M. (1999), Personality and religion among secondary pupils in Germany, *Panorama*, 11, 34–44.

Francis, L.J., Lankshear, D.W. and Pearson, P.R. (1989), The relationship between religiosity and the short form JEPQ (JEPQ-S) indices of E, N, L and P among eleven year olds, *Personality and Individual Differences*, 10, 763–769.

Francis, L.J. and Lester, D. (1997), Religion, personality and happiness, *Journal of Contemporary Religion*, 12, 81–86.

Francis, L.J., Lewis, J.M., Brown, L.B., Philipchalk, R. and Lester, D. (1995), Personality and religion among undergraduate students in the United Kingdom, United States, Australia and Canada. *Journal of Psychology and Christianity*, 14, 250–262.

Francis, L.J., Lewis, C.A. and Ng, P. (2002), Assessing attitude toward Christianity among adolescents in Hong Kong: the Francis scale, *North American Journal of Psychology*, 4, 431–440.

———. (2003), Psychological health and attitude toward Christianity among secondary school pupils in Hong Kong, *Journal of Psychology in Chinese Societies*, 4, 231–245.

Francis, L.J. and Montgomery, A. (1992), Personality and attitudes towards Christianity among eleven to sixteen year old girls in a single sex Catholic school, *British Journal of Religious Education*, 14, 114–119.

Francis, L.J. and Pearson, P.R. (1985a), Psychoticism and religiosity among 15 year olds, *Personality and Individual Differences*, 6, 397–398.

———. (1985b), Extraversion and religiosity, *Journal of Social Psychology*, 125, 269–270.

———. (1988), Religiosity and the short-scale EPQ-R indices of E, N and L, compared with the JEPI, JEPQ and EPQ, *Personality and Individual Differences*, 9, 653–657.

———. (1991), Religiosity, gender and the two faces of neuroticism, *Irish Journal of Psychology*, 12, 60–68.

Francis, L.J., Pearson, P.R., Carter, M. and Kay, W.K. (1981a), The relationship between neuroticism and religiosity among English 15- and 16-year olds, *Journal of Social Psychology*, 114, 99–102.

———. (1981b), Are introverts more religious? *British Journal of Social Psychology*, 20, 101–104.

Francis, L.J., Pearson, P.R. and Kay, W.K. (1983a), Neuroticism and religiosity among English school children, *Journal of Social Psychology*, 121, 149–150.

———. (1983b), Are introverts still more religious? *Personality and Individual Differences*, 4, 211–212.

Francis, L.J. and Robbins, M. (2000), Religion and happiness: a study in empirical theology, *Transpersonal Psychology Review*, 4 (2), 17–22.

Francis, L.J., Robbins, M., Santosh, R. and Bhanot, S. (2008), Religion and mental health among Hindu young people in England, *Mental Health, Religion and Culture*, 11, 341–347.

Francis, L.J., Robbins, M. and White, A. (2003), Correlation between religion and happiness: a replication, *Psychological Reports*, 92, 51–52.

Francis, L.J., Santosh, R., Robbins, M. and Vij, S. (in press), Assessing attitude toward Hinduism: the Santosh-Francis Scale, *Mental Health, Religion and Culture*.

COMPARATIVE EMPIRICAL RESEARCH IN RELIGION 151

Francis, L.J. and Wilcox, C. (1996), Prayer, church attendance and personality revisited: a study among 16- to 19-year old girls, *Psychological Reports*, 79, 1265–1266.

——. (1998), The relationship between Eysenck's personality dimensions and Bem's masculinity and femininity scales revisited, *Personality and Individual Differences*, 25, 683–687.

——. (1999), Personality and sex role orientation among 17–19 year old females in England, *Irish Journal of Psychology*, 20, 172–178.

Francis, L.J., Ziebertz, H.-G. and Lewis, C.A. (2002), The psychometric properties of the Francis Scale of Attitude toward Christianity among German students, *Panorama*, 14, 153–162.

——. (2003), The relationship between religion and happiness among German students, *Pastoral Psychology*, 51, 273–281.

French, S. and Joseph, S. (1999), Religiosity and its association with happiness, purpose in life, and self-actualisation, *Mental Health, Religion and Culture*, 2, 117–120.

Freud, S. (1950), *The Future of an Illusion*, New Haven, Yale University Press.

Hills, P. and Argyle, M. (1998a), Musical and religious experiences and their relationship to happiness, *Personality and Individual Differences*, 25, 91–102.

——. (1998b), Positive moods derived from leisure and their relationship to happiness and personality, *Personality and Individual Differences*, 25, 523–535.

Jorm, A.F. (1987), Sex differences in neuroticism: a quantitative synthesis of published research, *Australian and New Zealand Journal of Psychiatry*, 21, 501–506.

Jung, C.G. (1938), *Psychology and religion*, New Haven, Yale University Press.

Kay, W.K. (1981), Psychoticism and attitude to religion, *Personality and Individual Differences*, 2, 249–252.

Koenig, H.G., McCullough, M.E. and Larson, D.B. (2001), *Handbook of Religion and Health*, New York, Oxford University Press.

Lenski, G.E. (1953), Social correlates of religious interest, *American Sociological Review*, 18, 533–544.

Lewis, C.A. (1999), Is the relationship between religiosity and personality 'contaminated' by social desirability as assessed by the lie scale? A methodological reply to Michael W. Eysenck (1998), *Mental Health, Religion and Culture*, 2, 105–114.

——. (2000), The religiosity-psychoticism relationship and the two factors of social desirability: a response to Michael W. Eysenck (1999), *Mental Health, Religion and Culture*, 3, 39–45.

——. (2001), Cultural stereotype of the effects of religion on mental health, *British Journal of Medical Psychology*, 74, 359–367.

Lewis, C.A. and Francis, L.J. (2000), Personality and religion among female university students in France, *International Journal of Psychology*, 35, 229.

——. (2003), Evaluer l'attitude d'étudiantes universitaires françaises à l'égard du Christianisme: l'Echelle de Francis, *Sciences Pastorals*, 22, 179–190.

Lewis, C.A. and Joseph, S. (1994), Religiosity: psychoticism and obsessionality in Northern Irish university students, *Personality and Individual Differences*, 17, 685–687.

Lewis, C.A. and Maltby, J. (1995), Religiosity and personality among US adults, *Personality and Individual Differences*, 18, 293–295.

Loewenthal, K.M., MacLeod, A.K. and Cinnirella, M. (2001), Are women more religious than men? Gender differences in religious activity among different religious groups in the UK, *Personality and Individual Differences*, 32, 133–139.

Luckman, T. (1967), *The Invisible Religion*, New York, Macmillan.

Maltby, J. (1997), Personality correlates of religiosity among adults in the Republic of Ireland, *Psychological Reports*, 81, 827–831.

Maltby, J. and Lewis, C.A. (1997), The reliability and validity of a short scale of attitude toward Christianity among USA, English, Republic of Ireland and Northern Ireland adults, *Personality and Individual Differences*, 22, 649–654.

152 LESLIE J. FRANCIS

Maznah, I.R. and Choo, P.F. (1986), The factor structure of the Bem Sex Role Inventory, *International Journal of Psychology*, 21, 31–41.

Miller, A.S. and Hoffmann, J.P. (1995), Risk and religion: an explanation of gender differences in religiosity, *Journal for the Scientific Study of Religion*, 34, 63–75.

Miller, A.S. and Stark, R. (2002), Gender and religiousness: can socialization explanations be saved?, *American Journal of Sociology*, 107, 1399–1423.

Moberg, D.O. (1962), *The Church as a Social Institution*, Englewood Cliffs, New Jersey, Prentice-Hall.

Mol, H. (1985), *The Faith of Australians*, Sydney, George Allen and Unwin.

Munayer, S.J. (2000), The ethnic identity of Palestinian Arab Christian adolescents in Israel, Unpublished PhD dissertation, University of Wales (Oxford Centre for Mission Studies).

Robbins, M. and Francis, L.J. (1996), Are religious people happier? A study among undergraduates, in L.J. Francis, W.K. Kay and W.S. Campbell (eds.), *Research in Religious Education*, pp. 207–217, Leominster, Gracewing.

Robbins, M., Francis, L.J. and Gibbs, D. (1995), Personality and religion: a study among 8–11 year olds, *Journal of Beliefs and Values*, 16, 1, 1–6.

Rocklin, T. and Revelle, W. (1981), The measurement of extraversion: a comparison of the Eysenck Personality Inventory and the Eysenck Personality Questionnaire, *British Journal of Social Psychology*, 20, 279–284.

Roman, R.E. and Lester, D. (1999), Religiosity and mental health, *Psychological Reports*, 85, 1088.

Sahin, A. and Francis, L.J. (2002), Assessing attitude toward Islam among Muslim adolescents: the psychometric properties of the Sahin-Francis scale, *Muslim Education Quarterly*, 19(4), 35–47.

Schenk, J. and Heinisch, R. (1986), Self-descriptions by means of sex-role scales and personality scales: a critical evaluation of recent masculinity and femininity scales, *Personality and Individual Differences*, 7, 161–168.

Shuter-Dyson, R. (2000), Profiling music students: Personality and religiosity, *Psychology of Music*, 28, 190–196.

Stark, R. (2002), Physiology and faith: addressing the 'universal' gender differences in religious commitment, *Journal for the Scientific Study of Religion*, 41, 495–507.

Thompson, E.H. (1991), Beneath the status characteristics: gender variations in religiousness, *Journal for the Scientific Study of Religion*, 30, 381–394.

Vine, I. (1978), Facts and values in the psychology of religion, *Bulletin of the British Psychological Society*, 31, 414–417.

Wilcox, C. and Francis, L.J. (1997), Personality and religion among A level religious studies students, *International Journal of Children's Spirituality*, 1(2), 48–56.

Williams, E., Robbins, M. and Francis, L.J. (2005), When introverts ceased to be more religious: a study among 12- to 16-year-old pupils, *Journal of Beliefs and Values*, 26, 77–79.

Youtika, A., Joseph, S. and Diduca, D. (1999), Personality and religiosity in a Greek Christian Orthodox sample, *Mental Health, Religion and Culture*, 2, 71–74.

PART TWO

QUALITATIVE PERSPECTIVES

CHAPTER SEVEN

ADOLESCENTS' VIEWS OF DENOMINATIONAL IDENTITIES AND OF DIALOGICAL RELIGIOUS EDUCATION: AN EMPIRICAL STUDY FROM GERMANY

Friedrich Schweitzer

Summary

This chapter describes the results from a study on so-called cooperative or dialogical religious education in Germany. While the study as a whole included interviews with the students (applying qualitative and quantitative methods), classroom observations and analysis of syllabi, as well as interviews with teachers, principals and parents, the present chapter concentrates on the broadly Christian students' views and attitudes *vis-à-vis* different denominations and religions. The qualitative material presented in the article particularly allows for a detailed reconstruction of the adolescents' views of denominational identities, of ecumenical and, to some degree, interreligious relationships. Furthermore, the interview material covers students' reactions to the special kind of religious education that they came to experience in the context of the present project, that is, religious education based on cooperation and dialogue between Protestant and Catholic teachers or learning groups with the aim of dialogical learning. Finally, data gathered in different regions of Germany (north and south) shed new light on the question whether the religious presuppositions are really as different in different parts of the country as many educators suppose. The results suggest that the taken-for-granted assumption of such differences must be reconsidered. The present study demonstrates the possible contribution of empirical research to a more realistic view of the students' religious interests and presuppositions, and to improving the didactics of religious education as well as to policy making, especially concerning the model of religious education that should be preferred in the future.

Introduction

As in many countries in Europe and beyond, religious education has become a much contested subject in Germany (recent overviews: Schreiner, Pollard and Sagberg, 2006; Jackson, Miedema, Weisse and

156   FRIEDRICH SCHWEITZER

Willaime, 2007). As opposed, for example, to the United Kingdom where religious education is often taught in groups that comprise children and adolescents with different denominational and religious backgrounds (Jackson and O'Grady, 2007), the traditional German model presupposes separate groups for Protestant and Catholic religious education and, where there are enough students for this purpose, for Jewish religious education (Schweitzer, 2006: 81–96). Currently, Islamic religious education is being introduced in a number of places (although still on an experimental basis). In recent years, religious educators and other analysts from different fields have advanced several arguments against this traditional model and some have tried to establish alternative models, for example, in Hamburg with a type of religious education that is subject to Protestant guidelines but programmatically considers itself as open to all students independently of their denominational or religious background (Doedens and Weisse, 1997; Weisse, 2002). While some of the arguments against having separate groups in religious education are based on purely organisational considerations (the difficulty of organising the groups and of finding appropriate teachers for them), or on financial concerns (having separate groups is considered expensive), there are also educational arguments that have to be taken seriously. In my view, one of the most serious arguments concerns the need for dialogue and mutual understanding or respect in a society that is increasingly multicultural and multireligious. It should not be overlooked that religious educators in Germany have been aware of this need for quite some time, and that the existing curricula or syllabi make reference to interdenominational and interreligious learning and dialogue (overview: Schreiner, Sieg and Elsenbast, 2005). Yet it is also clear that the existing efforts hardly go far enough and that dialogue should not just be a topic to be talked about in class and in the absence of the other. Such dialogue should also become a praxis that has its place in the schools themselves.

It was for this reason that the Protestant Church in Germany (Kirchenamt, 1994) introduced the model of so-called cooperative religious education which, eventually, has also been endorsed, at least in part, by the Catholic Church (Die deutschen Bischöfe, 1996). Unlike the Hamburg model mentioned above, this model is based on a combination of working in separate denominational groups and of having the different groups come together for shorter or longer periods of time, sometimes even for a whole school year, in order to strengthen cooperation and dialogue. Although the cooperative model has only been put in practice with different Christian denominations on a broader scale so far, more limited examples as well as theoretical considerations have shown that it can also work with different religions (Schweitzer *et al.*, 2006: 174–184). This is why the cooperative model can also be called dialogical religious education—a designation that relates it more clearly to the need for dialogue between different cultures, denominations, and religions.

The understanding of dialogue and dialogical education has a long history. Most often, Martin Buber with his 'dialogical principle' and his emphasis of the 'I-thou-relationship' is quoted as the classic in this field (cf. Buber, 1973; Knauth, 1996: 123–163). Another source can be seen in the theory of communicative action of Jürgen Habermas (Habermas, 1981) who, with his concepts of discourse ethics, mutuality and respect, has influenced many educators and religious educators in Germany. A third source for dialogical education specific to the area of Christianity and religion consists in the Christian ecumenical movement, with its different models for Christian or ecclesial unity, on the one hand, and theological models for the relationship between different religions, on the other hand (for an overview cf. Nipkow, 1998). While many studies refer to the concept of dialogue and of dialogical religious education the concept is not very clear. Monographic studies have remained the rare exception (Thorsten Knauth's dissertation still is the major single study on dialogue and religious education, cf. Knauth, 1996; for an encyclopaedic entry see Knauth and Weisse, 2001). Most authors (including our own team, Schweitzer *et al.*, 2006) make use of the concept in order to indicate their interest in openness and mutuality between different religions, in tolerance and respect (Schweitzer, 2007), and in doing justice to different religious traditions and convictions or adherences in religious education (Weisse, 1996; Rickers and Gottwald, 1998).

There is no set organisational or didactical model that is connected to dialogical religious education. Yet the literature mentioned above agrees on a number of criteria that must be met by any model that claims to be dialogical. The model must actually bring together the students who should enter a dialogical relationship with each other. The setting must be such that students are encouraged to communicate their religious convictions and to listen carefully to others. The materials used in class should support dialogical activities rather than only individual forms of studying and learning. Teachers should clearly show their respect for children and adolescents with different religious backgrounds, without denying that they have backgrounds of their own.

The present chapter focuses on this kind of dialogical religious education, especially following the model of cooperative religious education with its combination of separate denominational groups, on the one hand, and having students with different denominational and religious backgrounds work together, on the other hand. One of the main purposes of our project was to find out if the dialogical-cooperative model really works in actual classroom situations and how teachers, students, and parents respond to it. Moreover, we were interested in identifying the presuppositions for successful cooperation and dialogue in religious education in terms of different didactical arrangements and organisational requirements. In doing so, we also had to face a number of major challenges and objections to the cooperative model of religious education. Some educators argued that the cooperative model could not work because it presupposes clear denominational or religious identities that, as a result of secularisation and religious pluralisation, no longer exist with today's students. Others argued that it could only work in the southern part of Germany, that is, in an area which is more traditional in respect to religion than northern Germany.

In the following, I will not give a full report on all the different parts of the research project. Instead I will focus on the question of how adolescents perceive and understand denominational identities and how they respond to dialogical religious education. This focus corresponds to our educational and theological point of view that emphasises children's or adolescents' needs as one of the decisive criteria in religious education (Schweitzer and Boschki, 2004). The concept of denominational identity used below refers to how the adolescents perceive and describe themselves: for example, if they identify themselves as Protestants, Catholics, members or followers of a non-Christian religion or—as some put it—as 'nothing'. Psychological and sociological theories of identity formation form a background to this understanding (Schweitzer, 2005), but none of them informs our use in the present context.

The present chapter will be limited to one age group—adolescents of the age of 15 to 16 years (ninth grade in German schools)—and will not include our data on children (cf. Schweitzer and Boschki, 2004) and younger adolescents (sixth grade/age 12), except for purposes of occasional comparison. The main source in the following will be interviews conducted with the adolescents. The other sources of the project—classroom observation, interviews with teachers and parents—will have to

ADOLESCENTS' VIEWS 159

remain in the background (for fuller descriptions, see our German publications: Schweitzer *et al.*, 2002; Schweitzer *et al.*, 2006).[1]

RESEARCH QUESTIONS AND METHODS

I have described the wider background of our study in the introduction. This background should be kept in mind in the following, even if I limit myself to three main questions:

(1) How do secondary students perceive the main Christian denominations present in Germany, that is, Protestantism and Catholicism, in relationship to their own identities and in relationship to non-Christian religions?
(2) How do they perceive and experience dialogical (cooperative) religious education?
(3) Is there a systematic difference between the religious presuppositions of the students in southern and northern Germany so that dialogical religious education can only work in southern Germany?

As will become clear in what follows, we had to break down these main questions into a fair number of more detailed questions in order to achieve meaningful results. At this point, however, it will be easier to remain at the level of the more abstract research questions that guided our procedure and our choice of methods.

Since very little research is available on all of our questions, we considered it important to work in an exploratory manner. This is why we decided to use semi-open interviews with small groups of adolescents (approximately 6 students per group). All interviews were conducted in a school context and were limited to the participants of religious education classes (in Germany students are allowed to opt out of such classes and attend ethics classes instead, if available). The interviewees

---

[1] The project was carried out by a team under the joint leadership of my Catholic Tübingen colleague Albert Biesinger and me as the Protestant Tübingen religious educator. The main researchers in the part of the project that focused on secondary schools were Jörg Conrad and Matthias Gronover, supported by a whole team of student researchers and by Rosemarie Ilg, a psychologist who did the statistical work. The project was funded by the *Deutsche Forschungsgemeinschaft* (German Research Association).

160   FRIEDRICH SCHWEITZER

were excused from class for the time of the interviews (20–25 minutes). Due to the model of dialogical (cooperative) religious education that, in the case of our project, had Protestant and Catholic religion groups as its starting point, most of the interviewees were Protestant or Catholic (it should be noted that about a third of them came from so-called mixed, Protestant and Catholic, parents). Some were not baptised (yet)[2] and had no formal religious affiliation. Some of the interview groups included children from non-Christian religions or children with dual (for example, Christian and Muslim) backgrounds. This composition of the groups participating in the project reflects the fact that denominational religious education groups typically are open to all students independent of their religious or denominational affiliation (legal clauses only concern the religious or denominational affiliation of the teacher, which must coincide with the Protestant, Catholic, etc., orientation of the respective class). In order to allow for possible developmental influences, we chose two different grade or age levels (sixth grade, age 12 to 13, and ninth grade, age 15 to 16; in our earlier study we worked with grades 1, 2, and 3, i.e., roughly between the age of 6 or 7 and 9: cf. Schweitzer *et al.*, 2002). The total number of oral interviews or transcripts was 134, including approximately 350 students. In the following, we will mostly focus on the 15- to 16-year-olds, that is, a sample of approximately 230 students. The interviewees came from the area around Tübingen (in the state of Baden-Wuerttemberg, in south-western Germany) where our research team was located (but not from Tuebingen itself because this is a university town that, due to the influences from the university, differs from other places in many respects). The general character of this area is urban, due to its proximity to the industrial Stuttgart area some 25 miles from Tübingen, but there are also a number of small villages that have maintained a somewhat rural character. The sample included about equal numbers of male and female students, from college bound and non-college bound tracks (the German *Gymnasium* and *Hauptschule*).

In order to gain insights into the second question—how the adolescents perceive and experience dialogical (cooperative) religious

---

[2] Some parents in Germany send their children to religious education classes in order for them to learn about religious matters, hoping that their children will become able to make an informed decision about their denominational or religious affiliation.

education—we had to make sure that the students interviewed had actually been exposed beforehand to dialogical religious education. We chose to interview them twice, at the beginning and at the end of the school year. We worked with a number of classes (ninth grade) in eight different schools. The state of Baden-Württemberg had officially introduced the model of dialogical religious education during the respective school year. In order to allow for influences from different types of schools (college bound and non-college bound, the German *Gymnasium* and *Hauptschule*), as well as for urban and rural contexts, we made sure that the schools involved were as different as possible in terms of these background variables. Since we were also interested in possible differences between students who had participated in dialogical religious education and those who had not (so-called non-participants), we also conducted similar interviews with students outside the cooperative model. Since comparative evaluations of this type raise special questions of their own, however, we will not include our observations from the interviews with nonparticipants in the present chapter except for the comparison between different parts of the country, the next step to be described.

We consider the oral interviews and their evaluations as an important data base in themselves, but they also formed the basis for a written questionnaire that we developed in order to include more students in the main location of our research (southern Germany). In addition to this, the written questionnaire could also be transferred to another location in a different German state, Northrhine-Westfalia in northern Germany, so that comparisons became possible (question 3 above, concerning possible systematic difference between the religious presuppositions of the students in southern and northern Germany and their implications for religious education). In doing so we had to face the difficulty that, according to state legislation, religious education in Northrhine-Westfalia has to be taught in separate denominational groups exclusively. Because of this legal requirement, we were not given permission to ask the students there about their views on dialogical (cooperative) religious education that is taught in a setting with the different groups together in the same classroom, bringing together students with different denominational and religious backgrounds. Consequently, our results in this part of the study only apply to the students' religious presuppositions and not to their responses to dialogical (cooperative) religious education.

162 FRIEDRICH SCHWEITZER

Given the financial restraints of our project, we did not achieve representative samples. Moreover, the two sub-samples for the quantitative study in southern and northern Germany were unequal in size: 1524 students from Northrhine-Westfalia compared with only 303 from Baden-Württemberg—a difference that had to be controlled statistically in a very careful manner. We cannot claim that our results allow for general statements about northern and southern Germany. As will become clear in the following, however, our results are such that they raise far-reaching questions concerning common assumptions. Since the overall structure of our project was rather complex it may be useful to summarise our sampling and interviewing in the following table 7.1.

The evaluation of the qualitative material was carried out by small groups of interpreters. As a first task, the interpreters developed categories for the interview evaluation from the interview material itself rather than presupposing the questions from the interview guideline. Once no new categories came up from the process of interpretation, the collection of categories ended and the categories selected could be used for the rest of the interviews. The procedure was informed by the current state of qualitative research (cf. Flick, Kardorff and Steinke, 2000) but it did not follow a particular model, for example, the

Table 7.1: The sample

	School year	School type	Pupils N	Pupils total
Group interviews at beginning of school year	9	kk	49	
	9	nk	16	
	6	nk	16	81
Group interviews at end of school year	9	kk	32	
	9	nk	16	
	6	nk	16	64
Questionnaire at beginning of school year	9	nk	129	
	6	nk	133	262
Questionnaire at end of school year	9	kk	57	
	9	nk (BW)	149	
	9	nk (NW)	652	
	6	nk (BW)	154	
	6	nk (NW)	872	1884

Note: kk stands for students from cooperative groups, nk for students from non-cooperative groups; BW = Baden-Wuerttemberg, NW = Northrhine-Westfalia.

set model of so-called content analysis that is now used very often in Germany (Mayring, 1983). The process of evaluating and interpreting the qualitative material remained hermeneutical, in line with the current standards for the evaluation of interview materials from semi-open interviews (Schmidt, 2000), carefully following the steps recommended for this procedure. Yet as described above, it was guided by clear questions and paid attention to frequencies in the students' responses.

RESULTS

Following the three questions described earlier, my main emphasis in the following will be on the results from the qualitative part of our study. Quantitative results will only be briefly taken up at the end of this section.

Different religions yet rather similar—Islam as borderline

Unlike the primary school children of our earlier study, all the adolescents interviewed by us were familiar with the terms 'Protestant' and 'Catholic'. Most of the adolescents, however, had difficulties explaining them in more detail. Many considered 'Protestant' and 'Catholic' as two 'religions'. The distinction between the concepts of 'denomination' and 'religion' was absent in their explanations, at least in most interviews. Nevertheless, they somehow seemed to understand that both 'Protestant' and 'Catholic', are Christian and, as a consequence, are different from other religions.

On the whole, the awareness of consensus or overlap between the two denominations was much stronger than that of differences and disagreements. According to the adolescents, the members of both denominations believe in God, pray, sing hymns, read the Bible, celebrate worship services, etc. In all these respects, the denominations look very much alike to them. Moreover, to them, possible differences appear to be limited to formal aspects while the content is the same. They perceived denominational identities as something external to the person that does not really affect the internal side. At the same time, such views seem not to be based upon considered judgements. When asked explicitly if they thought that the similarities between or the differences between the denominations were the more important, many of them became insecure and, in the end, opted for the differences even if they had claimed earlier that the denominations were very similar, if not identical. With respect to reunification of the different denominations—a possibility they did not want to exclude although they did not show much personal interest in this kind of Christian *ecumene*—they expected 'conflicts' because the differences would remain active with some of the people.

Another clear tendency in the adolescents' responses was the absence of theological aspects or interpretations. Many of them were aware of the eucharist being celebrated every Sunday in a Catholic Church as well as of the different patterns of worship in a Protestant Church. Yet they made no references to the meaning of such differences and consequently were not able to take a considered stance *vis-à-vis* such differences.

Altogether, most of the interviewees viewed the two denominations as 'rather the same' or pretty 'similar'. Since differences are only external, the denominations become interchangeable for them. In a certain sense, the choice between Protestant and Catholic comes to resemble the choice of a customer at a market with different providers offering basically the same goods or services. This image also fits very well with the remarkable statements of two sixth graders:

> It's just like in soccer. For example, if there is a team of the world with the best players of the world. They then can...they always need two teams. And then it is the best players of the world against the air because there is no more second team. That would be boring.
> If there are two companies and both produce the same. And if there is only one, then the prices cannot go down.

In these statements, the different churches or denominations are perceived as institutions operating in a market type situation. The adolescents themselves are described as possible customers who profit from the competitive situation. There is no inner or personal relationship between the adolescents and the Church. The Church is not understood as being composed of members. Rather, it appears like a bank or a supermarket that one can use without further commitment to its existence or more permanent involvement with it.

To repeat, denominational differences do not play any major role for the adolescents interviewed in our study. Yet this does not mean that there are no religious divisions for them at all. The line beyond which differences do become important is clearly marked by Islam, at least in many cases. Muslims believe in the 'same God' but in a different

ADOLESCENTS' VIEWS   165

way, so that in this case, for the interviewees, the differences turn into a real dividing line. This will become clearer once we look at what we call the adolescents' maps of the religious landscape.

Maps of the religious landscape

One of the most fascinating results of the interview study was the possibility of reconstructing and reading the internal maps of the religious landscape that the adolescents are working with in their statements. Their responses clearly indicate that they work with a limited set of categories that they use for giving a certain order to their impressions and observations in the field of religion. The terms 'map' and 'landscape' can capture this function. In describing the religious landscape, the adolescents seem to rely on two polarities that make up something like basic coordinates for their own orientation—the polarity of 'rigid' and 'relaxed', and of 'normal' and 'extreme'. While these adjectives are actually used by the adolescents themselves, they do not speak of 'religious landscapes'. The identification or reconstruction of such landscapes is the result of the work of interpretation and reconstruction. This is why the meaning of the terms 'rigid' and 'relaxed', 'normal' and 'extreme' has to be reconstructed from the interviewees' actual use of them.

In the interviews, the four coordinates—'rigid' and 'relaxed', 'normal' and 'extreme'—apply to the denominations. Many of the adolescents interviewed by us considered Catholicism as more 'rigid', while Protestantism was viewed as more 'relaxed'. Obviously they refer to the expectations that the denominations maintain for their members, that is, in the case of the Catholic Church, regular participation in the eucharist and a certain sort of moral behaviour. It should also be mentioned in this context that the adolescents sometimes offered descriptions that are clearly incorrect, for example, that Catholics did not believe in Jesus but only in Mary, or that Protestants did have the Bible but not the Old Testament.

The second polarity—'normal' and 'extreme'—is used across the denominations. In this case, the adolescents seem to be thinking of different intensities of belief or of religious ethics. In terms of the denominations this implies that the adolescents expected the differences between the denominations to become a problem only in case of 'extreme' believers, that is, with people who 'constantly' go to church, 'always' read the Bible, etc., to use their own words once again. For

166   FRIEDRICH SCHWEITZER

the interviewees, the prototype of 'extreme' faith can be found, among others, with the Muslims who express their faith in a visible manner in everyday life. Moreover, the adolescents also considered the generation of their grandparents as more 'extreme', especially compared with themselves who are quite 'normal'.

Friendship and religious adherence

With impressive unanimity, all of the adolescents interviewed maintained the view that being friends has nothing to do with being Protestant or Catholic. As one girl put it: "There happen to be some things where religion really does not play a role, and that is with love and friendship." According to the adolescents, being friends is a matter of 'trust', 'character', etc. That their friends belong to different denominations is known to the adolescents but they perceive it as completely 'normal'.

What they do not consider 'normal' are the influences of an 'extreme faith', which is often seen as related to a different nationality or to Islam. Friendship with a Muslim is possible but goes along with the experience of the friend as different. A Protestant girl reported: "Yes, one of my friends is Turkish and she also is a Muslim. With her you notice that these people are religious because they eat no pork, and you notice it when she is at my home. And that she cannot go out so often and is allowed to meet me only rarely."

So friendship has not much to do with religion except for certain situations or for the case of 'extreme' believers with whom they can not imagine being friends. Yet this is not the whole picture, as we can see once we include questions about marriage and about how the adolescents would raise children of their own.

Marriage and religious nurture

Marriage and the religious nurture of their own children are topics of a possible yet distant future for the adolescents. The interviewees did not seem to think about these topics very often. Yet their responses indicate that denominational identities and expectations play a much stronger role in this context than they do with friendship.

Much more than any religious motive it is personal love that, according to the adolescents, should be the basis for marriage. In this respect they repeated their convictions, described in the context of friendship above, about the absolute primacy of love in respect to all kinds of personal relationships. In their eyes, denominational membership is an additional aspect clearly subordinate to the interpersonal dimension. Consequently, marriage across denominational boundaries does not have to be a problem. Concerning the children from such a marriage the adolescents offered very different solutions that can be called pragmatic, like having one child baptised in the Catholic Church and the other one in a Protestant Church.

They expect problems, however, if one of the partners is 'strict' in his or her faith. Here we encounter again the distinction between 'strict' and 'relaxed' or 'normal' types of faith. Moreover, Islam again seems to mark a borderline for the adolescents. Most of the broadly Christian adolescents could not imagine marrying a Muslim partner. The parents seem strongly to support this expectation by sometimes directly advising their adolescent children against marriage across different religions.

Some of the adolescents interviewed clearly expressed their wish for a marriage with a partner of the same denomination. A Catholic girl said, for example: "I would like to marry a Catholic and my child will also be Catholic. That is clear for me from the beginning." She continued by pointing out the deep roots of her convictions that reach way beyond rational arguments: "I do not know why but I have made this decision somehow early."

Some of the adolescents advocate that the children should be allowed to make their own decisions and that one should not, for example, baptise children at a time when they cannot understand what is happening to them. Others would prefer the parents to make a first decision but to let the children decide by themselves later on.

Reactions to dialogical (cooperative) religious education

The overall reaction of the students to the cooperative and dialogical kind of religious education they had experienced during the school year was clearly positive. Many of them argued that it was new and interesting for them to get to know something about the other denomination. In some cases, they just thought that it was good to find out what topics were taken up in the other denominational religious education classes. In other cases, however, their interest was more profound. It referred to "what they believe, what differences there are and what is the same".

On the whole, the students perceived Protestant and Catholic religious education as very similar so that it did not make sense to them

168 FRIEDRICH SCHWEITZER

to have separate classes. Some students thought that it would be best to be together for certain topics and to work in separate groups at other times. The students' arguments indicate that they are aware of possible difficulties arising from different views within the respective denominations:

> Catholic student: Always together would not be so good...and always by ourselves is perhaps somehow boring...About the Pope, the others would have different opinions so that one could not really be together...then it would perhaps be rather inconvenient.

This student refers to what can be called dealing with different opinions or, to put it differently, dealing with conflicting religious truth-claims in a situation with members of different denominations who do not accept these claims. A small number of students expressed their apprehension that truth-claims could not be discussed anymore if everybody is together, independently of their convictions and denominational outlooks.

> Protestant student: I think they would not be allowed to ask the question if you have religious education with two different denominations...What is right in religion? What religion is right? Because I think both religions are true in their own way. Protestants find Protestant religion right and Catholics the Catholic religion. And if you have them together in religious education you couldn't ask the question because the Catholics would always say: the Catholic..., and the Protestants would say: the Protestant [religion]

These students seem to find it difficult to conceive of ways for dealing with conflicting truth claims in the presence of the other.

While the responses to dialogical religious education tended to be positive in most cases, there were a few exceptions that I do not want to suppress. They indicate that we should not assume that dialogue will automatically be experienced as enriching. One (Catholic) student was clearly opposed to being together with students from other denominations in religious education:

> When I do religion, I want to do my religion, not the religion of the others...Then I want Catholic, and that's it.

This student obviously is convinced that he is entitled to focus on his own beliefs and to enjoy the company of fellow believers, without having to bother with differing opinions or convictions.

In two of the interviews, the students reported conflicts that they experienced in their groups. Specifically they complained about Protestant students speaking negatively about the Catholic faith. This was hurtful to them.

One (Protestant) student described a confusing situation because the Protestant teacher and the Catholic teacher held different opinions so that the students 'got all confused'.

Critical statements of this kind remained a rare exception. They do not change the overall picture that the adolescents interviewed by us found the dialogical (cooperative) religious education they had experienced quite interesting and enriching. Moreover, a fair number of the students articulated profound reasons for this evaluation—wanting to learn about the others and find out about what they can share with them and what remains different.

Different presuppositions in different parts of the country?

As mentioned in the introduction, many religious educators in Germany tend to assume that cooperative or dialogical religious education is a model that might make sense in the southern part of the country with its more conservative religious presuppositions but that it could not work in northern Germany. Dialogue presupposes different identities—in the case of religious education, different denominational and religious identities—that these observers do not expect to be present in many parts of Germany. They assume that the students are not really familiar with different denominations and that they do not have a personal relationship to denominational traditions.

Some statements from teachers in a Northrhine-Westfalian study can illustrate this point of view. The teachers in this study (Hütte and Mette, 2003) argue for keeping all students together in religious education because they do not perceive any denominational influences with them. The authors of the study summarise their results referring to primary schools: "According to the interviews, basically nothing is known about the differences between Protestant and Catholic, so that an exchange is not possible." Similarly, concerning secondary schools, the teachers complained about "the lack of knowledge or the lack of religious socialisation of the students". Hütte and Mette report that most of the teachers were convinced that dialogue between the denominations or religions is impossible in religious education because the students are not aware of the differences between the denominations or religions (Hütte and Mette, 2003: 83).

The question of if and how a particular approach to religious education might be premised on the cultural and religious presuppositions in a given area is not only of interest within Germany. Similar questions can be raised for other countries or for larger bodies, like the European Union, that include countries with very different political and religious histories (cf. Jackson *et al.*, 2007). In such cases, comparative empirical studies on youth and religion can shed some light on the religious situation in different countries or regions. This kind of empirical work on a European scale has just begun (cf., as recent example, Ziebertz and Kay, 2005, 2006). It could play an important role in the future by providing us with a more in-depth understanding of the situation of religious education in Europe, the viability of different models and possibly even the effects of religious education.

In Germany, many people take it for granted that there are major religious differences between different parts of the country. This assumption does not only concern the well-known differences between the western part and the eastern part of the country, that is, the area of the former GDR with its 40 years of socialist and atheist education for which at least some research is available (for example, Engelhardt, Loewenich and Steinacker, 1997: 243–342). In respect to religious education, it also refers to differences within Western Germany. In this case, such assumptions are not based on any evidence other than occasional reports given by teachers, pastors, journalists, etc. In other words, they are not based on empirical data and, even more significantly, they are not even based on real comparisons in that practitioners tend to be very familiar only with their own local work. It is against this background that the third question above—whether there is a systematic difference between the religious presuppositions of the students in southern and northern Germany so that dialogical religious education can only work in southern Germany—has to be understood. In order to answer this question we gathered data not only in Baden-Württemberg, where our qualitative study took place, but also in Northrhine-Westfalia, a northern state with a strong influence from immigration.

With the help of our written questionnaire we interviewed students in both parts of the country. We did not have the means for doing a representative study because the main focus of our project was qualitative investigations around dialogical religious education. Yet we assumed that it would be better to have at least some empirical basis for comparative statements rather than having to depend exclusively on occasional impressions and intuitions. In Baden-Württemberg we had used the written questionnaire as an additional tool for including more students in our study than we would have been able to with oral interviews. Moreover, in order to find out about possible effects of dialogical (cooperative) religious education, we collected written data from 303 students who had not participated in the special cooperative setting of the project. Since there also is no cooperative religious education in Northrhine-Westfalia, this group of non-participants in Baden-Württemberg seemed to be most suitable for comparisons with the students there.

Northrhine-Westfalia is a state with both very urban and very rural areas. Moreover, some (mostly rural) areas are known as very Catholic in a traditional sense while others (urban areas) are considered secular or multireligious and multicultural. In order to do justice to such differences we had to include several different locations. Consequently, as mentioned above, our sample from Northrhine-Westfalia is much bigger than the one from Baden-Württemberg—a difference which had to be controlled for statistically in a very careful manner.

The results for the two parts of the country have been published in our German report (for a detailed description cf. Schweitzer *et al.*, 2006: esp. 62–76). In the present context I limit myself to what can be seen as the overall result of this part of our study. There were indeed a small number of differences of statistical significance between the responses from the two states. Yet contrary to all expectations, it was the students from the south who turned out to be less interested in the Church and who said that they are not convinced that denominational differences should play a role in marriage. The most important result, however, was definitely how similar the responses were in each part of the country. According to our data, the assumption of some kind of religious divide between northern Germany and southern Germany does not appear to be well-grounded.

To repeat: our data are not representative. Yet they could very well serve as a strong motive for doing more empirical work with representative samples in order to get a better basis for comparative statements, and for developing policies in the field of religious education.

INTERPRETATION OF THE RESULTS

The present study allows for insights in several respects. It includes arguments for why dialogical religious education is important and it offers a realistic view of students' presuppositions about this kind of teaching. It also proves that empirical research can inform educational policies by offering them a more solid basis than mere assumptions, for example, about the differences between the different areas of a country.

First, most of the students interviewed by us found dialogical religious education interesting and enriching. While some of them liked it for pragmatic reasons (because they liked the teacher better than in their regular classes) many students indicated reasons for their preference that are of educational value. This is especially true of their interest in getting to know other denominations or religions. Many of the interviewees considered a dialogical situation in which students with different backgrounds work together more suitable for this kind of learning. Even if there were a few exceptions to this positive response, and even if a small group of students explicitly did not like being exposed to religious convictions different from their own, this result is very encouraging for attempts to make religious education more dialogical.

The data also do not indicate that dialogical religious education might create confusion among the students—an argument that is often used in order to criticise dialogical religious education. Admittedly, there were a few cases in which students did report confusing effects of being faced with different opinions. Yet on the whole the adolescents seemed to be quite able to deal with religious differences. It should not be overlooked, however, that the adolescents found it quite difficult to conceive of ways for dealing with conflicting truth-claims in the presence of the parties involved. They assumed that each party would just argue for their own point of view while refusing the others. This indicates that dealing with such truth-claims is a topic that should be given more attention in religious education in the future. It is very important that students have a chance to understand and to experience how people can deeply disagree in important respects without hurting one another. Tolerance does not mean that there should be no more differences or that we should learn not to take differences so seriously; tolerance means that we can live together peacefully and respectfully without denying the differences between different people (cf. Schweitzer, 2007).

Does dialogical religious education foster such tolerance? How much prejudice—especially religious prejudice—do we have to expect with today's adolescents?

Second, dialogical religious education should be based on a realistic view of students' presuppositions in relationship to different denominations and religions. The students interviewed in our study show most of all the characteristics of religious individualisation and pluralisation. Clear denominational identities are rare with them. They hardly perceive any differences between the Christian denominations. However, there seem to be clear dividing lines once the relationship between different religions is concerned, that is, in the present case, in the relationship between Christianity and Islam. While Islam was not described in any generally negative sense, it was also obvious that certain generalisations or stereotypes were quite influential in our sample. It is easy to see how such stereotypes could turn into a full-blown type of prejudice once additional factors like biased media reports or the influence of certain groups come into play. Even if our study was not focused on the preventative effects of dialogical religious education against prejudice, there is at least a *prima facie* plausibility for the assumption that dialogical learning could be one of the ways towards more openness between denominations and religions. It should be noted, in this context, that recent larger studies on youth in Germany indicate that there are clear dividing lines between broadly Christian adolescents on the one hand and Muslim adolescents on the other (Fuchs-Heinritz, 2000). If this is true, dialogical religious education should not only be used as a model for bringing together different Christian denominations but different religions like Christianity and Islam as well (Schweitzer *et al.*, 2006: 174–184).

Our results also show, however, that denominational identities still play a role for today's adolescents in Germany: for example, in the context of marriage and of raising children. In this respect, the teachers' views of the religious presuppositions characteristic of their students were not supported indiscriminately by our interviews. On the basis of our study we can only speculate why teachers tend to assume that their students are less influenced by religious nurture and socialisation than they really are, at least according to their own statements (for similar results concerning primary schools cf. Schweitzer *et al.*, 2002). Possibly it is the role of the teacher that supports the perception of certain characteristics, while other characteristics tend to be overlooked. It is also possible that the small group situation of our interviews allowed for a type of personal communication that is less likely in a typical classroom situation.

If we take together our present study on adolescents with our earlier study on children (Schweitzer *et al.*, 2002), there are interesting differences between the age groups concerning dialogical religious education. Children seem to be in need of opportunities for identification with adults to whom they feel close. The sense of belonging to a certain teacher seems to be vital for them (Schweitzer and Boschki, 2004).

174   FRIEDRICH SCHWEITZER

This also explains why the children in our study often referred to their parents in talking about Christian denominations. The adolescents interviewed in the present study did not express such needs and orientations. For them, their peers are clearly more important. They never spoke of 'belonging' to a teacher. Moreover, when asked about Christian denominations, the adolescents answered by referring to a broader picture that included different denominations as well as different religions, something that we did not observe with the children in the earlier study. The religious horizon clearly seems to expand from childhood into adolescence, making different religions a much more pressing topic for them than for the children.

Third, the quantitative part of our study concentrated on a comparison of data from two different parts of the country. While it was not possible to present this part in any detail in the present chapter, this research is also a clear example for how empirical research can support political decision making. Although not representative and consequently not conclusive, our results are convincing enough to discourage any immediate assumptions about supposedly different religious presuppositions in the two parts of the country in question. Views taken for granted by many people will not necessarily stand the test of empirical evidence. It would be very interesting to have larger studies comparing different populations within the same country. So far, very little work has been done in this direction.

Another way of looking at the results from the comparison between northern and southern Germany could come from the understanding of contemporary adolescence (cf. Schweitzer, 2004: 40–63). The basic tendencies characterising today's adolescents—such as individualisation, pluralisation, globalisation—might exert a very strong effect in the direction of neutralising religious differences.

CONCLUSION

The claim that empirical research is able to inform political decision making, and that it can help us in becoming clearer about desirable models of religious education for the future, does not imply that empirical research will actually be allowed to play this role. State-related institutions as well as church-related institutions (who are involved in such decision making in Germany for legal reasons) each have their own agendas. Their decision making processes are often influenced

ADOLESCENTS' VIEWS 175

by factors like upcoming elections, media events, personal encounters, etc. In politics people often feel that they just cannot wait for empirical results because they have to take action now.

From my point of view, it would not be fair or justified to complain about this situation. Different fields tend to follow different rules. Yet, as researchers in the field of education, we should be aware of such differences no less than the differences that we actually study. Otherwise our empirical results will not achieve the effects we intended.

REFERENCES

Buber, M. (1973), *Das dialogische Prinzip*, Heidelberg, Lambert Schneider.
Die deutschen Bischöfe (1996), *Die bildende Kraft des Religionsunterrichts: zur Konfessionalität des katholischen Religionsunterrichts*, Bonn, Sekretariat der Deutschen Bischofskonferenz.
Doedens, F. and Weisse, W. (eds.) (1997), *Religionsunterricht für alle: Hamburger Perspektiven zur Religionsdidaktik*, Hamburg, Pädagogisch-theologisches Institut.
Engelhardt, K., Loewenich, H.v. and Steinacker, P. (eds.) (1997), *Fremde Heimat Kirche: die dritte EKD-Erhebung über Kirchenmitgliedschaft*, Gütersloh, Gütersloher.
Flick, U., Kardorff, E. von and Steinke, I. (eds.) (2000), *Qualitative Forschung: ein Handbuch*, Reinbek, Rowohlt.
Fuchs-Heinritz, W. (2000), Religion, in D. Shell (ed.), *Jugend 2000: Volume 1*, pp. 157–180, Opladen, Leske and Budrich.
Habermas, J. (1981), *Theorie des kommunikativen Handelns*, 2 volumes, Frankfurt am Main, Suhrkamp.
Hütte, S. and Mette, N. (2003), *Religion im Klassenverband unterrichten: Lehrer und Lehrerinnen berichten von ihren Erfahrungen*, Münster, LIT.
Jackson, R. and O'Grady, K. (2007), Religions and education in England: social plurality, civil religion and religious education pedagogy, in R. Jackson, S. Miedema, W. Weisse and J.-P. Willaime (eds.) (2007), *Religion and Education in Europe: developments, contexts and debates*, pp. 181–202, Münster, Waxmann.
Jackson, R., Miedema, S., Weisse, W. and Willaime, J.-P. (eds.) (2007), *Religion and Education in Europe: developments, contexts and debates*, Münster, Waxmann.
Kirchenamt der Evangelischen Kirche in Deutschland (ed.) (1994), *Identität und Verständigung: Standort und Perspektiven des Religionsunterrichts in der Pluralität, eine Denkschrift*, Gütersloh, Gütersloher.
Knauth, T. (1996), *Religionsunterricht und Dialog*, Münster, Waxmann.
Knauth, T. and Weisse, W. (2001), Interreligiöses Lernen, in N. Mette and F. Rickers (eds.) (2001), *Lexikon der Religionspädagogik*, pp. 874–881, Neukirchen-Vluyn, Neukirchener.
Mayring, P. (1983), *Qualitative Inhaltsanalyse: Grundlagen und Techniken*, Weinheim and Basel, Beltz.
Nipkow, K.E. (1998), *Bildung im Pluralismus Volume I: Religionspädagogik im Pluralismus*, Gütersloh, Gütersloher.
Rickers, F. and Gottwald, E. (eds.) (1998), *Vom religiösen zum interreligiösen Lernen: wie angehörige verschiedener Konfessionen lernen, Möglichkeiten und Grenzen interreligiöser Verständigung*, Neukirchen-Vluyn, Neukirchener.
Schmidt, C. (2000), Analyse von Leitfadeninterviews, in U. Flick, E. von Kardorff and I. Steinke (eds.), *Qualitative Forschung: ein Handbuch*, pp. 447–456, Reinbek, Rowohlt.

176 FRIEDRICH SCHWEITZER

Schreiner, P., Pollard, G. and Sagberg, S. (eds.) (2006), *Religious Education and Christian Theologies: some European perspectives*, Münster, Waxmann.

Schreiner, P., Sieg, U. and Elsenbast, V. (eds.) (2005), *Handbuch Interreligiöses Lernen*, Gütersloh, Gütersloher.

Schweitzer, F. (2004), *The Postmodern Life Cycle: challenges for church and theology*, St Louis, Missouri, Chalice.

———. (2005), Religiöse Identitätsbildung, in P. Schreiner, U. Sieg and V. Elsenbast (eds.) (2005), *Handbuch interreligiöses Lernen*, pp. 294–303, Gütersloh, Gütersloher.

———. (2006), *Religionspädagogik*, Gütersloh, Gütersloher.

———. (2007), Religious individualization: challenges to education for tolerance, *British Journal of Religious Education*, 29, 89–100.

Schweitzer, F., Biesinger, A., Boschki, R., Schlenker, C., Edelbrock, A., Kliss, O. and Scheidler, M. (2002), *Gemeinsamkeiten stärken—Unterschieden gerecht werden. Erfahrungen und Perspektiven zum konfessionell-kooperativen Religionsunterricht*, Freiburg and Gütersloh, Herder and Gütersloher.

Schweitzer, F., Biesinger, A., Conrad, J. and Gronover, M. (2006), *Dialogischer Religionsunterricht: Analyse und Praxis konfessionell-kooperativen Religionsunterrichts im Jugendalter*, Freiburg, Herder.

Schweitzer, F. and Boschki, R. (2004), What children need: co-operative religious education in German schools: results from an empirical study, *British Journal of Religious Education*, 26, 33–44.

Weisse, W. (ed.) (1996), *Vom Monolog zum Dialog: Ansätze einer interkulturellen dialogischen Religionspädagogik*, Münster, Waxmann.

———. (ed.) (2002), *Wahrheit und Dialog: theologische Grundlagen und Impulse gegenwärtiger Religionspädagogik*, Münster, Waxmann.

Ziebertz, H.-G. and Kay, W.K. (eds.) (2005), *Youth in Europe I: an international empirical study about religiosity*, Münster, LIT.

———. (eds.) (2006), *Youth in Europe II: an international empirical study about life perspectives*, Münster, LIT.

CHAPTER EIGHT

ORDINARY SOTERIOLOGY: A QUALITATIVE STUDY

Ann Christie and Jeff Astley

SUMMARY

The chapter first introduces the concept of 'ordinary theology', understood as the theology and theologising of those who speak of God reflectively, but who have received little or no theological education of a scholarly, academic or systematic kind. Ordinary soteriology, by extension, is the account of what Jesus does for human salvation that is offered by those who have received little or nothing by way of formal theological education.

Data on this topic were collected from forty-five regular Anglican churchgoers by means of in-depth interviews. Analysis of these data specified three main soteriological positions, identified as exemplarist, traditionalist and evangelical. The paper portrays and analyses each type, employing illustrations from the data, and discusses various soteriological issues in relation to each of them. It also explores a number of other soteriological difficulties.

The pastoral, theological, educational and evangelistic implications of the findings are briefly discussed.

INTRODUCTION

The concept of 'ordinary theology' arose in response to the questions, Where does theology belong? Who does it and who owns it?

At one time the answer would have been clear: theology is a clerical task, one of the parson's trades. But over many years in many countries the clergy have gradually lost their dominance over theology to an increasingly secular academy. This has been widely welcomed by the academy. Scholars reflecting on theological education routinely criticise the traditional 'clerical paradigm' that restricted the scope of theology to knowledge required by the Church's professional leadership. They are less tempted, however, to take up the radical plea voiced by Edward Farley for a return to an earlier view of theology as a fundamental dimension of *every* Christian's piety and vocation. He variously describes this feature as a 'disposition' or 'orientation', the 'personal knowledge' that attends salvation, and 'the wisdom proper to the life of the believer'. It was a form of theology that was not abstracted from its concrete setting. It was understood, rather, as personal knowledge of God, and was concerned with and developed within 'the believer's ways of existing in the world before God'. Farley claims that this enduring orientation, the 'sapiential and personal knowledge' that attends salvation, is 'a part of Christian existence as such'. This, he writes, is 'theology in its original and most authentic sense' (Farley, 1983: xi, 35–37; 1988: 81, 88).

That such a theology has no clerical restriction is clearly only part of the story; it is also not limited to the scholar or teacher. In this account of things, academic theology has no privilege or pre-eminence. Hence this form of theology may be *lay* in several senses: not only is it shared in by the whole Church, it is also the theology that typifies the non-expert—the person who has received little or no scholarly, academic theological education. In this latter sense it may be described as *ordinary theology*. In recent studies we have *defined* this type of theology, in terms both of content or outcome, on the one hand, and pattern or processes on the other, as *the theology and theologising of Christians who have received little or no theological education of a scholarly, academic or systematic kind* (Astley, 2002; Christie, 2005; Christie, 2007).

Those who wish to understand this phenomenon will need not only to recapture an earlier understanding of theology, but also to rid themselves of the derogative connotations of the word 'ordinary'. That which is ordinary is 'of the usual kind', it is 'normal' in one sense of that significantly ambiguous word—as 'regular' or 'typical'. In this sense there is nothing wrong with being ordinary. But to many, whatever is customary and widespread seems on that account commonplace, trite and inferior; and therefore to be dismissed as terminally uninteresting. Thus, while many definitions of theology begin in an admirably democratic way, unpacking the word in terms of a person's God-talk or reflective speaking of the divine, most of them then proceed to limit its arena of application to sophisticated and disciplined forms of reflection that are appropriate only to a minority of Christians—that is, to an intellectual élite. They permit only a nod in the direction of a more generic or broader sense of the word 'theology' that embraces the nonacademic.

We believe that we need to make more than a polite gesture in this direction for several reasons. From a pragmatic perspective, those who are engaged in Christian communication, pastoral care and worship need to know about the beliefs of those in their care, and their patterns and modes of thinking and believing. They need, therefore, to *listen* to them. Listening, of course, is routinely acknowledged (in theory at least) as a mark of respect and a deeply pastoral act. We would add, however, that our listening should include a dimension of *theological listening* that acknowledges that people's often halting, unsystematic and poorly-expressed words about their faith constitute a form of theology. (See Astley, 2002: 143–148.)

Is there a more theological justification for engaging in this study? One reason might be that understanding the nature of ordinary theology, especially by tracing better its origins and formative factors, can help us discover what it is about theology that *works* for people. Theology has somehow got to match up with people's experience, and ordinary theology includes insights and convictions that have been tested out in a wide range of circumstances by a wide variety of people. The Church offers a vast user-base that reveals how, when, where and to what extent theology 'touches down' on human experience and shows some sort of 'empirical fit' to life, to use Ian Ramsey's phraseology. The results of this testing process, however, will only be expressed in—and therefore only available to—the student of ordinary theology. In some such way, other people's ordinary theology might serve some of the needs of 'extraordinary', or academic theology. (See Astley, 2002: 148–162; Clark-King, 2004: 23–25.)

There is perhaps another reason for swallowing our contempt for ordinary theology. Just as a knowledge of children can teach adults about themselves, so a knowledge of ordinary theology can help those who engage in academic theology from a position of religious commitment to understand some of the more hidden dimensions, motivations and connections of their own theology. Why do I care so much for this topic or aspect of theology and remain untouched by that one? Why do I read Christ in this way? How and when did I learn to think like this, to frame my beliefs like this, to be this sort of Christian? Despite our academic theological education, the answers to such questions are frequently personal and autobiographical, sometimes embarrassingly so.

Our experience of ordinary theology leads us to make the paradoxical claim that it is often both fundamentally secular but also deeply religious and spiritual. Ordinary theology is typically secular in the sense of being grounded in our exercise of the everyday roles of ordinary life, perceived as being at the centre of the good life (see Taylor, 1989:

180 ANN CHRISTIE & JEFF ASTLEY

15–16, 23–24). It is also often characteristic of ordinary theology that it is religious, as a form of theology that keeps close to the religious impulses and especially to the spirituality that drives people and heals them. It is therefore 'meaningful' and 'significant' to the person who owns it, and hence frequently intensely personal. This personal tone of much ordinary theology is also not to be disparaged, for it is an indication that people are here *doing* theology first-hand, engaging in the *practice* of theology. They are thinking through and thinking with their own beliefs, and expressing their own feelings and reflections in their own language, rather than (as in far too much academic theology) operating in the second-hand mode of thinking *about* other people's theology. As we shall see, however, not all ordinary theology fully achieves this status of thought-through, first-hand theologising.

Method

We shall concentrate in this paper on ordinary theologians' views about Christian salvation. The research described here was carried out using a qualitative research method. Forty-five in-depth interviews were conducted with churchgoers from four Anglican churches in the rural English county of North Yorkshire. The style of Anglicanism in all four churches is best described as 'middle-of-the-road', with regular liturgical services. One of the churches has a sizable evangelical membership, however, and this enabled six evangelicals to be included in the sample of thirty women and fifteen men. The interviewees ranged in age from thirty-four to eighty-six, and came from a variety of educational and occupational backgrounds. The interviews were semi-structured, allowing the questions to be tailored to suit the needs of each individual, with probes or follow-up questions being used to achieve as full and complete an exploration of the theme as possible. The interviews generally lasted between sixty and ninety minutes and were recorded, transcribed and analysed.

The Church has never formulated a conciliar definition of soteriology in the way it has for christology. There is therefore no soteriological dogma, equivalent to the christological dogmas, against which ordinary soteriology can be tested. However, from New Testament times to the present day, the cross has always been pivotal to the Christian understanding of salvation. It was for this reason that we focused on the cross in these interviews. The main soteriological aim of the interview process was to explore what meanings, if any, the interviewees attached to the death of Jesus and the claim that Jesus is saviour. We were particularly interested in exploring the interviewees' understanding of what is most commonly perceived as the 'received' or 'traditional' theology of the cross, and the idea that we are saved or redeemed from sin and death by Jesus at the cost of his own suffering and death, which atoned for or expiated our sins. On this understanding, salvation *depends* on Jesus' atoning death.

Results and Discussion

Three main soteriologies were identified from the interviews: exemplarist, traditionalist and evangelical.

Exemplarist soteriology

Around twelve of the sample articulated some form of a clearly exemplarist theology of the cross, rejecting outright the traditional interpretation of Jesus' death as an atonement for human sin. On an exemplarist understanding, salvation is not dependent on what Jesus is said to have accomplished on the cross. Here the cross is purely illustrative (or 'subjective') not constitutive (or 'objective'). In other words, the cross only illustrates something of importance for humanity, it does not achieve something of importance for humanity—something without which salvation would not be possible (McGrath, 1994: 338–339). All of this group offer only an historical construal of Jesus' death, talking about Jesus as being a martyr to his cause which was to *"bring people back to God"* and *"show us a new way of living".*[1] Jesus' death was not necessary in order for a divine purpose to be accomplished, rather it was the inevitable consequence of the cause to which he gave his life: *"You can see how it all ended up like that."* Jesus' death was a function of the life he lived: *"He died to try and save us… to take us away from that sort of sinful behaviour."*

For some of this group, the crucifixion of Jesus *"shows man's inhumanity to man"* and exposes the sinful condition of humanity. Seen from this

---

[1] Quotes from interviewees are printed in italics, except in indented quotes. The notation '…' denotes a pause in speech. The notation '[…]' denotes an editorial omission of some of the interview text.

perspective, the cross can in itself cause repentance. The crucifixion of Jesus is also a symbol of historical evil trying to overcome good; of self-giving love; and of active fidelity and commitment to a cause. In exemplarist soteriology the emphasis is on the subjective impact of Jesus' death upon human beings and on salvation as a process in present human experience.

The impact of Jesus' death upon human beings can, of course, never be fully delineated. It may take the form of inspiration and encouragement to model themselves on the moral and/or religious example of Jesus:

> Kathleen   [Jesus] was a martyr for his cause, if you like. And I think that what [the cross] is saying is...even if it gets really difficult you shouldn't back-peddle just because it is expedient to do so.

Additionally or alternatively, it may take the form of inspiration and encouragement to persevere in situations of human suffering:

> Nora   Well we all suffer don't we through life, that's the thing, and I really think [the cross] shows us that we aren't on our own in this suffering really.

> John   [The cross] is symbolic of human suffering [...] Jesus represents humanity [...] he is us in that situation [so that] I really see myself on the cross, having stood up for something...like possibly during the war-time or whatever. [...]

> [Jesus' suffering] is something that I can share in, although I am not experiencing the full horror of it, and so in a way it is relieving something out of me. [...]

> [The cross] is a help. A release, I think, of the pressure that is on you...to share the experience of somebody else [...] If we share serious problems with other people then it will help and it is a pattern to follow.

For both Nora and John, identification with Jesus' sufferings is salvific, bringing release and healing into their own situations of suffering. On an exemplarist understanding the story of Jesus has power *in itself* to transform lives and effect salvation, and does not need to be hedged around by any kind of transactional atonement theory. Also the cross is not separated off from the rest of Jesus' life and made a datum of reflection on its own. Rather it is the whole of Jesus' life, and not just his death, that can *"open up new possibilities for us"* and empower new ways

ORDINARY SOTERIOLOGY: A QUALITATIVE STUDY

183

of living. The whole story of Jesus has the power to create courage, perseverance or hope in the believer, so that the believer finds herself *"set free"*. Exemplarist soteriology cannot thus be reduced, as it often is, to the mere claim that Jesus is an example to follow. There is much more to it than that, as the data clearly indicate.

The species of exemplarism discussed so far has focused on the power of Jesus' death (and life) to transform lives and thereby effect salvation. But there is another type of exemplarism present in the sample: one that focuses on the cross as a demonstration of the love of God. Several of the interviewees (nearly all of them women) mentioned the passion and death of Jesus as being revelatory of God's love, but their soteriological focus usually lay elsewhere. Like Peter Abelard, to whom the moral or exemplarist theory is usually traced, they were not pure exemplarists. But at least two of the women focus exclusively on the cross as a demonstration of the love of God and eschew all talk of Jesus' death as an atoning sacrifice. In both cases the cross, viewed as a demonstration of God's love, has had a profound impact on their lives:

> Hilary   I can't put into words the significance of that for me now...that Jesus was willing to give up his life...I find it hard to come to terms with that immense sacrifice. I just feel so grateful. I just feel such gratitude. [...]
>
>   Also to know that I am loved as well. I feel real comfort in that.
>
> Jill   I remember when I read...the part where it said, "And God so loved the world that he gave his only Son", and I thought...well it just meant so much to me to think that somebody could be willing to do that for somebody else.

In this kind of exemplarism, the cross primarily symbolises the love of God for humanity; so we may identify a shift in emphasis here, as the interpretation of Jesus' death takes a theological turn. Abelard emphasised the subjective impact of the love of God, insisting "that our hearts should be enkindled" and inspired to love by the love of God in Christ (Abelard, 1956: 283–284). In a similar way, for both Hilary and Jill, the story of Jesus' death and the notion of God that it embodies evokes from them a response of love and gratitude, and effects a profound change in their sense of self: *"To know that I am loved by God...it makes such a huge difference."* Again, the story—but this time a different aspect of it—is salvific in itself and does not require to be

184   ANN CHRISTIE & JEFF ASTLEY

theologised as an atonement for human sin. Their salvation theory is much simpler: Jesus saves by revealing the depth of God's love. Therein lies salvation.

Traditionalist soteriology

Around one third of the sample have what we will call a traditional*ist* (rather than 'traditional') soteriology. This adjective is borrowed from Robert Towler, who labels a particular type of Christian religiousness in this way. The very essence of traditionalism is 'unquestioning acceptance'. Traditionalists "believe in everything conventionally included in the Christian religion", but cannot explain "what they believe or why they believe it". They have an attitude of 'taking for granted' and the reasons for their beliefs are rarely examined (Towler, 1984: 80–93). What characterises this present group is their lack of any explicit atonement theology. They cannot articulate a theology of the cross at all, with questions about the cross eliciting little response beyond the repeating of set formulae.

In Christianity, atonement theology is carried in the language of the liturgy and hymns. All of this group, being regular churchgoers, are familiar with the discourse employed in these forms. When asked to comment on such language, however, most are at a loss and are unable to make any further theological comment beyond repeating the set phrases given by the tradition or saying, *"I just accept that"*, as if the discourse were self-explanatory. They *"just accept"* that Jesus came into the world to save sinners: *"that is what Christians believe".*

> Marion   Well that is what we are told in the Bible isn't it? He came to save us from our sins et cetera. And you just accept what is there don't you in a way...and you are brought up with it. [...]
>
> I think...he did save us. He came here to save us really, didn't he...through God. As I say, my faith really is quite simple. And I don't delve too much into it.
>
> Rose   Well I do think of him as being a Saviour I suppose, but...not too much about it. Um...I suppose you do think of him being a Saviour. [...]
>
> Yes. Saves us from...yes. I think...I suppose so [laugh]. I suppose he saves us from our sins, from whatever...[voice trails off].

It is axiomatic for members of this group that Jesus is saviour, but they cannot easily say in what way(s) Jesus *is* a saviour, or give an account of how the cross of Jesus is salvific. Jesus as saviour has personal, existential meaning for them, but they cannot conceptualise or articulate that meaning: their theology is hidden from immediate self-awareness and not readily available for inspection. So they use the language of the tradition, but *"don't think about what it means"*—and they do not seem to want to either. Consequently, they (like others in the sample) do not present any fully worked-out theologies of salvation. Instead, what we find here is a cluster of beliefs which coalesce around the death and resurrection of Jesus. But we also find that these beliefs do not form a logically coherent whole. Sociologists of religion have made the same point. For "the average believer", Towler argues, Christianity is in practice "much more like an amalgamation of beliefs and practices held together by their common association with the church rather than by their logical relation one to another" (Towler, 1974: 153). Academic theology seeks to systematise beliefs. Ordinary theology, on the whole, does not (Astley, 2002: 128–129). "Most people's practical belief is, probably, non-systematic", existing "in clustered bits and pieces" (Davies, 2002: 19, 21). What this group has is a story—the outline of the Christian mythos—which they keep in their heads in fragments, rather than as one overarching, coherent epic (see Sykes, 1997: xi–xii). They can be said to have a narrative- or story-soteriology, albeit a fragmented one, as opposed to a systematic or analytical soteriology.

It is significant that liturgy and hymnody, and the New Testament itself, are also rather short on explanations. It has been suggested that the New Testament utilises "clusters of idea-complexes" to explain the crucifixion, such as 'obedience' or 'sacrifice'. These provide a variety of 'explanatory hints' and suggestions as to how the event of the crucifixion plays a part in God's plan of redemption, but they are largely undeveloped there. Stephen Sykes contends that it is characteristic of theological communication in these contexts "to allude to, rather than spell out" the meaning of the idea-complexes or themes (Sykes, 1997: 15–17). Only in atonement *theories* are they fully developed.

We may assume that all these idea-complexes, together with the related 'sin-guilt-responsibility-freedom' nexus of ideas (Sykes, 1997: 42), will have been internalised by this group over many years of churchgoing. It does not seem to matter to them that they cannot expand on these ideas. It would seem that some people do not need explanations or atonement theories; they can manage perfectly well without them. Christianity 'works' for them, even though, *"I haven't really thought about it"*.

Hence this group's theology is more imagistic and metaphorical than conceptual (they have a *story* about Jesus' passion, not a *doctrine*), and it works primarily at the level of affect. The words of the liturgy and hymns have been described as providing "a series of pegs on which to hang conscious or unconscious recollections and reflections".[2] The familiar words of the liturgy and hymns ("Who on the same night that he was betrayed"; "he opened wide his arms for us on the cross") can surely carry "rich layers of meaning and emotion and a range of implication incomprehensible in its depth and indefinite in its extent" (Sykes, 1997: 13). The liturgy supports greater emotional than cognitive weight in the faith-experience of this group, and also for others in the sample. Questions about the cross therefore invariably evoked emotional rather than doctrinal (cognitive) responses, indicating that it is feelings rather than doctrines that are primarily associated with the cross. In this type of soteriology the cross is affect-laden rather than theory-driven.

Many in the group have learned to connect the death of Jesus with the forgiveness of human sin, but they are quickly in difficulty when asked to give an account of how or why the two are connected. Without an understanding of the Jewish atonement and sacrificial rituals, the explanations are not obvious. A few, however, like others in the wider sample (namely the exemplarists and some of those with soteriological difficulties), do not appear to connect their belief in a forgiving God with the event of the cross at all. Although God's forgiving is concentrated in the central event of the atoning death of Jesus in academic and liturgical theology, in much ordinary soteriology belief in God's forgiveness is largely independent of the death of Jesus. As we shall see presently, some in the sample explicitly reject belief in an atoning death because they find such a view morally unacceptable; but the majority seem not so much to reject belief in such a death as to fail to understand it. For them, asking for forgiveness is not complicated, whereas understanding how the shedding of Jesus' blood effects atonement is. In our contemporary world there is little natural understanding of the idea that "without the shedding of blood there is no forgiveness" (Heb. 9:22). As Sykes has observed, "without considerable and repeated explanations" (which

---

[2] Sykes is here talking about credal recitation, but the same principle applies to other liturgical language and hymnody.

most here have apparently not been given) modern congregations are unlikely to be able to understand such texts (Sykes, 1997: 4).

It would seem that people only take what they need in the realm of theology. That God freely and graciously forgives repentant sinners is sufficient for their religious needs and it is this simpler, but no less profound theology, that they have learned from scripture, the liturgy and Christian hymnody. The more complex atonement theology that is also adumbrated, and sometimes more explicitly represented in these media has essentially been ignored.

Evangelical soteriology

It is widely acknowledged that the substitutionary theory of atonement is a distinguishing feature of evangelicalism. [3] All those in our sample who explicitly declared themselves to be evangelicals subscribe to this theory. This is not surprising; what is surprising is that nobody else does. No other person in the sample speaks about the cross in the same way as the evangelicals. Admittedly, certain aspects of the theory are present in the theology of some of the traditionalists, but it always remains inchoate—a full-blown theory never emerges. The traditionalists never offer an *explanation* as to how the death of Jesus on the cross effects atonement and the forgiveness of sin; the evangelicals all do so, using a characteristic phraseology and theology which the following extracts illustrate.

> Paul Jesus died to pay the ultimate price for everyone's sins. Once and for all. [...]
>
> Jesus paid the penalty for all those things I had done wrong. [...]
>
> [Jesus] died for the sins; to set us free from the chains of bondage. [...]
>
> The reason that he was on the cross was that he could pay the debt for people that have done wrong things in their lives.
>
> Peter Our sin separates us, separates me from God. And this idea that God is holy and perfect and there has to be some way of dealing

---

[3] Thus the evangelical theologian, Paul Zahl, opines that "the content of theology is the substitutionary atonement of Christ." He describes it as "the fulcrum for all theology" (Zahl, 2000: 58, 52). In recent British debate, however, the substitutionary theory has been challenged by some evangelicals (see Chalke and Mann, 2003: 182).

> with the things that separate me from God...the fact that [sin] creates a barrier, a separation between us and God and that in order to deal with that barrier, to make the bridge if you like, Christ had to die on the cross to pay for our sins or to meet the demands of justice for our sins. [...]

> God through Christ paid that penalty. God pronounced what the penalty was, but at the same time he actually paid the penalty himself in order that we could actually...that there wouldn't be a barrier between man and God. So that is why the cross is so central, from my perspective, because without the cross the barrier would remain.

The extent of these extracts indicates that the evangelicals, in contrast to the majority of the sample, all had a lot to say about the cross. This is because substitutionary atonement is the cornerstone of their theology, and these extracts are peppered with the set phrases of this theory. The evangelicals have *explicitly* learned substitutionary atonement theology during their socialisation into evangelical Christianity. They have not just implicitly learned it from the liturgy or hymns. (As the data from the rest of the sample show, this implicit process rarely results in explicit soteriological theories.) Rather, they have been specifically taught it.

However, although evangelicals have a theology of the cross, they engage in systematic theological reflection no more than anyone else. Like many of the traditionalists, they too *"just accept"* the theology they have been given, and they are quickly in difficulty when pressed for further clarification. Paul, for example, after reciting the scheme he had been taught, then said, *"I've never actually thought about why Jesus had to die on the cross for our sins...An analytical mind might want to know. I just accept it."* No one in this group ever expressed any objection to the interpretation of the cross which they have been given. Indeed, they all considered substitutionary atonement to be the required theory for every true Christian. A Christian was *"someone who has accepted that Jesus paid the price for their sins on the cross"*.

However, the satisfaction and substitutionary theories of atonement face considerable pressure in theology today.

> In recent years the satisfaction theory has come under severe criticism for the following reasons: for its focus on the death of Jesus to the virtual exclusion of his ministry and resurrection, thus truncating the biblical witness; for its methodological mistake of literalizing what is meant to be, in truth, a metaphor, turning it into an ontological reality; for its promotion of the value of suffering, easily exploited to maintain situations of injustice; and for its effective history which has fostered the idea

of an angry God who needs to be recompensed by the bloody death of his Son (Johnson, 1994: 5).

When objections of this nature were raised in the interviews against substitutionary atonement, although the force of the arguments was generally acknowledged there was a reluctance to engage in discussion, since to do so *"would be threatening"* to faith. Since substitutionary atonement is an essential element of this version of Christianity, any challenge to its veracity will almost inevitably be treated with a good deal of suspicion, if not hostility. Substitutionary atonement will always appeal to some. Its simple message of transactional guilt is very effective and appealing, especially, as Julie Hopkins says, where feelings of guilt, insecurity and inadequacy are running high. Under such circumstances it can bring enormous relief to be told the 'good news' that Jesus' death takes away guilt, and that eternal damnation need not be feared because Jesus' blood has paid the price for sin (Hopkins, 1995: 48).

Substitutionary atonement is not, however, the whole of evangelical soteriology. Another key feature of this form of theology is the personal relationship with Jesus. All of the evangelicals, bar one, talked at length about Jesus as a present reality with whom they have a personal relationship.[4] Evangelical piety depends on knowing Jesus personally, directly and intimately in one's heart rather than in one's head. As such, one might argue that evangelical piety is a distinctive form of mysticism, involving an immediate and direct experience of Jesus as a loving and constant companion in one's inner life (see Inbody, 2002: 76–78). And this companion is *'everything'*. He is everything because he is the friend who is always to be relied upon, the constant companion who is always near, the healer and restorer who brings new life. But, in listening to these people speak, we noted that some will just as easily talk about *God* being with them as they do about Jesus. God and Jesus are often used interchangeably, suggesting that 'Jesus' is a label or a name for a felt experience. What really matters is the *experience*—the experience of love, acceptance, assurance, healing, intimacy and companionship. But the question remains: when believers say that Jesus is with them as their constant friend and companion, which Jesus do they have in mind?

---

[4] The experience of Jesus as a present reality with whom one maintains a personal relationship is not actually exclusive to the evangelicals. The piety of three other women, all of whom hold a traditionalist soteriology, also exemplifies this theme.

According to Harold Bloom, the Jesus who stands at the centre of American evangelical piety is a very solitary and personal American Jesus. Furthermore, he is the resurrected Jesus rather than the crucified Jesus or the Jesus who has ascended to the Father (Bloom, 1992: 32). Or, as Tyron Inbody puts it, "Jesus is the resurrected friend, walking and talking to me along the side of the road or 'beside the Syrian sea' or 'in the garden' in moments of private luminosity with the repentant sinner. 'He walks with me, and he talks with me, and he tells me I am his own'" (Inbody, 2002: 87). There is no direct evidence from our data to suggest that the Jesus with whom people inwardly converse is Jesus the resurrected friend, and more empirical work still remains to be done in this area. Quite what connections there are between the Jesus of the heart and the Jesus of the texts remains unclear. H.M. Kuitert likens the Jesus of the heart to a teddy bear: "Jesus has to be there for comfort, just as a child has to take its teddy bear to sleep peacefully." In the type of 'Jesus-mysticism' outlined above, Jesus becomes the vehicle "by which people can express their religious longings, their need for acceptance, for comfort"; its emotional value cannot be overestimated (Kuitert, 1999: 198–199). Our data clearly show that Jesus as a constant companion in one's heart or by one's side brings much reassurance, security and comfort. Knowing Jesus in this way is reported by our interviewees to be transformative, that is, salvific. So, for the evangelicals in our sample, Jesus saves in two main ways: he saves through his atoning death and he saves by being a constant companion.

Soteriological difficulties

Around one third of the sample admit to finding the cross *"very difficult to understand"* and can perhaps be described as possessing a confused theology of the cross. They all confess to being puzzled by many of the traditional soteriological affirmations; they cannot make sense of the language and they do not know what conclusions to draw from it. Terms like 'salvation', for example, appear to be virtually meaningless for many, as they have no sense of having been (or being) saved. *"Saved from what?"* they frequently ask. Several find it hard to make sense of the claim that Jesus came to save the world from sin, because of the lack of any empirical evidence to substantiate such a claim. Sin, evil and suffering, the perennial loci of the human predicament, have *not* been 'made well' through Jesus' death on the cross. Evil continues to stalk the world. So how can sin and evil be said to have been dealt with?

Atonement theology is based on the underlying premise that sin causes estrangement. But many in this sample have never felt that being 'a sinner' has prevented them from entering into a relationship with God. Because they experience God as one who is always willing to enter into a relationship with them, they do not understand why Jesus' death was necessary to enable God to accept sinners. If God is loving and forgiving now, and always has been, then why was Jesus' death necessary? Indeed, why is any specific act required in order for reconciliation to occur? The fact that this event is a *'hellish violent'* and *'gruesome'* death only exacerbates the problem.

The most frequently voiced query was, *"Why did Jesus have to die?"* The idea that Jesus' death was necessary for God to forgive sin is considered by this sub-group to be *'totally unnecessary'*, *'preposterous'* and *'so primitive'*. As we saw earlier, others in the sample have similar difficulties with any claim about the necessity of an atoning death, indicating that there is a quite widespread problem with this idea. If, as many contend, atonement (understood as the forgiveness of sins by the shedding of the blood of Jesus) is "the very heart of the faith" (Sykes, 1997: 6), then the fact that this idea is problematic for so many must surely be a cause for concern.

Yet the difficulties for this sample are obviously not that grave—after all they are all still regular churchgoers. The fact that the problems centred on such a key concept can so readily be laid aside by many Christian believers suggests that atonement is not the very heart of faith for *them*; they do not place as much emphasis on Jesus' death as academic theologians (or ordinary evangelicals) do. It may be said that they tend to circumvent atonement. They can do this because they have no need for a redeemer or mediator, substitute or representative to 'do something' about sin.

It does not follow from this, however, that they have a weak or inadequate understanding of sin—which is the charge that is usually levelled against non-constitutive theories of atonement. Rather, the data suggest that it is precisely because they take the power and persistence of sin and evil in the world so seriously that they cannot accept that somehow it has all been 'dealt with' on the cross. The feminist theologian, Christine Smith, writes that she "will never understand or embrace language that suggests that Jesus' death on a cross, or any death on a cross, breaks the power of sin, transforms human conditions or shatters evil" (Smith, 1992: 158). Our data suggest that many others would agree.

Puzzlement also arises, not only over this 'why' question, but also from the 'how' question concerning the *causality* of Jesus' saving work. How can the shedding of one man's blood actually effect forgiveness for the sins of the world? Michael Winter insists that what the modern enquirer needs is "a positive and cogent account of how humanity was liberated from sin, in order to make sense of an apparently senseless crucifixion" (Winter, 1995: 30). But, unlike Winter, none of this group feels the need to defend a constitutive view of atonement. They appear not to require *explanations* in the same way that constitutivists do. For many, Jesus' death is a senseless crucifixion: *"Why couldn't he have lived a lot longer?"* They find it very hard to see how a positive evaluation can ever be put on such a *'heart-breaking', 'violent', 'horrendous'* and *'cruel'* event. There is some evidence that the primary reason why some people (especially women) prefer *"not to think too much about [the cross]"* and its meaning is not because they have no need for an atoning death, although this certainly seems to be the case, but because they have an innate aversion to *"all that suffering".* The notion that something as *'awful'* and *'horrendous'* as the killing of Jesus could possibly accommodate a positive interpretation is something from which they also shy away. How can the suffering and death of Jesus be anything but evil? "What is good about Good Friday?", they seem to ask.

Inevitably, therefore, there is some resistance to the idea that Jesus' death and suffering was in any way *required* by God to make salvation effective, for what kind of God would that be? A God who expects or demands the death of his only Son is a *'big bully'*, or (as Hopkins puts it) "not a God of love but a sadist and a despot" (Hopkins, 1995: 50).

> Valerie   When Jesus cries from the cross, "My God, my God, why have you forsaken me?", I always think that that is the most sympathetic thing that he ever says. Because you do, you think, where the hell were you and why did you let him go through that?
>
> And sometimes I feel a little bit alienated from God in some of those...particularly when it comes to the Easter time, because it...is an horrific story. It comes down to, how could God put Jesus through that? And you always think, whenever you watch it or hear it, perhaps something will happen and he will get let off and he never has to be crucified. But maybe there is that masterful thing...about God being a bad person and a cruel Father-figure to actually put him through that. [...]
>
> So God as a sort of omnipotent big bully...that's never really left me.

It is the contention of many pacifist, black, feminist, and womanist theologians that the traditional sacrificial view of atonement, together with the satisfaction and substitutionary models, have promoted both violence and a punitive view of God. Certainly, for the likes of Valerie the cross does not function as a symbol of God's love, as it does for others in the sample (see above). She cannot see it that way, believing that a God of love would never have allowed Jesus to go through the crucifixion. Rather than demonstrating the love of God, the cross reveals God to be *'a cruel Father-figure'*. The difficulties with traditional atonement doctrine for Valerie stem from the interpretation of the death of Jesus as a sacrifice. For her, the language of sacrifice only has negative connotations; it is an unhelpful, dead metaphor that has no spiritual currency.

Conclusion

Our data clearly show that much traditional atonement theology and language is a stumbling block for many. Some find it offensive; most are simply puzzled by it. Either way, it is beyond dispute that the traditional ways of interpreting the cross do not communicate meaningfully to a number in this sample. Indeed, it would appear that the majority (i.e., those with soteriological difficulties, the exemplarists, and some of the traditionalists) do not consider the cross to be the pivotal point in time when God reconciled the human race to himself, nor do they perceive the crucifixion to be a necessary condition for the forgiveness of sin. They seem to have no felt need for an atoning saviour, and therefore they simply bypass what we have called the traditional theology of the cross as irrelevant to their religious needs. For this group of churchgoers, 'salvation without atonement' may be said to be their dominant theological position.

These findings have modest, but clear and significant, missiological and catechetical implications. If the ancient mythological stories of how Jesus saves have lost their power for many churchgoers, then what about those outside the churches? Hilary Wakeman asserts that traditional doctrines such as the divinity of Jesus, the fall, atonement and resurrection drive people away from the churches, and that new ways of expressing old beliefs are needed if Christianity is to capture again the imagination of our contemporary world (Wakeman, 2003). In other words, the Church needs to tell new stories of how Jesus saves—stories that address the religious needs of our contemporary world and that are credible and believable for modern minds.

In view of the fact that so many people have difficulty understanding how the death of Jesus can be said to save us, it is perhaps not surprising that these data show that Jesus as exemplar is *the* dominant soteriological theme, at least in this sample. A majority of the sample point to Jesus' life and teachings as the primary source of his salvific activity. Our data show that it is as believers engage with the story (or more accurately the stories) of Jesus that salvation can occur. Or to put it another way, the story of Jesus is salvific as it grasps people or impacts upon them in ways that are salvific. Once it is recognised that salvation comes through engagement with the story of Jesus, it becomes clear that Jesus' whole career is decisive for salvation and not just his death.

And this salvation will always be particular and personal, arising out of the various connections that are made between the believer's story and the story of Jesus. What 'saves' one, will not 'save' all. A particular Bible verse or story, for example, may have a profound salvific effect on some, yet leave others cold. Salvific encounters are always "diffuse and far-ranging in the experience of individual persons" and can never be fully explicable in terms of theoretical generalisations (Haight, 1999: 408). Patently, they are not dependent on a network of doctrines either; hence Jesus can and does save irrespective of whether one holds the right doctrine about him.

Further, when we 'look and see' what people's experiences of salvation actually are, we discover that salvation does *not* come through Jesus alone. God saves through Jesus, but he also saves in many other ways. In much of the ordinary soteriology of this sample the concept of salvation is not tied very closely to the life, death and resurrection of Jesus. There is no bifurcation here between God's general salvific and creative action, on the one hand, and the particular story of God's saving action in Jesus, on the other. This chimes in with the theological principle that wherever there is wholeness, wherever there is healing, whenever things go right, God is at work and salvation occurs. The data thus challenge the necessity of continuing to speak of Jesus as the only way of salvation. The believers in our sample may experience God's salvation primarily through Jesus but most do not conclude, and do not think that it follows, that God only saves through Jesus. To affirm that Jesus is the definitive or decisive revelation of God (which for Christians he is or should be) need not imply that Jesus is the only revelation of

God. Hence the findings from this study have not only missiological and catechetical implications, but also theological ones. They suggest that if Christianity is to gain a hearing in our contemporary world then it urgently requires some more circumspect (as well as more credible) accounts of how Jesus saves.

This claim might be said to reinforce the argument that there is a theological, in addition to a more pragmatic (ministerial) justification for promoting the study of ordinary theology. Academic Christian theology has too often legislated *a priori* for the implications that Christians must draw from their commitment to the gospel of, and about, Jesus. Descriptive empirical theology is less presumptuous. Its more modest aim is to seek to uncover the real depth grammar of the reflections of ordinary Christian believers. In performing this task, however, it is perhaps more likely to reveal a Christian theology that *works*, one that is undeniably *at work* in the everyday lives and worship of everyday believers. Academic theology should not be too proud to learn from its more ordinary cousin something more about the contours and the constraints of the big ideas of religion: in particular, what it means to be saved and what it means to be Christian.

References

Abelard, P. (1956), Exposition of the Epistle to the Romans, in E.R. Fairweather (ed. and trans.), *A Scholastic Miscellany: Anselm to Ockham*, vol. X, pp. 276–287, London, SCM.

Astley, J. (2002), *Ordinary Theology: looking, listening and learning in theology*, Aldershot, Ashgate.

Bloom, H. (1992), *The American Religion: the emergence of the post-Christian nation*, New York, Simon and Schuster.

Chalke, S. and Mann, A. (2003), *The Lost Message of Jesus*, Grand Rapids, Michigan, Zondervan.

Christie, A. (2005), *Ordinary Christology: a qualitative study and theological appraisal*, unpublished PhD thesis, University of Durham.

——. (2007), Who do you say that I am? Answers from the Pews, *Journal of Adult Theological Education*, 4(2), 181–194.

Clark-King, E. (2004), *Theology by Heart: women, the church and God*, Peterborough, Epworth.

Davies, D.J. (2002), *Anthropology and Theology*, Oxford, Berg.

Farley, E. (1983), *Theologia: the fragmentation and unity of theological education*, Philadelphia, Pennsylvania, Fortress.

——. (1988), *The Fragility of Knowledge: theological education in the church and the university*, Philadelphia, Pennsylvania, Fortress.

Haight, R., SJ (1999), *Jesus: symbol of God*, Maryknoll, New York, Orbis.

Hopkins, J. (1995), *Towards a Feminist Christology: Jesus of Nazareth, European women, and the christological crisis*, London, SPCK.

196 ANN CHRISTIE & JEFF ASTLEY

Inbody, T.L. (2002), *The Many Faces of Christology*, Nashville, Tennessee, Abingdon.
Johnson, E.A. (1994), Jesus and salvation, *Proceedings of the Catholic Theological Society of America*, 49, 1–18.
Kuitert, H.M. (1999), *Jesus: the legacy of Christianity* (trans. John Bowden), London, SCM.
McGrath, A.E. (1994), *Christian Theology: an introduction*, Oxford, Blackwell.
Smith, C.M. (1992), *Preaching as Weeping, Confession, and Resistance: radical responses to radical evil*, Louisville, Kentucky, Westminster/John Knox Press.
Sykes, S.W. (1997), *The Story of Atonement*, London, Darton, Longman and Todd.
Taylor, C. (1989), *Sources of the Self: the making of the modern identity*, Cambridge, Cambridge University Press.
Towler, R. (1974), *Homo Religiosus*, London, Constable.
——. (1984), *The Need for Certainty: a sociological study of conventional religion*, London, Routledge and Kegan Paul.
Wakeman, H. (2003), *Saving Christianity: new thinking for old beliefs*, Dublin, The Liffey Press.
Winter, M. (1995), *The Atonement*, London, Geoffrey Chapman.
Zahl, P.F.M. (2000), *A Short Systematic Theology*, Grand Rapids, Michigan, Eerdmans.

CHAPTER NINE

NARRATIVE COMPETENCE AND THE MEANING OF LIFE: MEASURING THE QUALITY OF LIFE STORIES IN A PROJECT ON CARE FOR THE ELDERLY

Thijs Tromp and R. Ruard Ganzevoort

Summary

How can we assess the ways in which people construe meaning in life? As part of a research project aimed at establishing and explaining the effects of narrative autobiographical life review methods, we are conducting brief narrative autobiographical interviews from elderly participants (age 80+) from both an experimental and a control group. As the overall study seeks to relate qualitative assessment of narrative competence with quantitative measures of well-being and quality of the caring relationship, we have developed a standardised multidimensional procedure for analysing interviews and measuring narrative competence. In our experimental design we will be able to capture development and change in the stories of an individual. This chapter presents the method for the narrative analysis of the quality of life stories, exemplifies it by a case study, and clarifies its implicit theological dimensions.

Introduction

It may seem slightly outlandish to present an empirical theological project on narrative competence and the meaning of life. Isn't the *meaning of life* an almost metaphysical concept, well addressed by catechisms and Monty Python, but too large and elusive for empirical measures? And is it possible to measure in any objective way the competence with which people construe and tell their life stories? Narrative methods, after all, are not particularly known for their sophistication in generating hard empirical evidence. These considerations bring us close to the theme of this volume as we are developing an instrument to move from texts to tables, from narrative material to standardised measures.

The vantage point of this project is the conviction that the narrative construction of meaning is essential in how people experience and live their lives. This reflects the narrative turn in, for example, social sciences and theology. One implication is that our research focuses on the particularities of individual autobiographies rather than on generalised aspects of a population. Another implication is that identity is seen as a dynamic process of constructing and reconstructing meaningful and viable life stories. That means that narrative competence becomes an important factor for understanding the ways in which individuals live and understand their lives.

The work presented in this chapter is part of a larger project on elderly care, in which we try to capture the development in life stories and their connection to well-being and quality of the caring relationship. The project has an experimental design with a control group, an intervention (writing a Life Story Book) and data collection (measurement immediately before and after the intervention and five months later). In this chapter we only present the methods we have developed for assessing narrative competence in the brief narrative interviews that are part of the project. We will demonstrate this method in a case study that is part of the larger project and discuss the theological ramifications. The results from the larger project will be presented at a later stage.

The structure of this chapter will be as follows: we first introduce and explain the methods we are developing. In a second step we demonstrate the method in a case study. Finally, we discuss the theological dimension of the project and instrument. In the appendix we give some context by outlining the design of the larger project.

Analysing the Narrative Autobiographical Interviews

Notwithstanding an increasing amount of research on developmental processes and the thematic contents of reminiscence among older adults, there is still no satisfactory understanding of why and how the contents of life review or recollections of past events contribute to the quality of the life story, narrative identity, and the experience of meaning. Until now the research on reminiscence and life review has mainly addressed the effects on the quality of life or subjective well-being. Research seeking to explain these effects is still in its infancy (see e.g. Haight and Hendrix, 1995; Schroots and Dongen, 1995; Bohlmeijer, 2007; Nieuwesteeg, Oste, Horn and Knipscheer, 2005). We have some insight in the correlation between types of reminiscence activities in life stories and successful aging. Wong (1995), Fry (1995) and others suggest that reminiscence has impact on the narrative organisation of personal identity. This may help us understand the mechanisms of reminiscence and life review work, but these authors provide only some indications of intrapersonal and extrapersonal factors that might be conditional for successful reminiscence.

The lack of a satisfactory explanation is a hindrance for the implementation of life history or life review methods. Time and again working with life history methods or doing life review work is discredited by the suggestion that it is just another way of giving attention to elderly people and that the narrative form has no additional value. A clarification of the mechanisms through which narrative methods are helpful may provide insights in the specific contribution of these methods to the well-being of elderly people. Furthermore, it may support an understanding that the life stories of care receivers are integral to health and care and not the exclusive domain of therapeutic or religious conversations.

The central question of the analysis of the life narratives in this project is: what are the effects of working with the life story book method on the construction of meaning in the life stories of old adults? We understand the construction of meaning in life stories as the way people order events and significances in telling about their life course. The way they give meaning to life can be understood in a narrative framework as the construction of a life story from a life course. Underlying our approach is a multidimensional model of narrative as developed by Ganzevoort (1998) and Ganzevoort and Visser (2007). In this model, six dimensions of narrative are described. Structure describes elements like time, place, causality, and degree of integration. Perspective addresses authorship and subjectivity. Role assignment deals with the roles that others (and the person him/herself) play in the story. Tone refers to emotion and genre. Next to these four dimensions of the story as text, we distinguish two dimensions of the story as a process of telling. Relational positioning deals with the performative actions through which the narrator seeks to shape the relationship with her/his audience. Justification finally describes how the narrator convinces the audience of the plausibility of the story. In this analysis we focus on the dimension of structure.

We regard the interviews as instances of the construction of meaning by the participant. The constructed meaning is not static, stable, or complete. It is, even in old age, the momentary outcome of an ongoing process. People do not tell their life stories in a fully developed and final form, but they construe meaning at their actual point in life, facing unique and real circumstances. In the case of these interviews the construction of meaning is influenced by the interview context. Furthermore, the momentary construction relates to the life course and its vicissitudes, on the one hand, and to the personal life view values, and/or ideological frames, on the other. Our focus on the narrative construction of meaning rests on our assumption that the construction of personal meaning takes place mainly on an intuitive non-discursive level. Talking about life vision and values is an abstraction that is not necessarily or directly connected to the actual life and self-image of the person. By analysing biographical narratives we hope to catch the construction of meaning 'by surprise'. We are, of course, aware that objectifying and quantifying narrative data is not very common in practical theology and other social sciences. Some would even claim that objectifying narrative data betrays the unique and subjective character of autobiographical stories. This is obviously true in one sense: the personal construction of meaning is not simply an example of a universal pattern. It is, however, not contrary to a subjective hermeneutical approach to life stories if we try to assess the structural aspects of stories. In our view these structural aspects are closely related to the unique content and the study of narrative quality supports other narrative investigations.

In conducting the brief narrative autobiographical interviews, we used an extremely open interview method. After informing the participants that the interview would last about 30 minutes, the interviewer commenced with one standardised question: "would you please tell me your life story?" The interviewer only intervened when the narrator came to a full standstill. The interventions were kept as minimal and open as possible: repeating the last sentence, asking whether there was anything else the person would like to add, or—in case the participant was still unable to continue the narration—a general opening question about a theme already mentioned by the participant. We had instructed our interviewers to use this last intervention only as a last resort. The reason for refraining from helping the participant telling his/her life story is that we want to establish the competence and the structure of the participant him/herself, and not a structure imposed on the story by the interviewer. This open starting question creates some tension at the beginning. After some hesitation, however, most participants start telling their life story.

The first analysis of the life stories shows that there is a similar narrative order in most of the stories. The first (and usually longest) part consists of a more or less chronological overview of the person's life. In two-thirds of the stories this first part is followed by a thematic section in which the narrator revisits some of the episodes in more detail or gives lively and illuminating anecdotes matching these episodes. In some cases, the narrator adds a new episode in this second part, usually an episode of shame or trauma. Most stories end with descriptions of what life is like in the nursing home.

CRITERIA FOR NARRATIVE QUALITY

Essential to our analysis is the assessment of changes in the narratives between the three moments we collected the stories and interpret them in terms of quality. For that purpose, we developed formal and material narrative categories that can be operationalised, objectified, and generalised so that they can be used in a larger sample. These categories need to be related to the issues of life review and narrative described earlier. Moreover, the categories should be open to both anthropological and theological reflections.

A first set of formal criteria is found in the work of personality psychologist Hubert Hermans. He states that three qualities of self-narratives account for well-being and psychological health: coherence, differentiation and flexibility (Hermans and Hermans-Jansen, 1995). The criterion of coherence is especially strongly supported by other life story researchers (Barclay, 1996; Brugman, 2000; Bruner, 1990; Klein, 1994; Klein, 2003; McAdams, 1988; McAdams, 1993; Schroots and Dongen, 1995; Schütze, 1983; Wong, 1995; Wong and Watt, 1991). Coherence refers to the semantic cohesion and logical ordering of the story. Fragmentation and unintelligibility are the opposites of this criterion. Differentiation refers to the different themes the narrator includes in the stories. Its opposite is massiveness. Flexibility finally refers to the degree the narrator masters the story, and is not blocked by obsessions or the fixation on only one theme. Its opposite is rigidity.

A second set of material criteria is found in the work of psychologist Ronnie Janoff-Bulman (1992). Based on her work with victims of trauma, she identified three fundamental assumptions that govern the self-narratives. Every narrator is faced with the challenge to construct the life story in such a way that it complies with these three fundamental assumptions. Many narrators are at pains to solve the conflicts in their story when they are unable to synthesise these three fundamental assumptions. They are tempted to save two of the assumptions at the expense of the third. A healthy and adequate life story covers all three fundamental assumptions. The first fundamental assumption is the meaningful coherence of the world. This is the assumption of order and significance that is threatened by chaos and coincidence. Narrators have to tell their story in such a way that their life and world make sense as a whole and that the world they live in is just. The second fundamental assumption is the benevolence of the world. This is the assumption of care and positive intentions in the social and natural context, countered by experiences of evil and neglect. Narrators have to tell their story in such a way that they can put trust in the people and structures they meet. The third fundamental assumption is self-worth. The narrator must tell the story in such a way that the individual existence is affirmed and valued positively. It is the challenge for narrators to create a meaningful story that fits the criteria of these three fundamental assumptions.

A Multidimensional Method for Analysis

For our analyses, we build on Barclay's (1996) distinction of three levels in any narrative: a phenomenal, an epiphenomenal, and a metaphenomenal level. We add a fourth, or preliminary, level that indicates the fluency in narrating; and rename Barclay's levels as linguistic, thematic, and plot-level. The first level in our analysis concerns the process of narrating. On the second level we look at linguistic characteristics of the narrative. On the third level we determine themes and storylines, in the topics. The fourth level is concerned with the overarching plot. Much research devoted to the quality of life stories is restricted to only one of these levels. Some focus on aspects of eloquence, some on grammatical characteristics, some on the quality of episodes or the coherence of storylines and some are confined to the nature of the plot. In our method for analysis we set out to establish changes on all four levels in order to examine the mutual dependency of the story levels.

Regarding the *narrating process*, we expect to find effects on the narrative competence in the sense that respondents would tell their story more fluently after the experimental intervention with the Life Story

Book Method, due to their practising telling their stories. We believe that this will be an indication of the narrative mastery of the narrator and the flexibility of the narrative. In terms of fundamental assumptions, we expect that a low sense of meaningful coherence or low self-worth can be inferred from specific types of resistance to narrating. An increase in trust and benevolence following the intervention is expected, resulting in a more fluent narration. That is, we expect an increase in narrative mastery.

On the *linguistic level* we expect that we will measure an increase in the frequency of terms of time, place, causality, evaluations, and subject-verb clauses. We regard this as a manifestation of increasing coherence (cf. Schütze, 1983; Barclay, 1996; Brugman, 2000; Klein, 2003). Self-worth changes are expected in the frequency of the use of first-person expressions. We further expect that the narrator, for whom the assumption of order is challenged, will use more words to describe an episode (Janoff-Bulman, 1991; De Vries, Blando and Walker, 1995).

On the *thematic level* we expect to find effects on the number of topics, the diversity, and the density of the storylines. This can be an indication of differentiation and coherence: that is, of order. On this level we also expect effects on what function the reminiscence has for the participant, for example, solely informing and entertaining, or evaluating and integrating. We believe this is an indication of the degree of integration, a formal characteristic of the material quality of the narrative. We further think that on the fundamental assumption of order something will occur according to the sequences of events, acts and experiences with positive or negative valuation. We distinguish between episodes with a redemption or contamination sequence (McAdams, Reynolds, Lewis, Patten and Bowman, 2001). Redemption sequence refers to a bad situation, followed by some kind of relief, and a contamination sequence is the reverse. This phenomenon is related to the plot-analysis. We expect an overall increase in benevolence, order, and self-worth following the intervention: that is, of narrative quality. Similar but smaller changes are expected in the control group because of the attention offered to people, but given the specific narrative aspects of the intervention, and the fact that the life story book remains available as a physical object, we expect that the values observed in the control group will return to baseline levels after some time, whereas we expect a lasting increase for the experimental group.

204 THIJS TROMP & R. RUARD GANZEVOORT

On the *plot-level*, we expect no substantial changes. Although McAdams (2006) and Freeman (1991) suggest that some change in the basic patterns of the personality structure is within the bounds of possibility, we don't expect our relatively light nontherapeutic intervention at high age to result in such changes on a level that is so close to personality structure. For the purpose of hypothesis testing, however, we formulate our hypothesis in positive form: the experimental group will show changes in plot after intervention with the Life Story Book Method.

Finally, because of the theological context in which this research project is located, we analyse the way ideological and religious language functions in the narratives. This will provide information about the contribution ideological language and religion make to the coherence and perhaps also to the differentiation of the narrative. Here the material criteria based on Janoff-Bulman will provide the backbone of the analysis. They can be considered to be the psychological correlates of elementary theodicy notions as we will demonstrate below. On both the psychological and theological level we see how existential themes are addressed. These existential themes allow for an interplay between the two disciplines.

Applying the Model: Mr Samuelson Finds Communion

It may be helpful to illustrate our analytical approach with the life narratives of one participant from the experimental group. We will present the narrative of Mr Samuelson, who is 85 years old. Like all participants, he told his life story three times: first, right before he started to make his life story book (t0); secondly, right after he completed the book (t1); and thirdly, 5 months after that (t2).

Mr Samuelson was born in a Jewish family in a German village and grew up facing the threat of the rising Nazi regime of Hitler. In his youth his parents moved to a larger town because they wanted to live closer to a Jewish community. At the age of fourteen he had to leave school because the Nazi regime did not allow him to continue his studies. He started working at a plumbing firm, got his diplomas and later joined a kibbutz in the northern part of Germany. He became an active member of the Zionist movement and considered emigration to Palestine, but was taken captive and held prisoner in Sachsenhausen. With help from the Dutch government he was freed and moved to the Netherlands. He again joined a Zionist youth movement. Soon after

NARRATIVE COMPETENCE AND THE MEANING OF LIFE

that war broke out in the Netherlands and he had to go into hiding. Despite the fact that he didn't have any money, his boss arranged a hiding place for him at a farm. There he met the daughter of the farmer and fell in love with her. After the war he tried to move to Palestine but he didn't succeed. He started a search for his parents, but no one from his family had survived. He then decided to return to his fiancé in the Netherlands. He married the farmer's daughter, fathered two daughters, lived a happy family life, and had a successful career as a metal worker. Following the death of his wife, he moved to a home for the elderly.

First level: narrating process

Regarding the process, we classified t0 as rather fluent, t1 and t2 as very fluent. On all three occasions little or no intervention was required. Mr Samuelson started and ended the story each time without external admonition. Silences sounded naturally. This indicates (according to our theoretical framework) a rather high narrative competence for all three interviews, and only a small increase of mastery and of experienced benevolence. We may expect from these results that the level of coherence on the linguistic level will not increase highly.

Second: linguistic level

At the linguistic level we score the density of terms of place (locality-index), time (time-index), causal connections (causality-index) and subject-verb clauses (subject-verb-index), with special attention to the proportion between first person and third person constructions. In the case of Mr Samuelson, both the time- and locality-index increase from t0 to t2 (time-index: 0.023 (t0) to 0.027 (t1) to 0.034 (t2); locality-index: 0.041 (t0) to 0.044 (t1) to 0.045 (t2)). The causality-index increases from t0 to t1 and falls back a little at t2 but not under the level of t0 (0.005 (t0) to 0.012 (t1) to 0.009 (t2)). The same holds for the subject-verb-index (0.099 (t0) to 0.115 (t1) to 0.112 (t2)). All this is, as we described above, an indication of increasing coherence, be it in a moderate way.

As for the proportion between first person and third person verb-constructions an increase of the first person subject-verb clause is established (0.034 (t0) to 0.039 (t1) to 0.048 (t2)). This can be interpreted as an increasing sense of narrative autonomy and thus of increasing self-worth. He tends to tell his life story more and more from his own perspective rather than from the perspective of other persons. The narrator focuses on his own contribution in his life story. We may expect that this will correlate with an increase of instrumental and integrative reminiscence, for these functions of reminiscence are used when people tell their stories from their own perspective and in an evaluating way.

Third: thematic level

At the thematic level we divide the story into episodes. The episodes are coded with general themes (the content of the episode), for example family, war, education, etc. In the analysis we attributed 48 (t0), 38 (t1) and 29 (t2) thematic labels to the episodes: 16 different labels at t0, 20 at t1 and 14 at t2. That means that the differentiation of the story is decreasing. Mr Samuelson is focusing his story on a smaller number of themes, possibly to select only the essential parts of the life story.

We have to keep in mind that the use of general themes does not give an adequate insight into the narrative significance of the contents. To account for this, we developed an additional approach of identifying storylines, closer to the narrative character, to establish the thematic coherence of the story. We summarised every episode in one sentence, a description of the microstory told at the episode (e.g. "Thanks to the support of my children and my best friend, I didn't break down when my husband left me"). This summary has to be isomorphic to the content and structure of the topic. That's why we call it a mini-plot. In a next step we order these miniplots in storylines consisting of episodes with comparable themes. This 'snap shot' provides information about the differentiation and coherence of the story. In the case of Mr Samuelson we discerned 10 storylines at t0, 11 storylines at t1, and again 10 storylines at t2, which leads to the conclusion that 'the thematic backbone' of his story is very stable. But when we look closer at the distribution of the episodes per storyline we discern that Mr Samuelson is thickening the story. He tells a similar story using fewer episodes (mean episodes per storyline: 2.4 (t0), 1.6 (t1), 1.4 (t2)). This means that Mr Samuelson is able to tell his story in fewer words and episodes, without losing essential elements of the content. This is an indication of a rather high and indeed growing narrative competence, and a high degree of coherence and flexibility. We may expect that this correlates with an increasing use of instrumental and integrative reminiscence. It is remarkable that the storylines containing most episodes (at all three interview moments) are about the war and the persecution of the Jews, and about his marriage and the death of his wife. We hypothesise that storylines containing many episodes regulate either to the essential material of the personal identity (e.g. work or family life) or to difficult themes the narrator has to cope with. In the case of Mr Samuelson, we think the latter will be the case, partly because he explicitly says so: "Actually, I'm thinking about the war and everything all my life."

The function of reminiscence changes over the three interviews. The percentage of informative reminiscence (just providing plain biographical information) decreases whereas the percentage of instrumental (telling about achieving personal goals) and particularly integrative reminiscence (evaluating and integrating the fruits of life) increases (informative: 71% (t0), 67% (t1), 36% (t2); instrumental: 21% (t0), 17% (t1), 29% (t2); integrative 8% (t0), 17% (t1), 36% (t2)). That means that Mr Samuelson tends to look back on his life with a more evaluating view. This correlates, as we expected, with the fact that he tells his story in a more concentrated way and more from his own perspective.

We also analysed the use of sequences in the episodes, using a sequence scoring instrument designed by McAdams and Reynolds *et al.* (2001). The percentage of contamination sequences (good situations turning to bad) slightly decreases and the percentage of redemption sequence (bad situations turning to good) increases, but only some months after the Life Story Book intervention (contamination: 21% (t0), 6% (t1), 7% (t2); redemption: 17% (t0), 17% (t1), 29% (t2)). That means that Mr Samuelson stresses more and more the good outcome in the episodes. This allows the interpretation that a relationship exists between focusing on essential parts, thickening the storylines, and stressing positive outcomes. Or, in other words: that episodes with positive outcomes facilitate coherency and integrative reminiscence. It could be expected that these findings at the thematic level may correlate with a change in plot, for the use of contamination sequences is related to a tragic or a romantic plot with a negative outcome, whereas the use of redemption sequences is related to a comic or romantic plot with a positive outcome.

Fourth: plot-level

In the case of Mr Samuelson the plot of t0 can be identified as romantic with a positive outcome. Mr Samuelson tells how he overcame the severe struggles he met in life and states solemnly that eventually he was fully integrated in Dutch society. He emphasises his own contribution to the relatively positive outcome of his life. This story therefore could be characterised as: "How Mr Samuelson found a home." The t1 and the t2 stories are similar in two aspects: he tells again about the struggles in life and the relatively possible outcomes. But he does not put emphasis on his own contribution to the positive outcome, as he did in t0. Instead he regards his life under a more passive perspective; things did turn out good or bad. He admits that his life has always been overshadowed by the war. "My life story is not very sparkling, it is overshadowed by the war" (t1) and "In fact, when I look back, my whole life was dominated by the war." The plot is a combination of a comic plot and a tragic plot. We interpret this as a sign that writing his Life Story Book has helped Mr Samuelson to forego his attempts to escape the tragic components in his life by construing a life story of conquering and finding a home. Instead the tragic aspects of his life are given more space, most importantly the loss of his family and the sense of not really being home.

Resumé

In terms of the fundamental assumptions, we see that Mr Samuelson tells the three stories with an increasing degree of self-worth, evident from the linguistic level, which indicates that he tells his story from his own perspective. Paradoxically, this increased autonomy on the side of the narrator goes hand in hand with the admission that the protagonist within the story seems less autonomous in determining his own life. It may be that an increase in narrative competence leaves room for the narrator to recognise the lack of autonomy in his life course. Increasing self worth of the narrator provides him with the power to face the dark sides of his life. On benevolence we see that Mr Samuelson does not focus only on the dark and malicious aspects of life, although he would have had reasons to do so. Instead he succeeds in telling his story as a benevolent one based on the positive experiences that he also encountered. In the first story he downplays the role of the malicious aspects. In the second and third story he integrates the comic and the tragic line and keeps them in tension, without losing the coherence of the story. The benevolent aspect is the most important factor in his overall plot at t1 and t2. On the aspect of order we see that his stories are very well organised with many parallels and causality. Although he maintains the order at t0 by diminishing the impact of some painful episodes at t0, episodes like the death of his parents and

THEOLOGICAL REFLECTIONS

Earlier, we stated that this investigation can be read as a study into lived religion (Failing and Heimbrock, 1998) or implicit religion (Bailey, 1997). Our focus is not so much on customary religious material, but on the structures of meaning subjects construct to develop a meaningful and adequate life story with which they can live their life. Obviously this need not be articulated in explicit, let alone traditionally calibrated, religious language. The life views, narrative constructions, evaluations, and metaphors that we encounter in the material are diverse and partly idiosyncratic, but they are dealing with the precise subject matter of religion and theology: the construction of significance and the meaning of life. The life stories collected are, therefore, expressions of the individual first order theologies of our participants (Ganzevoort, 2004). They are a much needed source for understanding human needs and longings, and inform our theories of aging, care, and human attribution of meaning.

This is not only an ideological justification of the project, it is part and parcel of the analysis itself. The categories derived from the work of Janoff-Bulman should be interpreted as existential or ultimately theological categories. The challenge for the narrator to create a meaningful narrative that complies with the three fundamental assumptions shows a perfect parallel to the classic dilemma of theodicy. The assumption of the meaningful order of the world, and therefore of the meaning of events, is an implicit articulation of the notion of creation and divine providence. It states that things happen for a reason, which offers the foundation for our trust in a safe and just world. Without this belief in the order of things, the world would be unacceptably threatening. A religious expression of this challenge is the question whether God has the power to rule and change the world, and whether the events of one's own life are willed by God. The assumption of the benevolence of the world is an implicit articulation of the notion of divine love and care. It states that we need not live in constant fear and paranoia, but can entrust ourselves at least partially to others and to the world.

Without this belief, the material and social world would be evil. A religious expression of this is the surrender to God's care and to the mercy that people express to one another, for example in elderly care. The assumption of self-worth is an implicit articulation of the notion of imago Dei, humans created after the image of God, which identifies them as invaluable in God's eyes. They are even interpreted as co-creators and name-givers, which stresses autonomy. This notion is specified in the individual value of the person, a notion that is fundamental in religious soteriologies that focus on personal redemption and not only on the continuation of human history. Finally, this assumption is essential for the merciful care of the sick, the old, and the needy, because receivers of care are seen as individuals, fellow humans that deserve our attention.

It is not our intention to exhaust the theodicy discussion here, but to clarify how the fundamental assumptions identified by Janoff-Bulman are the quintessence of religious meaning (Ganzevoort, 2005). The problematic constellation of the three in a life under stress triggers the stories that are intended to set things straight, but an adequate or successful life story is adequate precisely because it succeeds in accomplishing the interpretation of life as complying with the three fundamental assumptions. The solutions found for the theodicy dilemma are therefore only extrapolations of the structures of meaning constructed in every life story.

The narrative challenge that is addressed in this model of fundamental assumptions is further reflected in the context of elderly care and the appreciation of the narratives of the elderly. One approach to the elderly and their narratives is to see this life stage as an epilogue that reiterates some of the central themes but adds little of value to it. In this approach life stories are seen as only anecdotal, and accordingly elderly care is increasingly organised in a technical, medical, institutional way. Critics taking an ethics of care perspective would see this approach as dehumanising. In light of the fundamental assumptions identified here, we should say that this approach devalues human individuality and worth, and expresses little benevolence, although it may offer a lot of order. A second approach to elderly people and their narratives is to see old age as a finale, in which the life story culminates in possibly new and integrating meanings. This leads to the expectation that individuals will always have a new and richer story to tell. Life stories then are seen as essential, and elderly care needs to be organised in a reciprocal way. The health care institutions that espouse such a view try

NARRATIVE COMPETENCE AND THE MEANING OF LIFE 211

to offer an environment that is safe, well-ordered, just, and benevolent, and that affirms the individual worth and wishes of the elderly. That is, the identity of the institution is expressed in an intentional validation of the fundamental assumptions. The primary rationality in elderly care should be ethical or narrative, not technical, medical, or economic. It is not enough, then, to allow for Life Story Book methods within the organisation, the organisation itself will need to express these fundamental values. This includes organisational structures on the assumption of order, the benevolent attitude of caregivers on every level, and priority of the individual over the limitations of the institution. It is in examples like these that the moral implications and motivations of our research project come to the fore; but it may be clear by now that these are not detached from the empirical content.

The project we are involved in should be seen against the background of developments in elderly care in the Netherlands and elsewhere in Western societies. Although there is an increasing stress on medical and economical rationality in the ways our systems of care are organised, we also witness new attention to the 'softer' dimensions of emotional well-being, relational commitment, and existential meaning. In the Dutch context, healthcare professionals experiment with concepts of care structured by the needs, perceptions and wishes of the elderly. These 'new' concepts are labeled client-centered care, relationship-centered care, perception-oriented care, or 'warmhearted' care. All these approaches share an interest in personal meaning and relationship as the essential characteristics of good care. Effective care needs to attune to the meanings a client attributes to health, illness, relationships, everyday activities, etc. Solitude, for example, has different meanings for different people. Some people suffer existentially from solitude, or experience it as loneliness; others accept solitude as part of the elderly life or even prefer it from time to time. In order to provide good care, healthcare professionals need to be aware of the meanings clients attach to experiences in their lives. On this approach, the life story of clients is commonly seen as the main entrance to this dimension of giving meaning. It is not a surprise, then, that caregivers use reminiscence techniques to gather relevant information about the individual meaning structures of clients. One of the methods focusing on reminiscence and the life story is the creation of Life Story Books. Clinical experience shows that these methods may have a positive effect on well-being and the caring relationship (see e.g. Hansebo and Hihlgren, 2000; Clarke, Hanson and Ross, 2003; Huizing and Tromp, 2006; Kunz, 2006). There is also some empirical evidence about the benefit of reminiscence work (e.g. Bohlmeijer, 2007; see for a review Haight, Coleman and Lord, 1995). We lack, however, more systematic empirical evidence that can inform the management and policy of institutional elderly care. Our research project intends to provide that knowledge. Our decision to focus on actual life stories reflects our view of the significance of the individual construction of meaning for care-givers.

APPENDIX: THE LARGER RESEARCH PROJECT

For reasons outlined above, the Dutch governmental funding agency ZonMw decided to launch a project to assess the effects of narrative methods in the context of elderly care. The primary aim of our over-all research project is to establish and explain the effects of life review methods on well-being and the quality of care. The scientific aim is the validation of claims by narrative theorists and practitioners that narrative structures of meaning are crucial to well-being. This will contribute to theories of narrative in the contexts of health care and practical theology. The hypothesis of the project is that narrative approaches will yield positive effects and the explanation for the expected effects of the narrative method will be sought in the narrative nature of the intervention. Our main hypothesis, therefore, is that the effects of our intervention method on well-being and quality of the caring relationship will be the result of an improved quality of life narrative or narrative competence. We thus regard the quality of the life narrative as the mediating factor explaining the effects on well-being and relationships. The theological aim, finally, is to elucidate personal meaning and life view in connection to existential anthropological, ethical, and theological categories of meaning. This way, we contribute to theories of lived religion (Failing and Heimbrock, 1998), implicit religion (Bailey, 1997), religious coping (Ganzevoort, 2001), and an ethics of care (Tronto, 1993; Van Heijst, 2005).

The research design of the larger research project is experimental. We developed a life review method, more precisely a standardised life story book method 'Open Cards' (Huizing and Tromp, 2005).[1] Profes-

---

[1] To be published as *Mijn leven in kaart* (Huizing and Tromp, in press).

NARRATIVE COMPETENCE AND THE MEANING OF LIFE 213

sional nurses at the assistant level, trained in this method, engage in a series of seven encounters in which they talk with the elderly person about his or her life story. This is supported by a set of cards proposing a set of questions for seven different themes, like social relations, education-work-hobbies, religion-philosophy of life, etc.). Inbetween the sessions, the client, where possible with a family member, collects photographs and other important documents and objects that deserve a place in the Life Story Book. We used this life review method as the intervention in our experimental group (N=62), whereas we provided equal hours of extra attention for our control group (N=30). This extra attention took the form of taking a walk, shopping, having tea, or something similar, without any intentional or structured reminiscing activity. With three moments of interviewing for every participant (before (t0), immediately after (t1), and five months after the intervention (t2)), we effectively collected 220 brief narratives to be analysed for narrative competence and quality. With these narratives, we collected for each interview-moment quantitative data about the quality of life and quality of the caring relationship. We also asked the nurses and family members to complete questionnaires on motivation and satisfaction. The establishment of the effects of the life review intervention will be based on statistical analysis; the interviews and Life Story Books will be analysed qualitatively. In order to test the explanatory hypothesis, however, this analysis of the narratives needs to be standardised and eventually translated into quantifiable categories, so that they can be connected with the quantitative data. This chapter only focused on the method we developed for the narrative analysis.

REFERENCES

Bailey, E.I. (1997), *Implicit Religion in Contemporary Society*, Kampen, Kok Pharos.
Barclay, C.R. (1996), Autobiographical remembering: narrative constraints on objectified selves, in D.C. Rubin (ed.), *Remembering Our Past: studies in autobiographical memory*, pp. 94–127, Cambridge, Cambridge University Press.
Bohlmeijer, E. (2007), *Reminiscence and Depression in Later Life*, Utrecht, Trimbos.
Brugman, G. (2000), *Wisdom: source of narrative coherence and eudaimonia. A life-span perspective*, Delft, Eburon.
Bruner, J.S. (1990), *Acts of Meaning*, Cambridge, Massachusetts, Harvard University Press.
Clarke, E., Hanson, E. and Ross, H. (2003), Seeing the person behind the patient: enhancing the care of older people using a biographical approach, *Journal of Clinical Nursing*, 12, 697–706.

214 THIJS TROMP & R. RUARD GANZEVOORT

de Vries, B., Blando, J.A. and Walker, L.D. (1995), An exploratory analysis of the content and structure of the life review, in B.K. Haight and J.D. Webster (eds.), *The Art and Science of Reminiscing: theory, methods and applications*, pp. 123–137, Washington, DC, Taylor and Francis.

Failing, W.-E. and Heimbrock, H.-G. (1998), *Gelebte Religion wahrnehmen: Lebenswelt—Altagskultur—Religionspraxis*, Stuttgart, Kohlhammer.

Freeman, M. (1991), Rewriting the self: development as moral practice, in M.B. Tappan and M.J. Packer (eds.), *Narrative and Storytelling: implications for understanding moral development* (CD 54), San Francisco, California, Jossey-Bass.

Fry, P.S. (1995), A conceptual model of socialization and agentic trait factors that mediate the development of reminiscence styles and their health outcomes, in B.K. Haight and J.D. Webster (eds.), *The Art and Science of Reminiscing: theory, methods and applications*, pp. 49–60, Washington DC, Taylor and Francis.

Ganzevoort, R.R. (1998), Hoe leest gij? Een narratief model, in R.R. Ganzevoort (ed.), *De praxis als verhaal*, pp. 71–90, Kampen, Kok.

——. (2001), *Reconstructies: praktisch-theologisch onderzoek naar de verhalen van mannen over seksueel misbruik en geloof*, Kampen, Kok.

——. (2004), What you see is what you get: social construction and normativity in practical theology, in C.A.M. Hermans and M.E. Moore (eds.), *Hermeneutics and Empirical Research in Practical Theology: the contribution of empirical theology by Johannes A. van der Ven*, pp. 53–74, Leiden, Brill.

——. (2005), Als de grondslagen vernield zijn. Religie, trauma en pastoraat, *Praktische theologie*, 32(3), 344–61.

Ganzevoort, R.R. and Visser, J. (2007), *Zorg voor het verhaal: achtergrond, methode en inhoud van pastorale begeleiding*, Zoetermeer, Meinema.

Haight, B.K., Coleman, P. and Lord, K. (1995), The linchpins of a successful life review: structure, evaluation, and individuality, in J.D. Webster (ed.), *The Art and Science of Reminiscing: theory, methods and applications*, pp. 179–191, Washington, DC, Taylor and Francis.

Haight, B.K. and Hendrix, S. (1995), An integrated review of reminiscence, in B.K. Haight and J.D. Webster (eds.), *The Art and Science of Reminiscing: theory, methods and applications*, pp. 3–21, Washington, DC, Taylor and Francis.

Hansebo, G. and Hihlgren, M. (2000), Patient life stories and current situation as told by carers in nursing home wards, *Clinical Nursing Research*, 9(3), 260–279.

Hermans, H.J.M. and Hermans-Jansen, E. (1995), *Self-Narratives: the construction of meaning in psychotherapy*, New York, Guilford Publications.

Huizing, W. and Tromp, T. (2005), *Open kaart: met ouderen in gesprek over hun levensverhaal*, Utrecht, Reliëf.

——. (2006), Werken met levensboeken in de praktijk van de ouderenzorg, in E. Bohlmeijer, L. Mies and G. Westerhof (eds.), *De betekenis van levensverhalen: theoretische beschouwingen en toepassingen in onderzoek en praktijk*, pp. 401–414, Houten, Bohn Stafleu van Loghum.

Janoff-Bulman, R. (1991), Understanding people in terms of their assumptive worlds, in D. Ozer, J.M. Healy and A.J. Stewart (eds.), *Self and Emotion*, pp. 99–116, London, Jessica Kingsley Publishers.

——. (1992), *Shattered Assumptions: towards a new psychology of trauma*, New York, Free Press.

Klein, K. (2003), Narrative construction, cognitive processing, and health, in D. Hermans (ed.), *Narrative Theory and Cognitive Sciences*, pp. 56–84, Stanford, California, CSLI Publications.

Klein, S. (1994), *Theologie und empirische Biographieforschung: methodische Zugänge zur Lebens- und Glaubensgeschichte und ihre Bedeutung für eine erfahrungsbezogene Theologie*, Stuttgart, Kohlhammer.

Kunz, J.A. (2006), Using life story circles to change the culture of care, *Ageing Today*, 27, 1043–1084.

McAdams, D.P. (1988), *Power, Intimacy and the Life Story: personological inquiries into identity*, New York, Guilford Publications.

——. (1993), *The Stories We Live By: personal myths and the making of the self*, New York, Guilford Publications.

——. (2006), *The Redemptive Self: stories Americans live by*, Oxford, Oxford University Press.

McAdams, D.P., Reynolds, J., Lewis, M., Patten, A.H. and Bowman, P.J. (2001), When bad things turn good and good things turn bad: sequences of redemption and contamination in life narrative and their relation to psychosocial adaptation in midlife adults and in students, *Personality and Social Psychology Bulletin*, 27(4), 474–485.

Nieuwesteeg, J.J., Oste, J.P., Horn, L. and Knipscheer, C.P.M. (2005), *De Verhalentafel: een studie naar de effecten van de Verhalentafel op bewoners van zeven verzorgingshuizen/woonzorgcentra*, Amsterdam, Vrije Universiteit.

Schroots, J.J.F. and van Dongen, L. (1995), *Birren's ABC: autobiografiecursus*, Assen, Van Gorcum.

Schütze, F. (1983), Biographieforschung und narratives interview, *Neue Praxis: kritische Zeitschrift für Sozialarbeit und Sozialpädagogik*, 13, 283–92.

Tronto, J. (1993), *Moral Boundaries: a political argument for an ethic of care*, London, Routledge.

van Heijst, A. (2005), *Menslievende zorg: een ethische kijk op professionaliteit*, Kampen, Klement.

Wong, P.T.P. (1995), The processes of adaptive reminiscence, in B.K. Haight and J.D. Webster (eds.), *The Art and Science of Reminiscing: theory, methods and applications*, pp. 23–35, Washington, DC, Taylor and Francis.

Wong, P.T.P. and Watt, L.M. (1991), What types of reminiscence are associated with succesful aging?, *Psychology and Aging*, 6(2), 272–279.

CHAPTER TEN

THE THEOLOGICAL CASE FOR CHRISTIAN SCHOOLS IN ENGLAND AND WALES: A QUALITATIVE PERSPECTIVE LISTENING TO FEMALE ALUMNAE

Tania ap Siôn, Leslie J. Francis and Sylvia Baker

Summary

The new independent Christian schools developed by parents and evangelical churches in the United Kingdom since the late 1960s remain controversial among both Christian and secular educators. This study begins by examining the two faces of the educational and theological controversies. In response to these controversies, the present study traced 135 women who had graduated from these schools between 1986 and 2003 and analysed their evaluation of the education they had received in these schools within four main themes: the quality of the education; the context of Christian and moral nurture; the quality of relationships among the pupils, with the teachers, and with the wider world; and the preparation received for life after leaving school. Although there were some issues of criticism, the balance of opinion among the former pupils within all four areas was largely supportive of the new independent Christian schools, which were generally perceived as having prepared them well for life.

Introduction

The Christian churches have exerted a very strong influence on the development of schools within England and Wales. Long before the 1870 Education Act (Rich, 1970) established machinery through which schools could be built directly by the state, church-related initiatives had inspired the creation of the National Society (Anglican), the British and Foreign School Society (Free Church) and the Catholic Poor School Committee (Roman Catholic) to provide a network of denominationally distinctive schools (Cruickshank, 1963; Murphy, 1971; Chadwick, 1997). When state money was first voted by parliament to support schools in 1833, these funds were deployed by means of distribution through the voluntary church-based societies. Moreover, the establishment of Board Schools by the 1870 Education Act was intended to augment the denominational system, not to replace it.

The major restructuring of the educational system in England and Wales by the 1944 Education Act consolidated rather than threatened the partnership between the state and the churches in the provision of a national network of schools (Dent, 1947). There were two key components within this act of direct relevance to the future of Christian or church-related education. On the one hand, the place of church schools was protected by the creation of the two categories of voluntary controlled and voluntary aided status. In the controlled status, the state took over all ongoing financial responsibility in exchange for the churches relinquishing control over religious education and over staff appointments. In the aided status, the churches retained responsibility for a significant proportion of building and maintenance costs in return for retaining control over religious education and staff appointments. On the other hand, the churches were given a significant voice in determining the content of the religious education syllabuses for all state-maintained non-denominational and voluntary controlled schools, subject to the proviso that these syllabuses should not promote denominational teaching. As a consequence of the 1944 Education Act, the Free Churches largely withdrew from church schools, accepting that all state-maintained schools would promote appropriate religious education through the agreed syllabi; the Roman Catholic Church set about building more church schools, maintaining that only aided status would protect the future of the Catholic view of religious education; and the Anglican Church adopted different approaches in different dioceses, largely withdrawing from church schools in some areas, largely opting for controlled status in some areas, and largely striving for aided status in some areas (Francis, 1987). The 1988 Education Reform Act generally left unchanged the concordat agreed between the state and the churches in 1944 (Cox and Cairns, 1989).

In spite of the considerable investment of the churches in England and Wales in the state-maintained system of schools, there has been surprisingly little sustained theological reflection on why the churches are involved in schooling or on what they see as the goals of such involvement. The theology of education remains an under-developed and under-resourced discipline within England and Wales (Francis and Thatcher, 1990). From an Anglican point of view, the most sustained

THE THEOLOGICAL CASE FOR CHRISTIAN SCHOOLS   219

theological reflection on church schools was provided by *The Fourth R* (Durham Report, 1970). This report developed a theologically informed distinction between two different rationales for the involvement of the Church of England within the state-maintained system of schools, characterised as the church's general concern and the church's domestic concern. The general concern was to promote the education of all children, irrespective of the religious perspective of their parents, while the domestic concern was with the ongoing Christian education of the children of Anglican parents. The *Durham Report* recognised the irreconcilable tension between the two concerns and advocated that priority should be given to the general concern. Developing the ideas advanced in the *Durham Report* and working as an Anglican theologian, Francis (1990) challenged the Anglican Church to develop a threefold theological rationale for continued involvement within the state-maintained sector of education by: reconceptualising the general concern in terms of a theology of service; reconceptualising the domestic concern in terms of a theology of nurture; and developing a third rationale in terms of a theology of prophecy concerned with the radical Christian critique of an educational system which can only be undertaken from an informed insider perspective. The Church of England's most recent report on church schools, *The Way Ahead* (Dearing Report, 2001), remained surprisingly light on theological reflection.

From the outset the Roman Catholic perspective on church schools in England and Wales was shaped by a very different cultural context from that experienced by the Anglican Church. When the National Society was established in 1811, it was the intention of the Established Church to serve all the children of the nation (Burgess, 1958). When the Catholic Poor School Committee was set up in 1847, it was the intention of a socially-marginalised church to provide an alternative system of education for the children of Catholic parents. It was still this sense of protecting a minority (and potentially marginalised) faith community which inspired the Catholic Church's sacrificial investment in schools following the 1944 Education Act (Hornsby-Smith, 1978). The theological perspective of a minority faith-group continued to shape the influential Catholic theological reflection on church schools published in *Signposts and Homecoming* (Konstant, 1981), a report to the Bishops of England and Wales on "the educative task of the Catholic community". While recognising that Catholic education should be confined neither to the years of compulsory schooling nor to the Catholic school, this report reaffirmed the identity of the Catholic school as a believing and integrated Christian community. The report argues as follows:

> Within a Catholic school the ultimate distinctive element is that its life is based on the vision of Christ in which all learning, growing, service, freedom and relationships are seen as part of a growth in the knowledge, love and experience of God. In other words there is a deliberate hope that the experience of belonging to the school will encourage personal commitment to Jesus Christ, will mark an important stage in the process of conversion and will lead to the discovery of the Christian vocation (pp. 106–107).

Since the late 1960s a fresh theological perspective on church schools has developed in England and Wales, inspired by evangelical churches and by the independent Christian school movement. Since there is no one national body overseeing the development of independent Christian schools, commensurate with the national educational arms of the Church of England and the Roman Catholic Church, it is no easy task to trace the development of this movement. The early history has, however, been related by Deakin (1989), who maintains that the first school of this type was opened in Rochester in 1969. According to Deakin (1989), by 1988 the Christian Schools' Trust was in contact with 53 schools. The subsequent development of Christian schools in England and Wales has been chronicled (from the insider's perspective) by Watson and MacKenzie (1996) and Baker and Freeman (2005), and (from the outsider's perspective) by Poyntz and Walford (1994) and Walford (1994, 1995a, 1995b, 1995c, 2000, 2001a, 2001b, 2001c).

In his attempt to understand the theological and ideological motivation underpinning the independent Christian schools in the United Kingdom, Walford (1995a) conducted a series of semi-structured interviews with the headteachers of 11 of the 65 schools included in 1993 on the address list of the Christian Schools' Trust, and received completed questionnaires from 42 of the other 54 schools. Walford's data demonstrated considerable diversity in these schools, but also clear underlying themes which united them. On the basis of these data the following profile was offered by Walford (1995a:7).

> These schools share an ideology of biblically-based evangelical Christianity that seeks to relate the message of the Bible to all aspects of present day life whether personal, spiritual or educational. These schools have usually been set up by parents or a church group to deal with a growing dissatisfaction with what is seen as the increased secularism of the great majority of schools. The schools aim to provide a distinctive Christian

THE THEOLOGICAL CASE FOR CHRISTIAN SCHOOLS 221

approach to every part of school life and the curriculum, and, usually, parents have a continuing role in the management and organisation of the schools.

Much of the theology currently underpinning the Christian school movement is of the kind that Jeff Astley (2002) would describe as ordinary theology. It is not couched in the systematic form of the theological academy, but in the direct form of the evangelically-shaped believer. Within this genre good insight into the theological motivation behind Christian schools is provided by an analysis of Baker and Freeman's (2005) first-hand account of their personal involvement in the movement. The new Christian school movement is grounded in belief in the God who takes the initiative within the lives of the people of God to bring to fruition the purposes of God. Here is the God who communicates with individuals and with groups through the word of scripture, through pictures and words of prophecy. Here is the God who authenticates the message through answered prayer, through healing, and through the release of the necessary finances.

Flowing from this theological perspective, four main objectives can be identified in Baker and Freeman's (2005) account of the rationale of the new Christian schools. The first objective stands at the heart of schooling and concerns the *quality of education*. From the outset the new Christian schools emphasised the importance of academic achievement and set out to enable pupils to perform better than they might have done in their local state-maintained school. Small classes, dedicated teachers and good discipline were all seen as contributing to this goal of academic excellence. According to Baker and Freeman (2005: 133–134), within these schools quality education was to be promoted through a radically different curriculum and a radically different view of the child. In accordance with scriptural principles science education was to include creationism and (in the early days before a significant change in the law of the land) discipline was to include appropriate corporal punishment. In many ways school was to be conceptualised as an extension of the parental home, and quality education was to be furthered by extra-curricular experience as well as by the school environment.

The second objective stands at the heart of the gospel and concerns *Christian and moral nurture*. According to Baker and Freeman (2005: 27), "the greatest priority in children's education is for them to come to know the Lord". Coming to know the Lord involves character building and character transformation. Children educated in the new Christian schools are to be shaped in a Christian spirituality and in a Christian moral framework.

The third objective concerns the *quality of relationships* experienced by the children. At different points in their narrative Baker and Freeman emphasise three different aspects of relationships. Aspect one focuses on the relationships among pupils themselves, which should model Christian openness and inclusivity and reflect "training the children in the ways of orderliness, obedience, forgiveness, kindness and love" (pp. 27–28). Aspect two focuses on the relationship between pupils and teachers, "Teachers should pray for and with the children" (p. 132). Aspect three focuses on the relationship between pupils and the outside world. From the outset the new Christian schools tried both to model an alternative environment for their pupils and to equip their pupils to engage with the wider secular world.

The fourth objective concerns the role of education in *preparation for life* beyond the school-leaving age. Baker and Freeman (2005: 49) argue that "protection from destructive influences at an early age results in strength to withstand these when the child is older". The schools set out to provide "a good foundation on which pupils can build in the future" (p. 28).

Within the evangelical theological circles, however, the development of Christian schools is by no means uncontroversial. In particular, one strand of evangelical theology, well-represented by Brian Hill (1990, 1993), is strongly committed to 'deschooling' Christianity. For Hill, an educational rationale which combines education with Christian nurture, as exemplified by Christian schools, should be able to demonstrate its legitimacy by referring to relevant biblical directives or support ('biblical imperatives'), identifying a need arising from individual cultural and historical contexts ('cultural operatives'), and demonstrating the effects of such schooling through empirical research ('empirical indicatives'). In each of these three interrelated areas Hill argues that it is difficult to justify the existence of Christian schools. First, there are no biblical passages which either explicitly support or advise against the Christian school, although Hill points to biblical passages and themes which are, in his view, in opposition to the underlying principles and ethos of the Christian school (1990: 120–124). Secondly, when the present cultural and historical context is examined (in Hill's case Australia and comparable countries), he finds little justification for Christian schools in terms of need and effectiveness. For example, Christians benefit from

THE THEOLOGICAL CASE FOR CHRISTIAN SCHOOLS   223

and can offer more to others by living and acting in the non-Christian world, which provides opportunities to give testimony, to act as 'salt in the community', and to have faith challenged by others.

> There is no direct biblical command to set up Christian schools, nor any prohibition. What we do find in scripture are various principles of action, such as parental responsibility and the call to be salt in the community, which have to be weighed up in the light of one's own cultural situation at a particular time (1993: 247).

In addition, crucially for Hill, Christian schools are often set against the core values of the 'free' world, and the educational ideal of developing individual critical thinkers. Thirdly, Hill recognises the importance of empirical research detailing the development of Christian schools and their effects on pupils, noting that, "it takes time for the long-term effects of a particular theory of schooling to become apparent" (1990: 130).

The challenge posed by the perspective of empirical theology for the Christian school movement in England and Wales is to examine the extent to which the theological assumptions and theological assertions about the distinctiveness and effectiveness of Christian schools are reflected in practice. This broader challenge was properly focused by Robin Gill's pioneering work in the 1970s when he argued that theologians had a responsibility to check their claims about the social world by the best research techniques pioneered within the social sciences (Gill, 1975). In the case of theological claims about school-related education, this requirement for empirically-based research inevitably includes listening to the pupils themselves. As yet, however, only two studies in England and Wales have responded to listening to the pupils attending independent Christian schools.

In the first study, O'Keeffe (1992) administered the Francis Scale of Attitude toward Christianity (Francis, 1989) to 439 pupils between the ages of eight and 16 years attending six independent Christian schools. O'Keeffe (1992: 105) drew the following conclusions from her data.

> The main conclusion to emerge from this study is that schools are exercising a positive influence on their pupils' attitudes toward Christianity. The responses of pupils demonstrated that the majority of pupils hold positive attitudes toward God, Jesus, the Bible and personal prayer.

In the second study, Francis (2005) compared the values of the 13- to 15-year-old boys attending 19 independent Christian schools (usually providing quite small secondary facilities) with the boys attending the 114 non-denominational state-maintained schools included in the

Teenage Religion and Values project (Francis, 2001). The comparison was based on 136 boys in the independent Christian schools and 12,823 boys in the non-denominational state-maintained schools. Francis (2005: 139) drew the following conclusion from his data.

> The data provided by the present study [demonstrate]...that the values environment modelled by 13- to 15-year-old boys attending Christian schools is significantly different from that modelled by boys in the same age range attending non-denominational state-maintained schools.

According to these data, boys attending the Christian schools were more likely to be committed to belief in God and in the inerrancy of scripture. They were more likely to hold a positive view of the Church, to support the place of religious education in school, and to reject superstitious beliefs. They were less likely to hold liberal attitudes toward alcohol, tobacco and sex. They were less likely to be troubled by bullying and more likely to respect their teachers. They were more likely to feel good about life and about themselves.

While the empirical data provided by O'Keeffe (1992) and by Francis (2005) provide some clear evidence regarding pupils during their time at independent Christian schools, by their very nature these two studies were not designed to answer the equally important questions about the subsequent reflections and experiences of pupils after they had left school. The aim of the present study, therefore, was to listen to the views of young women who had studied for GCSEs or A levels in independent Christian schools, up to twenty years after they had graduated from these schools. As a pioneering study in this area the aim was to listen to their views as widely as possible, but then to analyse and to interpret their responses within the theologically informed framework generated from Baker and Freeman's (2005) account of the rationale of these independent Christian schools, as outlined above. According to this framework the four criteria against which the independent Christian schools should be assessed concern evaluations of: the quality of education provided; the implementation of Christian and moral nurture; the quality of relationships experienced with pupils, teachers and the wider world; and the preparation offered for life after leaving school.

Method

Procedure

All reasonable attempts were made to contact the female students who had graduated from 11 Christian schools after studying for GCSEs or A levels between 1986 and 2003, and to obtain from them responses to the survey questionnaire. This study reports on the first set of 135 thoroughly completed questionnaires.

Instrument

In an open-ended question pupils were also asked to comment freely on what they liked and disliked about the school. In addition to this broad question, the following more focused issues were raised: Did you enjoy your time at the school? Were you overprotected? Were you prepared for the next stage of your education/work? Did work/sixth form come as a shock? There were also some variations in the questionnaire in order to generate data of interest to specific schools,

Respondents

Respondents reflected a wide range of backgrounds in respect of age and career. For age, the oldest respondents were in their late twenties and the youngest had recently left school and were attending sixth-form colleges. For career, employment contexts were diverse and included occupations relating to teaching, childcare, medicine, law, academia, social services, business, public sector, private sector, mother and home-maker. Around 9% of respondents' careers were explicitly related to the Christian faith, being church or mission linked, and around 44% classified themselves as students, either in further education or higher education. A high proportion of respondents had remained commit-ted to the Christian faith, with 79% regarding themselves as practising Christians and 76% regarding themselves as members of a church.

Analyses

The data generated by the questionnaire were analysed to illuminate the four main theologically informed themes generated from Baker and Francis' (2005) account: the quality of the education; the context of Christian and moral nurture; the quality of relationships among the

226 TANIA AP SIÔN, LESLIE J. FRANCIS & SYLVIA BAKER

pupils, with the teachers, and with the wider world; and preparation received for life after leaving school.

RESULTS AND DISCUSSION

Quality of education

Comments made by the female graduates relevant to the quality of education that they had received in independent Christian schools reflected four main issues best described as: teaching and learning; curriculum breadth; extra-curricular experiences; and school environment. Although overlaps with other categories occur, all responses included in this section are connected explicitly with the quality of education in a broadly academic sense.

Teaching and learning includes comments concerned with academic standards or experiences within these two areas. Most responses referred to high academic standards achieved either in general or within examination contexts. Many responses made an explicit causal link between high standards in teaching and learning and small class sizes, dedication and quality of teachers, and the individualisation of the education process through teachers interacting with pupils on an individual basis and collaborative school-parent relationships which enabled pupils to achieve their potential. Some responses commented that small classes provided related benefits in relation to pupils' confidence and attitude, and some responses contrasted the academic educational benefits of their schools positively with those of other schools.

> The fact that our classes were...smaller meant we got more help and attention to help us with our studies.... Had better GCSE grades due to more help given in smaller classes than state schools.
> One thing that stood out from [the school] was the immense dedication given from the teachers. 100% I don't think I would have done as well as I did without them.
> [The classes were generally small] which made interaction a lot easier, this a[s] well as the high quality teaching tended to bring out the best in pupils—reflected in their results and attitude.

Many responses made positive references to specific subjects and teachers in relation to enjoyment of a subject as well as quality of teaching.

> C.D.T. was amazing, we got to build brilliant things and NAME was a good teacher.

THE THEOLOGICAL CASE FOR CHRISTIAN SCHOOLS 227

Weaknesses cited in teaching and learning included issues related to teachers, subjects, physical environment, and new developments. References were made to incompetent or inexperienced teachers, lack of teachers, and, in one school, there were qualified criticisms of SEN provision.

> [Disliked] Lack of teachers—many teach/were teaching too many subjects resulting in a work overload, stress etc. and so not being able to give each subject their all, and resulting in low morale. Some days nearly the whole day could be spent with one teacher (for different lessons).

Some subjects were disliked, considered uninteresting or not worthwhile and, in one school, religious education was criticised on this account. One female also criticised Christian teaching materials from the USA.

> I do think many opportunities were not taken advantage of. For example R.I. was the lesson that was hated by everyone. In a Christian school—so much could have been done through these lessons—discussions, real Bible teaching, an insight into other religions.

Other subjects should feature more prominently in the curriculum according to some females who felt that teaching on sex, drugs, alcohol, and other religions should either be improved or, in one school, included.

> Just to give some constructive criticism—I don't think the sex education I received was completely adequate.

The physical environment in terms of school size and lack of facilities is cited as having a negative impact on sports lessons.

> I work with a lady who sent her son for a trial day to the school and was very impressed with the school. The only reason she chose not to send him there, was because of the lack of sports facilities.... I appreciate though, it's difficult in a small school to create teams.

The new development of a sixth form in one school was criticised by a few females on account of poor examination results and the observation that the school was unprepared to expand its teaching provision.

> The worst: My lack of decent A-Level results, the obvious lack of preparation and facilities for a real 6th form.

In the same school a number of females complained about an over-emphasis on academic achievement.

When I started at [the school] there was too much emphasis on academic achievement.

Curriculum breadth includes comments relating mainly to choice of examination subjects, although there are references to the scope of the wider curriculum. Most responses are general comments about restricted subject choice at both examination level and wider curriculum level, although occasionally specific subjects are identified.

[Disliked] only limited choice and number of G.C.S.E's allowed or available.

Some females reported feeling forced or coerced to study particular subjects.

[Disliked] Being forced to take some subjects @ GCSE that I didn't want to take.

Some females reflected on the causes and implications of a restricted curriculum, and a few offered suggestions for improvements. Causes of a restricted curriculum included school size, limited funding, and lack of appropriately qualified teachers. The implications of a restricted curriculum were considered to have either a negative impact or no impact on the future careers of pupils.

I disliked or rather had trouble accepting that because our school was so small there was less opportunity for us to study the subjects we wanted to in Year 10 and 11. Lack of teachers meant some courses are unavailable. Also some teachers were not fully qualified to teach some subjects.
8 G.C.S.E's is not really sufficient—anyone wanting to do medicine or law finds it very difficult to get onto courses at universities of their choice based on their lack of G.C.S.E's.

Extra-curricular experiences include comments concerned with school trips, sporting activities, school productions, community service, and mundane or extraordinary events or experiences outside the normal curriculum framework. Many females recorded positive experiences of school trips in Britain or abroad. Similarly, many females referred positively to their experiences of school productions.

Some of my best memories are of projects we did as a class like the Joseph production.

Some females recorded positive experiences of sporting activities which included mainly outdoor pursuits, but also sports days, team events,

THE THEOLOGICAL CASE FOR CHRISTIAN SCHOOLS 229

athletics competitions, and water sports. One female commented that she had learnt to approach competition from a Christian perspective.

> I also loved the athletic competitions...I learned the spirit of competition from a Christian perspective.

A few females referred positively to their experiences of community service, both within the school community and outside.

> I have great memories of...painting the school buildings during the holidays.

Some females recorded enjoyable mundane experiences and some females recorded extraordinary, special experiences.

> [Great memories] The big waterfight we had in M5, going to the 'Ranch', the crazy trouble our class used to get into for doing stupid things like sticking hole reinforcers on each other's backs.

Negative comments relating to extra-curricular activities cited were comparatively few and referred to disliked activities or the desire to develop aspects of extra-curricular activities. Many of the comments related to disliked sporting activities or enthusiasm for more team sports and competitions.

School environment includes comments concerned with resources/facilities and school/class sizes. Only aspects of school environment which have not been referred to in the other quality of education sub-categories or other categories are exemplified here. With reference to resources and facilities, many females referred to the lack of resources/facilities generally or specifically in relation to ICT (Information Communications Technology), science, and sport. In addition, many females referred to the poor condition of resources/facilities relating to the state of accommodation, heating and water supplies, and uniform.

> The school seemed scruffy. I would tell people I went to independent school and others at state schools looked smarter. Everyone would wear different things for P.E. which let down because people expected you to be really smart.

A few females wrote of their hope for an increase in school budget.

> I would love to see greater financial provision for all staff. You all do such an amazing job in not the easiest circumstances. I would love to see the floodgates of God's provision flung wide open for you personally as well as for resources in the school itself.

However, some females from one school commented positively on school facilities, mainly in relation to school grounds.

> I loved the building and the grounds. To have a playground with fields, woods and orchards in was pretty good.

With reference to school and class sizes, many females referred positively to small class and school sizes, and the benefits derived from them. Most benefits related directly to quality of education and relationships, and these have been exemplified in their respective categories. However, many females commented on the disadvantages of small class sizes. Most responses related directly to the impact of small class size on relationships and one response linked small school size to limited subject choice, and these have been exemplified in their respective categories or subcategories.

Christian and moral nurture

Comments made by the female graduates relevant to the Christian and moral nurture that they had received in independent Christian schools are concerned mainly with the 'non-academic' part of pupils' education and refer to the schools' Christian context, provision, and faith development as well as other related 'non-academic' areas. Most responses in this category were positive comments concerning the quality of the Christian foundation and its impact on the development of their faith. Some females commented explicitly on the present or lifelong implications of their Christian education, and others wrote about putting what they had learnt into practice.

> The strong Christian faith and support from most of the teachers in the school, I think, has helped in laying the foundations of my own life as a practising Christian (for this, I am very grateful!).
> My Christian faith has been strengthened by the ability to think 'Christianly' and [the school] equipped me to approach life this way—it is especially important when making career choices.

In addition to Christian foundation and development, some females referred to related development in other 'non-academic' areas such as the spiritual, emotional, moral, political, social, and 'character' issues. Within this context, a few females compared the Christian school positively with other schools.

> I think it gave me a good grounding, giving me good morals and discipline—perhaps more so than if I'd been at a state school.

THE THEOLOGICAL CASE FOR CHRISTIAN SCHOOLS 231

> [The school] allowed me to develop a greater political awareness and social conscience which would not have been encouraged or honed within an ordinary state school environment.

Many females commented on their appreciation of the Christian environment and the opportunities it afforded such as being with other Christians, the integration of Christianity in all curriculum areas, freedom to be a Christian and explore their faith, regular experience of God, encouragement in their Christian walk, and protection as young Christians. Within this context, some females compared Christian schools positively with other schools either implicitly or explicitly.

> Easier to be a Christian than my other schools.
> Gave me the freedom to continue to explore/solidify my Christian faith.

Specific opportunities related to faith experiences were cited by many females. Most referred to enjoyment of assemblies, including some references to experiencing God's presence, and some referred positively to religious education lessons and regular prayer, for example before lessons and exams, for material provisions, and when pupils were injured. A significant moment for one female was when she spoke in tongues.

> I had regular first hand experience of the reality of a God who loves and provides for his children. Praying for finances for the school was a regular feature of school life. I never doubted that God would turn up with whatever the money was that was needed cos he always seemed to. I remember when Graham and Anne needed a car and God told them to pray specifically for what they really wanted and then he provided them with a huge hatchback!
> My best memory is when I was filled with the Holy Spirit and started to speak in tongues.
> Best memories—…assemblies—every now and then God's presence would really show up and lessons would be scrapped—they could go on all morning.

A few females commented on the non-coercive nature of faith development and the opportunity to be an 'individual' Christian. In addition, a few females commented on their appreciation of an educational context that reinforced the Christian principles of home and a desire to provide a similar foundation for their children.

> Since my parents were also Christians all the principles I learnt at home were supported by those at school.
> There was room for the realities of adolescence and in no way were we indoctrinated or forced into religion. We were given the best head

start and guidance up to a point, but all of my year, some earlier than others, had to make an individual choice of their beliefs. Not all of us are Christian now, but those who are, really are.

Many responses reflected positive aspects of an ethos or atmosphere characteristic of close communities, and words such as 'family', 'homely', 'friendly', 'happy', 'loving', 'safe', 'secure', 'caring', 'informal', and 'relaxed' featured prominently. In addition, some females commented on the open and accepting environment found in their schools.

I enjoyed the atmosphere—the freedom to be myself.

For a few females, their appreciation of the ethos or atmosphere was explicitly related to a school's Christian foundations.

I loved the atmosphere of the school, you can really feel the love of God in the building and the people.

For one female, motivated pupils created a positive atmosphere.

In comparison with the pupils I work with I feel that we were motivated which created a good atmosphere.

However, many females made negative comments concerning the quality and consequences of the schools' Christian aspects and pupils' faith development, and a few females suggested that spiritual elements should be voluntary. Most of these responses referred to schools' emphasis on external image and conformity, lack of opportunity for internal, individual spiritual development, 'spoon-feeding' of ideas or coercion, restricted opportunities for self-expression, difficulty living one's faith, and the need to engage with real issues.

I have a firm foundation in God, however, sometimes I have found that I believed Godly truths because I had been taught them not necessarily because I had experienced them for myself. But at least I am better off than some people who don't know them at all. My biggest concern is that people leave with a relationship with God that is theirs.

There were still problems of stealing, drinking and drugs among students, and I think a lot of this was out of rebellion to the faith they had been forced to live by.

The content of Christian teaching was criticised by a few females as fundamentalist, old fashioned, and strict, and for one female, this pushed her away from the Faith.

THE THEOLOGICAL CASE FOR CHRISTIAN SCHOOLS 233

> I am in no doubt that the school had our best interests at heart. Although they had a very strict Christian attitude, with very old fashioned morals.... I felt very oppressed as a lot of the Christian teaching was very much focused on the old testament message.

A few females commented that there was no context in which to 'outwork' their faith either at school or outside, and that faith needed to be challenged in a non-Christian world for it to develop.

> Although I found the spiritual input very valuable, I think that personally my faith would have grown more outside of [the] School. During my time there I had no non-Christian friends to challenge me in my faith, it was all 'spoon-fed' to me. For many of my friends this meant that their faith was not their own and when they left the school it no longer played a part in their life.

Some females recorded their dislike of assemblies or made constructive suggestions for improvement.

> Assemblies were generally good but there was a slight lack of practical, relevant advice—I consider myself a practical, realistic Christian and it would have helped to have this.

According to a few females, relationships were influenced by faith concerns and led to divisions among pupils following Christian/non-Christian and denominational lines. One female added that the Christian background of pupils did not necessarily improve relationships and another criticised the unreasonable standards of behaviour expected of pupils. Perceived divisions or barriers between Christian schools and the outside world have been included in the relevant relationships section.

> Quite often I would go home and burst into tears as a result of my fellow pupils (and even teachers!) ridiculing candles, altars, the role of Mary, wearing robes, saying set prayers etc. etc. It seemed so petty to focus on the miniscule things that divided us and at times this kind of attitude pushed me to 'give up' on [the school].

Another female contrasted her Christian school negatively with other schools, and one female advised the separation of education and Christianity at the higher stages of secondary school.

> Being a Christian school was very good, especially at primary level, for giving you a grounding in life, I think though that it's important to keep education and Christianity separate at the higher levels of senior school.

Quality of relationships

Comments made by the female graduates relevant to the quality of relationships that they had experienced in independent Christian schools reflected three main areas: relationships among pupils; relationships between pupils and teachers; and relationships between pupils and the outside world. Although overlaps with other categories occur, all responses included in this section are connected explicitly with the quality of relationships.

Responses in the relationships among pupils subcategory comment on experiences of friendships and relationships within individual classes or the school in general, and factors affecting their nature and quality. Most responses contained positive comments about the good friendships that existed while at school and many females also referred to the longevity and quality of friendships still extant.

> I still have many friends from my school days—not many of my peers can say that.

A few responses commented on the positive dynamics in whole class relationships.

> I particularly enjoyed my fifth yr as I think as a whole our class bonded well.

Many responses attributed the quality of friendships among pupils to small class sizes, providing a context for developing relationships. In addition, one female described how they were taught to 'mend', rather than 'sever' relationships, and another female attributed good relationships to the 'secure' ethos of the school.

> Where there was only a few people in each class (e.g. 5 girls 5 boys) it meant that you had to work harder at your friendships because otherwise you'd be on your own.

Implicitly associated with the small size of schools, some females commented that they valued knowing everyone, appreciated the interaction between year groups, and enjoyed acting as mentors to younger pupils.

> I liked that there was a range of ages at the school 0–16 and everyone knew everyone else.

A few females made positive comments about the lack of bullying or the effective handling of bullying at school.

THE THEOLOGICAL CASE FOR CHRISTIAN SCHOOLS   235

> Some children are bullied at school and at [my school] this is handled
> well and so does not exist in the same way.

However, some responses identified negative aspects of relationships
between pupils counterbalancing positive comments in this subcategory
or introducing new elements. In this context, some females reported
incidences of bullying, and were critical of how it was handled through
first hand or second hand experience. In addition, a few females commented negatively about the existence of cliques in the school as well
as disagreements with a particular friend.

> But I think sometimes I found it hard work relationally—lots of cliques
> groups, and no space available from people who could irritate you!!

Most negative comments were related to small class sizes, which exacer-
bated the impact of cliques, peer pressure, over-familiarity, personality
clashes, and disagreements as well as restricting the choice and number
of friends.

> Our small year group were together so long that we often got fed up
> with each other!
> I am the type of person who enjoys having lots of friends and having
> 6 girls and 4 boys in my year was too limiting for me.

Drawing on the Christian foundation of the schools, a few females
referred to the isolation of a non-Christian in small Christian classes,
pupils not adequately reflecting their Christian background, and the
observation that being Christian did not correspond to pupils being
'like minded'.

> I also found that some children from Christian homes were cocky and
> negative and hardened to the Gospel.

Responses in the relationships between pupils and teachers subcategory
contain mainly positive general comments describing the qualities and
characteristics of teachers and the relationship between pupils and
teachers. Words used to describe teachers in relation to pupils include
'approachable', 'encouraging', 'not critical', 'supportive', 'kind', and
'caring', 'friendly', and 'committed'.

> The teachers are fantastic, and really care, not just teach you.

In addition, a few characteristics of teachers were related to the Christian foundation of the school.

It is only when you attend another school i.e. for 6th form that you realise how blessed you were at [the school] with a team of teachers who pray for you and care so much about you.

Words used to describe the relationship between teachers and pupils include 'good', 'loving', 'relaxed', and a relationship marked by 'respect' and 'friendship'.

Good relationships with teachers were a very positive thing, a lovely balance of respect and friendship.

A few females contrasted these qualities and characteristics positively with other schools.

I always felt the staff at [the school] had a genuine care and concern for the pupils. I know this is not always the case in state schools.

For many females the way teachers understood, valued, and accepted pupils as individuals was significant. In addition, some females commented that the teachers' focus on the 'whole person' was distinctive and appreciated.

I had teachers that believed in me and helped to nurture the best in me. I am very grateful to each teacher and the school for all you did to encourage my walk with God and teach me with care, looking out for my spiritual and emotional development as well as the intellectual.

Small class sizes were seen to have a positive influence on relationships with teachers for a few females.

I loved the fact that the school's small size meant I was known as an individual, able to develop real relationships with my teachers.

A few females enjoyed the blurring of divisions between school, home, and church in respect of their relationships with teachers.

I loved the fact that all you teachers used to come around to my house for prayer meetings when I was little.

However, many females were critical of some aspects of their relationships with teachers. Most of the comments relate to poor or inconsistent discipline, and inappropriate rules, punishments or actions. In this context a few females commented negatively on the partiality shown by some teachers to particular pupils.

I hated the fact that I had money stolen from my bag and the person got let off! Issues like that should have been delt with more seriously.

THE THEOLOGICAL CASE FOR CHRISTIAN SCHOOLS 237

One female related a negative memory relating to corporal punishment.

> The worst time was when we used to have a debit and merit system and I ended up with my hand being smacked by a ruler for accumulating too many debits!

Other responses included critical comments about parents doubling up as teachers, too familiar relationships between teachers and their family, the intrusiveness of teachers, and restrictions in freedom.

> I did find it hard sometimes being taught by my Dad!!
>
> Teachers protected you too much. Wanted to know lots about you and stuff going on in lives which is OK sometimes but you don't want your teachers to know everything.

Individual females commented on the conservatism of teachers, teacher-pupil personality clashes, and teachers' lack of understanding of feelings.

Responses in the relationships between pupils and the outside world subcategory mainly contain comments about pupils' limited experiences of the outside world, its effect on pupils, and suggestions for improvement. Some females commented on the paucity of knowledge relating to the outside world and pupils' limited exposure to and interaction with its non-Christian elements.

> There was very little relevance to the 'real world'. Many there would have a shock at things that went on outside the school. Most had none or few non-Christian friends outside school.

A few females referred to the negative or misinformed image of the outside world presented by the school, and in this context one female commented that pupils were 'fed' opinions with no critical engagement with them.

> In fact, at that time, I felt that the school gave quite a negative impression of non-Christian people and almost looked down on them.

Some females commented on the effect that restricted knowledge and experience of the outside world had on pupils, which included 'slight fear' of the outside world and non-Christians, 'shock' on entering the outside world after leaving school, and challenges to faith.

> In some cases the 'outside [school] world' is too much of a shock!
>
> [Disliked] Sometimes there is a naivity about 'the real world' which can push pupils away from their faith.

Individual females referred to the ridicule experienced by those outside the school on account of the uniform, the need to raise the school profile in the wider community, and restrictions in music listening.

Suggestions for improvement made by some females included gradual introduction to the outside world, greater interaction with the outside world and secular schools, and teaching in respect of the outside world and living as a Christian within it.

> Not so good was the lack of understanding of the real world and how to understand not everyone shares your Christian belief. This therefore means training in allowing beliefs and friendships with others to exist without losing one of the [?] completely.

However, some females perceived benefits in their schools' restricted relationship with the outside world, including the advantage of protecting young Christians from the outside world during their formative years of faith development, and of allowing them to focus on study.

> I think that young Christians do need protecting and that a young, new Christian in a 'normal' school would be more easily affected, than affecting anyone else.

In addition, some females commented that they were not overprotected because they had experienced other schools and the presence of non-Christian classmates, and one female described the school as a 'microcosm' of the outside world.

> I joined the school at yr 7 so had experienced state schooling. I did see a difference with children who had been in school longer but would not look at that negatively.

Preparation for life

Comments made by the female graduates relevant to the preparation for life that they had received in independent Christian schools are concerned with the extent to which Christian schools were perceived explicitly to prepare pupils for life immediately after leaving school or for life in broader terms. Most females felt that their schools had prepared them well for the next stage of their education or life, although a few females wrote that they felt prepared through their own self-effort or out-of-school experiences. Some responses were general references recording positive connections between their Christian schooling and post-school lives, with a few females commenting generally on the foundation laid for the future.

THE THEOLOGICAL CASE FOR CHRISTIAN SCHOOLS 239

> I believe that [the school] gave me a personal strength in myself, an upbringing that was supportive and although it was protected from the 'real world' outside, [school] life gave me a solid foundation for meeting the 'real world' with clear focus and integrity.

Many responses referred to academic preparation in general with a few comments focusing more specifically on the benefits gained from the study of certain subjects such as debating skills and different world religions, and the instilling of higher expectations.

> One of the things I particularly value was the 'debating skills' that NAME and NAME taught us. This was not a conscious skill; but the confidence to challenge, analyse and be confident in my own personal convictions has been extremely important to my own personal and career development.

In addition, many females referred to non-academic positive effects of a Christian school education, relating to Christian faith education and enduring attitudes and qualities developed. Christian faith education led some females to set up Christian Unions at college, influenced career decisions, provided strength to cope with the next stage of life, and affected life/world perceptions. Attitudes, qualities, and skills developed included motivation, confidence, open-mindedness, optimistic outlook on life, social and communication skills, concern and appreciation of others and their needs, and responsibility.

> I would love to teach in a Christian school in the future. Since I am training as a teacher I have had some experience of state schools and have therefore been able to compare my experience and have realised the benefits of Christian schools.

Some females commented on the ease with which they made the transition from Christian to secular education, and for a few females shared similarities in ethos, size, and teacher-pupil ratio were perceived as contributory factors.

> I found a good group of friends—some Christian and sixth form was fairly strict and school had religious/moral ethos then—another school may have been different.

However, many females critically qualified their positive statements or identified areas where they felt unprepared. Most of these responses related to academic issues and problems encountered in the transition from GCSE to A-level. Problems cited included shock at increased workload and its difficulty, gaps in subject knowledge, effects of limited

GCSE opportunities, and difficulty in maintaining a balance between work and the new social world. One female suggested that sixth form learning approaches be introduced in the final year of school. Other females suggested that more education about sex, drugs, alcohol, and multicultural areas, opportunities for work experience, and more extensive career guidance would help to prepare pupils for life after their Christian school.

> Yes generally apart from science—we didn't cover some practical work that other schools did and I was expected to know at the start of the chemistry AS course.
> I think we were shielded from many of the issues which we would ultimately come into contact later. One of the most significant areas, in my opinion, was sex education, and particularly contraception. I was not told about the various forms of contraception available, but told more simply, just don't do it.... I think it is important to maintain a balance between providing a good moral foundation and 'street-sense'.

Adapting to the world outside of the Christian school was cited as problematic for many pupils who felt shocked and unprepared for the 'real world', issues with swearing, drugs, and alcohol, mixing with non-Christians, and living as a Christian in the world. A few females suggested that engagement with the outside world earlier would prove helpful to pupils.

> I think I was prepared in almost every way except what to expect about how my friends lived their lives.... I wasn't prepared for the concept that my friends would go out, get drunk, smoke pot, have sex yet still be nice people who weren't totally depraved with no sense of right and wrong.
> Not really able to experience the outside world. The only way we were allowed to was by going out to dinner and now that's being taken away. I remember in J4 we weren't allowed to go to the Egyptian museum because it was not Christian enough.... I know the museum is against what Christianity stands for. However the world outside of [the] school is not a Christian world so protecting us from a non-Christian environment is in no way preparing us for life after [school].

The contrast between the size of their Christian schools and sixth forms came as a shock for many females, and a few females commented on the lack of closeness in teacher-pupil relationships, the more limited support, help, and attention available from teachers, and the competitiveness of the secular school environment.

> [Shocked] Big school, real people, not close knit teacher-student relationship.

THE THEOLOGICAL CASE FOR CHRISTIAN SCHOOLS 241

Some females commented that they felt that they had been more protected or sheltered than those who had not attended a Christian school (although this was not necessarily viewed in a negative sense), and a few females referred to the shock of needing to be self-reliant after leaving a Christian school.

> I was glad that I was sheltered from the harsh realities of life; injustice and poverty, neglect and ignorance of many people. Maybe that makes those things harder to accept as an adult though.

Conclusion

Working within the discipline of empirical theology, the present study set out to identify the theologically informed rationale underpinning the development from the late 1960s of the new Christian school movement within the UK, and to test the consistency between the implicit objectives of these schools and the experiences of the female alumnae who could reflect back with the wisdom of hindsight both on their time at school and on the way in which school has or has not prepared them for life after leaving school. Four main theological objectives were identified within the rationale of these schools and the data provided by 135 female alumnae were analysed to evaluate the extent to which these objectives had been reflected in experiences of the pupils attending the new Christian schools. The following four conclusions can be drawn from these analyses.

The first theologically-informed aim of the independent Christian school sector concerned the importance of academic achievement and the provision of high quality education which would enable pupils to perform better than they might have done in their local state-maintained school. The data suggest that in many ways this aim was being achieved. Many former pupils praised the high academic standards achieved in their schools which they linked with small class sizes, dedicated teachers, close relationships between home and school and the individualisation of the education process. However, they were also well aware of the effect of limited and, at times, insecure finances, and small pupil numbers, which placed restrictions on subject choice and teachers as well as resources and facilities. One area which was highlighted by a number of pupils was the need to develop specific aspects of PSHE (personal, social, and health education) and cultural education, with particular reference to education concerning sex, drugs, alcohol and non-Christian religions.

The second theologically-informed aim of the independent Christian school sector concerned the importance of nurture in the Christian faith and in a Christian moral framework. The data suggest that in many ways this aim was being achieved. Most former pupils commended the presence and quality of their schools' Christian provision which set them apart from other schools. They felt that the school environment offered them the freedom, support, and security necessary to grow as young Christians, and many pupils appreciated the fact that their faith permeated all aspects of school life and ethos, making the school a homely, loving and safe place to be. Former pupils, however, were not uncritical of their experiences, and some offered positive suggestions concerning how this area could be developed, such as greater focus on linking faith to practice, more opportunities for self-reflection and self-expression, and opportunities to 'outwork' their faith in the outside world.

The third theologically-informed aim of the independent Christian school sector concerned the importance of the quality of the relationships experienced by the pupils. The data suggest that in many ways this aim was being achieved. Most former pupils appreciated the close relationships that they experienced with other pupils and with teachers. Teachers were concerned with the growth of the whole person, not just academic development, and most pupils valued this individual, whole-person approach, coupled with the love, friendship, and support that teachers provided. However, some pupils highlighted the disadvantages of small class sizes on relationships between pupils and the effect of some discipline issues on relationships between pupils and teachers. Where pupils commented on their relationship with the outside world, they often remarked that they had limited experience of it while at school, and offered positive suggestions about how to increase knowledge and experience of the outside world before pupils left school. Not all pupils, though, believed that their relationship with the outside world should have been developed further; some argued that young Christians needed to be protected in their formative years and others felt that they had sufficient opportunities to interact with the outside world.

The fourth theologically-informed aim of the independent Christian school sector concerned the importance of preparing the pupils for life beyond the school-leaving age. The data suggest that in may ways this aim was being achieved. Most former pupils felt that their schools had prepared them well for the next stage, and this was understood holistically in terms of academic preparation, faith preparation, and character preparation. Despite feeling generally well prepared for life beyond their school years, many pupils commented on the large step taken from a close, protective environment, characterised by distinctive Christian ideals, to a larger, more impersonal environment, characterised by pluralism in beliefs, values, and practices, without familiar supportive frameworks. Some pupils suggested that further developing education about sex, drugs, alcohol, and other religions and cultures would help this transition.

On balance, analyses of the reported experiences of female alumnae who attended 11 of the new independent Christian schools indicate that, according to these former pupils, their schools had been largely successful in meeting the four theological objectives identified within their rationale. Although critically reflective in their responses, many of the former pupils remembered their schools as places where academic achievement was of a high standard, the Christian and moral nurture provided was generally valued, positive relationships were formed, and, in many respects, preparation was good for the next stage of life. However, two significant areas for refinement are identified on the basis of the former pupils' responses. First, how may the transition from the distinctive culture of a Christian school to the very different cultures found in the 'outside world' be traversed with greater ease, without negatively affecting the Christian identity valued by so many of these former pupils? Secondly, in what ways could Christian schools benefit from comments made by former pupils about aspects of the Christian and moral nurture provided, and so further develop that which lies at the heart of their rationale? In a number of respects the usual divisions between the roles and responsibilities of the school and those of the family are opaque in the Christian school, and because of this, issues which are normally kept within the family domain come to the fore: when, how and for what purpose should aspects of the world outside the family be introduced to children, and what is the most appropriate way to nurture children in the family's beliefs and values?

REFERENCES

Astley, J. (2002), *Ordinary Theology: looking listening and learning theology*, Aldershot, Ashgate.
Baker, S. and Freeman D. (2005), *The Love of God in the Classroom: the story of the new Christian schools*, Fearn, Christian Focus.
Burgess, H.J. (1958), *Enterprise in Education*, London, National Society and London, SPCK.

244   TANIA AP SIÔN, LESLIE J. FRANCIS & SYLVIA BAKER

Chadwick, P. (1997), *Shifting Alliances: church and state in English education*, London, Cassell.

Cox, E. and Cairns, J.M. (1989), *Reforming Religious Education: the religious clauses of the 1988 Education Reform Act*, London, Kogan Page.

Cruickshank, M. (1963), *Church and State in English Education*, London, Macmillan.

Deakin, R. (1989), *The New Christian Schools*, Bristol, Regius Press.

Dearing Report (2001), *The Way Ahead: Church of England schools in the new millennium*, London, Church House Publishing.

Dent, H.J. (1947), *The Education Act 1944: provisions, possibilities and some problems* (third edition), London, University of London Press.

Durham Report (1970), *The Fourth R: the report of the commission on religious education in schools*, London, National Society and SPCK.

Francis, L.J. (1987), *Religion in the Primary School: partnership between church and state?* London, Collins Liturgical Publications.

——. (1989), Monitoring changing attitudes towards Christianity among secondary school pupils between 1974 and 1986, *British Journal of Educational Psychology*, 59, 86–91.

——. (1990), Theology of education, *British Journal of Educational Studies*, 38, 349–364.

——. (2001), *The Values Debate: a voice from the pupils*, London, Woburn Press.

——. (2005), Independent Christian schools and pupil values: an empirical investigation among 13- to 15-year-old boys, *British Journal of Religious Education*, 27, 127–141.

Francis, L.J. and Thatcher, A. (1990) (eds.), *Christian Perspectives for Education: a reader in the theology of education*, Leominster, Fowler Wright.

Gill, R. (1975), *Social Context of Theology*, London, Mowbray.

Hill, B.V. (1990), Is it time we deschooled Christianity?, in L.J. Francis and A. Thatcher (eds.), *Christian Perspectives for Education: a reader in the theology of education*, pp. 119–133, Leominster, Fowler Wright.

——. (1993), Christian schools: issues to be resolved, in L.J. Francis and D.W. Lankshear (eds.), *Christian Perspectives on Church Schools*, pp. 246–257, Leominster, Gracewing.

Hornsby-Smith, M.P. (1978), *Catholic Education: the unobtrusive partner*, London, Sheed and Ward.

Konstant, D. (1981), *Signposts and Homecomings: the educative task of the Catholic community*, Slough, St Paul Publications.

Murphy, J. (1971), *Church, State and Schools in Britain 1800–1970*, London, Routledge and Kegan Paul.

O'Keeffe, B. (1992), A look at the Christian schools movement, in B. Watson (ed.), *Priorities in Religious Education*, pp. 92–112, London, Falmer Press.

Poyntz, C. and Walford, G. (1994), The new Christian schools: a survey, *Educational Studies*, 20, 127–143.

Rich, E.E. (1970), *The Education Act 1870*, London, Longmans.

Walford, G. (1994), Weak choice, strong choice and the new Christian schools, in J.M. Halstead (ed.), *Parental Choice and Education: principles, policies and practice*, pp. 139–150, London, Kogan Page.

——. (1995a), *Educational Politics: pressure groups and faith-based schools*, Aldershot, Avebury.

——. (1995b), The Christian schools campaign: a successful educational pressure group? *British Educational Research Journal*, 21, 451–464.

——. (1995c), Faith-based grant-maintained schools: selective international policy borrowing from the Netherlands, *Journal of Educational Policy*, 10, 245–257.

——. (2000), *Policy and Politics in Education: sponsored grant-maintained schools and religious diversity*, Aldershot, Ashgate.

——. (2001a), Evangelical Christian schools in England and the Netherlands, *Oxford Review of Education*, 27, 529–541.

THE THEOLOGICAL CASE FOR CHRISTIAN SCHOOLS 245

——. (2001b), The fate of the new Christian schools: from growth to decline? *Educational Studies*, 27, 465–477.

——. (2001c), Building identity through communities of practice: evangelical Christian schools in the Netherlands, *International Journal of Education and Religion*, 2, 126–143.

Watson, K. and MacKenzie, P. (1996), The new Christian schools in England and Wales: an analysis of current issues and controversies, *Journal of Research on Christian Education*, 5, 179–208.

PART THREE

QUANTITATIVE PERSPECTIVES

CHAPTER ELEVEN

FAITH OR MORALITY? 'THEOLOGICAL SEDIMENTS' DEPENDING ON THE CENTRALITY, CONTENT, AND SOCIAL CONTEXT OF PERSONAL RELIGIOUS CONSTRUCT SYSTEMS

Stefan Huber and Constantin Klein

Summary

The study tried to analyse to what degree traditional denominational doctrines influence the personal beliefs of Christians today. The analysis was led by the assumption that personal beliefs are—to some degree—influenced by common traditional doctrines that are taught in preaching, lessons, and talks about religious issues, and can be understood as a kind of 'theological sediment' in today's beliefs. In this study, the issue at stake was whether there exists a 'typical Catholic' and a 'typical Lutheran' belief in justification. Reflecting historical denominational doctrines and notions of justification several theoretical positions for Catholics and Lutherans were proposed, discussed and operationalised.

Because it is plausible that the influence of traditional doctrines depends strongly on the salience of one's religiosity, the explicit differentiation between the centrality and the contents of personal religious construct systems (Huber, 2003, 2007) was integrated into the theoretical framework. It was hypothesised that the more important and central is one's religiosity, the greater should be the impact of traditional doctrines.

A comparison was made of beliefs concerning justification between Roman Catholics and Lutherans in Germany. The relevance of the centrality of their religiosity was also analysed. It was found that there is a small but significant difference in the beliefs concerning justification depending on religious affiliation. There is, in accordance with the theoretical hypotheses, an interaction between the centrality of one's religiosity and one's religious affiliation: while the Catholics always see both faith and doing good works as of equal importance, Protestants rate faith more highly the more central their religiosity. There is some evidence that traditional doctrines can still influence personal religious beliefs today.

Introduction

At the end of the nineteenth century, the founders of modern sociology started to consider the societal impact of religious traditions and ideas. Probably the best known example is Max Weber's analysis of *The Protestant Ethic and the Spirit of Capitalism* (Weber, 1920/1988).[1] In this famous essay, Weber argued that the uncertainty of Protestants about their personal eternal status of belonging to the category of the saved or the damned, especially for those denominations that accept the Calvinist doctrine of predestination to salvation or damnation, led them to work as hard as they could to 'prove' their belonging by their economic success in the present life. The theological justification for doing so has particularly been Jesus' saying in Matthew 7:16: "You will know them by their fruits" (quoted according to New King James Version). Other biblical quotations that have been interpreted in the same direction include Isaiah 3:10; Matthew 3:8–10; Luke 3:8, 9; John 15:16 and 2 Corinthians 9:10. According to Weber, the ethical principle of hard work was important in the evolution of modern capitalism, especially in the Protestant regions and nations in the Western world. Weber concluded that this ethical principle still persisted in secular times as the secular relict of a religious idea, as 'the Spirit of Capitalism'.

Although Weber's study was heavily discussed and criticised, in particular with regard to the empirical evidence of his analysis (cf. the critiques and Weber's reactions in Weber, 1987), it nevertheless became a classic of the sociology of religion (Seyfarth and Sprondel, 1973). Although it has been nearly a century since Weber first published his essay, there has been little pertinent empirical research, although an operationalisation of his concept was first developed by sociologists in the sixties (Goldstein and Eichhorn, 1961). Nearly all empirical research since then has been done in the field of psychology (Blood, 1969; Buchholz, 1978; Hammond and Williams, 1976; Ho, 1984; Mirels and Garrett, 1971; Ray, 1982; Maes and Schmitt, 2001; Wollack, Goodale, Wilting and Smith, 1971). Although Weber's theory of the Protestant ethic clearly dealt with a *theological* concept, the question of justification and salvation, little attention has been given to him by empirical theologians.

---

[1] For further information about Weber's essay see Tyrell, 1990; Guttandin, 1998.

Weber's stimulating idea—to search for secular orientations which developed from religious and theological beliefs during a long process of a 'sedimentation'—was re-invented from a theological perspective by Claudy. Claudy (2005: 59–60) introduced the term 'anthropological sediment' to express the claim that interpretations of human existence always use, implicitly or explicitly, already current anthropological concepts. These are present in the surrounding culture, which may be conscious or unconscious, and either well developed theoretically or not developed at all. According to Claudy, these sediments are rooted in specific beliefs about the nature of humankind that have been elaborated during history in the scriptures and teaching of leading thinkers as well as in popular stories, legends, fairy tales, or in ordinary, everyday language. Such beliefs remained plausible over time at least for many people, because of their common and relatively simple plausibility. They therefore serve as cognitive guidelines that help to interpret the ways in which people think, talk and act in specific situations. They may once have been elaborated in a clear and sophisticated way, but their persistence was due to their relatively easily understandable and popular argumentation. So they 'sedimented' down the ages and became part of a commonly shared anthropology. As an example, one might think about the golden rule, which is well-known in Jesus' popular formulation in Luke 6:31 but is also present in many other forms in diverse cultures and languages.

Claudy himself analysed successful and popular contemporary movies in search of anthropological sediments which he discussed from a hermeneutic-theological point of view. In Claudy's analyses, the sediments are more complex but also more diffuse, because he searched for story motifs such as the mission for a special challenge (saving people in cases of catastrophes or crimes as in 'Alien' or 'Die Hard') or predestination for a heroic life always fighting against all evil (as in 'Harry Potter' or 'Spiderman'). The aim of Claudy's studies was to find existential motifs of a popular anthropology inductively and to employ them as an important challenge to contemporary theological-anthropological reflection. It is not the goal of this study to discuss the plausibility of Claudy's analyses. It is only important here to notice two things: first, Claudy described processes like the change from a theological doctrine to a popular economic approach to life that Weber analysed a century earlier precisely with his concept of 'sedimentation'. Second, Claudy completely inverted the direction of Weber's perspective—from *a sociologist's view on the religious and theological phenomenon* of a specific Christian belief, to *a theological perspective on a secular modern mass phenomenon.*

Although this change of perspectives is quite interesting, for a theological study it still might be worth considering religious beliefs from a theological perspective, and employing the concept of sedimentation to look for some kind of 'theological sediments' in modern Christians' beliefs. This approach—facing *religious beliefs influenced by traditional theological doctrines* (Weber's topic of interest) *from an (empirical-) theological perspective* (Claudy's perspective)—seems, at least for us, to be a very suitable procedure for an empirical-theological study with a historical interest. Our question is whether the beliefs of Christians today are still influenced by common traditional Christian doctrines. If the personal beliefs of Christians are to some degree still influenced by such doctrines, which are taught in preaching, lessons, or talks about religious issues in families, bible groups, etc., it should be possible to uncover theological sediments that result from these influences. The present study seeks to explore such a 'sediment' using the Structure-of-Religiosity-Test (S-R-T: Huber, 2006, 2008, in press) as a measure. This was especially designed for systematic research in comparative religious studies and empirical theology.

The basic structure of the S-R-T is defined by Glock's five core dimensions of personal religiosity (Stark and Glock, 1968; Huber, 1996): the intellectual, the ideological, the devotional, the experiential and the ritual dimension. The measurement of these dimensions systematically differentiates between the centrality and content of religiosity. The concept of *centrality* overlaps with concepts such as intrinsic motivation, salience, and importance of religion. These all deal with the effect of religion on somebody's personality, the impact of religious contents on one's experiences and behaviour. The concept of *content* is related to the direction of religion. Religious contents can be beliefs, schemas, styles, and orientations. They are always related to a certain direction to which religion leads a person. The differentiation between centrality and content of religiosity reflects the theological distinction between the *fides qua creditur* and the *fides quae creditur*. In a theological perspective, the S-R-T tries to heed Van der Ven's demand for the development of measurement instruments for an empirical theology (cf. Van der Ven, 1990: 179). Software is available (see www.XPsy.eu) for the computerised elicitation, analysis, and depiction of S-R-T-scales, and other scales.

This study is a post-hoc analysis using data from studies on German samples which were conducted to validate the S-R-T. Belief in

FAITH OR MORALITY? 253

the sinner's justification (a traditional theological concept nearly as 'classic' as Weber's object of interest, the belief in predestination), was thought to be analysable using the given data. So the aim of this study was to analyse whether traditional doctrines of justification influence the beliefs of contemporary Christians, which could be interpreted as empirical evidence for a 'theological sediment'. In addition, adopting a methodological perspective, the study seeks to test the usability of the concept and measures of the S-R-T for empirical-theological research on ecclesiastical-historical issues.

DENOMINATIONAL DOCTRINES OF THE SINNER'S JUSTIFICATION IN ECCLESIASTICAL HISTORY

The doctrine of justification is clearly a denominational issue because it originally marked the beginning of the Reformation and became the classical bone of contention between the Roman Catholic and Protestant Churches. It should therefore be possible to find characteristic differences between the beliefs of today's Catholics and Protestants on justification.

Germany is a good place for an empirical-theological study of characteristic denominational beliefs in justification, for two reasons. First, the Reformation began in Germany and became important for the whole of Germany's subsequent history. Thus processes of sedimentation could have taken place there. Second, as a result Germany is still denominationally divided today. While in many other nations the denominational conflicts and wars of the sixteenth and seventeenth centuries resulted in the dominance of one specific Christian denomination, such as Roman Catholics in France or Lutherans in the Scandinavian countries, in Germany today there exists an equally strong Roman Catholic and mainline Protestant (mostly Lutheran) tradition. Each spans about one third of the German population, with those without a denomination making up the other third (Wolf, 2001; Terwey, 2003; see also the reports of the Roman Catholic Church: Sekretariat der Deutschen Bischofskonferenz, 2005; and of the Protestant Church in Germany: Kirchenamt der Evangelischen Kirche in Deutschland, 2005).

Although the denominational differences are probably not as important as they used to be, it could be assumed that there are still differences in the religious culture and, therefore, in religious thinking and behaviour between the two large groups of the Roman Catholics and Protestants as a result of a process of theological sedimentation. Both Catholic and Protestant theologians still have to deal with these differences in theology, pastoral practice and religious education, for instance in ecumenical dialogue (Kühn and Pesch, 1991), or in situations of denominational diaspora (e.g. Rehm and Wagner-Friedrich, 2006). It would seem to be interesting, therefore, to discover to what degree the theological differences between Catholics and Protestants over the doctrine of the sinner's justification are reflected in the religious beliefs of German church members.

As part of the theoretical background for the operationalisation of the empirical study below, it is necessary to study ecclesiastical history to uncover the classic denominational doctrines of justification (for overviews see Herms, 1992; McGrath, 2005; Müller, 1977; Pesch and Peters, 1994). Since Paul's letter to the Romans, and especially since Augustine's victory over Pelagius in the fifth century, the principle of *sola gratia*, the belief that humankind can only be justified by God's endless grace, was the canonical Christian doctrine. Augustine, whose position became dominant during the following centuries, argued most explicitly in his *Ad Simplicianum de Diuersis Quaestionibus* (397/1970) that God alone is able and willing to justify the human sinner (see also Drecoll, 1999). But in the late period of medieval theology it became a common belief that God would not refuse his grace to someone who tries to achieve justification on their own, showing their sincere intention by doing 'good works' (Dettloff, 1963; Ebeling, 1989). The idea of acquiring justification by good works spread and was the origin of the selling of indulgences.

This practice led Martin Luther to write his famous 95 theses and to reconsider the notion of justification. Luther referred to both Paul and Augustine and revived the view that humankind could only achieve justification by God's grace. Luther's notion of the sinner's justification is particularly described in his *De servo arbitrio* (1525/1908), and in shorter versions it became a popular part of the Lutheran confession in the *Confessio Augustana* (CA 4) and in the *Apology of the Confessio Augustana* (ApolCA 4,80) (both reprinted in *Lutherisches Kirchenamt*, 2000, Nr. 10 and Nr. 111. For a Catholic perspective on Luther's notion of justification, cf. Bogdahn, 1971). According to Luther, individuals are justified while they are still sinners. In Luther's concept, the Christian is always both sinner and justified, *simul iustus et peccator*. Justification indeed is possible only for those who believe (*sola fide*), but faith is thought to be a consequence of God's grace as well. As a result of his justification, man starts to do good works which are seen as the fruits of his life of faith. While good works in this sense may be seen as an expression of faith, they do not have any relevance for justification. In Luther's eyes, good works have no significance at all for one's relationship with God, but are only important for the relationship with one's neighbour. Although this is an important part of Christian existence too, the Lutheran tradition may be said to show a tendency to set faith against good works, because the term 'justification by faith alone' became a keyword through the centuries and could therefore be a proper candidate for a theological sediment in today's beliefs.

In reaction to the critique expressed in the Reformation, the Roman Catholic position was redefined during the Council of Trent in 1547. The so-called Tridentinum highlighted the importance of divine grace and declared that there could be no justification without God's forgiving grace (cf. the 'Decree on justification' in the Council's decrees, 1547/ Denzinger, 1997). The ability to believe was thus seen to be exclusively dependent on justifying grace. But in Catholic doctrine a person still has the freedom to agree to inspiring grace, the 'gratia praeveniens', and therefore to acquire justifying grace. But his agreement is no longer a merit. Merits are good works which permit sanctification to a justified person (for Luther sanctification occurs at the same moment as justification—'simul iustus et peccator'). In Catholic doctrine man has the chance to gain merit by doing good works which will be taken into account on the Day of Judgement. This means that, from the Catholic point of view, an individual can participate actively in his sanctification. It could be presumed, therefore, that in the Roman Catholic tradition there is a much stronger tendency than in the Lutheran tradition to regard both faith and works as almost equally important. For example, the prominent Catholic theologian Karl Rahner (1965) spoke in this sense about the direct relationship between loving God and loving one's neighbour.

Although these doctrines were formulated in the sixteenth century, it is important to add that the notion of justification is still of interest today. Indeed, only a few years ago there was an intense discussion between Catholic and Lutheran theologians, especially in Germany, about the *Joint Declaration on the Doctrine of Justification* (between the Roman Catholic Church and the Lutheran World Federation: Lutherisches Kirchenamt der VELKD, 1999; see also Jüngel, 2006; Thönissen, 2000). This represents a current attempt by the denominations to come closer to each other over the critical points of the doctrine of justification.

256 STEFAN HUBER & CONSTANTIN KLEIN

Before coming to the empirical study, a third possible position on the problem of justification should be described. During the Enlightenment the theological dimension of justification became less important. More attention was given to the question of rational moral behaviour. Moral behaviour could be seen as the next step in human development, the 'religion of reason', leaving the traditional religious beliefs behind. This was the perspective taken by David Hume in *The Natural History of Religion* (1757/1993; see also Flew, 1969; Gaskin, 1978). But it also remained possible to recognise 'religion within the limits of reason alone', which was the position of the German philosopher Immanuel Kant (1793/2003; Kant, 1987; see also Lötzsch, 1976; Wagner, 1975; Walsh, 1965; and Wood, 1970; for a comparison of the positions of Hume and Kant, cf. Levener, 1969). Both Hume and Kant emphasised the superior impact of moral behaviour, but Kant saw the important rational function of traditional religion particularly in leading people to study moral behaviour. Since the Enlightenment, it has become possible in the liberal Protestant tradition to understand the classic theological notion of justification as a symbolic expression of the demand for correct moral behaviour (which, on a religious level, God wants for humankind). Thus, the upgrading of good works—seen as moral behaviour—became possible from a non-religious as well as from a religious point of view.

Altogether, then, three possible ideal options may be distinguished in the question of humankind's justification, each of which is theologically reasonable and therefore a possible result of a theological sedimentation process (cf. Figure 11.1). It is possible to see faith as most important; this would be a 'typical Lutheran' position. It is possible to lay an equal emphasis on faith and good works; this would be a more 'typical Catholic' position. And, finally, there is the possibility of rating good works as being the more important in terms of correct moral behaviour; this would be a liberal religious position as well as a completely non-religious position.

METHOD

The aim of the empirical study was to explore the statistical evidence for these theoretical options. A post-hoc analysis was therefore done using the data from the sample of the validation study for the S-R-T. The respondents were German church members and churchgoers.

The inquiry took place in Bad Kreuznach, a town with about 45,000 inhabitants which is very typical of the western part of Germany with regard to social structure, the distribution of church affiliation, and political attitudes. The complete sample consisted of 706 individuals. A total of 417 of them were women and 289 men; 364 were Roman Catholics and 342 mainline Protestants (nearly all of them Lutherans). Their ages ranged from twelve to 92 years, with a mean of 50.7 (SD = 18.2).

The analysis concentrated on the following question: "Many religions expect people to do good and to trust God. Which of these two is, in your opinion, more important?" As possible answers, five categories were given as follows: it is most important to do good (1); both are important, but doing good is more important (2); both are equally important (3); both are important, but trusting God is more important (4); it is most important to trust in God (5). The issue at stake was whether there are theological sediments such as a 'typical Catholic' and a 'typical Lutheran' belief in justification. The question quoted above was taken as a dependent variable and religious affiliation as an independent variable. First, the mean difference between the denominations was examined. According to the theoretical scheme, Catholics were expected mainly to rate faith and good works as equally important, while Protestants were expected mainly to rate faith more highly. The option of rating good works more highly remained unclear, because it could be interpreted in a religious way as well as in a non-religious way. Thus, no hypothesis was formulated about this third option with reference to denominational membership.

The question about the typical attitude towards justification is primarily a descriptive question. But in an analytical sense, it is important to understand which (other) elements of religiosity also determine the belief in justification. Thus, as a framework for operationalising religiosity factors that are influential for the belief in justification, the S-R-T model of religiosity was employed. As described above, this model distinguishes between the centrality and the content of religiosity to reflect the theological distinction between the *fides qua creditur* and the *fides quae creditur*. In addition to the concepts of centrality and content, the social environment of a religious person can be added as a contextual factor. Searching for typical denominational beliefs focuses on the social religious environment. Thus the social dimension of one's religiosity was operationalised by the religious affiliation of the study participants, either Roman Catholic or mainline Protestant (Lutheran).

To analyse the importance of the two factors of centrality and content, several S-R-T measures were used as further independent variables and covariates. To measure the centrality of religion, the S-R-T's core scale, the 'Centrality Scale' (Huber, 2003, 2004, 2007), was used. The 'Centrality Scale' consists of 10 items measuring the intellectual, ideological, devotional, experiential and ritual dimension of personal religiosity. The scale has been applied in numerous studies with about 7000 respondents since 1999. In most of the samples its internal consistence is higher than .90 (Cronbach's alpha). The 'Centrality Scale' delivers not only a linear measurement of the centrality of the religious construct system in personality, but also a categorical measurement of three distinct ideal types of religiosity. The typology depends on the position of the religious construct-system in the cognitive architecture of personality: in a central, a subordinate or a marginal position (for a theoretical discussion of the three ideal types and their empirical operationalisation, see Huber, 2003: 257–264; 2004: 93–99; 2007: 220–227). This typology is the basis for the calculations referred to below.

It was hypothesised that the more central one's religiosity, the more relevant would be one's denominational identity. Thus, a bigger difference in the estimation of faith (in Protestants) or of faith and morality (in Catholics) might be expectable in accordance with the degree of centrality. On the other hand, it seems plausible that the less central one's religiosity, the more likely it will be to find a higher estimation of good works. Either somebody is not very religious, when there is no reason for them to trust God but as an ethical person they will still do good works; or somebody takes the Kantian position, in which religion is subordinate to morality. Therefore a higher estimation of good works among people with low religiosity was expected. Because of these interrelations between religious affiliation and centrality, an interaction effect of both factors was also expected: Protestants with a high centrality of religiosity were expected to elevate the importance of faith, while Catholics with a high centrality of religiosity should regard both doing good and trusting God as equally important.

Because the dependent variable, the estimation of good works and/or faith, can be seen as part of religiosity's contents, further religious contents were conceptualised as covariates in the theoretical model. To measure such contents, two more indices were employed. The first was a single item representing the ideological dimension of religiosity, asking whether participants believe in a personal God. This item was part of an inventory measuring nine different images of God. The general

FAITH OR MORALITY? 259

instruction in the inventory was: "*People have very different ideas about God. Therefore, in this section we are putting the word 'God' in quotation marks. Please indicate to what extent the individual statements meet with your own personal ideas about 'God'.*" The wording of the item concerning the personal image of God was: "*In my view, 'God' is like a person.*" As possible answers, five categories were given ('*not at all*', '*hardly*', '*a bit*', '*quite a lot*', '*very*'). The second measure was a 9-item-scale of 'positive emotions towards God' (EtG+: Huber and Richard, in review) representing religiosity's experiential dimension. This scale was part of an inventory with 16 different emotions towards God, positive as well as negative. The general instruction of the inventory was: "*How often do you experience situations in which you have the following feelings with regard to God?*" As possible answers, the following five categories were given ('*never*', '*seldom*', '*sometimes*', '*often*', '*very often*'). The nine positive emotions towards God (EtG+) were: *trust, awe, joy, protection, happiness, hope, gratitude, reverence, and release from guilt.*

The EtG+ scale has an internal consistency (Cronbach's alpha) of .93 ($N = 706$). It was hypothesised that both contents, the belief in a personal God and positive emotions towards (this) God, should increase the tendency to rate faith more highly, because they express the object of faith and the personal relation to this object so that they correspond to an expectation of personal justification.

Altogether, the operationalised model contained two independent variables (church affiliation, centrality) and two covariates (belief in a personal God, positive emotions towards God) to explain the variance of the item asking whether doing good or trusting God is more important. Single effects for each independent variable and covariate were hypothesised, and the independent variables were expected to interact. To test the described model statistically, a univariate ANOVA was employed to analyse the degrees of variance explanation.

RESULTS

As a first result, a slightly significant mean difference in the estimation of faith or good works could be found between Catholics and Protestants (Table 11.1). As expected, the mean answer of the Catholics was almost exactly in the middle rating (3), seeing both faith and good works as equally important. The mean answer of the Protestants was slightly higher, at about 3.2, which corresponds to the hypothesis that Protestants may tend to upgrade faith—their result is located between

STEFAN HUBER & CONSTANTIN KLEIN

Table 11.1: Mean difference between Catholics and Protestants

Church affiliation	N	Mean	SD
Roman Catholics	364	2.98	1.06
Mainline Protestant (Lutheran)	342	3.18	1.22
Total	706	3.08	1.15

Dependent variable: doing good/trusting God; t(704) = −2.40; P = .017

ratings 3 and 4, but still very close to the middle rating (and therefore still close to the Catholic position). Therefore, in answer to the first question, it might be concluded that there is a small tendency towards typical denominational beliefs regarding justification.

But it should be noticed that the denominational difference really is quite small. Hence, the analytical question asking for other elements of religiosity that determine the belief in justification becomes even more important. Looking for the results of the ANOVA, which tested the advanced theoretical model, it can be concluded that there are even more important factors (Table 11.2). The model has an adjusted R^2 of .354 so that in total 35% of the variance can be explained by the chosen variables. Most of the independent variables and covariates explain variance in a significant way, but church affiliation alone does not reach a significant level. But, as expected, the centrality is highly significant and has a partial eta^2 of .041, so that it would explain about 4% of the variance. Thus, people with a more central religiosity tend to attribute a similar importance to faith as they do to doing good, or even to rate faith as more important.

With regard to the covariates, they can be found to be significant, too. The 'Positive emotions towards God' scale explains the major part of the variance in the model, with a highly significant partial eta^2 of .092. The belief in a personal God is significant as well, but has the smallest partial eta^2 with .015. But the statistical significance of both covariates demonstrates the potential importance of religious issues in the question of faith and/or good works. Overall, most of the model hypotheses can be confirmed, except the one according the church affiliation.

But this factor had been the major point of interest. Does church affiliation indeed have no impact? Although church affiliation is not itself significant, as expected a significant interaction was found between

FAITH OR MORALITY?

Table 11.2: ANOVA Results

	F	p	partial eta^2
Independent variables			
Church affiliation	.91	.341	.001
Centrality of religiosity	14.90	<.001	.041
Interaction	6.54	.002	.018
Covariates			
Belief in personal God	10.40	.001	.015
Positive emotions towards God	71.05	<.001	.092

Dependent variable: doing good/trusting God

church affiliation and centrality. It has to be admitted that its partial eta^2 is only .018, so there is only a relative impact of the interaction between church affiliation and centrality. In studying the interaction, the two denominations and the three levels of religiosity's centrality have to be distinguished (cf. Table 11.3 and Figure 11.1). Interestingly, the interaction between centrality and church affiliation is stronger among Protestants: at the level of low centrality, they are more likely to rate doing good highly than are Catholics at the same centrality level. But the more central is a personal religious construct system, the more the respondents tend to regard faith as of similar importance or more important than good works. At the middle level of personal religious construct systems, a similar mean for Protestants and Catholics can be found. Both denominations are located near the middle rating, attributing an equal importance to both faith and good works. At the level of a central religious construct system, Catholics remain at the level of rating three, while Protestants reach a higher level, located right in the middle between rating of three and four. Thus, Protestants with a central religious construct system tend to evaluate faith more highly, as they were expected to do according to the assumption of a theological sediment corresponding with the traditional Lutheran doctrine.

Overall, therefore, individual differences in beliefs about justification seem to be explainable by a model combining centrality and religious content, and, to a lesser degree, the denomination as an additional contextual factor.

Table 11.3: Interaction between church affiliation and centrality of religiosity

Church affiliation	Centrality	N	Mean	SD
Roman Catholic	low	19	1.42	.77
	middle	170	2.76	1.06
	high	175	3.36	.87
Protestant (Lutheran)	low	18	1.06	.24
	middle	182	2.86	1.15
	high	142	3.87	.83
Total	low	37	1.24	.60
	middle	352	2.81	1.11
	high	317	3.59	.88

Dependent variable: doing good/trusting God

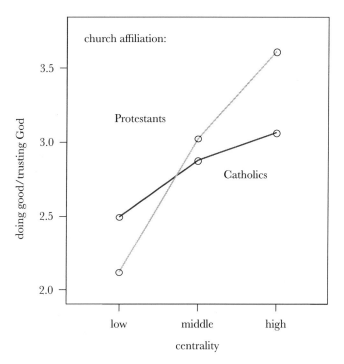

Figure 11.1: Interaction between church affiliation and centrality of religiosity

Discussion

All in all, belief in justification does not seem to be an exclusive denominational feature. Although there is a significant mean difference, the results of the ANOVA indicate that theological sediments like 'typical Catholic' or 'typical Protestant' beliefs can be found only to a low degree, and that they depend strongly on the centrality of one's religiosity. According to the ANOVA, the centrality of a personal religious construct system seems to play a key role. The more religious someone is, the more a sediment of the denominational doctrine seems to be present, and the more likely that person is to vote on the importance of faith and/or good works according to his or her denominational doctrine. Central religiosity seems to correspond with a clearer denominational identity.

The contents of specific religious feelings (such as positive emotions towards God) and beliefs (such as the belief in a personal God) seem to increase the tendency to upgrade faith. The more that somebody experiences positive emotions towards God, and the clearer his image of God as a personal partner, the stronger he seems to view trusting God as more important than doing good works. Lower religiosity has clearly been associated with the tendency to regard doing good as more important than trusting God. Therefore, in the sample investigated of many highly religious people the Kantian position of regarding morality as the main function of religiosity seems to be rare. A lower centrality of religiosity can be associated either with the unimportance of faith (and justification) or, if the impact of positive emotions towards God is taken into account, with an uncertainty about one's own faith and justification. Assurance of justification seems to be more likely in people with central religiosity; most of them seem to be 'securely' religious.

Although the interaction effect is much smaller than the effect of centrality or of the 'Positive emotions towards God' scale, it illustrates that the denominational tradition is of some importance. In the present study the denomination-caused sedimentation seems to be clearly limited and to depend strongly on the different levels of centrality; otherwise a single effect would have occurred. But this finding might be due to the operationalisation of denominational tradition by the single item concerning church affiliation.

It is important to be aware of several limitations of this study. First, consideration has to be given to the problems associated with the scales and items. Church affiliation (as independent variable) and belief in a personal God (as covariate) have only been assessed by single items, and consequently it has not been possible to generate a broader variance. For example, if characteristic denominational beliefs had been studied with a complete scale including several items instead of the single demographic item 'church affiliation', perhaps a single effect in the ANOVA would have been found here too. Second, there are clear limitations to the operationalisation of belief in justification. Asking what is more important, doing good or trusting God, is only rarely operationalised in the complex arguments over the classical denominational doctrines mentioned above. Therefore, consideration of the theological sediments of the doctrines of justification also remains partial. Third, it has to be recognised that there are problems concerning the sample. In particular, the analyses of the relevance of centrality are affected by the small number of participants of low centrality. This group only contained 37 individuals, while the groups with a middle level and a high level of centrality consisted of 352 and 317 individuals respectively. This arises from the fact that investigations were only made among church members and churchgoers. On the other hand, these specific samples have been necessary due to the study's goal to consider a greater number of highly religious respondents. Finally, the main reason for the limitations listed here is that the study was conducted *post hoc*, so that the theoretical assumptions had to be tested with already existing measurements and data. Taking these limitations into account, the study merely constitutes an initial step in the empirical analysis of distinct personal religious construct systems as a consequence of a sedimentation process in an ecclesiastical-historical perspective in this case by focusing on denominational differences in religious thinking. Yet, the results found even with this limited sample and operationalisation may possibly provide some impulse for future research.

Conclusion

As the mean difference between Catholics and Protestants and the interaction effect between religious affiliation and religiosity's centrality indicate, there is some evidence that traditional doctrines can still influence personal religious beliefs today. Although the belief in justification is probably not that important anymore, in the beliefs of persons with a central religiosity there really seem to be 'theological sediments' of traditional denominational doctrines. Recognising such sediments might

FAITH OR MORALITY? 265

help to understand the religious beliefs even of modern Christians, and therefore it seems worth considering them in future research.

The interaction between church affiliation and the centrality of personal religiosity provides evidence regarding the notion of a differentiation between contents and centrality, and therefore for the concept of the S-R-T. Thus the S-R-T seems to be a useful tool for comparative research in different religious traditions, and one that is also sensitive to developments in ecclesiastical history. According to the ANOVA result, the 'Centrality Scale' in particular has been helpful in detecting the impact of both the centrality of religiosity and, in the interaction effect, of the traditional doctrines. While Protestants seem to vote quite 'Catholic' on the level of a simple mean difference, distinguishing between the three levels of religiosity's centrality illustrates that Protestants also respond to the question of faith versus morality according to their denominational tradition—but only if their religiosity is on a high, central level. Further research might be done to confirm these results.

REFERENCES

Aurelius Augustinus (397/1970), *Ad Simplicianum de diuersis quaestionibus*, CChrSL, 44, 7–91.

Blood, M. (1969), Work values and job satisfaction, *Journal of Applied Psychology*, 53, 456–459.

Bogdahn, M. (1971), *Die Rechtfertigungslehre Luthers im Urteil der neueren katholischen Theologie*, Göttingen, Vandenhoeck and Ruprecht.

Buchholz, R. (1978), An empirical study of contemporary beliefs about work in American society, *Journal of Personality and Social Psychology*, 46, 1132–1141.

Claudy, T. (2005), *Die Gegenwart—das unentdeckte Land: systematisch-theologische Hermeneutik populärer Filmkultur*, Leipzig, Evangelische Verlagsanstalt.

Denzinger, H. (ed.) (1997), *Enchiridion Symbolorum Definitionum et Declarationum de Rebus Fidei et Morum/Kompendium der Glaubensbekenntnisse und kirchlichen Lehrentscheidungen, Griechisch/Lateinisch—Deutsch*, hrsg. von H. Denzinger [electronic resource], Freiburg/Berlin, Herder.

Dettloff, W. (1963), *Die Entwicklung der Akzeptations—und Verdienstlehre von Duns Scotus bis Luther: mit besonderer Berücksichtigung der Franziskanertheologen*, Münster, Aschendorff.

Drecoll, V.H. (1999), *Die Entstehung der Gnadenlehre Augustins*, Tübingen, Mohr Siebeck.

Ebeling, G. (1989), *Lutherstudien*. Bd. 2. *Disputatio de homine. Dritter Teil: die theologische Definition des Menschen. Kommentar zu These, 20–40*, Tübingen, Mohr.

Flew, A. (1969), *Hume's Philosophy of Belief*, London, Routledge, Kegan and Paul.

Gaskin, J.C.A. (1978), *Hume's Philosophy of Religion*, London, Palgrave Macmillan.

Goldstein, B. and Eichhorn, R. (1961), The changing Protestant ethic: rural patterns in health, work, and leisure, *American Sociological Review*, 26, 557–565.

Guttandin, F. (1998), *Einführung in die Protestantische Ethik Max Webers*, Opladen, Westdeutscher Verlag.

266 STEFAN HUBER & CONSTANTIN KLEIN

Hammond, P. and Williams, R. (1976), The Protestant ethic thesis: a social psychological assessment, *Social Forces*, 54, 579–589.

Herms, E. (1992), Gnade, in E. Herms (ed.), *Offenbarung und Glaube: zur Bildung des christlichen Lebens*, pp. 1–19, Tübingen, Mohr.

Ho, R. (1984), Development of an Australian work ethic scale, *Australian Psychologist*, 19, 321–332.

Huber, S. (1996), *Dimensionen der Religiosität*, Bern, Verlag Hans Huber.

——. (2003), *Zentralität und Inhalt: ein neues multidimensionales Messmodell der Religiosität*, Opladen, Leske and Budrich.

——. (2004), Zentralität und multidimensionale Struktur der Religiosität: eine Synthese der theoretischen Ansätze von Allport und Glock zur Messung der Religiosität, in C. Zwingmann and H. Moosbrugger (eds.), *Religiosität: Messverfahren und Studien zu Gesundheit und Lebensbewältigung: neue Beiträge zur Religionspsychologie*, pp. 79–105, Münster, Waxmann.

——. (2006), The structure-of-religiosity-test, in Research Institute for Spirituality and Health (ed.), *European Network of Research on Religion, Spirituality, and Health—Newsletter April 2006*, 1, 1–2 (http://www.rish.ch/pdf/Newsletter 2006-2.pdf).

——. (2007), Are religious beliefs relevant in daily life?, in H. Streib (ed.), *Religion Inside and Outside Traditional Institutions*, pp. 211–230, Leiden, Brill Academic Publishers.

——. (2008), Der Religiositäts-Strukur-Test (R-S-T): Kernkonzepte und Anwendungsperspektiven, *Prävention Zeitschrift für Gesundheitsförderung*, 31(2), 38–39.

——. (in press), Der Religiositäts-Strukur-Test (R-S-T): Systematik und operationale Konstrukte, in W. Gräb and L. Charbonnier (eds.), *Individualisierung und die pluralen Ausprägungsformen des Religiösen: Studien zu Religion und Kultur*, volume 1, Münster, Lit-Verlag.

Huber, S. and Richard, M. (in review), *The Inventory of Emotions towards God (EtG): validation and relation to centrality of religiosity.*

Hume, D. (1757/1993), *Dialogues Concerning Natural Religion and the Natural History of Religion*, Edited with an introduction by J.C.A. Gaskin, Oxford, Oxford University Press.

Jüngel, E. (2006), *Das Evangelium von der Rechtfertigung des Gottlosen als Zentrum des christlichen Glaubens: eine theologische Studie in ökumenischer Absicht*, Tübingen, Mohr Siebeck.

Kant, I. (1987), *Die Religion innerhalb der Grenzen der bloßen Vernunft*, hrsg. von Rudolf Malter, Stuttgart, Reclam.

——. (1793/2003), *Die Religion innerhalb der Grenzen der bloßen Vernunft: mit einer Einleitung und Anmerkungen*, hrsg. von Bettina Stangneth, Hamburg, Meiner.

Kirchenamt der Evangelischen Kirche in Deutschland (ed.) (2005), *Evangelische Kirche in Deutschland: Zahlen und Fakten zum kirchlichen Leben*, Hannover, Kirchenamt der Evangelischen Kirche in Deutschland.

Kühn, U. and Pesch, O.H. (1991), *Rechtfertigung im Disput. Eine freundliche Antwort an Jörg Baur auf seine Prüfung des Rechtfertigungskapitels in der Studie des ökumenischen Arbeitskreises evangelischer und katholischer Theologen: Lehrverurteilungen-Kirchentrennend?*, Tübingen, Mohr.

Leuener, H. (1969), *Hume und Kant: systematische Gegenüberstellung einiger Hauptpunkte ihrer Lehren*, Bern, Francke.

Lötzsch, F. (1976), *Vernunft und Religion im Denken Kants: Lutherisches Erbe bei Immanuel Kant*, Köln, Böhlau.

Luther, M. (1525/1908), De servo arbitrio, *WA*, 18, 600–787.

Lutherisches Kirchenamt der Velkd (ed.) (1999), *Die gemeinsame Erklärung zur Rechtfertigungslehre: alle offiziellen Dokumente von Lutherischem Weltbund und Vatikan*, Hannover, Lutherisches Kirchenamt der Velkd.

Lutherisches Kirchenamt der Velkd (ed.) (2000), *Unser Glaube. Die Bekenntnisschriften der Evangelisch-Lutherischen Kirche: im Auftrag der Kirchenleitung der Vereinigten Evangelisch-Lutherischen Kirche Deutschlands* (Velkd), hrsg. vom Lutherischen Kirchenamt, bearbeitet von Horst Georg Pöhlmann, Gütersloh, Gütersloher Verlagshaus.

FAITH OR MORALITY? 267

Maes, J. and Schmitt, M. (2001), *Protestantische-Ethik-Skala (PES). Messeigenschaften und Konstruktvalidität: Berichte aus der Arbeitsgruppe Verantwortung, Gerechtigkeit, Moral 146*, Trier, Universität Trier.

McGrath, A. (2005), *Iustitia Dei: a history of the Christian doctrine of justification*, Cambridge, Cambridge University Press.

Mirels, H.L. and Garrett, J.B. (1971), The Protestant ethic as a personality variable, *Journal of Consulting and Clinical Psychology*, 36, 40–44.

Müller, G. (1977), *Die Rechtfertigungslehre: Geschichte und Probleme*, Gütersloh, Gütersloher Verlagshaus Mohn.

Pesch, O.H. and Peters, A. (1994), *Einführung in die Lehre von Gnade und Rechtfertigung*, Darmstadt, Wissenschaftliche Buchgesellschaft.

Rahner, K. (1965), Einheit von Nächsten—und Gottesliebe, *Geist und Leben*, 38, 168–185.

Ray, J. (1982), The Protestant ethic in Australia, *Journal of Social Psychology*, 116, 127–138.

Rehm, J. and Wagner-Friedrich, J. (eds.) (2006), *Evangelische gibt's hier nicht: eine Spurensuche in und um Bamberg*, Memmelsdorf, Genniges Buch.

Sekretariat der Deutschen Bischofskonferenz (ed.) (2005), *Katholische Kirche in Deutschland. Statistische Daten 2003: Arbeitshilfen 193*, Bonn, Sekretariat der Deutschen Bischofskonferenz.

Seyfarth, C. and Sprondel, W.M. (eds.) (1973), *Seminar Religion und Gesellschaftliche Entwicklung: Studien zur Protestantismus-Kapitalismus-These Max Webers*, Frankfurt/M., Suhrkamp.

Stark, R. and Glock, C. (1968), *American Piety: the nature of religious commitment*, Berkeley, Los Angeles, University Press.

Terwey, M. (2003), Kirchen weiter auf der Verliererstraße: Inferno und Aberglauben im Aufwind, *ZA-Information*, 52, 93–119.

Thönissen, W. (2000), Dialog auf neuer Basis: was kommt nach der gemeinsamen Erklärung zur Rechtfertigungslehre? *Theologie und Glaube*, 90, 559–572.

Tyrell, H. (1990), Worum geht es in der Protestantischen Ethik? Ein Versuch zum besseren Verständnis Max Webers, *Saeculum*, 41, 130–177.

van der Ven, J.A. (1990), *Entwurf einer empirischen Theologie*, Weinheim, Deutscher Studien Verlag.

Wagner, H. (1975), Moralität und Religion bei Kant, *Zeitschrift für philosophische Forschung*, 29, 507–520.

Walsh, W.H. (1965), *Kant's Moral Theology*, London, Oxford University Press.

Weber, M. (1920/1988), *Gesammelte Aufsätze zur Religionssoziologie*, Bd. 1, Tübingen, Mohr.

——. (1987), *Die protestantische Ethik*, hrsg. von Johannes Winckelmann, Bd. 2. *Kritiken und Antikritiken*, Gütersloh, Gütersloher Verlagshaus Mohn.

——. (1996), *Die protestantische Ethik und der Geist des Kapitalismus. Textausgabe auf der Grundlage der ersten Fassung von 1904/05 mit einem Verzeichnis der wichtigsten Zusätze und Veränderungen aus der zweiten Fassung von 1920*, hrsg. und eingeleitet von K. Lichtblau und J. Weiss, Weinheim, Beltz.

Wolf, C. (2001), Empirische Befunde zum Prozess der religiösen Pluralisierung in der Bundesrepublik Deutschland, in M. Klöcker and U. Tworuschka (eds.), *Handbuch der Religionen: Kirchen und andere Glaubensgemeinschaften in Deutschland*, Bd. 5, Ergänzungslieferung, pp. 1–20, München, Olzog.

Wollack, S., Goodale, J., Wilting, J. and Smith, P. (1971), Development of the survey of work values, *Journal of Applied Psychology*, 55, 331–338.

Wood, A.W. (1970), *Kant's Moral Religion*, Ithaca, New York, Cornell University Press.

CHAPTER TWELVE

SOCIALISATION AND EMPIRICAL-THEOLOGICAL MODELS OF THE TRINITY: A STUDY AMONG THEOLOGY STUDENTS IN THE UNITED KINGDOM

Mark J. Cartledge

SUMMARY

The socialisation of Christian doctrine is an area of empirical-theological research that has received very little attention. Therefore this study begins to highlight this avenue of research by considering the impact of specific socialisation factors on certain Trinitarian beliefs. It investigates this relationship through an analysis of quantitative data collected from a sample of 244 theology students training at 11 residential theological institutions in the United Kingdom, representing Ecumenical, Evangelical, Pentecostal, and Adventist educational contexts. The aim of this chapter is to test the ways in which Trinitarian beliefs are transmitted via socialisation. The key research question can be stated thus: what is the influence of socialisation factors on empirical-theological models of the Trinity in the context of specific background variables? From a theoretical account of socialisation, which includes a discussion of the reference group, significant others, environment and media, and the individual, the impact of socialisation on the key models of the Trinity is tested. These Trinitarian models are: (1) orthodox-exclusivist; (2) pneumatic-social; (3) modalist; (4) subordinationist; and (5) transgender. The findings of this research are important and show that gender, educational qualifications, Christian age (how long a person has been a Christian) and educational contexts all influence Trinitarian beliefs (especially orthodox-exclusivism and modalism) via the specific socialisation factors of famous preachers, magazines, audio and video tapes, and personal bible study. It is hoped that this study shows the importance of such an enquiry and suggests possibilities for future research.

INTRODUCTION

Socialisation refers to the process whereby individuals become members of a particular social group and adopt certain roles and behaviour, in other words, become actors or agents in the various scenarios of life in particular cultures. It is a process that usually begins within a family context (referred to as primary socialisation) and continues throughout the life-span of individuals as they move through formal education and on into the world of work (referred to as secondary socialisation). Standard sociological textbooks will normally outline a number of theoretical perspectives, for example role theory, associated with the structural-functionalist tradition, symbolic interactionism and psychoanalytic theory (Fulcher and Scott, 2003). This chapter begins by offering a brief outline of these broad traditions before identifying key socialisation factors that are important to the enquiry.

Role theory stresses the requirements and obligations of roles as defined by different cultures, and socialisation is the process through which individuals learn how to enact them. This is achieved not only by external definition but by the internalisation of social expectations so that they are understood and embraced by the person. The degree of freedom that individuals have to adopt a role is debated within the literature. It is increasingly recognised that social roles are more akin to loose frameworks within which people can and do improvise through their actions (Fulcher and Scott, 2003). The importance of socialisation is that it enables an account to be given of the process whereby individuals within a given social and cultural context play certain accepted social roles and embody particular attitudes appropriate to those roles (Mayer, 1970). In role theory the goal of socialisation 'is to bring the individual to a proper regard for the limits of desirable and acceptable behaviour in various situations and relationships' (Danzinger, 1971: 22). Understandably we think of children being born within a family unit and being socialised through their upbringing into the beliefs, values and practices of the wider community. The family, school, university, and other institutions, such as the Church and voluntary organisations, provide contexts in which such socialisation occurs (White, 1977). The physical environment, the mass media, including literature and the internet, also contribute to the learning process. Indeed, it could be argued that any process whereby an individual transfers from one culture to another and becomes a member of that second cultural group necessarily involves some mechanism of socialisation. Therefore, social mobility and major social changes involve the re-socialisation of people of all ages and the transference from one social world to another is made increasingly possible and desirable (Berger, 1969).

Symbolic interactionism is associated with the work of George Herbert Mead (1964) and Erving Goffman (1963) and the social construction of meaning. Meaning, it is argued, is decided through communication and negotiation of different meanings both within and between social groups. Reflecting on how children develop their identities in their early years, Mead observed that individuals monitor their own actions as they develop a sense of their own self. It is through the process of socialisation, that is, through the interaction of the individual with others, that the self is constructed. And it is through the reflection on this interaction, and in particular the ability to assess the reaction of others, that the self develops. The most important people are the 'significant others', such as the parent, teacher or youth worker. In Mead's terms the 'I' is the social agent and the source of action, whereas the 'me' is the social self. This is "constructed through interactions with others and reflecting the attitudes that they adopt" (Fulcher and Scott, 2003: 135; Mead, 1964). By moving from significant others to 'the generalised other' children take on the attitudes of wider society, objectifying them as norms with moral authority and becoming socialised members of broader society (Van der Ven, 1998). Social interaction also includes props, for example the use of a white coat and a stethoscope worn around the neck by medics. The symbolic purpose of the props is to persuade the patients of the doctor's professional competence. Therefore, in social interaction there is a 'self-presentation' for others to observe and with which to cooperate (Goffman, 1963).

Psychoanalytic theory focuses on the emotional meanings as explained by the relationship of the conscious to the unconscious dimensions of the mind. The unconscious drives motivate people to act and their consciousness is dominated by their attempts to control these drives. Sigmund Freud understood that unconscious mental processes are rooted in biological drives, such as the desire for pleasure, and that human action is shaped by the struggle between unconscious emotional drives and conscious rational control. According to this theory, biological drives are repressed by the conscious mind and thus converted to socially acceptable behaviour. This can mean that certain drives, if ignored, can return to consciousness in distorted ways, for example slips of the tongue (Freudian slips) or via dreams or anxiety. This dynamic between the unconscious and the conscious can be understood as creative or destructive (Fulcher and Scott, 2003). Freud believed that as the child interacts with his or her family certain drives are satisfied. Through the experiences of satisfaction or frustration the child becomes aware of him/herself as an individual. Children develop a sense of anxiety concerning the reactions of others and guilt for behaviour that is met with disapproval. The handling of anxiety and guilt are regarded in this tradition as critical in socialisation and the development of the personality. Parental prohibitions imposed on children mean that they develop a sense of morality as boundaries define that which is permissible, and these understandings are internalised in terms of right and wrong (Fulcher and Scott, 2003).

Given this theoretical context, this chapter is interested in the ways in which beliefs and therefore meanings are transmitted. It is concerned with the process of socialisation as an explanation for the transmission of 'cognitive meaning' from one generation to the next, and from those on the inside to those on the outside, so that they can come into a society or group and a consensus of meaning can be maintained (Berger, 1969). Of course, the transmission of meaning occurs via the establishment and maintenance of a set of social relationships that enable shared attitudes and commonly understood roles to be owned by the individual (Furniss, 1995). Through this process of socialisation other people's beliefs become those of the individual, that is, they are internalised. As Berger states: "He [*sic*] draws them (meanings) into himself and makes them *his* meanings. He becomes not only one who possesses these meanings, but one who represents and expresses them" (Berger, 1969: 15). It is this representation and expression that is important in the retention of members within a particular culture or group. We are all familiar with the disillusioned person who fails to attend church regularly. Gradually she or he attends less frequently, stops meeting church friends, stops receiving the church newsletter and eventually disengages and may also cease all personal devotional practices if, that is, they were practised in the first place (McGuire, 2002). The loss of representation and expression occur throughout the process of disengagement. There are also people who live at the margins: they prefer the periphery to the centre because you can be less representational and less expressive at the periphery than the centre, but with a certain cost. By contrast, the marginal who are brought into the centre of power and influence are often seen to conform to the social expectations of the group with surprising speed.

The aim of this chapter is to consider an aspect of socialisation, the transmission of cognitive meaning, via an instrument measuring church socialisation in relation to five empirical-theological models of the doctrine of the Trinity that have been tested with a sample of theology students in the United Kingdom. The chapter will focus on the ways in which adults belonging to different church cultures and backgrounds are influenced by certain socialisation factors and thus adopt specific Trinitarian beliefs.

KEY FACTORS IN SOCIALISATION

Theoretically there are a number of key factors that influence the acquisition of new beliefs and values, and enable people to become new members of a different society or group and be retained by that group.

Reference group

A reference group is a key ingredient in the process of transformation (Furniss, 1995). It is the peer group or the community that offers support and encouragement in the new beliefs and values and demonstrates certain practices consonant with them. Peer groups are normally associated with adolescents as significant contributors to the formation of behaviour and values, but the reference group in a broader sense is vital to socialisation (White, 1977). This is because it mediates to newcomers a new culture of meaning and enables outsiders to be integrated into different social practices. It also reinforces behaviour and values and functions as a mechanism of retention. Therefore the impact of a reference group, however small, must not be underestimated in the acquisition of a new culture, beliefs and norms, and indeed in the maintenance of societal values. A reference group maintains shared meaning among its members but enables that shared meaning to be 'taken-for-granted' (McGuire, 2002: 37). In this sense it has been called the 'chorus' group that routinely affirms one's place in the general scheme of things (Berger and Luckmann, 1967). In many cases, it is also a group that is consciously chosen because within contemporary society there are so many reference groups with which to associate (Furniss, 1995). Arguably in the age of the internet and cyberspace there has been a loss of certain kinds of face-to-face reference groups and a replacement by 'virtual' reference groups.

Significant other

Like the notion of a reference group, the concept of a 'significant other' is often associated with the theory of 'plausibility structures', that is, "a set of social institutions and social networks whose functioning and day-to-day reality render belief plausible" (Aldridge, 2000: 82). In this discussion it is a useful idea and indeed it could be argued that 'plausibility' is an important dimension of socialisation (Berger, 1969). In this context, a significant other is a leader within a social group who reinforces a particular worldview and contributes to its maintenance as 'reality' (Furniss, 1995). Therefore there is always an important dialectic between the significant other and the reference group as they interact and confirm each other (Berger and Luckmann, 1967). The significant other may weld authority in an officially legitimated way and function in an office as priest or minister, or s/he may be someone who is gifted and to whom the group looks for guidance and assistance in the maintenance of the reference group's ethos and its social culture. Typically in churches, significant others are people with enormous influence in the shaping of corporate beliefs and values. They are also usually the gatekeepers and monitor the boundaries of the group and its culture. If there are members who do not conform to the social expectations then they can be treated in such a way that they feel constrained to conform. The other side of social integration, of course, is social discipline and sanctions if the social controls administered by the significant others as representatives of the institution involved in socialisation are breached (Richards, 1970). Socialisation and social control are inevitably correlated to a certain degree and the person who strays can be considered a fool, a knave or even mad (Berger, 1969). Interestingly, Frances Ward in her ethnographic account of an Anglican congregation describes how the members managed the influence of their priests by the mechanism of 'resistance' expressed through silence, gossip and illness (Ward, 2004).

Environment and media

In addition to people and the mediation of cultural values by interpersonal processes, there are cultural artefacts and literature that enable identity to be formed. Church buildings are significant symbols of Christian subcultures. A Norman cathedral says a number of things about God (God is transcendent, wholly other and remote—and perhaps absent), compared with a converted warehouse now used by a New Church and furnished with a stage, carpets and movable seats (God is immediate, utilitarian and perhaps a little cosy). Both are used for worship and tell very different stories regarding the kind of God that is worshipped. In the same way, the type of literature read, the music listened to and the language spoken can reinforce a particular understanding of God, the world and the purpose and meaning of life. How values are communicated via such means is an important factor in the overall understanding of the processes involved. Various media are the chief means by which the message of a particular group is explained and elaborated. This is why radio and television, cinema and newspapers, books and magazines are so important within the process (White, 1977). Their power and ubiquity are culturally sanctioned and religiously endorsed by different kinds of groups (Danziger, 1971).

Individual differences and personal commitments

It is easy to locate the processes of socialisation in the social structures and to forget the impact that individual differences and personal commitments make to the process. Individuals embrace a new culture with different degrees of commitment, and sometimes societal values can be embraced with so much commitment that the self becomes a tough task master with high expectations of success and conformity (White, 1977). It has been suggested that an overly socialised individual treats the limits of acceptable behaviour anxiously, thus stifling individuality and creativity and being overly dependent, while the under-socialised frequently oversteps conventional boundaries and makes unreasonable demands on others, thus exhibiting impolite or aggressive tendencies (Danziger, 1971). There is always going to be a delicate balance between the public and private worlds of individuals in this regard. George Herbert Mead's suggested dynamic between the social-taking self (Me) and the choice-making self (I) can be noted here (Mead, 1964; Furniss, 1995), although it has been argued elsewhere that *both* the 'I' and the 'Me' are socially conditioned, and not just the 'Me' (Van der Ven, 1998). There are public events in which people participate and there are more private rituals and habits that people embrace. It may be that the reference group upholds these practices and values as important, or it may be that there is a strong psychological attachment to certain items or practices, which enables greater commitment to be displayed by some rather than others. Indeed, each learner's experience is unique and therefore the individuality of socialisation must also be noted (White, 1977). Although self-identity is social and is developed through a continual interaction with others, the influences of the reference group, significant others and the media are never entirely deterministic because there is always the dimension of human agency

(McGuire, 2002). Thus the individual is a participant in a protracted conversation with the wider society and social group, and this must continue if the person's identity is to be maintained (Berger and Luckman, 1967; Berger, 1969). Van der Ven conceives of this interaction as pluralistic and consequently proposes the notion of a 'dialogical self' which embodies the voices of the various roles that the self plays on the stage of life (Van der Ven, 1998: 108).

Empirical-Theological Literature

In previous studies an instrument measuring socialisation has been employed in order to understand the process whereby Pentecostal or Charismatic Christians acquire glossolalia. The first study showed that the charismatic church context provides statistically significant support for the understanding of glossolalia in terms of particular theological symbols (beauty, awe, power, intimacy, faith-building, and vulnerability) (Cartledge 1999a; 2002). The second study developed material from a previously published qualitative study (Cartledge, 1999b), with additional quantitative data (Cartledge, 2003). In this further study, a number of socialisation factors (famous preachers, church leaders, friends, conferences, books, magazines, audio tapes, video tapes and personal bible study) were tested in relation to the frequency of speaking in tongues and the purposes of glossolalic speech as: prayer, prophecy, worship, or spiritual battle. The results showed that, with the exception of friends, all the factors are associated with the frequency of glossolalic speech. These factors are also associated with the purpose of glossolalia as prayer, prophecy, worship, and spiritual battle. In particular, the role of church leaders and personal bible study must be noted as the most significant socialising factors. These studies suggest that the theory of socialisation invites further work in relation to empirical research in theology. Therefore, the same instrument is employed in this study and reflected upon at the end of this chapter.

Models of the Trinity

This research project has attempted to test certain theological models of the doctrine of the Trinity. These models have been reported elsewhere (Cartledge, 2006), and research from that study will be used to complement and inform this discussion. Since the focus of this enquiry is the socialisation process, these empirical-theological models are merely summarised briefly.

The doctrine of the Trinity seeks to give an account of the doctrine of God in the light of New Testament Christology and pneumatology as interpreted by the early Church Fathers. How can the one God of Israel be conceived as three persons, Father, Son and Holy Spirit? It is a key doctrine and one that has witnessed revived interest by theologians in recent years. Discussions of the doctrine often emphasise either the one-ness of God, as in the Augustinian tradition, or the three-ness of the persons, as in the Cappadocian tradition. Therefore all of the models are based on this basic tension between notions of unity or plurality (Brown, 1984). *Modalism* gives priority to the unity of God at the expense of the plurality as the same God acts chronologically through different *persona* or masks. Today functional modalism is popular, as God is conceived as creator, saviour and sustainer (Thompson, 1994). *Subordinationism* and a *Social* doctrine of the Trinity give priority to plurality but in different ways. Subordinationism suggests that there is some form of hierarchy in the Godhead, either ontologically representing an inequality of essence, or functionally in terms of the economy of salvation. A Social doctrine emphasises the equality and reciprocity of the persons of the Godhead, understanding unity to be established via *perichoresis* (mutual indwelling) rather than a common substance (Cartledge, 2004). It stresses the dynamic interaction between the three persons of the Trinity.

In order to engage with the most recent scholarship, items have been added to measure the feminist critique regarding traditional Trinitarian language. This aspect also features as a theological model, namely transgender (Cartledge, 2006).

METHOD

Sampling and data collection

The survey aimed to sample theology students from institutions training people for lay and ordained Christian ministry in the United Kingdom. Initially it started with a survey of Anglican institutions and was expanded to include all United Kingdom institutions training people for Christian ministry. This was conducted over the years 2003 to 2005. Intentionally it focused on students who had some understanding of the doctrine of the Trinity at undergraduate level two. Therefore undergraduate level two (or 'Intermediate') and level three (or 'Honours') students form part of the sample. The overall sampling frame was constructed from the *UK Christian Handbook* (Brierley and Wraight, 1995) that lists all theological education institutions. However, the number of institutions used was modified by the application of two criteria. Only those institutions were approached that were able to provide theological education: first at undergraduate level two (that is, normally, second year undergraduate level in the United Kingdom); and, second, in a residential setting. These criteria were applied because of the nature of the study, since the doctrine of the Trinity requires some understanding of theology before the questionnaire could be understood. They were also applied because of the need to obtain a useful response rate. It is easier to administer a questionnaire to a class of students in a single place and time than to distribute it to part-time and distance students.

From the 43 institutions that were approached, 11 replied positively and supported the research by administering the questionnaire: 244 usable questionnaires were obtained from this sample. It is estimated that there are approximately 1500 theology students in residential training for Christian ministry at undergraduate level in the United Kingdom in any given year. Therefore this sample represents 16.2% of that population. If the level one (or 'Certificate') students—amounting to a third of that population—are removed, then in terms of level 2/3 students this sample amounts to 24.4% of the remaining population.

The participating institutions represent four main theological contexts in which education for Christian ministry takes place: Ecumenical, Evangelical, Pentecostal and Adventist. Three institutions representing the Ecumenical context (training for ministry in the Church of England, Methodist, Roman Catholic and United Reformed Church) provided responses from 60 students. Four institutions representing the Evangelical context provided responses from 81 students. Two Pentecostal institutions provided responses from 68 students. One Adventist institution provided responses from 35 students. This study is therefore uniquely able to compare the different educational contexts and traditions, as well as the implications for such contexts in the training of people for Christian ministry.

Participants

In this sample 60.2% are men and 39.8% are women. It is a young sample with the majority (92.2%) of the students aged under 50 years: 25.8% are under 25 years, 33.2% are between 25 and 39 years, and a further 18.9% are between 40 and 49 years. Of these students, 53.7% are single, 41.4% married and 3.7% divorced. The majority have educational qualifications greater than GCSE, with 22.5% obtaining Advanced levels, 14.3% diplomas in Higher Education or equivalent, 36.1% with degrees in Higher Education, 9.8% with Masters and 1.2% with Doctoral level qualifications. Therefore, although the *theological* level of engagement is at level two or three, many of the students bring with them significant educational skills from other institutions and contexts.

The students identified themselves as having been Christians over a number of years: 7.4% for less than 5 years, 12.3% between 5 and 9 years, 20.1% between 10 and 14 years, 15.6% between 15 and 19 years, 19.3% between 20 and 24 years, 7.8% between 25 and 29 years, and 6.6% between 30 and 34 years.

Measures

As noted above, the instrument has been tested in a previous study and proved to be a reliable scale (Cronbach alpha of .81 for a nine-item measure, Cartledge, 2002). It was used in this study because of its previous reliability.

In the context of church socialisation the significance of the 'reference group' is measured by the items 'friends' and 'conferences'. The 'significant other' is measured by the items 'famous preachers' and 'church leaders'. These items cover local, national and international influences on Christians. The 'environment and media' are measured by the items 'books', 'magazines', 'audio tapes' and 'video tapes', and 'personal bible study'. Individual differences and personal commitments permeate all of these other areas as the person interacts with the reference group, significant others and the environment and media. They cannot be measured directly but must be understood as embedded in what is seen through these other areas, but especially in terms of 'personal bible study'.

The instrument asked the question: How much have the following helped you to understand the nature of God? Please circle the

280 MARK J. CARTLEDGE

Table 12.1: The socialisation scale: item rest of test correlations

	r
Famous preachers	.47
Church leaders	.39
Friends	.30
Conferences	.42
Books	.44
Magazines	.50
Audio tapes	.55
Video tapes	.50
Personal bible study	.37
Alpha	.76

appropriate number and answer for all the items. Each item was followed by the options: 'very little 1 2 3 4 5 very much'. The items were: famous preachers, church leaders, friends, conferences, books, magazines, audio tapes, video tapes and personal bible study [PBS].

The Cronbach alpha coefficient of .76 reinforces the reliability of the measure as established in the earlier study (see Table 12.1 for details of the item rest of test correlations). However, this study is interested in the influence of the individual items rather than the scale as a single measure.

Principal components analysis was used primarily to identify latent factors that could function as theological scales for the models of the Trinity. Each of the factors identified by the analysis was subsequently refined in terms of their reliability as scales of measurement (DeVellis, 1991). Some of the items contained in the factor analysis were omitted in order to obtain the highest reliability score according the Cronbach alpha coefficient. Only measures that were able to generate alpha coefficients of .70 or greater were retained for further analysis (Cartledge, 2006). The following Trinitarian scales were retained: orthodox-exclusivist (O-E), which refers to traditional and orthodox theology combined with an exclusivist Christology (12-item measure, alpha = .73); pneumatic-social (P-S), which combines a pneumatological accent with a social doctrine of the Trinity (nine-item measure, alpha = .70); modalist (M, three-item measure, alpha = .80); subordinationist (S, three-item measure, alpha = .83); and transgender (TG), which expresses gender interchange relating to God-language (two-item measure, alpha = .74) (Cartledge, 2006: 158–160).

Research questions

There are four main research questions arising from the discussion and which guide the exploration of the data. First, are men and women socialised differently in relation to Trinitarian beliefs? If so, what are the socialisation factors that influence men and women? Second, what background variables are associated with the socialisation of Trinitarian beliefs? What are the most significant socialisation factors? Third, are students from the various educational contexts socialised differently in relation to Trinitarian beliefs? If so, what are the most significant socialisation factors? Fourth, how are the models of the Trinity socialised in relation to each other? What are the most significant factors in the socialisation of the different theological models?

RESULTS

Identifying the context of socialisation factors

Table 12.2 shows that there is a statistically significant difference between men and women in relation to the socialisation factors of famous preachers, friends and conferences. Men regard famous preachers as more influential than do women, and women regard friends and conferences as more influential than do men. For the rest of the socialisation factors there is no statistically significant difference between the two groups.

Table 12.3 shows that there are a number of statistically significant correlations between socialisation factors and the background variables of age, educational qualifications and Christian age. There are negative correlations between age and church leaders, friends, conferences and video tapes. Therefore, the younger the person, the greater the association with these items. There are also negative correlations between Christian age and friends, conferences, audio tapes and video tapes. This suggests that these socialisation factors are stronger for younger Christians than for older ones. Finally, there are negative correlations between educational qualifications and church leaders, friends, conferences, magazines, audio and video tapes and personal bible study. Therefore the less educated the person is the more influence these factors have, especially magazines and video tapes.

282 MARK J. CARTLEDGE

Table 12.2: T-test: comparison of men and women for socialisation factors

	Men			Women				
	N	M	SD	N	M	SD	t	p<
Preachers	147	3.18	1.3	96	2.59	1.3	3.45	.001
Friends	146	3.71	1.0	95	4.05	1.1	−2.48	.05
Conferences	147	2.76	1.2	94	3.16	1.3	−2.49	.05

Table 12.3: Correlations of background variables and socialisation factors

	Age	Educational Qualifications	Christian Age
Preachers	−.010	−.101	.028
Leaders	−.157*	−.149*	−.086
Friends	−.142*	−.158*	−.156*
Conferences	−.154*	−.165*	−.140*
Books	−.076	−.128	−.045
Magazines	−.058	−.176**	−.065
Audio tapes	−.058	−.145*	−.135*
Video tapes	−.156*	−.279**	−.218**
PBS	−.090	−.162*	−.120

Note * = p< .05; ** = p< .01.

Table 12.4 shows that there is a statistically significant difference between the educational contexts of the students and the socialisation factors. The association with famous preachers is generally positive, but especially so for Pentecostal and less so for the Ecumenical contexts. The association with church leaders is positive but again more so for the Pentecostal but less so for the Adventist context. The association with conferences is positive and again this is more for Pentecostal than for Adventist and Evangelical contexts. The association with magazines is quite weak and this is especially so for the Ecumenical context, the strongest influence being found in the Adventist context. The association with audio tapes is neither strong nor weak, but the Pentecostal context is more strongly influenced by this factor compared with the Ecumenical context. The association with video tapes is quite weak, especially for the Ecumenical and Evangelical contexts, with the Adventists showing the strongest preference. The association with personal bible study is generally very strong and is the strongest of all the factors explored, with the strongest association in the Adventist and Pentecostal contexts.

SOCIALISATION AND EMPIRICAL-THEOLOGICAL MODELS 283

Table 12.4: One-way ANOVA: educational context by socialisation factors

	Ecumenical		Pentecostal		Evangelical		Adventist		F	p<
	M	SD	M	SD	M	SD	M	SD		
Preachers	2.5	1.2	3.4	1.2	2.9	1.4	3.2	1.4	5.08	.01
Leaders	3.4	1.1	4.0	1.0	3.5	1.2	2.8	1.3	7.66	.001
Conferences	2.6	1.3	3.4	1.1	3.0	1.2	2.4	1.1	8.09	.001
Magazines	1.8	1.0	2.2	1.2	2.0	1.1	2.5	1.2	3.26	.05
Audio tapes	2.0	1.2	2.9	1.3	2.4	1.2	2.7	1.4	6.30	.001
Video tapes	1.8	1.1	2.5	1.3	1.8	1.0	2.8	1.3	8.86	.001
PBS	4.2	1.0	4.6	0.8	4.3	0.8	4.7	0.6	3.95	.001

Socialisation factors and empirical-theological models of the Trinity

Table 12.5 shows the statistically significant associations between the socialisation factors and empirical-theological models of the Trinity. Famous preachers, audio tapes and personal bible study are most positively associated with the Orthodox-exclusivist model. Famous preachers, magazines, audio tapes and personal bible study are most positively associated with the pneumatic-social model. The factor of audio tapes is most positively associated with the subordinationist model. Famous preachers, magazines, audio and video tapes are most positively associated with the modalist model. All of these associations suggest that the greater the influence of these factors the greater the preference for these models. However, the factor of audio tapes is negatively associated with the transgender model, thus suggesting that the weaker the influence of this factor the greater the preference for this model.

DISCUSSION

There are a number of important findings from this investigation that have been guided by the research questions.

First, it is clear that there are statistically significant differences between men and women in relation to three of the socialisation factors: famous preachers, friends and conferences. For men, the category of the significant other is more important and especially in relation to preaching. Therefore the role of the preacher is more influential in the acquisition of Trinitarian beliefs for men than women. This particular form of significant other renders beliefs more plausible for men than for women. Women are more influenced by friends and conferences than

284   MARK J. CARTLEDGE

Table 12.5: Correlations of socialisation factors and Trinity model

	O-E	P-S	S	M	TG
Preachers	.222**	.188**	.045	.144*	−.117
Leaders	.096	.026	.084	−.006	−.116
Friends	.083	.010	−.026	−.002	.013
Conferences	.082	−.009	.061	.122	−.037
Books	.117	.118	−.011	−.072	.058
Magazines	.061	.138*	−.068	.182**	−.041
Audio tapes	.205**	.227**	.205**	.155**	−.160*
Video tapes	.036	.057	−.047	.270**	−.010
PBS	.178**	.156*	.023	.029	−.065

Note * = p< .05; ** = p< .01. O-E = Orthodox-exclusivist model; P-S = Pneumatic-social model; S = Subordinationist model; M = Modalist model; TG = Transgender model.

men, thus indicating that the impact of the reference group is more important for them. From the earlier complementary study (Cartledge, 2006), the data suggest that men prefer subordinationism compared with women, and that this theological attitude is mediated via famous preachers. Women are different, preferring the transgender model, which is mediated via friends and conferences. Thus Trinitarian beliefs and meanings are mediated more strongly via peers for women than they are for men. This finding would appear to be significant because it highlights the possible differences between men and women in relation to how authority is mediated (hierarchically or socially) and how beliefs are transmitted (pulpit or pew). This may reflect the gender bias of famous preachers, but in an era of women ministers and priests that cannot be assumed. In any case, this finding has important implications for Christian educational practice.

Second, the background variables of chronological age, educational qualifications and Christian age (how long a person has been a Christian) are significantly associated with the socialisation factors. The variable of chronological age is negatively correlated with church leaders, friends, conferences and video tapes. This suggests that the three factors of the reference group, significant other and media are important here. The younger the persons are the greater the influence these factors are seen to exercise. This finding coheres with what we know about the role of peer groups for adolescents and young adults, and reinforces that understanding. To some extent Christian age mirrors age in general. The younger people are in Christian terms, the greater is the influence of peers (friends and conferences) and the electronic media (audio and video tapes). Therefore, even though a person may be in mid-life, if that person is young in Christian years s/he draws on the same support factors (peers and electronic media) as younger people do. The only difference is that younger people in general are more reliant on a significant other (church leader) than older people, which reflects the difference in personal maturity. Educational qualification is negatively correlated with peer groups (friends and conferences), significant others (church leader) and media resources (magazines, audio and video tapes and personal bible study). The greater the educational attainment, then the less the person associates with these factors. This suggests that more educated people are more independent in their thinking and less reliant on these factors. Interestingly, though, books are not statistically associated with educational attainment, suggesting that theology books do not necessarily fill the socialisation gap, even for theology students. Earlier research discovered that the only Trinitarian model to be associated with the variable of educational qualification was the transgender model (Cartledge, 2006). That association was negative, indicating that both the least socialised and the least educated prefer this model, and this is especially the case for women. Perhaps this is an indication of how certain individuals are alienated from church culture and language and, thus, for them the transgender model represents a discourse of resistance.

Third, the educational context is statistically significant in relation to all except two of the socialisation factors (friends and books). Significant others are generally regarded positively for all of the groups, but especially for Pentecostals (famous preachers and church leaders). With the absence of the factor of friends, the reference group is represented by the conference item and again this is most significant for Pentecostals. In relation to electronic media, the Pentecostals (audio tapes) and Adventists (video tapes) display the greatest affinity, although these are relatively weak. The influence of literature is observed in relation to the Adventists (magazines, although the influence is quite weak) and by Adventists and Pentecostals (with regard to personal bible study, which is strong across the groups). It appears that the educational contexts appear to socialise most strongly for the Pentecostals and the Adventists. However, when you look at these factors for the Adventists, it is clear that they have the lowest association with church leaders and conferences and the highest associations with magazines, audio and video tapes and personal bible study. This suggests that socialisation is most reliant on famous preachers, denominational material and personal piety, perhaps mediated through the educational context. In general terms for all of the groups, the factors most associated are church leaders and personal bible study, suggesting that the role models of significant others (preachers/leaders = teachers) and personal spirituality (personal bible study) drive the socialisation across the different contexts. The Ecumenical context is by far the least strongly socialised and displays weak socialisation in relation to significant others (famous preachers), the reference group (conference) and electronic media (audio and video tapes). It also displays the lowest score in relation to literature (magazines and personal bible study). What is surprising is that the Evangelical educational contexts do not appear to socialise strongly in all the ways one would expect. Famous preachers, church leaders and personal bible study show approximately average scores in the sample, which is a surprising finding and suggests that further research is required to begin to explain these differences. In terms of the Trinity models, the complementary study showed that the orthodox-exclusivist model is socialised strongly across the different educational contexts, especially for Pentecostals (via preachers, leaders and conferences). The modalist model is also strongly socialised and is most noticeable for the Adventists (via preachers, media and personal bible study). Subordinationism is most strongly socialised again for the Pentecostals (again via preachers, leaders and conferences), while the transgender model, although socialised weakly, is most prevalent within the Ecumenical context (Cartledge, 2006).

Fourth, it is clear from the associations of the socialisation factors with empirical-models of the Trinity that the reference group plays no apparent role in the socialisation of Trinitarian beliefs. This is not a surprise since most people would not be confident in interpreting this doctrine to their peers. The most important factors are significant others (famous preachers) and media—especially magazines and audio tapes, although video tapes is significant (once) and personal bible study (twice). The single most influential factor is audio tapes, suggesting that either sermons or teaching material is circulated most successfully via this medium. The orthodox-exclusivist model is socialised most strongly via famous preachers, audio tapes and personal bible study. The pneumatic-social model is socialised most strongly via famous preachers, magazines, audio tapes and personal bible study. Subordinationism is only socialised via audio tapes. Modalism is socialised most strongly via famous preachers, magazines, audio and video tapes, but (interestingly) not personal bible study. The transgender model is negatively

SOCIALISATION AND EMPIRICAL-THEOLOGICAL MODELS   287

correlated with audio tapes, suggesting that this model clashes with all other models as they are mediated through this means. These findings indicate the importance of preaching, the role of popular media such as magazines and audio tapes in particular, and the way personal bible study supports certain models. The fact that modalism is the most socialised model through popular level media is unsurprising since it can be considered the dominant popular understanding of the doctrine today (Latham, 2002; Shuster, 2002).

Conclusion

This chapter has explored the role of socialisation in the acquisition of Trinitarian beliefs as measured by means of five empirical-theological models. Theoretically, it has done this with respect to the key socialisation factors of the reference group, the significant other(s), environment and media. Empirically, the use of a reliable measure of socialisation by means of its component items enabled this exploration to take place. In its current form it is able to be used to paint a picture of how theology students from four different types of educational contexts are socialised in their Trinitarian beliefs as part of the web of meanings that constitute their beliefs and values.

A number of conclusions can be drawn from this study. First, men are most strongly socialised via a particular kind of significant other, the famous preacher, which in turn is associated with orthodox-exclusivist, pneumatic-social and modalist models of the Trinity. Second, younger students are most strongly socialised via the reference group, the significant other of church leader and video tapes, which in terms of models of the Trinity means that modalism is the only mediated model transmitted via video tapes for this group. Third, younger Christians are similar to young people but have all the models mediated to them via audio tapes, with the exception of the transgender model. Fourth, the greater the educational qualifications, the less likelihood there is of socialisation in relation to the reference group, the significant other of church leader, or literary and electronic media. This means that for the less well educated there is a greater likelihood of socialisation via these means in relation to all the models of the Trinity, with the exception of the transgender model. Fifth, the Pentecostal context is the most strongly socialised context, especially in relation to famous preachers, church leaders and conferences and via these factors to orthodox-exclusivist,

288   MARK J. CARTLEDGE

pneumatic-social and modalist models of the Trinity. This would be especially the case for Pentecostal men and the influence of famous preachers. Sixth, the most strongly socialised model of the Trinity in general is modalism. Clearly these findings are preliminary and further research is necessary to test the nature of socialisation in relation to key Christian doctrines, including the doctrine of the Trinity.

METHODOLOGICAL REFLECTION

A reflection on the use of this quantitative instrument for measuring socialisation is offered here as a means of critically evaluating the tool that has been used in this research project.

It is important to set this instrument within its original context. The instrument was designed approximately ten years ago as part of a congregational survey and emerged from an interaction between the literature on the socialisation of glossolalia (the focus of study) and my own inductive case studies of two churches (Cartledge, 1999a; 2002). It is obviously limited by being shaped by the social science literature on how glossolalia is acquired and by the specifics of two case studies. It now feels slightly dated even though it is still useful and reliable. From its use within this present study a number of changes can be suggested to improve the instrument for wider use within congregational surveys.

First, the influence of the reference group could be nuanced by suggesting a number of other categories that clarify the nature and influence of sub-groups within the congregational setting. For example these could be: youth, house, study, men's and women's groups. Also, large networking influences could also be identified, for example holiday camps or seasonal conventions (such as Spring Harvest and New Wine in the United Kingdom).

Second, the influence of the factor 'significant others' is also limited and could be improved by a wider selection of possibilities, for example by specifying: clergy, lay leaders, youth workers, school teachers, worship leaders, musicians, spiritual directors and prayer partners. Defining preachers in terms of 'famous' preachers is probably too restrictive and therefore should be simply 'preachers'. The category of 'church leader' is too vague and some of the above categories should provide greater precision.

Third, the items relating to the media are now dated with the advent of CDs and DVDs. I would therefore suggest adding these items to the existing list, along with the internet, Christian TV channels, TV generally and radio. I would also add a specific item, 'sermon tapes', because of the influence of recorded sermons within some congregations and the importance of preaching generally. There is nothing in the existing instrument relating to the physical environment: this should be remedied by the inclusion of at least one item concerned with the building or location of worship, musical and liturgical traditions.

Fourth, the personal agency of the individual is not measured in the current instrument, except perhaps via 'personal bible study'. This needs to be measured more explicitly through items such as: 'personal choices' and 'individual decisions'. In this way we can at least identify the self-perception of personal agency, which can be set within a broader theoretical and empirical socialisation framework.

It is hoped that this study and further projects developing instruments of measurement can usefully contribute to the advancement of socialisation research within empirical theology.

References

Aldridge, A. (2000), *Religion in the Contemporary World: a sociological introduction*, Cambridge, Polity.
Berger, P. (1969), *The Social Reality of Religion*, London, Faber and Faber.
Berger, P. and Luckmann, T. (1967), *The Social Construction of Reality: a treatise in the sociology of knowledge*, London, Penguin.
Brierley, P. and Wraight, H. (eds.) (1995), *United Kingdom Christian Handbook*, London, Christian Research.
Brown, D. (1984), *The Divine Trinity*, London, Duckworth.
Cartledge, M.J. (1999a), *Tongues of the Spirit: an empirical-theological study of charismatic glossolalia*, PhD dissertation, University of Wales.
———. (1999b), The socialisation of glossolalia, in L.J. Francis (ed.), *Sociology, Theology and the Curriculum*, pp. 125–134, London, Cassell.
———. (2002), *Charismatic Glossolalia: an empirical-theological study*, Aldershot, Ashgate.
———. (2003), *Practical Theology: charismatic and empirical perspectives*, Carlisle, Paternoster.
———. (2004), Trinitarian theology and spirituality: an empirical study of charismatic Christians, *Journal of Empirical Theology*, 17(1), 76–84.
———. (2006), Empirical-theological models of the Trinity: exploring the beliefs of theology students in the United Kingdom, *Journal of Empirical Theology* 19(2), 137–162.
Danziger, K. (1971), *Socialization*, Harmondsworth, Penguin.
DeVellis, R.F. (1991), *Scale development: theory and applications*, London, Sage.
Fulcher, J. and Scott, J. (2003), *Sociology* (second edition), Oxford, Oxford University Press.
Furniss, G. (1995), *Sociology for Pastoral Care: an introduction for students and pastors*, London, SPCK.
Goffman, E. (1963), *Behaviour in Public Places: notes on the social organization of gatherings*, London, Collier Macmillan.

Latham, R. (2002), The Trinity—yesterday, today and the future, *Themelios*, 28(1), 26–35.

Mayer, P. (ed.) (1970), *Socialization: the approach from social anthropology*, London, Tavistock.

McGuire, M.B. (2002), *Religion: the social context* (fifth edition), Belmont, California, Wadsworth Thomson.

Mead, G.H. (1964), *On Social Psychology: selected papers*, edited and with an introduction by Anselm Strauss, Chicago, Illinois, University of Chicago Press.

Richards, A.I. (1970), Socialization and contemporary British anthropology, in P. Mayer (ed.), *Socialization: the approach from social anthropology*, pp. 1–32, London, Tavistock.

Shuster, M. (2002), Preaching the Trinity: a preliminary investigation, in S.T. Davis, D. Kendal and G. O'Collins (eds.), *The Trinity: an interdisciplinary symposium on the Trinity*, pp. 357–381, Oxford, Oxford University Press.

Thompson, J. (1994), *Modern Trinitarian Perspectives*, Oxford, Oxford University Press.

Van der Ven, J.A. (1998), *Formation of the Moral Self*, Grand Rapids, Michigan, Eerdmans.

Ward, F. (2004), The messiness of studying congregations using ethnographic methods, in M. Guest, K. Tusting and L. Woodhead (eds.), *Congregational Studies in the UK*, pp. 125–137, Aldershot, Ashgate.

White, G. (1977), *Socialisation*, London, Longman.

CHAPTER THIRTEEN

RELIGIOUS SOCIALISATION IN THE FAMILY: A MULTI-DIMENSIONAL AND MULTI-LEVEL PERSPECTIVE

Sabine Zehnder Grob, Christoph Morgenthaler and
Christoph Käppler

SUMMARY

Understanding processes of religious socialisation in the family is a long-standing interest in empirical research on religion. In this chapter, we expand upon previous investigations on parents' influence on children's religiosity by considering families' self-organisation on different systemic levels and its impact on children's religiosity. Four types of family influence on the centrality and different dimensions of religion for children are examined (individual influence by mother and father, influences of parents' religious agreement, religious family climate and transgenerational transmission of religion). The data set is based on a Swiss survey of 393 families of which both parents and one child (average age 11.9 years) completed a paper and pencil questionnaire. Results show substantial effects of all the family variables on children's religiosity, both on the centrality of religion and on its different dimensions (intellect, ideology, devotion, experience, ritual). The individual influence of mother and father seems of paramount importance, but the actual and perceived spousal agreement concerning religion, the religious family climate and influences from the mothers' and fathers' families of origin also show a significant effect on children's religiosity. The theoretical implications of these effects are discussed, both as they contribute to research on religious socialisation and empirical research in theology.

INTRODUCTION

Families are significant contexts for religious development and the transmission of religion from generation to generation, even in comparison with the impact of peer-group, school, Church, radio and television (de Hart, 1990; Grom, 2000). Religion is transmitted, developed and stabilised, but also filtered, questioned, or ignored in the context of the family. Parents are of paramount importance in this family processing of religion. There is a long research tradition—especially in Great Britain and the USA—of stressing the parents' influence on children's religious attitudes and practices (cf. Beit-Hallahmi and Argyle, 1997: 99; Hood, Spilka, Hunsberger and Gorsuch, 1996: 74). Interestingly enough, one rarely encounters studies that analyse the impact of families as separate social systems on religious socialisation, treating more than the one-to-one relationship of parent and child. In the introduction to their book *The Psychology of Religion*, Hood, Spilka, Hunsberger and Gorsuch (1996) revealingly concede that the family of origin and the extended family are potentially very important in affecting one's socialisation and functioning in a number of systems, including (but not limited to) religion. They continue, however, "Although we recognise that parental influence may take place within the broader context of the family or a small community, we focus here specifically on parental influence" (75). In our own study, we also focused on parents and their influence on children. In addition, we hypothesised that this influence interacts with the families' religious self-organisation on higher systemic levels. In order to understand the influence of parents on children's religiosity, this influence should be integrated within the broader framework of religious family dynamics.

A serious research gap prompted this study as well. Sociological research which maps out the religious landscape of Switzerland is well-established (Dubach and Campiche, 1993; Campiche, 2004; Dubach and Fuchs, 2005). Strangely enough, the same is not true for psychological research on religion, in particular on religious socialisation in families. This is virtually non-existent. This paucity of psychological research on religion holds true for all German-speaking countries and has its own historical background. It would, therefore, be very interesting and significant to discover answers to the following questions: How do the social contexts of pluralisation and de-standardisation of religion, diagnosed by sociologists of religion, influence the processing of religion in Swiss families? Are religious convictions and practices still transmitted from one generation to the next in Switzerland today? Or, by contrast, are Swiss families increasingly abandoning their role as transmitters of established religious institutions and predominant religious traditions? Are families becoming religious 'factories' of their own for the assemblage of different religious bits and pieces and the forging of a meaningful life, which has been a basic tenet of German sociological research since the 1970s (Vascovics, 1970; Wössner, 1968; Ebertz, 1988)?

Levels of Family Religion and Religious Socialisation

We assume that religious convictions and practices can be important for families and family socialisation on several levels of family organisation. The following four-level model of the processing of religion in family was developed.

Individual religion

At this level, we focus on the individual religious construct systems of the parents (and also the children's constructs as dependent variables). Parents bring these individual religious constructs into their marital relationship. These construct-systems were forged by many processes, among them the parents' religious socialisation in their own families of origin, thereafter appropriated and developed through the life cycle. As we can gather from many surveys, these individual attitudes brought into marriage differ more and more between the spouses. Individualisation and pluralisation of religion in our society penetrate families as well. It is important, therefore, to scrutinise closely the individual religiosity of the spouses if we want to understand religious socialisation in the family context. Drawing on a notion of individual religiosity that takes into account both the content and the centrality of religious concepts in the individual's belief system (Huber, 2003, 2004), we developed the following assumptions concerning the motivational impact of religion on parents. The centrality of religious constructs—its more or less central position in the parents' system of personal constructs—determines its efficacy, that is the extent to which religion influences daily matters, making religion a motivational factor of its own. An important facet of a parent's daily life is the education of children. Therefore high centrality of religious concepts would result in a higher and more consistent pattern of religious socialisation from the maternal and/or paternal side. Consequently a first hypothesis can be derived.

> *Hypothesis 1:* Children's religious attitudes and practices are influenced by the centrality of religious constructs for each parent.

Focusing on that level of influence means taking seriously the pluralisation of religious convictions in today's Swiss families. Focusing on that level alone, however, would also mirror an overemphasised individualistic stance with regard to religion in families. We would thus ignore the trivial fact of the parents influencing each other in this process of religious socialisation. Parents have to find a way of cooperating in religious education as in other areas of common life. If their individual religious convictions differ too much, they can inhibit each other in significant ways in the transmission of religious attitudes and practices to their children. Moreover, children are much more than dependent creatures to be moulded by parents. They increasingly become partners in the interactive self-organisation of families, contributing a great deal to family dynamics as well as to the systemic religious self-organisation of families. We have therefore included three additional levels in our study.

Dyadic construct validation

The parents' individual religious construct systems become part of processes of explicit and implicit validation and questioning in the couple's development of a common dyadic construct system. Establishing a common plausibility structure and shared constructs is an essential part of the development of a viable environment for marital life (Willi, 1991). The religious attitudes and practices brought into cohabitation are also negotiated in this process of construct-validation (and de-validation) and—at least some of them—become part of the common construct system of a couple. High religious centrality of both parents would result in a greater presence of religious constructions in the life of the couple. The frequency of these religious constructions, and the effects on the self-definition as a couple and on daily functioning, would then vary according to the degree of individual religious centrality. Differences in centrality and in the different religious dimensions would complicate the development of such self-definitions, and would reduce the effect of religion on daily functioning (the same holds true, of course, in situations in which both parents' religious construct systems are peripheral). A double effect could be at work in these situations of marital religious disagreement: if religious centrality is different for the partners, then the probability of misunderstandings mounts, together with the tendency to withhold religious convictions from the couple's daily conversation (and, in effect, from the family). Children can sense differences on that level, reacting with some uncertainty about how to orient themselves in an incongruent environment (Hoge and Petrillo, 1978; Nelson, 1981; Cavalli-Sforza, Feldman, Chen and Dornbusch, 1982; Dudley and Dudley, 1986; Erikson, 1992). A second basic hypothesis follows from this.

Hypothesis 2: Children's religious attitudes and practices are influenced by the outcome of the dyadic religious construct validation of their parents as partners.

Triadic religious construct validation and family climate

The process of dyadic construct validation and development is taken to a new level by the arrival and growth of a child. Children also prompt parents, at first by their very presence, then by their maturing, experiencing, thinking and questioning, to explain parts of their religious construct system and to live up to their responsibility in this area of parenting, as in others. Again, as was hypothesised on the spouse's level, the higher the parents' centrality of the religious construct system, the more intensive are their religious attitudes and practices and, therefore, the more autonomous the functionality of religion. As time goes on, these processes create—as Klaghofer and Oser (1987) have hypothesised—distinctive modes of the religious family climate. We therefore attempt to assess the family's religious self-perception in four dimensions: family coping, family integration, family discourse and religious socialisation as functions of religion. We assume these dimensions to be stronger in families where religion is also established on the family level as an important reference, the centrality of the religious construct system depending on the following factors:

- religion is perceived to be important by all family members;
- all family members participate in its (re-)construction;
- it influences self-perception and self-definition of a family and its members;
- its effects can be seen in relevant areas of family life.

Families are not only reference groups for pre-adolescents. Families are the main surrounding networks for children up to age 10 or 12, and the main place where religion is processed, constructed and reconstructed. There is an assumption borrowed from constructivism underlying this reasoning: families do not adopt religion as it is represented by religious institutions and do not transmit it unchanged from one generation to the next. In a plural social context, in particular, traditional religious practices must be re-constructed if not co-constructed by parents and children if they are to remain plausible (Morgenthaler, 2005). In the context of increasing religious plurality within Swiss society, this assumption takes the functional autonomy of families into account. A third hypothesis follows from this.

Hypothesis 3: Children's religious attitudes and practices are influenced by the outcome of the family's religious construct validation.

Transgenerational transmission and validation of religious constructs

A fourth level of influences and validation may be postulated. In many families in today's Western societies, grandparents are still very much alive and play a considerable role at least in the lives of young families. In addition, empirical studies show an amazing continuity of the parents' influence on religion into middle adulthood (Glass, Bengston and Dunham, 1986). Religion is processed along these trans-generational lines in families as well.

Hypothesis 4: Children's religious attitudes and practices are influenced by transgenerational transmission and influences.

In order to gain an adequate picture of religion's importance in family life and socialisation, all four levels of family self-organisation have to be considered. Of course, the model just developed is much too simple to account for all the different multifaceted family types established in our societies. And, of course, there are other factors which influence the impact of parents' religion on children, as a long series of empirical studies has shown. Parents' influence on children is stronger under the following conditions: the more important religion is for the parents; the more the child likes, identifies with, and has a close relationship with the parent (Erickson, 1992; Hoge, Petrillo and Smith, 1982); when both parents share the same religious beliefs (Hoge, Petrillo and Smith, 1982); when parents support and control children (Weigert and Thomas, 1972; Bjarnason, 1998); when parents frequently talk with their children about religious issues (De Hart, 1990; Herzbrun, 1993); when parents desire the child to be religious (Flor and Knapp, 2001); for children with a secure attachment style (Granqvist, 1998; Granqvist and Hagekull, 1999); for first-born children (Clark, Worthington and Danser, 1988); when children are younger (Francis and Brown, 1991); when parents are younger (Hoge, Petrillo and Smith, 1982). Despite its limitations, however, the model was adopted to examine religion and religious socialisation in Swiss families with children.

Research Design and Methods

Sample

The chapter presents data from an empirical study of families in the German-speaking part of Switzerland. A questionnaire was completed by 702 schoolchildren of both sexes in their school classes in different cantons of Switzerland. The fathers and mothers of the participating children were also each asked to respond to a questionnaire and send it back independently. More than 900 parents responded. Different data sets could be differentiated with questionnaires received from: child only (192), child and mother (103), child and father (14) and child, mother and father (393).

The subsequent sections of the chapter refer to the fourth data set, comprising 393 families of which both parents and one child completed the questionnaire, which can be characterised as follows. The age of children (46.3% girls and 53.6% boys) averages 11.9 years (SD .65, ranging from 9.3 to 14.1 years). The mothers' ages range from 32 to 61 (mean 41.7, SD 4.36) and represent the following denominations: Reformed/Protestant 57.3%, Catholic 29.3%, other Christian denominations 7.5%, other religion 1.6%, no denomination 4.3%. The fathers are 44.1 years of age on average (SD 5.15, ranging from 30 to 60 years) and represent similar denominations: Reformed/Protestant 52.4%, Catholic 30.3%, other Christian denominations 7.4%, other religion 1.4%, no denomination 8.5%. Analyses of variance of all scales used in the study revealed that there are only very few and slight differences between the four groups of the sample, (e.g. with regard to the sub-scale 'intellect' of the S-R-T there is a slightly significant difference between children of subgroups 1 and 4 and subgroups 2 and 4 (independent samples t-test)).

Research instruments

Religious centrality and sub-dimensions: centrality scale of the S-R-T
The 'Structure-of-Religiosity-Test' (S-R-T) is a comprehensive test designed for multidimensional and comparative interreligious research in the field of religion as well as for practical use in psychotherapy. The basic structure of the S-R-T is defined by Glock's five dimensions of religiosity (Stark and Glock, 1968): intellectual, ideological, devotional, experiential, and public religious practice. According to the new multidimensional model for the measurement of religiosity (Huber, 2003), the measurement of these dimensions differentiates between centrality

and content of religiosity. The concept of centrality is related to the efficacy of religion. The more central the religion is, the greater is its impact on the experience and behaviour of a person. The Centrality Scale used in this study consists of 15 items. Each of Glock's 5 dimensions are operationalised through 3 items that measure the intensity of these dimensions on a very general level, ten items being expressed in theistic and five in non-theistic religious terms.

A pre-test indicated that the items of the Centrality Scale of the S-R-T were too difficult for the children to understand. We therefore had to adapt the phrasing of the items to the children's comprehension, carefully conserving the content of the items but simplifying the grammatical structure of each. Thereafter, the adapted version of the Centrality Scale of the S-R-T was also used for the parents. Parents' and children's scores could thus be compared directly. The adapted version of the Centrality Scale shows the same good psychometric qualities as the original version of the questionnaire (Cronbach's alpha for the 10-item scale, theistic religion: children .89, mothers .91, fathers .93).

Spousal Religious Agreement Scale (S-R-A-S) and construct difference
We have not found a scale suitable for our purpose for assessing the spouses' explicit and perceived agreement on religious issues. We therefore developed our own scale, covering three possible religious dimensions of marital life: a cognitive component (2 items, one inverted), close to the first Glock dimension of 'intellect'; an action-oriented component, close to the fifth Glock dimension of 'ritual'; and a component concerning the common responsibility of the parents for the religious education of their children, representing an aspect of daily family life where efficacy of high individual centrality in religion can be assessed. The spouses were asked to indicate on a four-point scale how close to or how different from their partner they felt with regard to the following statements (not true at all = 1, a little true = 2, fairly true = 3, very true = 4): (1) "We differ very much in our interest in religious matters" (inverted); (2) "We go to worship together"; (3) "We both attach value to the religious education of the children"; (4) "My partner and I agree on religious issues" (Cronbach's alpha for the perceived agreement scale: mothers .75, fathers .72; this is an acceptable reliability for group comparisons).

In addition to this perceived religious agreement, we measured the 'real' differences in parents' religiosity by comparing the parental scores concerning religious centrality and the religious sub-dimensions (numeric distance of the scores by subtraction).

Religious Family Climate (R-F-C)
Items of the religious family climate scale developed by Klaghofer and Oser (1987) were adopted. In their empirical work, Klaghofer and Oser define the religious family climate as the experiencing and evaluation of the possibilities of religious discourse and religious action in a family. A positive family climate implies a certain amount of religious acting and religious meaning-making, helping to resolve basic imbalances in the children's development of faith. A positive climate allows the reconstruction of experiences under religious auspices and the reflection of the respective processes. We asked parents and children about explicit religious discourse and religious education in the family, and about religion being a means of family integration and coping in difficult life situations, entertaining the hypothesis that the religious family climate would create a family context influencing the religious development of children and as well as the centrality of the children's religious constructs.

For theoretical and methodological reasons, we chose four out of more than twenty items. Parents and children were asked to indicate how they think about their family on a 4-point Likert scale (not true at all = 1, a little true = 2, fairly true = 3, very true = 4): (1) "In our family, we all speak out when it comes to religious matters"; (2) "The faith we share knits our family together"; (3) "It is important to me (to my parents) to bring up my (their) children in a religious way"; (4) "In our family, religion helps us to cope with difficult situations such as illness, accidents and quarrels" (Cronbach's alpha for the scale: children .85, mothers .82, fathers .85).

Transgenerational Transmission of Religion (T-T-R)
We have not directly collected data from the grandparents of the children. However, we asked parents to answer two questions, aiming at the importance of religious socialisation and religious discourse in their family of origin: (1) "How important to your parents was your own religious education?" (1 = not at all, 2 = a little, 3 = moderate, 4 = pretty much, 5 = very: mothers' mean = 3.56 (SD 1.24); fathers' mean = 3.45 (SD 1.29)); (2) "How often were religious issues discussed in your family of origin?" (1 = never, 2 = rarely, 3 = sometimes, 4 = often, 5 = very often: mothers' mean = 3.10 (SD 1.04); fathers' mean = 2.99

300 GROB, MORGENTHALER & KÄPPLER

(SD 1.07)). The scales for fathers and mothers were of satisfactory quality (Cronbach's alpha .83).

Data analysis

The four basic hypotheses mentioned in the theoretical outline of our study were empirically tested in the following way. Centrality of children was taken as the dependent criterion variable whose relation to the four levels of religious family self-organisation was analysed. Regression analysis was used to test the impact of the four levels of religious family organisation on children's religiosity. Predictor variables entered into the equation were: centrality of the parents' religiosity (Centrality Scale of the S-R-T for parents), perceived spousal religious agreement (S-R-A-S), religious family climate (R-F-C) and the transgenerational transmission of religion (T-T-R). Additional exploratory analysis was done on all levels, using zero order correlation analysis and stepwise regression analysis. The data analysis was conducted using SPSS Software (Statistical Package for Social Sciences, v. 12).

RESULTS

Findings of the study will be presented as follows: first, referring to the different dimensions of parents' and children's individual religions; secondly, an analysis of the impact of the levels of family religion on children's religiosity; and, finally, an analysis integrating relevant results as predictors in a comprehensive regression model.

Parents and children: Religious centrality and the five religious sub-dimensions

Parents' and children's multidimensional religiosities on the first, that is on the individual level, exhibit the following properties (see table 13.1). There is a significant gender difference in every dimension for both mothers and fathers, and girls and boys, with female respondents showing—as expected—higher scores in the religious sub-dimension and in centrality of religion. This difference is more prominent on the parental than on the children's level (mean difference .20 for parents, .11 for children). In an intergenerational comparison boys show slightly higher scores than fathers, mothers higher scores than girls. Mothers, fathers, girls and boys score highest in the ideology dimension (with

RELIGIOUS SOCIALISATION IN THE FAMILY 301

Table 13.1: S-R-T, Religious centrality and dimensions: summary of means and standard deviations, theistic religious items

Centrality	Mothers		Fathers		p-s	E.S.	Girls		Boys		i-s	E.S.
Subscales	M	SD	M	SD	t		M	SD	M	SD	t	
Intellect	2.34	.53	2.16	.57	***	0.32	2.17	.56	2.10	.54	ns	0.13
Ideology	2.47	.56	2.18	.70	***	0.46	2.40	.51	2.35	.60	ns	0.08
Devotion	2.17	.70	1.90	.75	***	0.37	2.13	.67	1.99	.72	*	0.02
Experience	1.86	.61	1.71	.62	***	0.25	1.85	.60	1.77	.58	ns	0.15
Ritual	1.90	.62	1.77	.64	***	0.21	2.00	.63	1.83	.62	**	0.03

Note: scales of SRT ranging from 1 (never/not at all) to 3 (often/entirely).
E.S. = Effect Size (here and in all following tables are Cohen's d).
p-s = paired samples, i-s = independent samples.
* = p< .05; ** = p< .01; *** = p< .001; ns = not significant.

devotion as the second highest); the experience dimension, on the other hand, comes last for all respondents.

The table 13.2 depicts the scores for the items of the S-R-T, which taps into the centrality of non-theistic traditions for respondents. The parents' means in table 13.2 seem to be comparatively low. The highest scores are found with regard to the feeling of all-encompassing unity. It is interesting to see that this is different from the parents' answers in the theistic tradition, where 'experience' is the dimension lowest in acceptance. This idea seems to be nearer to the respondents' experience than the idea of a God speaking to people, or even of a God intervening in one's life. With regard to the theistic items, women show significantly higher scores than men (reincarnation p< .001, E.S. = .27; meditation p = .007, E.S. = .19; all-encompassing unity p = .024, E.S. = .16; rituals from other religions p< .001, E.S. = .11; all comparisons assessed by paired-samples t-tests).

Believing in reincarnation is more widely accepted among children than among fathers and mothers (mothers-children p< .001, E.S. = .30; fathers-children p< .001, E.S. = .58), but there exists no significant difference between parents and children with regard to meditation. As with the parents, children's scores on the non-theistic scale are significantly lower than their scores on the theistic scale. This analysis suggests that non-theistic religious traditions have by no means permeated Swiss families, and do not surpass theistic traditions in influence. They seem of limited importance, in some areas compensating the loss of plausibility of ideas of the theistic traditions (i.e. afterlife and experiential relation to God).

302 GROB, MORGENTHALER & KÄPPLER

Table 13.2: S-R-T, Summary of means and standard deviations for mothers, fathers, children, non-theistic items

	Mothers		Fathers		Children	
	M	SD	M	SD	M	SD
Belief in reincarnation (theology)	1.49	.69	1.32	.57	1.70	.73
Mediation (devotion)	1.21	.45	1.13	.39	1.19	.44
Feeling of all-encompassing unity	1.68	.54	1.59	.59	–	–
Rituals from other religions (ritual)	1.15	.38	1.11	.34	–	–

Note: scales of SRT ranging from 1 (never/not at all) to 3 (often/entirely).
– items omitted from children's questionnaire.

In the following sections we will restrict our analysis to the five religious dimensions in the theistic traditions.

Parents' and children's centrality in relation to dimensions of religion

Turning to one of the main research questions, "How is the children's religiosity related to the different levels of family religion?", we will initially focus on the individual level. We hypothesised that the construct system of each parent would be related in a unique and direct way with the centrality of the children's construct system. As a first step, children's religious centrality was predicted by parents' religious centrality. Regression estimates for the influence of parents' religious centrality on children's religious centrality yield 43.4% of the explained variance. Mothers' and fathers' centrality are good predictors for children's centrality, mothers' centrality being of slightly higher relevance than fathers' (beta for mothers .370; beta for fathers .355). Thus, the data support the first main hypothesis.

Additional statistical analysis was executed with regard to the five sub-dimensions. The data presented in tables 13.3 and 13.4 resulted from a bivariate correlation analysis. As hypothesised, all correlations are highly significant, indicating positive associations. (The authors are aware that the correlation-structure between the different aspects assessed indicate an underlying general (g-)factor which was also confirmed by factor analysis.)

Centrality as a whole is highly correlated between parents and children, but the correlations in the different dimensions of religion are also high or rather high. This can again be interpreted as an indicator of the socialising power of the parents' religious construct system,

RELIGIOUS SOCIALISATION IN THE FAMILY 303

Table 13.3: Correlations of religious centrality and religious sub-dimensions of children and mothers

Mothers	Children					
	Intellect	Ideology	Devotion	Experience	Ritual	Centrality
Intellect	.35	.32	.39	.23	.33	.40
Ideology	.26	.42	.44	.26	.34	.43
Devotion	.37	.43	.57	.29	.44	.53
Experience	.30	.40	.46	.31	.40	.47
Ritual	.40	.42	57	.31	.62	.58
Centrality	.41	.49	.60	.34	.53	.60

Note: all correlations significant p< .001.

Table 13.4: Correlations of religious centrality and religious sub-dimensions of children and fathers

Fathers	Children					
	Intellect	Ideology	Devotion	Experience	Ritual	Centrality
Intellect	.39	.32	.45	.29	.38	.46
Ideology	.44	.38	.53	.30	.41	.52
Devotion	.41	.37	.55	.32	.45	.53
Experience	.39	.36	.49	.31	.39	.49
Ritual	.42	.36	.53	.29	.56	.55
Centrality	.48	.42	.61	.36	.52	.60

Note: all correlations significant p< .001.

assessed according to the five dimensions of individual religiosity and (in particular) of centrality.

A second pertinent impression is the similar pattern and size of the correlations between the five dimensions of religion in tables 13.3 and 13.4. Mothers' and fathers' religious centrality are connected to the children's centrality, having similar tendencies in the different dimensions of centrality.

Correlations are highest in the devotional and ritual dimensions, and this holds true for boys and girls. This is another striking feature of the data. It seems that prayer and attendance at religious worship were the areas of religious family life in which parents' and children's statements seem to converge most. Attendance at worship by parents and children was also strongly related in previous research (cf. De Hart, 1990; Francis and Brown, 1991; Hoge and Petrillo, 1978). Even more important for families with children of that age is devotion, that is prayer. This religious dimension shows the highest correlations with almost all other dimensions (with the exception of the ritualistic dimension). The ritual and the devotional dimensions both bear strong behavioural components: prayer and attendance at worship both imply visible religious practice, involving common actions of the family; whereas attitudes and beliefs—characterising the other dimensions—can more easily be kept secret or at least separated from open processing in the family. Learning mechanisms such as modelling and positive reinforcement can also be more effective in the dimensions that involve open behaviour (Grom, 2000).

If we compare these correlations with other studies, we find that the results are in the expected range. Thus, our findings confirm those of similar studies in Great Britain and the US (e.g. Hunsberger, 1985; Hoge, Petrillo and Smith, 1982; Potvin, Hoge and Nelson, 1976; Dudley and Dudley, 1986; Gibson, Francis and Pearson, 1990; Francis and Brown, 1991; Cavalli-Sforza, Feldman, Chen and Dornbusch, 1982). Similar correlations date back to the first of these studies: Newcomb and Svehla (1937) found correlations between .58 and .69. Our data, however, come from empirical research done from ten to 70 years later in a country whose religious pluralisation and individualisation in the last decade has been amply demonstrated. The 'generation gap' between parents and children, which has been alleged for decades, can be detected neither in these data nor in the earliest empirical studies, showing that such differences are small or non-existent (cf. Hood, Spilka, Hunsberger and Gorsuch, 1996: 77).

For further exploratory purposes stepwise regression analysis was also conducted. The children's Centrality Scale was inserted into the equation as a criterion variable, and the fathers' and mothers' scores in the different sub-scales were inserted as stepwise predictor variables. The factors on the maternal side bearing some weight in this equation reflect the correlations. It is interesting to see, though, that fathers are important with their religious intellectual and ideological stances concerning an afterlife (in the more 'theoretical' dimensions of religion), whereas mothers seem influential in the more 'practical' and community-oriented dimensions of devotion and ritual. Both mothers and fathers seem to be important persons for children with respect to religion, mothers outweighing (but not eliminating) fathers in their influence.

Can we therefore conclude, with Hoge and Petrillo (1978), that "the most powerful social background predictor of a person's religious

RELIGIOUS SOCIALISATION IN THE FAMILY

Table 13.5: Regression estimates for the effect of the parents' religious sub-dimensions on children's centrality (stepwise)

Model	Sub-dimensions of parents	R^2	Beta	p<
1	mother: sub-scale ritual	.370	.608	.000
2	mother: sub-scale ritual	.442	.473	.000
	father: sub-scale ideology		.301	.000
3	mother: sub-scale ritual	.459	.368	.000
	father: sub-scale ideology		.267	.000
	mother: sub-scale devotion		.178	.001
4	mother: sub-scale ritual	.467	.337	.000
	father: sub-scale ideology		.201	.000
	mother: sub-scale devotion		.184	.001
	father: sub-scale intellect		.122	.021

involvement appears to be the religious involvement of his or her parents"? There is ample evidence for a clear-cut 'yes' to that question. But let us turn to the other levels of religious family organisation before closing the files.

Construct difference and perceived religious difference on the parental level and its relation to children's religiosity

Children's religious attitudes and practices are influenced by the outcome of the dyadic religious construct validation of the parents as spouses. This refers to our second main hypothesis.

Two approaches to an empirical test of this hypothesis were chosen. On the one hand, we directly addressed parents, asking how they themselves would assess spousal agreement with regard to religious issues. We hypothesised perceived spousal agreement to be more influential for the socialisation of children than mere similarity of the religious construct systems, because spousal agreement presupposes processes of explicit religious communication in the marital relationship, which influences religious communication with the children. On the other hand, we assessed similarities and dissimilarities between the parents' religious constructs, using the data of the Centrality Scale and sub-dimensions that we collected from both parents. We analysed closeness of the parents with one another, regarding their individual construct systems, assuming that the socialisation effects would be higher in families with

306 GROB, MORGENTHALER & KÄPPLER

high spousal similarity of religious constructs than in families with high dissonance on this level.

Perceived religious similarity/dissimilarity of the spouses

Some of the characteristics of the data collected from the spousal religious agreement scale are presented in tables 13.6 and 13.7. Do parents assess their religious agreement with their partners in similar ways? Table 13.7 shows high or very high and significant correlations between the explicit religious agreement assessed by husband and wife. Additional statistical analysis showed that mothers and fathers do not differ systematically from each other in their assessment of religious similarity with their partners.

It is interesting to see that correlations are again higher in the dimensions involving common action and reflection than in the two other dimensions that are more related to individual religious predispositions. To test our main hypothesis we again conducted a regression analysis, entering the perceived agreement of mothers with fathers and of fathers with mothers as predictors. Perceived religious agreement between the spouses is important for children's religiosity: 28.3% of the variance of children's religious centrality is explained by this predictor (compared to 42.3% predicted by the parents' religious centrality). In this case, the fathers' perception of religious agreement with mothers seems to be slightly more important than the mothers' perceptions (beta for fathers .310; beta for mothers .255).

Construct differences between the spouses

Let us now turn to the 'objective' aspects of both parents' religious constructs. How close to or distant from one another are the parents with regard to the centrality of religion and the five religious sub-dimensions? These data are presented in table 13.8. Again, as emerged earlier, the Centrality Scale and the sub-scale ritual (attendance at worship) are the two scales revealing the strongest agreement between the spouses. The two ways of assessing parental religious consent (perceived agreement and construct difference) are negatively correlated, as expected (from mothers r = −.44, p< .001; fathers r = −.49, p< .001).

In the next exploratory step we compare the directly measured 'real' differences between the parents' religious constructs with the spouse's subjective perception of these differences and their respective relations to children's religiosity. Table 13.9 shows the correlations relating to

RELIGIOUS SOCIALISATION IN THE FAMILY

Table 13.6: Spousal religious agreement: summary of means and standard deviations for mothers and fathers

	Mothers		Fathers		t	
	M	SD	M	SD	p-s	E.S
Agreement concerning interest in religious issues (inverted)	3.14	.97	3.17	.94	ns	.03
Agreement concerning attendance of worship services	2.36	1.19	2.38	1.18	ns	.02
Agreement concerning religious education	2.62	1.07	2.65	1.08	ns	.03
Agreement concerning religious unanimity	2.99	.90	2.98	.91	ns	.01

Table 13.7: Correlations between religious similarity, perceived by fathers, and religious similarity, perceived by mothers

Item	r
Perceived agreement with spouse concerning religious interest	.49
Perceived agreement with spouse concerning going to worship together	.77
Perceived agreement with spouse concerning importance of religious education	.73
Perceived agreement with spouse concerning religious questions	.54

Note: all correlations significant p< .001.

Table 13.8: Summary of numeric differences between parents' centrality scores

	M	SD
Centrality scale	.37	.32
Sub-scale intellect	.41	.46
Sub-scale ideology	.51	.52
Sub-scale devotion	.49	.53
Sub-scale experience	.48	.46
Sub-scale ritual	.31	.38

direct comparisons. Of special importance for the children's centrality and their religiosity in all sub-scales is their agreement on religious education, as perceived by both mothers and fathers. The parents' agreement scale as a whole is also moderately correlated with the

308 GROB, MORGENTHALER & KÄPPLER

Table 13.9: Correlations of parents' perceived and numeric religious construct differences with children's religious centrality and dimensions

Agreement rated by Mothers

Centrality children	Intellect	Church attendance	Religious education	Religious issues	Agreement summary
Intellect	.17**	.35**	.42**	.18**	.38**
Ideology	.14**	.33**	.44**	.15**	.36**
Devotion	.14**	.48**	.57**	.15**	.46**
Experience	.11**	.26**	.39**	.12**	.29**
Ritual	.17**	.50**	.55**	.16**	.48**
Centrality	.18**	.49**	.59**	.19**	.50**

Agreement rated by Fathers

Centrality children	Intellect	Church attendance	Religious education	Religious issues	Agreement summary
Intellect	.11*	.31**	.43**	.18**	.36**
Ideology	.08	.30**	.45**	.18**	.35**
Devotion	.16**	.43**	.57**	.22**	.49**
Experience	.11*	.26**	.35**	.13**	.30**
Ritual	.16**	.45**	.51**	.21**	.47**
Centrality	.16*	.44**	.58**	.23**	.50**

Numeric differences with regard to Religious Centrality and Sub-dimensions

Centrality children	Intellect	Prayer	Ideology	Church attendance	Experience	Centrality
Intellect	−.10*	−.05	−.21**	−.07	−.01	−.08
Ideology	−.11*	−.02	−.17**	−.06	.02	−.05
Devotion	−.14**	−.05	−.25**	−.04	.00	−.08
Experience	−.14*	−.02	−.11*	−.04	−.07	−.04
Ritual	−.14**	−.12*	−.22**	−.06	−.04	−.11*
Centrality	−.16**	−.07	−.24**	−.07	.00	−.09

children's sub-dimensions and centrality. The other dimensions show slight or moderate correlations as well; all are significant.

'Real' numeric differences between both parents concerning religious centrality and religious sub-dimensions show the expected negative correlations with children's religious centrality and religious sub-dimensions. Of special importance for the development of children's religious centrality is parental disagreement in the dimensions of intellect and ideology. Most of the correlations in this part of the table are insignificant.

The two parts of the table each mirror a distinct pattern of correlations. The two approaches to measuring parental religious accord seem to assess two different aspects of the dyadic construct validation. The perceived difference is, as expected, more important for the children's religious centrality and the religious sub-dimensions than is the mere numeric difference between the spouses' religious constructs. These findings are corroborated by regression analysis presented in table 13.10. Here again, perceived agreement is more apt to explain variance in religious centrality than is the numeric construct-difference. But the 'real', directly measured difference is also of limited importance.

Summarising our findings, we could say that the spousal level of religious family organisation is important for religious socialisation as well. Perceived religious agreement between the spouses is of special importance for the religious centrality of children. However, detecting substantial correlations between parental construct differences on the 'objective' level and the religious centrality of children is also rather interesting. These data seem to corroborate our second hypothesis: Children's religious attitudes and practices are related to the outcome of the dyadic religious construct validation of the parents. Let us now turn to the third level of religious family organisation, to religious family climate. Here, the factor to be analysed is the systemic power of families on their members.

Religious family climate and its relation to children's religiosity

Children's religious attitudes and practices are influenced by the family's validation of religious constructs. This is the third of our basic hypotheses, tested by the religious family climate scale (R-F-C). According to table 13.11, mothers show significantly higher scores than fathers, with the exception of religious education where the difference is not significant.

310 GROB, MORGENTHALER & KÄPPLER

Table 13.10: Regression estimates for the effects of parents' religious agreement and construct differences on children's religious centrality (stepwise)

Predictor variables of parents	R^2	Beta	p<
Father: agreement with mother	.306	.354	.000
Mother: agreement with father		.308	.000
Construct differences		.183	.000

Table 13.11: Religious family climate: summary of means and standard deviations for mothers and fathers

Items of religious family climate	Mother		Father		p-s	
	M	SD	M	SD	t	E.S
In the family we all speak out when it comes to issues of religion	3.25	.86	3.12	.93	**	.15
Religious education is important	2.17	1.02	2.09	1.06	ns	.08
Religion helps us to cope with difficult situations	2.80	1.00	2.60	1.02	***	.20
Faith knits the family together	2.31	1.13	2.13	1.07	***	.16
R-F-C-total scale	2.63	.81	2.49	.85	***	.17

Note: Scales ranging from 1 (not at all) to 4 (entirely).

Again a regression analysis was performed to classify the impact of the religious family climate perceived by mothers, fathers and children on children's centrality. The variance of children's centrality explained by this predictor is nearly as high as the variance explained by the parent's centrality (43.4% compared to 41.9%; beta for mothers .392; beta for fathers .300). This finding supports our third hypothesis concerning the systemic power of families for the religious socialisation of children. Besides the one-to-one relation of the parents' and children's individual religiosity, families have an influence on children's religiosity as social units of a higher order.

Exploratory correlation analysis showed high correlations of the religious family climate, as perceived by mothers and fathers, with children's religious centrality (fathers .62; mothers .59). Surprisingly, correlations of children's centrality with their own assessment of religious family climate were even higher (.74). In order to explore this connection on a deeper level, an additional stepwise regression analysis with the four sub-dimensions of the religious family climate was performed (table 13.12). The perceptions of the religious family climate by all family members

RELIGIOUS SOCIALISATION IN THE FAMILY 311

Table 13.12: Regression estimates for the effects of the items of the R-F-C Scale (child, mother and father) on children's religious centrality (stepwise)

Model	Variables of children and parents	R^2	Beta	p<
1	child: religion helps us to cope with difficult situations	.451	.672	.000
2	child: religion helps us to cope with difficult situations	.556	.500	.000
	mother: religion helps us to cope with difficult situations		.366	.000
3	child: religion helps us to cope with difficult situations	.603	.348	.000
	mother: religion helps us to cope with difficult situations		.313	.000
	child: faith knits the family together		.283	.000
4	child: religion helps us to cope with difficult situations	.618	.269	.000
	mother: religion helps us to cope with difficult situations		.265	.000
	child: faith knits the family together		.235	.000
	child: religious education is important		.191	.000
5	child: religion helps us to cope with difficult situations	.626	.254	.000
	mother: religion helps us to cope with difficult situations		.216	.000
	child: faith knits the family together		.211	.000
	child: religious education is important		.173	.001
	father: faith knits the family together		.125	.005

contributes as predictors to the children's centrality, the children's and mothers' perceptions being more important than the fathers' perception of the religious family climate. 62.6% variance of children's centrality is explained, again providing strong support for the third hypothesis concerning the systemic influence of families on children's religiosity. The children's own perception of the religious family climate seems to be of special importance for their religiosity. This is in agreement with a systemic view, children being interaction partners in their families and thus contributing to their own socialisation. As on the parental level, the perception (in this case of the family climate) is essential for the effects of interactively processed religion in the family.

Summarising the findings of this section, we can say that the third hypothesis is also supported by our data. As social units characterised by intimacy and intensity of exchange and construct validation, families seem to influence the religious socialisation of children. Of particular importance for practical work is the children's own assessment of religious family climate (cf. Hoge and Petrillo, 1978; De Hart, 1990: 70ff; and for adolescents, Acock and Bengston, 1978). This confirms our theoretical assumptions: if children experience and evaluate religious issues as important in their families, and if they can cope with cognitive imbalances (as Klaghofer and Oser, 1987 put it) they are enabled to develop their religious practice and interpretation of reality more than they can in a family context that is cleaved or ignorant with regard to religious issues.

We only have space to glance at the fourth level of religious family organisation: the transgenerational dynamics of family life.

Multi-generational transmission of religion and children's religious socialisation

There have been surprisingly few empirical studies integrating data from three generations (cf. Glass, Bengston and Dunham, 1986; Scheepers and Van der Slik, 1998). In the present study, parents assessed the importance of religious education and the frequency of religious discourse with regard to their own families and to their family of origin. We can compare the generations on a descriptive level first, focusing on some striking results. Whereas only 8.5% of the fathers say that religious education was of no importance in their family of origin, 38.0% regard religious education as not being important in their own family. 6.6% of the mothers think that religious education in their own family of origin was not important at all, but 31.2% say that it is not important in their own family. From one generation to the next, the irrelevance of religious education has quadrupled according to the parents' estimation. The opposite, but not very prevalent, tendency can be seen in these parents' answers to the question about religious discourse in their families of origin and their own families. Here, 34.9% of the fathers and 30.4% of the mothers indicate that religious issues were never or only rarely discussed in their families of origin, but only 26.0% of the fathers and 20.7% of the mothers think that this is true for their own families. These data point to a remarkable increase of families in which (formal) religious education is no longer considered

RELIGIOUS SOCIALISATION IN THE FAMILY 313

Table 13.13: Regression estimates for the effects of the family-of-origin religiosity by mother and father on children's religious centrality (stepwise)

Predictor variables of parents	R^2	Beta	p<
Mother: religiosity in family of origin	.150	.217	.000
Father: religiosity in family of origin		.279	.000

Table 13.14: Importance of religious education (line 1) and religious discourse (line 2)

	Mothers	Fathers	Maternal grandparents	Paternal grandparents
Children	.54**	.54**	.25**	.36**
	.23**	.28**	.20**	.14**
Paternal grandparents	.39**	.47**	.25**	
	.19**	.27**	.12**	
Maternal grandparents	.39**	.34**		
	.17**	.20**		
Father	.66**			
	.41**			

to be an important responsibility of the parents. But we could also say that the mode of representation of religion in families changes between these two generations from a more socialisation-oriented type of transmission to a more discourse-oriented type of representation of religious themes within family life.

Again, a regression analysis was performed, entering the perceived religiosity of the families of origin into the equation (table 13.13). The explained variance of the children's religious centrality is 15.0%, a value much lower than on the other levels of family organisation presented above. The influences on the paternal side seem stronger than the influences on the maternal side. A zero order correlation analysis corroborates this result and yields additional information.

With regard to religious discourse, the correlations between children and parents are only slightly stronger than the ones between children and grandparents. Correlations between fathers and their parents are slightly higher than associations between mothers and their parents. Correlations of the importance of religious education are slightly stronger than with respect to those of religious family discourse. Again, correlations between children and their parents are slightly higher than

Table 13.15: Regression estimates for the effects of grandparents' and parents' assessment of religious education and discourse on children's religious centrality (stepwise)

Model	Variables of children and parents	R^2	Beta	p<
1	father: importance of religious education	.320	.567	.000
2	father: importance of religious education	.371	.365	.000
	mother: importance of religious education		.305	.000
3	father: importance of religious education	.377	.327	.000
	mother: importance of religious education		.290	.000
	paternal grandparents: importance of religious education		.103	.027
4	father: importance of religious education	.384	.342	.000
	mother: importance of religious education		.280	.000
	paternal grandparents: importance of religious education		.212	.002
	paternal grandparents: religious discourse		.144	.027

between grandparents and their children. Associations between fathers and their parents are also higher than the ones between mothers and their parents.

For further exploratory purposes, we also entered the parental and grandparental scores touching on religious education and religious discourse in their respective families, in a stepwise regression analysis, the religious centrality of the children being the criterion variable (table 13.15).

Summarising the results from our analysis of transgenerational influences on children's religious centrality, we conclude that the importance of religious education for the parents is most prominent in a multigenerational perspective. However, it is a noticeable finding that the father's (and not the mother's) family of origin seems to influence the grandchildren's religious centrality in both dimensions of education and discourse.

Impact of the four levels of family religion on children's religious centrality

We have tried to evaluate independently the relations of the different levels of family religion to the centrality of the children's religiosity, finding a decreasing amount of the children's religious centrality explained by the different levels of family self-organisation. Is this finding supported

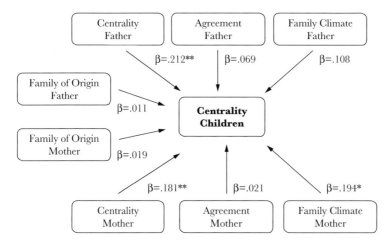

Figure 13.1: Regression estimates for the effect of parents' religion (all predictors) on children's centrality

by our final analysis? Following our theoretical model we attempt, as a last step, an assessment of the relative impact of the different facets of the religious family organisation on children's religiosity. For further exploratory purposes a stepwise regression analysis contributes to the following model (figure 13.1).

Entering all predictors, the model explains 46.0% of the variance of children's religious centrality. The centrality of father and mother show the highest beta, and both are significant. Family climate is also important, the mothers' perception being of higher importance (showing a stronger level of statistical significance) than the fathers'. Families of origin seem to be of mixed and small predictive value: father's beta is small and mother's beta is actually negative. In the equation the small betas of the perceived spousal agreement can be interpreted theoretically. Spousal consent is one of the bases for the development of religious family climate. It can be hypothesised that there is, besides a direct influence of spousal agreement, also an indirect influence on children's centrality, transmitted through the religious family climate.

For further exploratory purposes a stepwise regression analysis contributes to the following models (table 13.16). Table 13.16 again corroborates our main tenet: children's religiosity is on the one hand influenced by both parents' religiosity in a direct way. On the other hand, the systemic influence of the family—assessed by the parents' perception

Table 13.16: Regression estimates for the effects of all predictors on children's religious centrality (stepwise)

Model	Variables of children and parents	R^2	Beta	p<
1	father: centrality scale.	.376	.613	.000
2	father: centrality scale	.426	.409	.000
	mother: perception of religious family climate		.303	.000
3	father: centrality scale	.438	.361	.000
	mother: perception of religious family climate		.193	.015
	mother: centrality scale		.187	.015
4	father: centrality scale	.442	.252	.003
	mother: centrality scale		.272	.000
	mother: perception of religious family climate		.222	.005
5	father: centrality scale	.446	.255	.003
	mother: perception of religious family climate		.121	.150
	mother: centrality scale		.206	.008
	father: perception of religious family climate		.125	.047

of the religious dimensions of their family life—is of importance for the children's religiosity as well, although this influence seems less strong than the direct influence of individual parent religiosity. Both parents' perceptions of the family climate are important. The second level of our model, the spouses' consent in religious matters, is of no additional explanatory value. Again, we can assume an indirect influence of spousal consent on the religious family climate.

CONCLUSIONS

The findings presented in this chapter show that Swiss families are still important agents of religious socialisation for children on the fringes of pre-adolescence, despite religious pluralisation and de-standardisation. Thus, our results refute the hypothesis of a marked generation gap in the transmission of religious convictions and practices, and in the capacity to construe life situations in a religious mode—a capacity connected with the centrality of the religious construct system. A caveat, however, should be added to avoid giving a mistaken impression at this point: not only religious centrality but also distance from religious issues seems to be transmitted from one generation to the next in the family context.

Our data show the predominant influence of the mothers' and fathers' individual religious construct systems on their children's religious centrality. Religion is transmitted from parents to children on the first level of our model in highly individualised ways. Nevertheless, the three other levels of the religious family organisation that we differentiated are also related to the children's religiosity in meaningful and important ways. Integrating these different levels of analysis seems essential if we want to develop an adequate picture of the function of religion in the systemic self-organisation and socialisation of the family.

On the spouses' level of religious construct validation, perceived similarity or dissimilarity is more important for the socialisation of children than the actual religious differences, assessed by the centrality-scale of the S-R-T. A similar phenomenon can be observed with regard to the five sub-dimensions of religion. Socialisation effects seem most important in the dimensions implying overt and common behaviour. The perceived agreement between the spouses connected with open communication (and not the 'real', directly measured construct differences) seems important for children's religious centrality. There are also high correlations between the children's perception of the religious family climate and their centrality of religious constructs. Making religion tangible, visible, audible and working in action seems to be an important factor influencing religious socialisation in families (cf. De Hart, 1990). This thesis is supported by our data in many ways.

The position of fathers is especially intriguing. Their importance for religious socialisation in today's Swiss families is rather surprising, although previous research has yielded similar results (Kieren and Munro, 1987). Our data do not support the sole and dominant influence of mothers for religious socialisation. For children in the age group 9 to 14 in Swiss families, fathers (and even their families of origin) seem to be important reference points in religious matters as well. Their function in the process of religious socialisation has to be elucidated by further research. It might be a 'gate-keeping' function: as long as mothers do not deviate too much from fathers in the intellectual and ideological dimensions, they can deploy their more devotional and experiential religiosity with their children; otherwise their influence is censured. It might also be that fathers "may serve as role models for continued religiousness, or for rejection of religion after initial religious socialisation" (Hood, Spilka, Hunsberger and Gorsuch, 1996: 81), a salient issue for children of that age. A third explanation could be changes in gender roles, with fathers increasingly accepting their responsibility in areas (such as religion) that mothers were responsible for in the past.

Due to limited space we had to restrict our analysis to some prominent features of the data. Our study is cross-sectional. Thus, a first limitation is its restricted value for causal explication, which is only possible in a longitudinal design. Correlation and regression analyses were used in this stage of research. Due to limitations in resources we did not distribute a questionnaire to the children's grandparents. This extension would certainly make it possible to reach additional important insights into the transgenerational transmission of religion, and into the changing priorities of the generations concerning religious issues. The children in our study are still in pre-adolescence. The next stage in their development is connected with severe strains not only for the adolescents themselves, but also for their families as social units. It would be very interesting to learn more about the development of religious centrality and of multidimensional religion during that period, and to analyse how family religion changes in that period of the family life cycle, and also to perceive how the different levels of religious family organisation are adapted to the next stages of development.

REFERENCES

Acock, A.C. and Bengston, V.L. (1978), On the relative influence of mothers and fathers: a covariance analysis of political and religious socialization, *Journal of Marriage and the Family*, 40, 519–530.

Beit-Hallahmi, B. and Argyle, M. (1997), *The Psychology of Religious Behaviour, Belief and Experience*, London, Routledge.

Bjarnason, T. (1998), Parents, religion, and perceived social coherence: a Durkheimian framework of adolescent anomie, *Journal for the Scientific Study of Religion*, 37, 742–755.

Campiche, R.J. (2004), *Die zwei Gesichter der Religion: Faszination und Entzauberung*, Zürich, TVZ.

Cavalli-Sforza, L.L., Feldman, M.W., Chen, K.-H. and Dornbusch, S.N. (1982), Theory and observation in cultural transmission, *Science*, 218, 19–27.

Clark, C.A., Worthington, E.L. and Danser, D.B. (1988), The transmission of religious beliefs and practices from parents to firstborn early adolescent sons, *Journal of Marriage and the Family*, 50, 463–472.

de Hart, J. (1990), Impact of religious socialisation in the family, *Journal of Empirical Theology*, 3, 59–87.

Dubach, A. and Campiche, R.J. (eds.) (1993), *Jede(r) ein Sonderfall? Religion in der Schweiz: Ergebnisse einer Repräsentativbefragung*, Zürich, Basel, NZN.

Dubach, A. and Fuchs, B. (2005), *Auf der Suche nach dem verlorenen Sinn: Ergebnisse der zweiten Sonderfallstudie als Horizont für eine lebensdienliche Kirche*, Zürich, TVZ.

RELIGIOUS SOCIALISATION IN THE FAMILY 319

Dudley, R.L. and Dudley, M.G. (1986), Transmission of religious values from parents to adolescents, *Review of Religious Research*, 28, 3–15.

Ebertz, M.N. (1988), Heilige Familie? Die Herausbildung einer andern Familienreligiosität, in L. Konrad (ed.), *Wie geht's der Familie? Ein Handbuch zur Situation der Familien heute*, pp. 403–413, München, Kösel.

Erickson, J.A. (1992), Adolescent religious development and commitment: a structural equation model of the role of family, peer group, and educational influence, *Journal for the Scientific Study of Religion*, 31, 131–152.

Flor, D.L. and Knapp, N. (2001), Transmission and transaction: predicting adolescents' internalization of parental religious values, *Journal of Family Psychology*, 15, 627–645.

Francis, L.J. and Brown, L.B. (1991), The influence of home, church and school on prayer among sixteen-year-old adolescents in England, *Review of Religious Research*, 33, 112–122.

Gibson, H.M., Francis, L.J. and Pearson, P.R. (1990), The relationship between social class and attitude towards Christianity among fourteen- and fifteen-year-old adolescents, *Personality and Individual Differences*, 11, 631–635.

Glass, J., Bengston, V.L. and Dunham, C.C. (1986), Attitude similarity in three-generational families: socialisation, status inheritance, or reciprocal influence?, *American Sociological Revue*, 51, 685–698.

Granqvist, P. (1998), Religiousness and perceived childhood attachment: on the question of compensation or correspondence, *Journal for the Scientific Study of Religion*, 37, 350–367.

Granqvist, P. and Hagekull, B. (1999), Religiousness and perceived childhood attachment: profiling socialized correspondence and emotional compensation, *Journal for the Scientific Study of Religion*, 38, 254–273.

Grom, B. (2000), *Religionspädagogische Psychologie*, vollst. überarb. 5. Aufl., Düsseldorf, Patmos.

Herzbrun, N.B. (1993), Father-adolescent religious consensus in the Jewish community: a preliminary report, *Journal for the Scientific Study of Religion*, 32, 163–166.

Hoge, D.R. and Petrillo, G.H. (1978), Determinants of church participation and attitudes among high school youth, *Journal for the Scientific Study of Religion*, 17, 359–379.

Hoge, D.R., Petrillo, G.H. and Smith, E.I. (1982), Transmission of religious and social values from parents to teenage children, *Journal of Marriage and the Family*, 44, 569–580.

Hood, R.W. Jr., Spilka, B., Hunsberger, B. and Gorsuch, R. (1996), *The Psychology of Religion: an empirical approach* (second edition), New York, Guilford.

Huber, S. (2003), *Zentralität und Inhalt: ein neues multidimensionales Messmodell der Religiosität*, Opladen, Leske and Budrich.

——. (2004), Zentralität und Inhalt. eine Synthese der Messmodelle von Allport und Glock, in C. Zwingmann and H. Moosbrugger (eds.), *Religiosität: Messverfahren und Studien zu Gesundheit und Lebensbewältigung. Neue Beiträge zur Religionspsychologie*, pp. 79–105, Münster, Waxmann.

Hunsberger, B. (1985), Parent-university student agreement on religious and nonreligious issues, *Journal for the Scientific Study of Religion*, 24, 314–320.

Kieren, D.K. and Munro, B. (1987), Following the leaders: parents' influence on adolescent religious activity, *Journal for the Scientific Study of Religion*, 26, 249–255.

Klaghofer, R. and Oser, F. (1987), Dimensionen und Erfassung des religiösen Familienklimas, *Unterrichtswissenschaft*, 2, 190–206.

Morgenthaler, Ch. (2005), ...habe ich das halt für mich alleine gebetet (Mirjam 6-jährig). Zur Ko-Konstruktion von Gebeten in Abendritualen, in A. Biesinger, H.-J. Kerner, G. Klosinski and F. Schweitzer (eds.), *Brauchen Kinder Religion? Neue Erkenntnisse—praktische Perspektiven*, pp. 108–121, Weinheim, Basel, Beltz.

Nelson, H.M. (1981), Gender differences in the effects of parental discord on preadolescent religiousness, *Journal for the Scientific Study of Religion*, 20, 351–360.

Newcomb, T.M. and Svehla, G. (1937), Intra-family relationships in attitude, *Sociometry*, 1, 180–205.

Potvin, R.H., Hoge, D.R. and Nelson, H.M. (1976), *Religion and American Youth: with emphasis on Catholic adolescents and young adults*, United States Catholic Conference, Washington DC.

Scheepers, P. and van der Slik, F. (1998), Religion and attitudes on moral issues: effects of individual, spousal, and parental characteristics, *Journal for the Scientific Study of Religion*, 37, 678–692.

Stark, R. and Glock, C.Y. (1968), *American Piety: the nature of religious commitment*, Berkeley, California, University of California Press.

Vascovics, L.A. (1970), *Familie und religiöse Sozialisation*, Wien, Notring.

Weigert, A.J. and Thomas, D.L. (1972), Parental support, control and adolescent religiosity, *Journal for the Scientific Study of Religion*, 11, 389–393.

Willi, J. (1991). *Was hält Paare zusammen? Der Prozess des Zusammenlebens in psychologisch-ökologischer Sicht*, Reinbek b.H, Rowohlt.

Wössner, J. (1968), Kirche—Familie—Sozialisation, in G. Wurzbacher (ed.), *Die Familie als Sozialisationsfaktor*, pp. 308–352, Stuttgart, Enke.

CHAPTER FOURTEEN

APOSTOLIC NETWORKS IN BRITAIN: PERSONALITY AND PRAXIS

William K. Kay

SUMMARY

Personality theory has already shed light on the functioning of Christian denominations. There are special difficulties, however, in the application of personality theory to new Christian groups. This is because new Christian groups are often imprecisely defined. Attention needs to be given to the characteristic roles and practices of these groups. Following the charismatic movement of the 1960s, apostolic networks grew up in the 1970s. No published empirical research has been carried out on their congregations. The survey-based evidence presented here suggests that extraversion and neuroticism function among congregational leaders of these groups in ways similar to those found among Pentecostal leaders, but that psychoticism is associated with church planting and ministry to drug addicts. The chapter argues that personality theory may have a useful part to play in establishing the classification of religious groups.

PERSONALITY AND RELIGION

In recent years sustained attempts have been made to relate aspects of personality theory to dimensions of the church (e.g. Francis, Craig and Butler, 2005; Francis and Jones, 1996; Francis, Payne and Jones, 2001; Francis and Pearson, 1985a, 1985b, 1991; Francis, Pearson, Carter and Kay, 1981a, 1981b). The theoretical account of this relationship is made difficult by the range of personality theories on offer and by the range of denominations, churchmanships, and cultural contexts in which churches are situated.

Preliminary considerations

Clearly, in order to make a proper assessment of the impact of personality theory on clergy, it is necessary to clarify exactly how groups of clergy may be composed. The most obvious method of classifying clergy is by identifying them with their denomination. Personality theory can be applied to groups of Baptists, Methodists, Anglicans, and so on, exploring the correlations between different personality dimensions or types of each of these groups of clergy and their beliefs and priorities (Kay and Francis, 1996). The assumption here is that core doctrinal traditions are sufficiently strong to give each group of clergy a slightly different identity. Yet this is by no means the whole story, since there is considerable variation within the larger and older Christian denominations. The notion of 'churchmanship' encapsulates these variations, and the best shorthand distinction between different types of churchmanship is often theological. Basic theological tenets are interpreted in markedly different ways. Typically, theological liberals are inclined to interpret core beliefs symbolically and with acknowledgement to the flexibility built into their tradition. Typically, theological conservatives are inclined to interpret core beliefs literally and without acknowledging the possibility of flexibility. This means that a comprehensive classificatory system of clergy will take account not only of their denominational affiliation but also of their theological conservatism or liberalism (Randall, 2005).

Like any classificatory system of this kind, there are difficulties in applying it to clergy who are in new and emerging groups. For instance, it becomes difficult to apply the system to a minister who was once in a Baptist setting, worshipped for a while in an Anglican church and then joined a network. The charismatic movement of the 1960s saw many pilgrimages across the theological spectrum. The concern of this chapter is for those who ended up in what have variously been called 'house churches', 'new churches' or, more accurately, 'apostolic networks', which emerged mainly from Pentecostal and Baptist churches though with a mixture of Anglican, Roman Catholic and others as well (see Kay, 2007 for more details). Theological conservatism and liberalism are harder to assess in these circumstances because relics of older belief systems may be partially retained.

For this reason it is probably more appropriate to direct personality theory to specific *roles* and *practices* within apostolic networks. For instance, the role of the minister in evangelism or church planting may crucially distinguish between one network and another, or between the networks and the churches out of which they grew. Similarly, the practice of prophecy (extempore inspired utterance) within apostolic network congregations may provide measurable distinctives that are far more salient than conventional features relating to liturgy or statements of belief. As the historical outline below indicates, evangelism, church planting and prophecy are all prevalent and important within apostolic networks and, as previous research has indicated (Kay and Robbins, 1999; Kay, 2000a, 2000c, 2001), these roles and practices can be correlated with personality.

Emergence of apostolic networks

Apostolic networks in Britain grew up as a result of the second phase of the charismatic movement. The onset of the charismatic moment at the beginning of the 1960s was, theologically and experientially, a replication of the process that had occurred nearly 60 years before when the Pentecostal movement in Britain was launched (Harper, 1965). Theologically, the charismatic movement emphasised the unmediated work of the Holy Spirit within the life of individuals and, subsequently, collectively within congregations. Charismatic gifts were claimed and manifested; worship was revitalised and modified; lay leadership was empowered; interdenominational gatherings on a large-scale were enabled. The theological impact of the charismatic movement was at first limited to a greater general emphasis upon the Holy Spirit, but gradually there were other influences and divergences over Christian initiation and eschatology (Tugwell, 1975, 1977; Virgo, 1980). Ultimately more important than these, however, there came to be theological disagreements about the purpose of the charismatic movement as a whole. The movement could be seen as a divinely intended renewal of the existing order that was not intended to lead to institutional or structural change but simply to revitalise spirituality (Bittlinger, 1975). Alternatively, it could be seen as the start of a more radical, institutional and thoroughgoing challenge to the existing ecclesiastical order (Walker, 1998).

Experientially the charismatic movement in Britain reached across most of the Protestant spectrum apart from within Presbyterians in Northern Ireland and elements of the Federation of Independent Evangelical Churches in England. Nearly every Protestant group was touched in some way (Kay and Dyer, 2005). Equally, Roman Catholic congregations and individual priests were also affected though their influence on the apostolic networks, when they arrived, was marginal (Hocken, 1998).

To understand the divergent interpretations of the purpose of the charismatic movement it is necessary to go back at least to the 1950s. In a series of meetings and publications with widening readerships

Arthur Wallis (1923–88) began to enunciate a vision for the church that was based upon what looked like Brethren ecclesiology coupled with charismatic gifts (Wallis, 1956, 1961). Brethren ecclesiology was a stripped down and simplified form of Protestantism. There were no full-time clergy and Christian life within Brethren circles was inclined to sectarianism in its abstention from civic voting and lack of contact with most other Christians. It adopted a cessationist position with regard to spiritual gifts and assumed that they had died out in the providence of God once the canon of Scripture had been formed (cf. Budgen, 1989). Within each town or city only one Brethren assembly could exist: theoretically, the believers within a geographical area should unite round a single communion table. Into this strict and unadorned ecclesiology, Wallis wished to fit revivalism that was fired by charismatic gifts operating according to a New Testament pattern. It logically followed from Wallis' theological position *vis-à-vis* spiritual gifts that the work and office of apostles and prophets should also exist in the contemporary Church—there was no disagreement about the appropriateness of pastors, evangelists and teachers. Apostles and prophets were quite another matter and the claiming of apostolic functions was seen to be controversial, not to say arrogant. For, if apostles and prophets existed, they had the authority to overturn existing theological and denominational structures however historically hallowed they might be.

Arthur Wallis' radical views came gradually to be heard by charismatics (Wallis, 1991). Some of these became discontented with the charismatic movement. They thought that the spiritual impetus of the movement was consistently blocked by denominational barriers erected by tradition, and they were no longer willing to operate within these constraints. They were strengthened in their analysis by the commanding preaching of Martyn Lloyd-Jones.

In 1963 Martyn Lloyd-Jones (1899–1981) addressed the Westminster Fellowship of ministers. Going back to first principles, he questioned the value of specialist societies and associations and asked whether evangelicalism "should ever be based on anything but the church" (Lloyd-Jones, 1989: 172). Shunning sociological or conventional definitions he contended that the church "is a gathering of men and women who have believed the preaching of the Gospel" (p. 179) who form a spiritual society with the Holy Spirit as their companion. Such a society not only preaches the gospel but practises church discipline (p. 182). Three years later, at the National Assembly of Evangelicals organised

APOSTOLIC NETWORKS IN BRITAIN: PERSONALITY AND PRAXIS   325

by the Evangelical Alliance in London in 1966, Lloyd-Jones was asked to give the opening address on evangelical unity. The leaders of the Alliance were familiar with his views but had asked him to present them publicly, perhaps to stimulate discussion and bring known differences into the open (Murray, 1990: 522). They could hardly have expected his impassioned oration demanding that evangelicals leave their denominations to form a new pan-evangelical body.

It is my contention that these two preachers, Arthur Wallis and Martyn Lloyd-Jones, prepared the ground for the emergence of apostolic networks, the former in terms of ecclesiology and pneumatology and the latter in terms of an uncompromising mindset willing to throw aside cooperation with denominational evangelicals. The crucial piece of evidence here is that one of the key leaders of the new networks, Terry Virgo, attended Martyn Lloyd-Jones's congregation while he was a student in London. The new networks were made up of completely new congregations or of existing congregations that were severed from their denominational moorings and reconfigured. None of this took place without pain and confrontation but, by the early 1970s, new groupings of churches were being established under the leadership of evangelistic figures who later came to see themselves as apostolic. It is these apostolic figures and the subsidiary leaders of their networks who are the subjects of this chapter.

Twelve separate apostolic networks were founded in the fifteen years from 1970–85. They are: Bryn Jones and Harvest Time/Covenant Ministries (c. 1975);[1] Tony Morton and Cornerstone, later c.net (c. 1980); Terry Virgo and New Frontiers International (1979 under the name Coastlands); Barney Coombs and Salt and Light (1982); Gerald Coates and Pioneer (from 1970); John Noble and Team Spirit; Roger Forster and Ichthus (1974); Stuart Bell and Ground Level (c. 1981); Colin Urquhart and Kingdom Faith (c. 1979); Colin Dye and Kensington Temple/London City Church; John Mumford and Association of Vineyard Churches (1986); Noel Stanton and the Jesus Army/Jesus Fellowship (c. 1973).

---

[1] The founding date is not always easy to pin down. In several cases (e.g. Salt and Light or Cornerstone), the network began with the establishment of a large and thriving congregation that spread its networking tendrils out in a way which became formalised by the formation of a new trust deed and charitable name. Where a precise date is given, it is almost always the date of the registration of a new trust deed.

326 WILLIAM K. KAY

Each network is centred on an apostolic figure who functions, in denominational terms, like a founding bishop. The apostolic figure provides advice, strategy, experience, impetus, direction and is a symbol of unity and identity. Each apostolic figure has between 15 and 500 churches connected with himself (all the apostolic figures are male) and, as a point of principle, relationships between churches and their apostle are as free of bureaucracy as possible. Everything hinges on the personal connection between the apostle and the leaders of local congregations. In each case apostolic figures are charismatic personalities in both the general sense (that they are high profile leaders) and in the more technical New Testament sense (that they accept the operation of charismatic gifts for today and feel that their own ministries are inspired by the Holy Spirit).

All the new networks have come into existence within the last 40 years. At the beginning the apostolic figures were subject to implicit and explicit criticism from Pentecostals and other evangelicals. In overcoming this criticism the apostolic figures have shown themselves to be men of enduring confidence and determination, but it would be a mistake to consider them to be sectarian since many of them collaborate with other churches, and have done so for many years.

For survival purposes the apostolic networks have had to grow and they have done this by evangelism, church planting and by giving attention to the structure of their congregations in such a way as to facilitate increasing numbers. In terms of doctrine and experience, the apostolic networks are very similar to the mainline Pentecostal churches that have been in Britain since 1915—indeed some of the apostolic figures started life within the classical Pentecostal denominations. Others began as Baptists or Anglicans. As already indicated, classificatory systems do not easily apply to these new churches both because the liberal-conservative dimension does not properly fit (all the churches are conservative in orientation while avoiding fundamentalism) and because denominational identities (if the networks can be considered to be embryonic denominations) are still being shaped.

Personality theories

While Jungian psychology has provided insight into theologically expressed differences between denominations and helped explain why certain personality profiles prefer certain denominations (see Francis, 2005, for a succinct summary) earlier, and in some respects simpler, studies have made use of the Eysenckian personality model (Francis and Pearson, 1985a, 1985b, 1991; Francis, Pearson, Carter and Kay, 1981a, 1981b). The Eysenckian model is based upon presumptions about human physiology (Funder, 1997). The autonomic nervous system controlling breathing, digestion and other involuntary functions is separate from the central nervous system. Because the involuntary system deals with the release of enzymes and controls heartbeat, it also functions in relation to fear, anxiety and the stabilisation of the body after threat. Neuroticism and stability are functions of this nervous system. On the other hand the extraversion-introversion functions are said to be linked to the ability of the brain to accept stimulation. Where the brain is over-stimulated inhibition sets in as a protective mechanism (Eysenck, 1967). Extraverts are those whose brains are characteristically under stimulated with a consequence that extraverts seek further stimulation. Introvert brains by contrast are already stimulated and tend to avoid excessive and additional stimulation. This results in the personality traits of the party-going, risk-taking, noisy extravert and the quiet, risk-averse introvert. The psychoticism/tendermindedness factor is thought to be a consequence of either male sex hormones or a rudimentary forebrain. In the Eysenckian scheme the three factors—neuroticism-stability, extraversion-introversion, psychoticism-tendermindedness—devolve into a series of traits measurable by self-assessed questionnaires (Kay and Francis, 1996).

Previous research on the personality of the clergy (Francis, 1991, 1992; Francis and Jones, 1997, 1998; Francis and Kay, 1995; Kay, 2000a) has detected the importance of tendermindedness in relation to attitude to Christianity and the positive impact among Pentecostal ministers of extraversion within pastoral and evangelistic work, especially in relation to church growth. Indeed church growth may be connected with the prevalence of extraversion and charismatic gifts (Kay, 2000b: 295 and passim). Francis and Robbins (2004) have data suggesting that ministers in apostolic networks may be even more extraverted that Pentecostals. The foregoing discussion leads to three theoretical questions.

1. Do personality factors work in the same way among apostolic networks as they do among Pentecostal ministers?
2. Can personality theory be applied more widely to take account of activities less relevant to Pentecostal ministers?
3. Can personality theory contribute to classificatory schemes describing Christian groups?

328 WILLIAM K. KAY

METHOD

The standard statistical texts enumerating church groups in the UK are published by Christian Research and authored by Peter Brierley (e.g. 2001). In these he indicates that there are approximately 2094 New Churches in the UK with 2385 ministers. Closer inspection and email correspondence both with Peter Brierley and with church leaders suggest that these figures are either overestimated or else include churches that stand outside the apostolic sphere and are therefore not relevant to this project.[2] There are various websites available by which fuller information can be gathered but these also do not give accurate or complete pictures.[3] A more detailed analysis indicates that there are some 12 relevant networks with 675 congregations (Kay, 2007).

The questionnaire used in this study was made up of 6 sections. The first section asked questions about age, gender, training, church size, annual rates of births, baptism, deaths, marriages, church structure, growth, decline and congregational charismata. The second section dealt with the frequency of ministerial charismatic and evangelistic activities. A third section gave 150 statements on doctrinal issues and offered respondents five options from agree strongly to disagree strongly on each issue; these varied from Christology to ecclesiology, from cell church to belief in 'apostolic ministry'. A fourth asked leaders about the roles they prioritised in ministry. A fifth asked leaders to complete the revised and abbreviated Eysenck Personality Questionnaire (Francis, Brown and Philipchalk, 1992). The questionnaire as a whole was designed to allow comparison between the leaders of apostolic network and the Pentecostal leaders surveyed by Kay (2000b).

Table 14.1 gives details of distribution and returns and of the overall response rate of 36%. Questionnaire results were analysed by SPSS 14.0.

---

[2] 5520 churches resulted from a Google search for 'community church' based on the http://www.findachurch.co.uk/ site (28/01/2005). There is no way of knowing if they are network churches, denominational or independent without detailed closer inspection.

[3] For example Evangelical Alliance's Website, http://www.upmystreet.com, http://www.churchesuk.co.uk, http://www.findachurch.co.uk/.

APOSTOLIC NETWORKS IN BRITAIN: PERSONALITY AND PRAXIS 329

Table 14.1: Network returns of questionnaire

Network	sent	replied	
	n	n	%
Cornerstone	50	16	32
New Covenant Ministries	12	3	17
Ground Level	77	29	38
Ichthus	45	13	29
Jesus Fellowship/Multiply Network	53	11	21
Kingdom Faith	13	9	69
Kensington Temple	54	10	19
Lifelink	6	3	50
New Frontiers	200	82	41
Salt and Light	50	21	42
Spirit Connect/Pioneer	12	8	67
Vineyard	75	26	35
Unclassified		8	
Total	647	239	36

Sample

Respondents were congregational leaders and in some cases included apostolic figures, but for purpose of comparison the bulk of the survey is analogous to a survey of full-time clergy and lay leaders.

Of the 239 respondents who completed the questionnaire, 93% were male. Their mean age was 48 years and the mean length of time in the ministry was 14 years. As many as 22% of respondents were unpaid by their congregations and 51% were in paid secular employment. Only 9% were in sole charge of a congregation although 41% were in charge as senior ministers and 27% as part of a team. The median annual number of baptisms conducted by each respondent was three, the median number of marriages one and the median number of funerals one. Overall, 63% of these ministers looked after a congregation of less than 100 adults but 9% looked after a congregation of more than 200 adults; 9% cared for church congregations of less than 25.

As many as 95% of these respondents believed that "the baptism in the Spirit is a distinct experience" though only 17% believed that tongues (glossolalia) are the "initial evidence" for Spirit-baptism. About a third (36%) were creationists and believed that the world was made in six 24-hour days. All respondents (100%) believed that Jesus died for their sins and he rose again physically from the dead. Over half these respondents (51%) believed that women should have the same opportunities as men for ministry.

In an earlier study of this sample Kay and Dyer (2005) showed that a huge proportion of leaders within the networks (85%) believed that "apostolic leadership is vital to the 21st-century", and an even larger number (89%) agreed with the statement "I believe in the authority of apostles today". Nearly all respondents (95%) were able to say "I believe in the ministry of apostles". The role of the apostle was clearly highly valued.

Prior to further analysis the EPQ items were tested for reliability. Extraversion (alpha .837) and neuroticism (alpha .748) were satisfactory but psychoticism, as is often the case, was less robust (alpha .363).[4] However, in respect of the figures relating to psychoticism upon which most weight is placed in this study, significances were high (Table 14.2). Thus, the lower reliability of the psychoticism scale is compensated for by two highly significant beta weights.

FINDINGS

Multivariate analysis was used to disentangle the effect of network, gender and personality. This is because networks do not have similar proportions of female leaders and because, in any case, there are differences between them in respect of their composition and function. For instance, Ground Level is made up of churches that are not only part of the Ground Level network but also of churches that retain membership with other groups or denominations. The same may be said of Kingdom Faith which, as part of its policy, offers help to churches of almost any kind without insisting that these churches leave their denominations. Kingdom Faith takes the view that its help is non-governmental whereas other groups like Covenant Ministries are more exclusive in their membership. Consequently there will be greater diversity within those networks which take congregations from a variety of sources, especially if these congregations maintain dual membership.

---

[4] Cronbach's alpha could be raised to .492 by dropping one item in the psychoticism scale. When this was done and the multiple regression equations re-computed, all the significances in Table 2 remained in place or improved and the R squared figure increased in every case.

APOSTOLIC NETWORKS IN BRITAIN: PERSONALITY AND PRAXIS   331

Table 14.2 presents the findings related to a series of stepwise multiple regression computations, where gender and network were always entered into the equation before personality variables. The table gives the size of beta weights and F values together with their significances. The purpose of this form of analysis is to assess the significance of personality variables only after sex and the network differences have been taken into account.

DISCUSSION

Table 14.2 shows that a respondent's frequency of prophecy is associated with extraversion and that females and the tenderminded are more likely to consider that prophecy causes congregational disorder. Introverts are significantly more inclined to agree that Christians should not drink alcoholic beverages while extraverts are significantly more likely to think that Christians should be baptised in water by immersion. There are significant differences between networks in relation to the worries of individual members and those who score highly on the neuroticism scale worry more than do stable individuals. Extravert respondents are significantly more inclined to judge that their congregations have grown in the previous 12 months. Women and extraverts are significantly more inclined to offer to drive a new person to church. Extraverts are significantly more inclined to invite someone to church. Females and stable individuals are significantly more inclined to see Christian TV and radio as important to the future of the church, and toughminded individuals are significantly more inclined to believe that their church ought to be fully involved in giving practical help to the poor, including drug addicts. Ministry to drug addicts is supported more highly by extraverts, and extraverts are more likely to find their own ministerial priorities lie in evangelism. Pioneering is associated with extraversion and also with toughmindedness and varies significantly between networks. A sense of burnout is significantly associated with neuroticism.

It is arguable that the greater willingness of women to drive a new person to church is linked with the smaller number of opportunities (as compared with denominational churches) women have for ministry within churches associated with apostolic networks, and a similar argument might be made for the higher valuation placed upon Christian broadcasting.

Table 14.2: Multiple regression showing beta weights, R^2 and F values

Dependent variables	Independent variables							
Items	Sex	Network	E	N	P	R^2	F	p<
Prophesying (respondent's frequency of)			.206**			.059	2.378	.04
Prophecy causes congregational disorder	−.146*				−.142*	.080	3.308	.01
Christians should not drink alcoholic beverages			−.210**			.068	2.601	.03
I believe that Christians should be baptised in water by immersion			.172*			.067	2.818	.02
I am worried about the future of my network (denomination)		−.159*		.169*		.100	4.178	.00
By what percentage would you judge the number in your ministerial care has grown in the last twelve months			.250***			.104	4.371	.00
Offered to drive a new person to church (respondent's frequency of)	.185**		.169*			.072	2.955	.01
Invited someone to church (respondent's frequency of)			.189**			.066	2.688	.02
Christian TV is important to the future of the church in Britain	−.200**			−.156*		.062	2.510	.03
Christian radio is important to the future of the church in Britain	−.202**			−.153*		.060	2.430	.04
Interdenominational gatherings of local Christian leaders are more important than denominational structures		−.166*				.056	2.282	.05
My church ought to be fully involved in giving practical help to the poor					.191**	.056	2.235	.05
My church ought to be fully involved in giving practical help to drug addicts			.167*		.167*	.059	2.405	.04
Respondent's ministerial priority as: evangelist			.284***			.089	4.194	.00
Respondent's ministerial priority as: pioneer		.138*	.265***		.239***	.157	7.982	.00
I feel burned out by my ministry here				.341***		.138	6.128	.00

Note: * p< .05, ** p< .01, *** P< .001; n = 237; female coded 1, male coded 2.

There are variations in the extent to which leaders worry about the future of their network. There are also variations in the extent to which networks value interdenominational gatherings of local Christian leaders, and we may take this finding as a proxy for more or less ecumenical and therefore flexible orientations.

Turning to the personality variables, extraversion is the most potent predictor of individual behaviour. Those who score highly on the extraversion scale are more likely to prophesy, to invite a new person to church and to offer to drive a new person to church. They are also more likely to believe that Christians should be baptised by immersion and that their church ought to be involved in giving practical help to drug addicts. Similarly, extraverts are more likely to report a growing congregation or pastoral group. All these activities are in keeping with the extravert predisposition for sociability and public notice. Prophecy within a congregation requires the confidence to speak to large gatherings in an impromptu way; inviting new people to church requires the ability to reach out to strangers; baptism by immersion requires adults or teenagers to expose themselves to the public show of being immersed in water. None of these findings is completely unexpected, but what is surprising is that extraverts are significantly inclined to see the importance of helping drug addicts to recover though, in this case, this is linked with higher levels of psychoticism (see below). Moreover, and in keeping with a series of other findings on the importance of personality within Christian ministry, extraverts are more likely to see themselves as evangelists and pioneers than introverts and, indeed, to function more easily in these roles than introverts (Kay, 2000b). It is not surprising, given all these engagements with people of many kinds, that extraverts also report themselves to be experiencing growth in the numbers of people within the ambit of their pastoral care.

Those who score high on the neuroticism scale show themselves to be more worried about the future of their network and to feel more burned-out ministerially. It is hardly unexpected that high neuroticism scorers are inclined to worry since, almost by definition, this is characteristic of them. Those who are prone to anxiety find the stresses of ministry psychologically challenging. Equally, such people are less likely to think that Christian broadcasting holds the future of the church. We can express this the other way round by saying that those who are more psychologically stable are more inclined to believe that Christian broadcasting is going to be important to the future of the church in Britain, and this conviction is also more associated with women than men.

In relation to psychoticism, those who score more highly on this scale are more inclined to believe their churches should contribute to the poor and help drug addicts. Such individuals are also more inclined to see themselves as pioneers than do others. These findings are supported by the notion that those who score high on the psychoticism scale are likely to have the ability to function outside social support systems. Moreover, other studies indicate that any drug-takers may themselves be high on the psychoticism score which suggests that these leaders who wish to help drug addicts may themselves have come from this kind of background, or at least sense compatibility with it (Eysenck and Eysenck, 1975). Earlier findings about psychoticism show that, while high scorers may be particularly toughminded, their willingness to engage in compassionate social action may spring from a tendency to see the world in terms of a struggle between good and evil according to which charitable acts are conceivable as weapons on the side of the good (Kay, 1998). Tenderminded individuals, by contrast, are more suspicious of the impact of prophecy which, in congregations attached to apostolic networks, tends to be spontaneous and unpredictable. Tenderminded individuals are more inclined to think such outbursts cause disorder and dislike them.

The findings reported here are broadly in accord with those already reported concerning Pentecostal ministers. There is evidence to suggest that extraversion is linked with church growth and with public interactive behaviour of a charismatic, practical and evangelistic kind. The linkage between extraversion and charismatic manifestations and church growth is similar to that reported by Poloma in 1989 and replicated by Kay in 2000 (Kay, 2000b). The mechanisms bringing about church growth within the congregations belonging to apostolic networks appear to be similar to those at work within Pentecostal congregations on both sides of the Atlantic. What is new and arresting is that psychoticism appears to be important in connection with pioneering or ground-breaking activity and in relation to the tougher forms of ministry connected with drug addiction and poverty. Thus there is some evidence that, within Pentecostal and charismatic contexts, psychoticism is harnessed to the overriding aims of such churches rather than being excluded from the spectrum of personality characteristics found among Christians. Neuroticism appears to be linked more strongly than introversion with a tendency to burnout.

When apostolic networks are viewed through the lens of personality, the data indicate that the personalities who flourish in Pentecostalism would also find apostolic network congregations conducive to them. Whatever may be the case with regard to doctrine or history, personality variables join most apostolic network churches more strongly to the Pentecostal than to the charismatic wave. Further research reported in Kay (2007) shows that finer distinctions can be made between the networks in terms of their ecumenical orientations and suggests that these orientations are explicable in terms of the life history of the founding apostle.

Conclusion

The following main conclusions can be drawn in relation to the three research questions. First, there is preliminary evidence that personality factors do work in the same way among members of apostolic networks as among Pentecostals. Extraversion is associated with growing congregations and with the exercise of spontaneous charismatic gifts. The consonance between Pentecostals and members of apostolic networks is shown especially in the important area of church growth. Here the same dynamics seem to apply.

Second, there is also preliminary evidence that personality theory can be applied more widely than has been the case with Pentecostal churches. This is because certain kinds of ministry (e.g. to drug addicts and in church planting) are far less common in settled and established Pentecostal denominations. Where these ministries exist in a Pentecostal context, they are much more likely to operate in parachurch settings than as off-shoots of congregational life. In any case toughmindedness has a beneficial effect on various kinds of ministry and does not simply function to dampen positive attitudes to Christianity.

Third, the classification of new religious groups is intrinsically problematic and personality theory can help to demonstrate the existing denominations with which new groups have affinities. So, although there are historical and theological connections between Pentecostal churches and new apostolic networks, it is when we find that there are similar linkages between extraversion and charismatic gifts, or extraversion and church growth, that we begin to have further confidence that the historical linkages have a basis, not only in spiritual reality but also in psychological reality. Or, to put this another way, we can begin to build up a classificatory scheme for new religious groups by using the tools of historical and theological scholarship and *then confirm or disconfirm*

336 WILLIAM K. KAY

these results using the tools of personality theory (and this provides the answer to our third research question). It should not be thought that we are reducing new religious groups simply to their personality components because we find that within new religious groups some dimensions of personality may function differently from the way they function within established groups. Pioneering and church planting, activities that require toughmindedness, can be shown to be associated with significant psychoticism levels within the respondents examined here. Consequently we can argue that one of the drivers behind the success of apostolic networks is their ability to utilise a personality factor not normally prominent within other Christian groups.

ACKNOWLEDGEMENT

This research was supported by a grant by the Arts and Humanities Research Council.

REFERENCES

Bittlinger, A. (1975), The function of charismata in divine worship, *Theological Renewal*, 1, 5–10.
Brierley, P. (ed.) (2001), *UK Christian Handbook: religious trends 3*, London, Christian Research.
Budgen, V. (1989), *Charismatics and the Word of God*, Durham, Evangelical Press.
Eysenck, H.J. (1967), *The Biological Basis of Personality*, Springfield, Illinois, Charles Thomas.
Eysenck, H.J. and Eysenck S.B.G. (1975), *Manual of the Eysenck Personality Questionnaire*, London, Hodder and Stoughton.
Francis, L.J. (1991), The personality characteristics of Anglican ordinands: feminine men and masculine women? *Personality and Individual Differences*, 12, 1133–1140.
——. (1992), Is psychoticism really a dimension of personality fundamental to religiosity? *Personality and Individual Differences*, 12, 645–652.
——. (2005), *Faith and Psychology: personality, religion and the individual*, London, Darton, Longman and Todd.
Francis, L.J., Brown, L.B. and Philipchalk, R. (1992), The development of an abbreviated form of the Revised Eysenck Personality Questionnaire (EPQR-A): its use among students in England, Canada, the USA and Australia, *Personality and Individual Differences*, 13, 443–449.
Francis, L.J., Craig, C.L. and Butler, A. (2005), Understanding the Parochial Church Council: dynamics of psychological type and gender, *Contact*, 147, 25–32.
Francis, L.J. and Jones, S.H. (eds.) (1996), *Psychological Perspectives on Christian Ministry: a reader*, Leominster, Gracewing.
——. (1997), Personality and charismatic experience among adult Christians, *Pastoral Psychology*, 45, 421–428.
——. (1998), Personality and Christian belief among adult churchgoers, *Journal of Psychological Type*, 47, 5–11.

Francis, L.J. and Kay, W.K. (1995), The personality characteristics of Pentecostal ministry candidates, *Personality and Individual Differences*, 18, 581–594.

Francis, L.J., Payne, V.J. and Jones, S.H. (2001), Psychological types of male Anglican clergy in Wales, *Journal of Psychological Type*, 56, 19–23.

Francis, L.J. and Pearson, P.R. (1985a), Extraversion and religiosity, *Journal of Social Psychology*, 125, 269–270.

——. (1985b), Psychoticism and religiosity among 15-year-olds, *Personality and Individual Differences*, 6, 397–398.

——. (1991), Religiosity, gender and the two faces of neuroticism, *Irish Journal of Psychology*, 12, 60–68.

Francis, L.J., Pearson, P.R., Carter, M. and Kay, W.K. (1981a), The relationship between neuroticism and religiosity among English 15- and 16-year-olds, *Journal of Social Psychology*, 114, 99–102.

——. (1981b), Are introverts more religious?, *British Journal of Social Psychology*, 20, 101–104.

Francis, L.J. and Robbins, M. (2004), *Personality and Pastoral Care: a case study of empirical theology*, Cambridge, Grove Books.

Funder, D.C. (1997), *The Personality Puzzle*, London, Norton and Company Ltd.

Harper, M. (1965), *As at the Beginning*, London, Hodder and Stoughton.

Hocken, P.D. (1998), *Streams of Renewal* (second edition), Carlisle, Paternoster.

Kay, W.K. (1998) A demonised worldview: dangers, benefits and explanations, *Journal of Empirical Theology* 11, 1, 17–29

——. (2000a), Job satisfaction in Pentecostal ministers, *Asian Journal of Pentecostal Studies*, 3(1), 83–97.

——. (2000b), *Pentecostals in Britain*, Carlisle, Paternoster.

——. (2000c), Role conflict and British Pentecostal Ministers, *Journal of Psychology and Theology* 28, 2, 119–124.

——. (2001), *Personality and Renewal*, Cambridge, Grove Books.

——. (2007), *Apostolic Networks in Britain*, Carlisle, Paternoster.

Kay, W.K. and Dyer, A.E. (2005), The Pentecostal and Charismatic movements and theological training in the UK, *Quadrant*, Jan, 2.

Kay, W.K. and Francis, L.J. (1996), *Drift from the Churches*, Cardiff, University of Wales Press.

Kay, W.K. and Robbins, M. (1999), A woman's place is on her knees: the pastor's view of the role of women in Assemblies of God, *Journal of the European Pentecostal Theological Association*, 18, 64–75.

Lloyd-Jones, D.M. (1989), *Knowing the Times*, Edinburgh, The Banner of Truth Trust.

Murray, I.H. (1990), *D Martyn Lloyd-Jones: the fight of faith 1939–1981*, Edinburgh, Banner of Truth.

Poloma, M.M. (1989), *Assemblies of God at the Crossroads*, Knoxville, Tennessee, University of Tennessee Press.

Randall, K. (2005), *Evangelicals Etcetera: conflict and conviction in the Church of England's parties*, Aldershot, Ashgate.

Tugwell, S. (1975), *Did you Receive the Spirit?* London, Darton, Longman and Todd.

——. (1977), Is there a 'pentecostal experience'?, *Theological Renewal*, 7, 8–11.

Virgo, T. (1980), review of Iain H Murray's *The Puritan Hope*, Banner of Truth, in *Restoration*, January/February, 11.

Walker, A. (1998), *Restoring the Kingdom* (fourth edition), Guildford, Eagle.

——. (1956), *In the Day of Thy Power: structural principles of revival*, Arlesford, Christian Literature Crusade.

——. (1961), The divine idea of the local church, in A. Wallis (ed.), *The Divine Purpose of the Church: an enquiry*, privately printed.

Wallis, J. (1991), *Arthur Wallis: radical Christian*, Eastbourne, Kingsway.

CHAPTER FIFTEEN

XENOPHOBIA AND RELIGIOUS PLURALISM: AN EMPIRICAL STUDY AMONG YOUTH IN GERMANY

Hans-Georg Ziebertz and Ulrich Riegel

SUMMARY

After the Second World War Germany, as other European countries, developed into a multicultural and multireligious country. In the public discourse the experience of cultural, ethnic and religious pluralism is often seen as reason for xenophobic attitudes and behaviour. This chapter analyses theoretical concepts of xenophobia and draws a picture of current German society. We describe the social context of an empirical inquiry with 1923 young people of 16 to17 years of age and analyse their attitudes towards xenophobia and religious pluralism. Background characteristics studied include gender, personality, church membership, religious self-perception and attitude towards inter-religious relationships. The analysis shows that young Germans are not afraid of foreigners and appreciate the cultural and religious plurality of German society. The female youngster without a mono-religious point of view shows these attitudes most strongly. A comparison of the German sample with those from Poland, Israel and Sweden displays the importance of national background in this context.

INTRODUCTION

Xenophobia is often related to the presence of foreigners, but it is a problem more generally between people and groups who differ in a number of attitudes and behaviours, ethnicity and race, culture and religion. Nevertheless, it is particularly appropriate to study the 'strange' as an object of xenophobia when the focus is on foreigners. Different groups of foreigners in a country represent pluralism, and this implies the need for foreigners and autochthonous people to define their relationship. In this chapter we analyse the attitudes towards foreigners and towards religious plurality of young Germans. We first reflect on the concept of xenophobia before providing a brief description of the political and religious situation in Germany. We then develop our research question,

Xenophobia in a Theoretical Context

describing the empirical concepts and their operationalisation. Lastly, we analyse the data and discuss the findings.

Xenophobia in a Theoretical Context

Xenophobia is a fact, in Germany as well as in other European countries. Riedl (1994) mentions the following causes, which are present in the public discourse: a natural drive towards xenophobia, a lack of education in the family, the failure of schools in training secondary virtues, a late consequence of Nazi Germany, a result of the years of public debate about asylum, as of madness, as of the impact of the 1968-generation, or as some terrible fate. Most of these causes suggest that xenophobia is an 'accident' which could have been prevented by more attention to education and discipline.

A general definition of xenophobia is 'fear against strangers'. Its etymological roots lie in the Greek 'xenos' (strange, foreign) and 'phobos' (fear). Fear can have different causes; it can be based on ideas (ideologies), stereotypes and prejudices, but also on interpersonal experiences with 'other people' which have been evaluated as negative by the individual. The term 'stranger' highlights differences, mostly expressed as differences of nationality, religion, culture and race. Therefore the term xenophobia is narrowly related to racism and ethnocentrism. Racism was traditionally understood as "ideology that claims the fundamental inequality and hierarchical order of different biologically defined races" (Rydgren, 2003: 48). In the recent history of Germany, Hitler's Nazi ideology was based on distinguishing people as good or bad through biological differences. In opposition to the Germanic ideal (tall and blond male with blue eyes: the superior 'Herrenmensch') other races were defined as people of lower value (the inferior 'Untermensch'). The Nazi ideology allowed the first to annihilate the second. A similar ideology, known as apartheid, operated for a long time in South Africa. Recent expressions of racism are not solely based on biological arguments but on cultural differences as well. Cultural racism "stresses the insurmountable difference between culturally defined ethnies" (Rydgren, 2003: 48). The concept of ethnicity (and ethnic) is based on the distinction between in-group and out-group. Ethnocentrism can be understood as a set of attitudes in which the in-group is positively and the out-group negatively evaluated (Scheepers and Gijsberts, 2005). The meaning of xenophobia is closely related to cultural racism and can include elements of ethnocentrism. If xenophobia is developed with a manifest concept of ethnicity it can turn into ethnocentrism. Latent xenophobia is developed less consciously and takes certain stereotypes and prejudices 'for granted'. With Rydgren we may conclude that the wide spread of cultural racism "is an 'ideologicalized' form of manifest xenophobia" (2003: 48). Latent xenophobia is a non-reflected 'scheme' which guides people's behaviour and gives direction to their evaluation of experiences of the 'strange'.

In order to explore deeper and ask what causes xenophobia, we summarise three theoretical approaches: the first stresses the importance of human nature, the second the relevance of psychological development especially in childhood and youth, and the third focuses on the socialising power of society and culture.

The sociobiological approach

The sociobiological theory explains xenophobia within the context of evolution (Wahl, Tramitz and Blumtritt, 2001; Guha, 1991). The difference between ontogeny and phylogeny is important. Etymological roots of ontogeny are the Greek 'oos' (essence) and 'genesis' (development). Social sciences like sociology, pedagogy and psychology have developed basic concepts and theories such as socialisation, behaviourism, social learning theory and several more which can be understood within the frame of ontogeny. The development of attitudes and behaviour is seen as fundamentally connected with the societal 'Überbau' consisting of norms. Its influence on classes and individuals can be reconstructed in a historical context, so it implies the dimension of time. The etymological roots of phylogeny are the Greek 'phylos' (tribe) and 'genesis' (development). This approach claims that behaviour is innate and steered by evolutionary processes. Most authors distinguish between innate and determined. Only a few would say that behaviour is wholly determined.

What is the origin of this concept? It recalls that human beings look back on a tribal history of several million years. In this historical process changes in behaviour develop and are genetically inherited. The forces that impinge on this process are mutation and selection. Mutations allow a change in adaptation to the environment that may aid survival; such mutations are likely to be promoted by selection. Many hold that neither nature nor culture is determined. These two forces do not act independently of one another but interact. In social history mutation can be interpreted as innovation and the unexpected idea; selection as tradition, experience and something that is learned. Guha summarises: without selection, there would be chaos; without mutation, there would be stagnation (1991: 71). Proponents of the sociobiological theory state that xenophobia cannot be understood without the interaction between ontogeny and phylogeny. They refer to the importance of instinct for optimal adaptation to the environment. Among animals it is still normal to reject other species: the reaction is spontaneously aggressive. This behaviour is appropriate, because it claims space and keeps others at a distance. For the survival of a species the inheritance of this instinct was crucial. For a long period this was essential for hominids, too, and it can be found in many cultures in our present time. Hence the sociobiological theory calls xenophobic behaviour 'universal'. For people today threat is not based on actual experiences, but imagination can create experiences that are deemed real. Right-wing parties make use of it when foreigners are stigmatised as causing many problems like violence and unemployment. A lack of resources is likely to stimulate xenophobic behaviour, especially when people or groups claim the same space or goods.

Is there no way to overcome congenital xenophobia? Representatives of this concept do not deny that learning takes place. But they would not say that learning exhaustively explains xenophobic attitudes and behaviour. The central cause of xenophobia must be taken into account: that is, the long-term influence of evolution with its steering function on personality and emotions. Alongside cultural development and enlightened consciousness, old transmitted patterns are still working in the human brain and must be seen as interrelated with social learning processes. When we reflect on the survival of humankind we do it under the conditions of modernity and globalisation. Old patterns of defining 'what is strange' and 'how to beat the strange' can be inefficient. 'Distance' has a different meaning nowadays than it did thousands of years ago. In consequence, xenophobia may not be a proper trait or attitude to guarantee one's own survival today. In fact, it is the opposite: widespread and strong xenophobia can cause destruction. In other words, congenital patterns that had a positive function in the past can have a negative one in the future. For survival in the modern globalised environment, solidarity and willingness to cooperate seem to be more important than defending boundaries and securing a limited habitat. Therefore, in the long run of evolution, a plausible scenario is that humankind has a better chance to survive with a lower degree of xenophobic attitudes than with a higher one. The question is how far education can support this process by encouraging non-xenophobic attitudes. However, the relation between evolution and social context is circular; it is not one of direct causality. One can therefore claim that xenophobia is congenital but not determined by the evolutionary process.

The psychological approach

Xenophobia is a frequently researched phenomenon in psychology. The psychological perspective is focused on individual and interindividual processes: how people deal with fear, what experiences they have had with strangeness, and what behaviours result from handling alienation and fear (e.g. aggression). A key concept of developmental psychology is the process of dissolution of the symbiosis of a child with its mother, the gradual replacement of the mother and the progressive separation of the individual during childhood and youth (Klosinski, 1994). Separation is a process with an open end. A child must learn to distinguish between proximity and distance. The first task is to handle the relationship between child and mother, and then this task extends to other relationships. The developmental goal is that the relation between proximity and distance is not just an either-or but that both can coexist. For developmental psychology this learning process is essential so that an individual can deal with aggression (Winnicott, 1965). The experience of childhood is that separation either results in distance and 'cold relations' or that an empathic relation is nevertheless still possible. Explorations of strangeness will succeed when a safe environment exists to which a child can return. In adolescence, when the self is fragile a fantasy of omnipotence develops.

As Erdheim (1992) stresses, omnipotence is a concept inherent in nationalistic and ethnocentric attitudes. Adolescents ascribe negative images to an out-group, while the positive images are identified with the in-group. Referring to findings from group dynamics, Klosinski (1994: 271–272) pointed out that four rules are relevant in this context: the tendency to exclude what is strange from the daily life of a group; a group hierarchy which is based on power and aggression; the tendency to define opponent groups or individuals (and therefore the need for an objective); and, finally, the more a group feels threatened and the more significant the fear is, the more ready it is to join in the defensive fight. The concrete expression of these processes is dependent on specific situations. It is important to recognise here the laws by which group processes are guided. These considerations show that the balance between closeness and distance, and between the definition of the self and strangers, is potentially connected with aggression. This is quite normal: when people cope with fear they fall back on aggression. Therefore, it is possible to argue that even from the perspective of psychology a disposition towards xenophobic behaviour exists. Whether and to what extent this occurs depends on the stage of the individual's development, his and her personality and the characteristics of reference groups. The general insight is that groups tend to define demarcation lines. A common enemy stimulates a positive in-group feeling because commonality is important to ward off an enemy. To strengthen demarcation lines in order to defend oneself from the other is a coping mechanism for fear. Foreigners and what is perceived as strange are excellently suited to be projections of fear. Concentrating on a foreign group helps to cover or ignore problems in one's own group. Fear is one of the key concepts used by developmental psychologists to explain xenophobic behaviour: fear of personal loyalty, the future, inferiority, social status, unemployment, social order, and the fear of uncertainty about the validity of our values and religious truth in a context of cultural pluralism.

The socialisation approach

The third group of theories diagnoses the main reason for xenophobia as the social and societal environment in which people live. Young people acquire these attitudes by socialisation. According to Rippl (2004) there are four modes in which xenophobia can be developed by socialisation. The first is called a transmission mode, which implies more or less a direct transfer of the attitudes of parents to the worldview of a child or adolescent. Early adolescence is understood as an important time of openness to the acquisition of patterns of attitudes. In most cases this process is not based on actual political discussions within the family, but the experience of parental talk during daily life. In these cases socialisation is understood as social learning and learning via models. A second mode relates to the study of authoritarian personality by Adorno, Frenkel-Brunswick, Levinson and Sanford (1950) after the Second World War. What is important here is not the content that parents express but the style of interaction between parents and child during education. An emotionally deprived style of education with a strong regime of punishment will create a problematic personality structure. Its effect is that subsequent interactions, especially with weaker people, are based on aggression, resulting in a disposition to xenophobia. A third mode draws attention to the fact that during adolescence not only parents but also reference groups are important for the development of political attitudes. Political rigour and right-wing orientations often include xenophobic attitudes. Insofar as young people come into contact with such groups, or with right-wing music, culture or literature, their clear and hierarchical worldview can seem attractive in the context of a pluralistic environment. A fourth mode focuses on individual experiences of social disintegration. Here the real problem of integrating youth into modern society is not transmission from parents or reference groups, understood as a force towards xenophobic attitudes. In many cases unemployment is central, which often coincides with experiences of meaninglessness, a decline of participation, a loss of norms and values, a lack of opportunity to have a better life, social isolation, and so on. Under these circumstances individuals look for compensatory activities.

If the causes of bad living conditions have nothing to do with individual ability, an external enemy is sought. Xenophobia offers a valve for this. The concepts are not clear cut but show some overlap; what they have in common is that societal causes stimulate xenophobia. Riedl (1994) follows that line in saying that xenophobic behaviour may be seen, not as something personal, but as something caused by the political-societal system in which young people grow up. Theories of this type state that, in the interaction of individuals and society, the environment has a very strong influence on the formation of a worldview. According to Riedl, xenophobic behaviour is an instrument to cope with a crowded society because it offers strength, superiority, and emotional security. Xenophobia is then based on the ideology of inequality which allows a totalitarian understanding of values, and an exclusion of people with a certain nationality, ethnicity or religion, because the individual is placed at the top of a natural hierarchy. At the centre of a societal justification of xenophobia is the social system which stimulates and supports the development of rigid attitudes and behaviour.

These theoretical approaches do not exhaust the concepts needed to explain xenophobic attitudes and behaviour. However, the approaches referred to show a continuum of xenophobia as a natural reaction of humans to the influence of the social environment. Regardless of the differences in explanation, if the motive power for xenophobia is natural or contextually based, it reduces fear and anxiety and helps people feel more confident. This is especially needed in situations where individuals are confronted with diversity. In the following section we will focus our atttention on religious diversity in current German society.

Xenophobia and Religious Pluralism in Germany

German society currently incorporates a good portion of individuals with a non-German background (www.destatis.de). In 2007, 7.3 million allochthon people lived in Germany, most of them from Turkey, the former Yugoslavia and Italy. This represents 8.8% of the German population. Most of these people live in the big cities of Berlin, Hamburg and the 'Ruhrgebiet' or the industrial regions of Baden-Württemberg and Bavaria. By contrast, in all the federal states from the eastern parts of Germany the percentage of people with a non-German background is less than 3%. Accordingly, in their daily life young Germans experience foreign cultures mainly via the media and by consuming foreign food (Münchmeier, 2000). Personal contacts take place in school, but less so during their leisure time. Although 73% of students share their classroom with at least one or two contemporaries with a different ethnic background, in their leisure time only 30% of the young Germans meet foreign youngsters, mostly in sport activities. One may assume that many of these contacts happen occasionally. There are regional differences, as in the Eastern parts of Germany there are hardly any foreigners. Most young people who live in the former GDR do not meet allochthonous contemporaries, either at school or in their leisure time.

In terms of religious belonging, 62% of Germans are Christians, 4% Muslims, 1% Jews and 33% without religious affiliation in 2004 (www.fowid.de). Half of the Christians were Roman Catholics and half were Protestants, mainly Lutheran. Citizens who belong to an Orthodox Church had a predominantly non-German background. The majority of Muslims are Sunnites or Shiites; only a few of them had a German background. Cultural and religious pluralism in Germany is most visible in the differences between Christians and non-Christians. This pluralism is represented in the bigger cities and the industrial regions in the West and the South, but less so in the rural areas. In urban centres the experience of religious difference in daily life arises around political and cultural issues of public relevance. Thus there is continuous public discussion related to Islamic-motivated terrorism. Another controversial discussion in Munich and Cologne received national attention in

2007, because new big mosques were planned for city centres. (Since the 1960s mosques have been located mostly at the peripheries of the cities.) Religious pluralism is not exclusively related to Islam, but the presence of Islam is the most relevant content of pluralism. Germany is also divided into religiously and nonreligiously affiliated people. This demarcation primarily follows the former border between the FRG and the GDR: most of the people without religious belonging live in the Eastern parts of Germany, 75% non-affiliated to 25% affiliated. In Western Germany these proportions are reversed.

Since the 1980s a public debate has been going on discussing the question whether there has been a shift towards xenophobic attitudes in German society. Research supports the idea that an ideological transformation is occurring. In terms of social consent, until the 1980s there was a social boundary with regard to public discussion of right-wing nationalistic opinions. In view of the historical legacy, a public proscription of such positions was natural. For some time this boundary seems to have been eliminated or at least to have been notably lowered. This shows itself in the re-awakening of the radical right-wing. In the last decade, nationalistic parties won seats in federal parliament in five out of 16 federal states. The media constantly reports attacks against businesses, homes and houses of prayer. Although violence against foreigners remains the exception statistically, an habituation effect has set in for many people. Not only are foreigners the targets of right-wing hatred, so also are German citizens who show solidarity with non-Germans. Finally, certain xenophobic attitudes are popular among young people in Germany (Münchmeier, 2000): 62% think that there are too many foreigners living in the country; 30% cannot imagine marrying an allochthonous partner. Again there are regional differences. Young people from the Eastern parts are more xenophobic than their contemporaries from the West. Other markers of difference are gender and education. Males are slightly more xenophobic than females, and so are students with a low level of education compared with those who go to university.

Is this ideological transformation related to religious pluralism? Here we only have some empirical data which does not draw a coherent picture (www.fowid.de). On the one hand, religious orientation is not correlated with political orientation. Neither the self-perception as religious nor religious belonging affect sympathy with any particular political party or programme. On the other hand, 68% of Germans agree that people with very strong religious beliefs are often too intolerant of others. In empirical inquiries among youth we find a correlation between ethnocentrism and the monoreligious conviction that one's own belief was the only true one (Ziebertz and Van der Ven, 1994; Ziebertz, 2005a, 2005b).

According to David Herbert, religion is a bearer of cultural identity that can transform heterogenity to unity (community). In his reflection on Islamism, he identifies Islam as a 'master signifier' (2004: 160), able to establish communal identity across different societal subsystems. Using the concept of 'umma', Muslims are able to define their position in a heterogeneous world. Connecting power is an implicit potential in every traditional religion, as Durkheim has stated. As sources of societal cohesion, religions like Christianity, Judaism, or Islam carry convictions and values which go beyond religious discourse. They are able to bridge the structural differentiation of contemporary society and offer a narrative capable of supporting cultural belonging.

In light of this scenario, xenophobia may be related to religion in two ways. First, religion may be used as a marker of cultural difference. Establishing community and marking difference are coincidental characteristics. Just as community is related to shared convictions, values and practices, the difference of the other may be construed by the lack of these convictions, values and practices. For instance, according to Mary Perkins, the birth of a European identity is strongly related to its delimitation from Islamic cultures (2004). In this process Islam has been taken as an out-of-date culture, not meeting the requirements of modern times. Religion is a criterion of difference that is easily handled. As a 'master signifier', which overlaps societal subsystems and shapes individual life-styles, a person's religious affiliation characterises the whole person and her/his cultural background. In this regard religion is a single and clear-cut criterion of cultural difference. Second, religion may be a moderator of cultural difference. This can happen either in a positive or in a negative manner. Religion is first a source of solidarity and a recognition of the difference of the other. Every religion provides narratives of solidarity with people who do not belong to their own culture. At the same time, peace is highly valued by different religions. On the other hand, religious convictions and values turn out to be the cause of conflict and terror. Exclusive truth claims contain the potential to be defended, even by aggression, against other truth claims. In this regard religion may moderate or exacerbate xenophobia.

Method

Research questions and assumptions

In this study we examine the empirical relationship between xenophobia and religious pluralism. In modern German society both attitudes may be correlated, but this correlation is not obvious. Understanding secularisation as the process of the growing meaninglessness of religion, one could assume that religion has no relevance to xenophobia. To explore this claim we add three religious variables to the analysis: the formal category of religious belonging, the subjective category of religious self-perception, and attitudes towards interreligious differences (relationship between the religions). These variables will substantiate the role of religion in the relationship between xenophobia and religious pluralism. Finally, we will analyse our findings on a national bias. Germany has a peculiar history in the period of 1933 to 1945. In reaction to Germany's peculiar history, every student has to undergo special lessons at school which deal with German history and personal relationships towards foreigners. As a result of this educational effort, it may be that the German findings represent a national exception. Our research questions are as follows.

1. What attitudes do young Germans have towards foreigners?
2. What attitudes do they have towards religious plurality?
3. Is there a correlation between attitudes towards foreigners and attitudes towards religious plurality?
4. Do religious belonging, religious self-perception and attitudes towards the relationship between religions correlate with xenophobia and religious plurality?
5. Do these correlations depend on the German national context?

Because of the explorative character of this study, we do not want to describe our research expectations as hypotheses, but rather more cautiously as research assumptions. Because of the character of the sample (better educated young people) we presume that the degree of xenophobia will be low among students attending a Gymnasium or Comprehensive School (question 1). Further, we expect a positive attitude towards plurality (question 2). The reason for these assumptions is that better educated youth will not mirror an ideology which legitimises attacks on foreigners and members of other religions. They could have learned to change their perspective and to engage in differentiated thinking. In regard to question 3, we assume that xenophobia and attitudes towards religious pluralism are negatively correlated. This contradicts the notion that religion is not a factor of social relevance. According to the predictors employed in our study (religious belonging, religious self-perception and attitudes towards the relation between religions), we assume that only religious concepts of exclusiveness correlate positively with a xenophobic attitude, whereas the acceptance of multireligiosity correlates positively with religious pluralism (question 4). Finally, we expect some disparity when comparing German youth with others (question 5). Germany has a specific historical and cultural background and the attitude towards foreigners will be affected by this.

Theoretical concepts and their operationalisation

This contribution mainly focuses on attitudes of young people towards xenophobia and religious pluralism, and whether there is a relationship between these two attitudes.

Xenophobia. Xenophobia and fear of strangers is not a modern phenomenon. However, xenophobia has a modern face that takes on ugly characteristics, when hatred of foreigners spread, or even more extreme, for example when violent attacks are carried out on foreigners. All European countries are familiar with this problem. In our survey we used a xenophobia scale published by Nurmi (1998). This breaks down xenophobia into different levels. Besides unspecific attitudes towards the presence of foreign citizens ("There are too many foreigners in this country"), it contains items concerning the economy ("The foreigners take away jobs from the natives because they work for less money"), personal relationships ("I try to stay away from foreign young people") and matters of social life ("Foreigners who don't want to conform to this country shouldn't stay here"). All in all, the 10 items form a reliable one-dimensional scale (Cronbach alpha = .90).

Religious plurality. Religious plurality is a social-cultural normality in Western countries. Pluralisation takes place both within a culture and over cultural borders. Convictions of belief, values and lifestyles can no longer be attached to a single, overarching worldview. Demands of exclusivity do not remain unchallenged, and must be explicitly justified. Christian religions find themselves in contention with other religions and worldviews not only over the appropriate interpretation of reality, but also over the influence of the social and cultural process.

Individuals can experience plurality differently. On the one hand, it stands for liberality and choices; on the other hand, it is exactly this openness that can become a problem if certainties are put into question and orientation frameworks are abandoned. In our survey we used a scale with 12 items, from which we here present three sample reactions to plurality. First, a positive reaction in which plurality is greeted as welcome ("It is good that we encounter so many different religions and worldviews in our society"); second a negative reaction in which plurality is connected with insecurity and unrest ("In our society, there are so many religions and cultural influences that you don't know in which direction to go"), and third a neutral position that it does not make a difference to individual and collective life whether there is diversity or not ("The many religions in our country make life neither more nor less difficult"). A factor analysis (main component analysis with varimax rotation and eigenvalue > 1) reduced the number of items leading to one reliable factor: four items of the positive concept remained and one of the negative concept, which showed a negative factor loading and was recoded before producing the scale. The one-dimensional scale is reliable (Cronbach alpha $= .75$) and represents a positive attitude toward religious pluralism.

Besides the relation between xenophobia and attitudes towards religious pluralism, we are interested in the role of religion with regard to these attitudes. In our study we include three elements: religious belonging, religious self-perception and attitudes towards the relationship between religions. Religious belonging is a formal category. It depends on membership in a religious community and provides no insight concerning religious commitment. In our chapter we distinguish between members and nonmembers. Religious self-perception represents the individuals' understanding of their own religiousness. It gives information about the subjective perspective, which in a modern society is theoretically independent of church membership. In our survey religious self-perception was assessed by the item "I regard myself as a religious person" which could be answered on a 5-point Likert scale. The relationship between the religions refers to the plurality of religious truth claims. Plurality is a problem for most religions. Religious communities like Judaism, Islam and Christianity raise exclusive demands regarding belief in religious truth and approaching the revelation of God. Nevertheless, it belongs to the essence of plurality that one at least recognises the existence of alternative interpretations, even if one dismisses them critically. We refer to three typical points of view on this matter. The first point of view is a monoreligious one: "Only in my religion do people have access to true redemption." This statement excludes other religions as pathways to salvation. The second point of view refers to the phenomenally, sociologically, or psychologically inspired analysis of all religions as finally equal, as identical in their social functions and as different social-historical forms of expression of the search for happiness and perfection. This multireligious claim is represented by the item "Religions are equal to each other; they are all directed at the same truth." A third alternative is given by the interreligious point of view. This does not neutralise the conviction implicit in the content of each religion to challenge faith. But when a tradition claims superiority without any further details, and as not everything that exists can be equally important and equally meaningful, then dialogue is needed in order further to explore religions in one's own search for God and to come closer to the recognition of truth. The relevant item in our study is "The real truth can only be discovered in the communication between religions."

Finally, we compare the German findings with other national contexts (Israel, Poland, and Sweden). Nationality represents the historical and socio-cultural background of the individual. The Israeli society represents a Jewish culture surrounded by Arabic neighbours. Poland is a thoroughly Catholic society, which has undergone fundamental economic and social changes since the 1990s. Sweden is well settled within the EU economic system with a predominantly Protestant cultural background. In terms of religious belonging, Germany is a mixed country, which on the one hand is well integrated into the EU, and on the other hand has to handle the economic and cultural differences between its Western and Eastern parts. In general the countries selected represent four specific national scenarios.

Sample

These data are taken from a cross European study "Religion and Life Perspectives" (RaLP) which included ten countries with about 10000 respondents (Ziebertz and Kay, 2005, 2006; Ziebertz, Kay and Riegel, 2008). It focuses on teenagers attending secondary schools with a good academic background (e.g. grammar school). The study was carried out in medium sized towns. On the one hand, these are less influenced by tradition, convention and custom compared with rural areas; on the other hand, there is a lower level of individualisation here than in bigger cities. All of the cities also have a good portion of nonChristian religious communities.

To answer research questions (1) to (4) we used the German subsample. In Germany the investigation took place in 53 schools (Gymnasium and Gesamtschule) in seven cities (Augsburg, Dortmund, Dresden, Aachen, Hildesheim, Rostock, and Würzburg) with a sample survey of 1923 people in total. The average age is 17 years. Of those surveyed 1470 declare that they belong to a Church or religious community, and 418 of those surveyed deny this. Catholic youths are the majority (N = 954) and Lutherans are the second largest group (N = 463); 36 of those surveyed have a Muslim background, 13 describe themselves as Orthodox, 5 belong to a different religious community. In the German sample there is a slight majority of girls (54%) as opposed to boys (46%).

To answer research question (5) we also examined sub-samples from Israel, Poland and Sweden. The sample from Israel (N = 851) has a small majority of female youngsters (54%); the average age is 19 years and everyone surveyed is Jewish. The Polish sample (N = 797) has an average age of 18.5 years; it represents almost exclusively Catholic youth (97.6%), with more girls (58%) than boys (42%). The Swedish sample (N = 757) is mostly Lutheran (65%), and youngsters of no denomination (32%); the average age is 19.8 years, and again there are more females (57%) than males (43%).

To analyse attitudes towards xenophobia and religious plurality we used the statistical routines of frequencies, descriptives, and correlations. To construct the scales we used factor analysis (main component analysis, varimax-rotation, eigenvalue > 1) and reliability routines (Cronbach alpha). All scales are reliable in all of the four samples. The statistical routines were run on the SPSS software. To describe the means we use the following formula: 1.00–2.19 = strong disagreement; 2.20–2.79 = disagreement; 2.80–3.20 = uncertainty; 3.21–3.80 = agreement; 3.81–5.00 = strong agreement. We interpret the correlation values and β-values of the regression analysis according to the following formula: 0.00–0.14 = very weak; 0.15–0.29 = weak; 0.30–0.44 = medium; 0.45–0.59 = strong; 0.60 and higher = very strong.

RESULTS

The presentation of the results follows the sequence of research questions.

Xenophobia

Strangers and foreign people are a visible expression of plurality. However, they can also be seen as projections of fears connected with the experience of plurality. In this study a scale was used in which the issue of the presence of foreigners was raised in several ways and youngsters asked to what extent a feeling of threat was connected with this.

There is one item which is clearly approved by German youngsters (table 15.1): they wish to deport foreigners who turn to crime (m = 3.56). They also agree that foreigners who do not conform should not stay (m = 3.22). There is slight agreement that foreigners should not act provocatively in public (m = 3.18). All these items emphasise the importance of conforming to the cultural norms of the majority. The other items concern the rejection of foreigners. Remarkably, the young people clearly reject all the economic items as well as the items regarding personal relationships. Teenagers attending German high schools are not afraid of being jobless because foreigners work for less money (m = 2.33), and they do not think that the economy would do better with fewer foreigners living in Germany (m = 2.30). Nor do they seek to avoid contacts with foreigners (m = 1.93) or reject intercultural marriages (m = 1.40). Both the economy and personal relationships are relevant topics for 17-year-olds, who are to finish school soon and need to find a reliable partner. All in all, German youngsters with a good education are not afraid of foreigners. This result is also reflected in the mean of the total scale: 2.55 represents disagreement with xenophobia. But two aspects should be kept in mind. First, the respondents claim that foreigners should conform to the cultural standards in Germany. Second, the high value of the standard deviation indicates some variance in attitudes towards strangers. So the answer to the first research question is: average young Germans, attending good schools, are not xenophobic, but they expect strangers to observe the cultural standards of the majority.

XENOPHOBIA AND RELIGIOUS PLURALISM

Table 15.1: Xenophobia

	N	Mean	SD
Foreigners who turn to crime in my country should be deported immediately	1919	3.56	1.27
Foreigners who don't want to conform to this country shouldn't stay here	1916	3.22	1.28
Foreigners shouldn't act so provocatively in public	1910	3.18	1.29
A lot of foreigners have it too good in this country	1918	2.61	1.27
There are too many foreigners in this country	1870	2.55	1.33
Most politicians in this country care too much about foreigners, and not enough abut the people who have always lived here	1909	2.46	1.22
The foreigners take away jobs from the natives because they work for less money	1919	2.33	1.21
The economy would do a lot better in this country if there were fewer foreigners	1918	2.30	1.13
I try to stay away from foreign young people	1913	1.93	1.09
People from this country should not marry foreigners	1915	1.40	0.79
Descriptive statistics of the total scale	1922	2.55	0.87

Note: 1 = disagree strongly; 2 = disagree; 3 = not certain; 4 = agree; 5 = agree strongly.

Religious plurality

As several cultures and religions are present in German society, the current political debate concerning mainstream German culture is over how Germany's youth view religious plurality. Four items were approved by the students (table 15.2). All regard religious plurality as positive and valuable. The youngsters perceive cultural plurality as interesting and colourful (m = 3.94 and m = 3.77), and they do not feel unease when confronted by different religions (m = 3.59). Instead of undermining one's orientation (m = 2,78), religious plurality is perceived as enriching (m = 3.27). The item representing a negative statement about religious plurality tends to be rejected by the respondents. They do not think that a broad variety of religious and cultural influences will lead to disorientation (m = 2.78). This recognition of religious plurality is also represented by the mean of the total scale (m = 3.61). Looking at the standard deviations, there is an apparent rise if only religious plurality is concerned. The biggest variance occurs with the items suggesting that the presence of many religions does not matter (sd = 1.17), and that the variety of religious beliefs is enriching (sd = 1.16). This indicates that some of the teenagers consider religious plurality a problem.

356 HANS-GEORG ZIEBERTZ & ULRICH RIEGEL

Table 15.2: Religious plurality

	N	Mean	SD
The fact that there are so many cultures is good for our society and makes it colourful	1915	3.9	1.04
It is good that we encounter so many different religions and worldviews in our society	1916	3.77	1.08
It really doesn't matter that there are so many religions in our country	1916	3.59	1.17
The variety of religious beliefs in this country is enriching			
In our society, there are so many religions and cultural influences that you don't know in which direction to go*	1916	2.78	1.07
Descriptive statistics of the total scale	1922	3.61	0.87

Note: 1 = disagree strongly; 2 = disagree; 3 = not certain; 4 = agree; 5 = agree strongly; * reverse coded.

However, German young people with a good education in general feel well prepared to cope with religious plurality—which is the answer to our second research question.

The relationship between xenophobia and religious plurality

In this section we raise the question whether xenophobia is correlated to attitudes towards religious plurality. On the one hand, fear of strangers in most cases equates to a fear of the unknown and the different. This would imply a negative relationship between xenophobia and plurality. On the other hand, religious plurality within a secularised society might show no correlation to xenophobia because religion is not perceived as relevant. The empirical data does not support the latter assumption. Xenophobia and attitudes towards religious plurality are clearly negatively correlated ($r = -.49^{***}$). Those who appreciate religious plurality are less xenophobic, and those afraid of foreigners do not regard the presence of many religious traditions as a positive and enriching fact. So the answer to the third research question is that xenophobia and a positive attitude towards religious plurality simply exclude each other.

Xenophobia and plurality according to religious belonging and religious attitudes

To be able to substantiate the relevance of religion with regard to xenophobia more precisely we included some additional religious variables

XENOPHOBIA AND RELIGIOUS PLURALISM

Table 15.3: Xenophobia and plurality according to religious belonging and religious attitudes (correlations)

	Xenophobia	Religious plurality
Religious belonging (being a member)	.06**	–
Religious self-perception	–	–
Multireligiosity	–	.12***
Interreligiosity	–.13***	.28***
Monoreligiosity	.21***	–.27***

Note: ** p< .01; *** p< .001

into the analysis. These are the categories of religious belonging, the statement whether one regards oneself as religious or not, and three characteristic attitudes towards the relationship between religions (multireligiosity, interreligiosity and monoreligiosity).

Religious belonging is positively correlated with xenophobia, but the correlation is very weak (r = .06**; table 15.3). Further, there is no relationship between religious self-perception and xenophobia or attitudes towards religious plurality. How one thinks about foreigners or about the plurality of religious beliefs and practices is independent of one's own religious assessment. Both variables, religious belonging and religious self-perception, are of no importance with regard to xenophobia and religious plurality. This changes with attitudes towards the relationship between religions. A multireligious as well as an interreligious attitude is positively correlated to the appreciation of religious plurality (r = .12*** and r = .28***). Those who regard all religions as equal and those who are convinced that real truth is only gained through dialogue between religions tend to think positively about religious plurality—and vice versa. Interreligiosity is negatively correlated to xenophobia (r = –.13***). The fear of foreigners and the will to contact foreign religions do not fit together properly. Finally, a monoreligious attitude correlates positively with xenophobia (r = .21***) and negatively with the appreciation of religious plurality (r = –.27***). Those who regard their own religion as an exclusive path to salvation tend to be afraid of foreigners and tend to assess the presence of different religions as negative—and vice versa. Although these correlations are weak or very weak, they draw a coherent picture, which will answer the fourth research question. Whereas the mere fact of religious belonging or being religious or not is of no importance with regard to xenophobia and attitudes towards religious plurality, the assessment of the relationship between religions is important. A xenophobic attitude is positively related to an exclusivistic religious stance (monoreligiosity) and negatively related to the will to engage in interreligious dialogue (interreligiosily). So it is not the fact of being religious but the quality of the religiosity that is significant.

The relevance of the national context

The last research question focuses on the national context. With Germany, Israel, Poland and Sweden we have chosen four samples with different characteristics (see above). The empirical data about xenophobia and attitudes towards religious plurality support these characteristics (table 15.4).

In the main, the Swedish respondents do not share xenophobic attitudes (m = 2.42), although the relatively high standard deviation indicates that there are some Swedes who are unhappy about the presence of foreigners (sd = 1.06). Swedish teenagers appreciate religious plurality (m = 3.53). All in all the Swedish findings are similar to those in Germany. By contrast, the Polish respondents are uncertain with regard to xenophobia and attitudes towards religious plurality. Most of them do not know whether the presence of foreigners is good or not (m = 3.16), nor how to evaluate religious plurality (m = 3.10). The Israeli sample shows a good portion of xenophobic thinking (m = 3.52). These teenagers are uncertain whether religious plurality is enriching or leads to disorientation (m = 3.02). Turning to the correlation analysis, as in Germany xenophobia and the appreciation of religious plurality are correlated negatively in all three countries. Within the four countries Poland is an exception, because here the correlation is very weak. Accordingly in Poland there is only a slight chance that the unease in the presence of foreigners is based on the rejection of religious plurality—and vice versa.

Given these different national contexts, do they result in relevantly different stances towards the relationship between the religions? They do, but only in the case of Israel (table 15.5). Evidently the effect of those attitudes is highest in Israel. In both cases they declare more variance than in Germany, Poland and Sweden. The difference in the declared variance is especially remarkable with respect to xenophobia. Turning to the β-values, in Israel xenophobia is related in a moderate strength to a monoreligious attitude (β = .46***). The other β-values are weak or very weak. They fit the well-known picture that multireligious and interreligious attitudes support the appreciation of religious plurality,

XENOPHOBIA AND RELIGIOUS PLURALISM

Table 15.4: Xenophobia and religious plurality in Poland, Israel, and Sweden (descriptive analysis and correlations)

	Poland		Israel		Sweden	
	Mean	SD	Mean	SD	Mean	SD
Xenophobia	3.16	0.72	3.52	0.85	2.42	1.06
Religious plurality	3.10	0.62	3.02	0.71	3.53	0.77
Correlation xenophia/ Religious plurality	−.14***		−.40***		−.58***	

Note: N Poland = 797, N Israel = 851, N Sweden = 7 57. 1 = disagree strongly; 2 = disagree; 3 = not certain; 4 = agree; 5 = agree strongly.
* p< .05; ** p< .01; *** p< .001.

Table 15.5: Xenophobia and plurality according to religious attitudes by national context (regression analysis)

	Xenophobia				Religious plurality			
	GER ß	POL ß	ISR ß	SWE ß	GER ß	POL ß	ISR ß	SWE ß
Multireligiosity			−.08*	−.16***	.06*	.24***	.20***	.25***
Interreligiosity	−.11***		−.10**		.26***	.09**	.17***	.08*
Monoreligiosity	.21***	.19***	.46***	.24***	−.25***	−.18***	−.26***	−.29***
r	.24	.19	.54	.28	.39	.36	.49	.39
Declared variance	6%	4%	29%	8%	15%	13%	24%	16%

whereas a monoreligious attitude supports xenophobia. In more detail, in Germany and Poland a xenophobic attitude is independent of the multireligious stance that all religions are equal. The same is true with regard to an interreligious attitude in Poland and Sweden. But these details change the overall picture. To sum up, Germany, Poland and Sweden represent similar cases. There are some effects of attitudes towards relationships between the religions with regard to xenophobia and the appreciation of religious plurality. But these effects only explain a small part of the variance. In Israel xenophobia is based to a significant extent on a monoreligious attitude and the effect of all of these attitudes explains a good portion of the variance. So the answer to the fifth research question is that national context is only relevant in the particular case of Israel. The European countries of Germany, Poland and Sweden do not differ significantly. In terms of the relationship between xenophobia and religious pluralism Germany is not a European exception.

Conclusion

In this chapter we researched the relation between xenophobia and religious pluralism. We have investigated whether this relation is affected by religious character and attitudes. A number of research assumptions have stuctured the analysis.

First, we expected that young people who receive a better education will show a positive attitude towards religious plurality and reject xenophobic thinking. This expectation has been confirmed. The young Germans in our study do not show xenophobic attitudes and they experience religious plurality as enriching and stimulating. Pluralism is part of their experience of daily life, they have learned to cope with it and to accept the consequences that emanate from pluralism. These findings confirm results from previous studies (Ziebertz, 1990; Heitmeyer, 1992; Münchmeier, 2000; Ziebertz and Kay, 2005). One reason for this could be that better levels of personal resources (a better education) enable individuals to deal with plurality.

Second, we expected that xenophobia and religious pluralism would be negatively connected: that xenophobic people evaluate pluralism negatively and vice versa. Third, we expected that religiosity is a sensitive indicator towards both attitudes. These assumptions were also confirmed. Fear of strangers is an attitude which is not combined with the perception that plurality is enriching. Xenophobic respondents experience religious plurality and difference as a cause of unease and anxiety. The remarkable fact is that it is religious plurality which is related to unease and anxiety where foreign customs are concerned. This notion is backed up to some extent by the finding that xenophobia is weakly correlated to attitudes towards relationships between religions. The monoreligious attitude is based on exclusivistic patterns. This attitude fits into a xenophobic habitus and does not fit into a pluralistic one. The interreligious attitude is focused on the dialogue between the religions. It appreciates religious plurality. This finding may help to delineate how religion re-emerges as a social force. In a modern society the formal fact of belonging to a religious community is of no significance—at least as far as Christianity is concerned, which is the major religion in Germany. Religious self-perception is of no relevance, either. The thing that matters is the way in which religiosity is perceived and realised.

Fourth, we expected that the national context would show differences. According to our findings this is only true in the case of Israel.

Although the societies of Germany, Poland, and Sweden differ in their religious character and their historical background, they show similar relations between xenophobia and religious attitudes. The different situation in Israel can easily be explained by the conflict with the Palestinians, in which religion is a significant criterion of difference between the opponents. Therefore, at least in Europe, the relationship between xenophobia and religious pluralism does not depend on the national context.

How might we interpret these findings? There is no doubt that religious pluralism represents a key feature of the current social environment. Pluralism can be understood as a direct expression and consequence of modernisation. Religious pluralism defines the context in which individual thinking and behaviour seeks acceptance and acknowledgment. This is not a trivial notion, if one takes into account that the process of secularisation could weaken or diminish the relevance of religion as a factor of the social environment. Our findings show that xenophobic attitudes are not well adapted to this social context. They are positively correlated with exclusivistic religious claims, which contradict the idea of any equality between the religions. One may argue that, in the long run, xenophobic attitudes will vanish. People will predominantly favour low xenophobic attitudes, because they would be better adapted to the requirements of modern society. But one may imagine a different scenario as well. In this scenario xenophobia has a superior character because it is a bearer of identity and a source of orientation in a pluralistic environment. Today xenophobic attitudes may be marginalised by society, but in the long run they will establish strong communities of individuals that are able to overcome the mentality of anything-goes within a pluralistic society. In the sociobiological framework both scenarios are possible.

This brings us to the psychological framework. In this framework personal and social resources are essential for how an individual copes with her/his role and position in society. In this context the negative correlation between xenophobia and religious pluralism can be explained by a lack of relevant resources. Whoever is afraid of strangers is not able to compete with the variety of options typical in a pluralistic society. Instead, she or he will stress exclusivistic attitudes, which establish the individual's orientation as the normative one. In a psychological framework this condition is not a matter of fate. It can be treated in different ways. One may look back into the biography of the individual and counsel him or her about traumatic experiences. One may promote socialisation and education in families to improve self-esteem and the relation between proximity and distance. One may establish educational programmes to train social strategies, which diminish the relevance of in-group and out-group strategies. All of these processes equip the individual for coping with a pluralistic context. The success of these initiatives depends on the character of the relationship between xenophobia and religious pluralism. In this survey we interviewed youth attending *Gymnasium* or *Gesamtschule* who should or could be rich in personal and social resources. Does this condition turn the relationship between xenophobia and religious pluralism more fundamental?

In the social-constructive framework the relation between xenophobia and religious pluralism is directly affected by the social context. This framework takes into consideration the fact that religious convictions and practices offer norms, values, and—in general—orientation within a pluralistic society. Religions represent a specific worldview and propose ethical guidelines. They imply criteria to categorise plurality. According to our findings, this condition is a European one and in this area relatively independent of national peculiarities. Within this context religion can resume being a relevant social factor and two scenarios are possible. On the one hand, religion as a source of orientation may be used to exclude what is not part of one's own religious convictions. This is the case with xenophobic teenagers who prefer a monoreligious attitude. On the other hand, religion as a source of orientation may also be used to categorise plurality and bring different claims into dialogue. This is the case with non-xenophobic teenagers who show interreligious attitudes. Both scenarios are possible—and according to our findings it is the religious attitude which marks the difference regarding xenophobia and the evaluation of religious plurality in a modern society. Of course, most of the youngsters surveyed think in the second way.

These findings allow an optimistic view of the future. The limitation could be that we have only interviewed students from Gymnasium and Gesamtschule. We do not have data from teenagers with fewer personal and social resources or from nonChristian youngsters. These limitations of our study underline that all of our other reported interpretations are tentative and emphasise the need for follow-up research.

REFERENCES

Adorno, T.W., Frenkel-Brunswick, E., Lavinson, D.J. and Sanford, R.N. (1950), *The Authoritarian Personality*, New York, Harper and Brothers.

Erdheim, M. (1992), Das Eigene und das Fremde: über ethnische Identität, *Psyche*, 46(8), 730–744.

Guha, A.-A. (1991), Xenophobie: oder warum gibt es Fremdenfeindlichkeit? *Vorgänge. Zeitschrift für Bürgerrechte und Gesellschaftspolitik*, 30(1), 69–80.

Heitmeyer, W. (1992), *Rechtsextremistische Orientierungen bei Jugendlichen*, Weinheim, Juventa.

Herbert, D. (2004), Islam, identity and globalisation, in S. Coleman and P. Collins (eds.), *Religion, Identity and Change: perspectives on global transformation*, pp. 155–173, Ashgate, Aldershot.

Klosinski, G. (1994), Fremdenfeindlichkeit, Rassismus und Gewaltbereitschaft bei Kindern und Jugendlichen, in G.E. Becker and U. Coburn-Staege (eds.), *Pädagogik gegen Fremdenfeindlichkeit: Rassismus und Gewalt*, pp. 267–279, Weinheim, Beltz.

Münchmeier, R. (2000), Miteinander—nebeneinander—gegeneinander? Zum Verhältnis zwischen deutschen und ausländischen Jugendlichen, in Dt. Shell (ed.), *Jugend 2000, 13, Shell Jugendstudie*, Opladen, leske+budrich.

Nurmi, J.-E. (1998) (eds.), *Adolescents, Cultures, and Conflicts: growing up in contemporary Europe*, New York, Garland Publishing.

Perkins, M. (2004), *Christendom and European Identity: the legacy of a grand narrative since 798*, Berlin, De Gruyter.

Riedl, A. (1994), Ideologie der Ungleichheit und Gewaltakzeptanz als Orientierungsmuster von Jugendlichen, in G.E. Becker and U. Coburn-Staege (eds.), *Pädagogik gegen Fremdenfeindlichkeit: Rassismus und Gewalt*, pp. 280–295, Weinheim, Beltz.

Rippl, S. (2004), Eltern-Kind-Transmission: Einflussfaktoren zur Erklärung von Fremdenfeindlichkeit im Vergleich, *Zeitschrift für Soziologie der Erziehung und Sozialisation*, 24(1), 17–32.

Rydgren, J. (2003), Meso-level reasons for racism and xenophobia, *European Journal of Social Theory*, 6(1), 45–68.

Scheepers, P.L.H. and Gijsberts, M. (2005), *Religiosity and Ethnocentrism in Comparative Perspectives*, Leiden, Brill.

Wahl, K., Tramitz, C. and Blumtritt, J. (eds.) (2001), *Fremdenfeidlichkeit: auf den Spuren extremer Emotionen*, Opladen, Leske und Bundrich.

Winnicott, D.W. (1965), *The Maturational Processes and the Facilitating Environment*, London, Hogarth.

Ziebertz, H.-G. (1990), *Moralerziehung im Wertpluralismus*, Weinheim, Dt. Studienverlag.

———. (2005a), A Move to Multi? Empirical research concerning attitudes of youth toward pluralism and religion's claims of truth, in D. Pollefeyt (ed.), *Interreligious Learning*, pp. 3–24, Leuven.

———. (2005b), Models of inter-religious learning: an empirical study in Germany; in L.J. Francis, M. Robbins and J. Astley (eds.), *Religion, Education and Adolescence: international empirical perspectives*, pp. 204–221, Cardiff, University of Wales Press.

Ziebertz, H.-G., and van der Ven J. (1994), *Religiöser Pluralismus und interreligiöses Lernen*, Weinheim, Dt. Studienverlag.

Ziebertz, H.-G. and Kay, W. (eds.) (2005), *Youth in Europe. Volume 1: an international empirical study about life perspectives*, Münster, LIT.

———. (eds.) (2006), *Youth in Europe. Volume 2: an international empirical study about religiosity*, Münster, LIT.

Ziebertz, H.-G., Kay, W. and Riegel, U. (eds.) (2008), *Youth in Europe. Volume 3: an international empirical study about the relationship between religiosity and life perspectives*, Münster, LIT.

CHAPTER SIXTEEN

A CHURCH DIVIDED BY THEOLOGY AND PRACTICE: THE CASE OF THE ADMISSION OF CHILDREN TO COMMUNION IN THE CHURCH IN WALES

Keith Littler

SUMMARY

This study examines the way in which change in theology and practice takes place in the Anglican Church by focusing on the case of the admission of children to communion through the eyes of clerics in the Church in Wales. Surveys were conducted in 1993 and 2003, and to accommodate the changed status of clergywomen between 1993 and 2003. The data recorded is confined to clergymen. The chapter begins by examining the classic locus of Anglican teaching on admission of children to communion, and the ways in which the teaching has been challenged and modified by Anglican reports and local practice since the publication of the influential Ely Report in 1971. The chapter proceeds by proposing that changing perspectives in Anglican teaching are likely to be mediated at the local level through the personal beliefs and attitudes of the local parish clerics who are often responsible for teaching the laity and for determining local practice. In turn, it is maintained that the views of the local clergy may be shaped both by personal factors and by churchmanship factors. Regarding personal factors, it is likely that older clergy may be more resistant to change than their younger colleagues. Regarding churchmanship factors, it is likely that Catholics and Evangelicals hold significantly different views on key aspects of Christian initiation.

INTRODUCTION

The New Testament is not particularly helpful in providing information about children and communion. Certainly there is evidence that children were present at worship from the earliest times and this may well have included the eucharist. Strange (1996) has suggested that if the earliest Christians saw some similarities between the eucharist, which commemorated the sacrifice of Christ whom Paul described as 'our Passover Lamb' (1 Corinthians 5:7), and the Passover celebration already familiar to them, then we might expect that children would partake of the Christian meal as they had done of the Jewish one (Exodus 12:21–27). It is a fair point but lacks the support of solid evidence.

More revealing is the effect that another New Testament reference (John 6:53) would seem to have had upon St Augustine. John's Gospel comment, that "unless you eat the flesh of the Son of Man and drink his blood you can have no life in you", appears to have persuaded St Augustine that there could be no halfway house between the baptised and the communicant. From this axiom, St Augustine built a powerful case for the admission of children to communion (Strange, 1996). The admission of children to communion in the Eastern Church became defined from this time onwards and remains so. In the West, however, the situation has been less straightforward and, despite Augustine's weighty support, a combination of custom and theology have worked together against the acceptance of child communion.

By the late Middle Ages, a growing reverence for the sacrament of holy communion meant that the eucharist had become virtually a privilege for the priesthood. It is hardly surprising, therefore, that children were debarred from participation in the sacrament. Indeed, the place of children in the theme of things was prescribed in a detailed way when in AD 1215 the Fourth Lateran Council linked the taking of holy communion with the child's arrival at years of discretion (Lowther Clarke, 1932). Thus the Council ruled that children should not be permitted to communion until they had arrived at an age which would allow them to distinguish clearly the elements of the communion from ordinary food. The appropriate age was initially thought to be around seven years, but was later pushed back to between ten and fourteen years. This was the first time a specific age was set on receiving communion.

Despite a good deal of subsequent repudiation of the theology of the Fourth Lateran Council, the Council's ruling was reinforced by the Catholic Reformation of the sixteenth century and the Council of Trent condemned out of hand any suggestion of child communion. Holeton (1981) shows how in the Protestant Churches, despite sporadic efforts to revive the primitive practice of child communion, a pattern has developed for communion to be associated with the process of growing up, while Fisher and Yarnold (1989) demonstrate the manner in which the three parts of the rite of initiation (baptism, confirmation, and communion) became separated one from another. By the sixteenth century infant baptism had become so common that liturgical books

A CHURCH DIVIDED BY THEOLOGY AND PRACTICE 367

ceased to include a separate rite for adults. It was not uncommon for baptism to be expected within a week of the birth of a child as a result of which baptism began to be regarded as a naming ceremony. What is more, some baptism rites, including the Sarum Rite (Whitaker, 1970), included an admonition to the godparents to teach their godchildren to pray and to ensure that they were in due course confirmed. Baptism by the presbyter had become the general practice with the gift of the Holy Spirit linked with confirmation and conferred by the bishop when the child was at least seven years old. Meanwhile, reverence for the eucharist led to the postponement of the first communion to a similar age. Thus the practice has been for baptism to take place in infancy and for confirmation to take place during adolescence, preceded by preparation and followed by communion.

This does not, of course, alter the fact that the legitimacy of the process has continued to be marked by controversy, as illustrated by the diametrically opposed positions of Mason (1893) and Lampe (1967) concerning the rite of confirmation. Although, as Fisher (2005) maintains, the history of discussion about the access of children to communion is of more than antiquarian interest and remains extremely relevant to the current debate, for the purposes of the present study it is developments since the *Ely Report* of 1971 and subsequent attempts to formulate an acceptable theology in relation to the access of children to communion that are of special interest.

THE ELY REPORT AND AFTER

In 1969 a commission was appointed by the archbishops of Canterbury and York with the Right Revd Ted Roberts, the Bishop of Ely, as its chairman. The resulting *Ely Report* (1971) declared its conviction that all the blessings of initiation necessary for access to communion are received at baptism in a single sacramental moment and the commission found no evidence for the existence of confirmation before the time of Irenaeus in the late second century; a point reiterated by the later *Toronto Statement* (Holeton, 1991). Since the *Ely Report* regarded confirmation as primarily a service of commitment and commissioning, it saw no reason to insist that confirmation precede communion. It recommended that the Anglican Church make explicit its recognition that baptism is the full and complete rite of Christian initiation and

368 KEITH LITTLER

may, therefore, be followed by admission to communion. The Bishop of Ely, in introducing the report to the Church of England Synod, pressed for an early decision (Church of England, 1971). Had the report been fully accepted by Synod it would have represented a radical change in the accepted pattern of initiation and a major break with the Catholic past. In fact the *Ely Report* has failed to settle the Anglican debate about access to communion precisely because it came down heavily on one side of the theological argument. In consequence it has aroused opposition from many who adhere to the belief that confirmation is a sacramental rite conveying the gift of the Holy Spirit and is necessary to the fullness of initiation and to access to communion.

It is within this context that the *Report of the Doctrinal Commission of the Church in Wales on Christian Initiation* (Church in Wales, 1971) was published and argued that it is possible to meet the legitimate desire of some of the clergy to introduce baptised children to the communicant life at a pastorally appropriate age. No question arises regarding their qualifications to receive the sacrament. Such children are recognised as members of the Church in a formal sense (Holeton, 1998). Avery (1992: 129) is categorical in the statement, "All grace for a Christian is given in his or her baptism. There is no need to add anything to baptism."

Binfield (1994), through his persuasive summary of an experiment in the involvement of children at the eucharist, asks why, if children are baptised should they be refused communion? Fowler suggests that positive damage to children's faith development may result from refusing them access to communion:

> We are endowed at birth with nascent capacities for faith. How these capacities are activated and grow depends to a large extent on how we are welcomed into the world and what kinds of environment we grow in. Faith is interactive and social; it requires community, language, ritual, and nurture. Faith is also shaped by initiatives from beyond us and other people, initiatives of spirit and grace. How these latter initiatives are recognised and imaged, or unperceived and ignored, powerfully affects the shape of faith in our lives. (James Fowler, cited by Meyers, 1995: 160)

Johnson (1999) writes from personal experience of children at the eucharist and concludes with conviction that it is not only desirable but clearly right for all who are baptised to be granted access to communion.

There is evidence of children being welcomed to communion in most Church of England dioceses (Harden, 2004). Craven (2005) advises us

A CHURCH DIVIDED BY THEOLOGY AND PRACTICE 369

that since 1974 children from the age of seven have been welcome to receive the bread and wine, alongside adults, in the Diocese of Southwark. Similarly, the dioceses of Peterborough and Manchester were officially admitting children to communion from an early date (Church of England, 1997), while by 2004 most Church of England dioceses were doing so (Church of England, 2005a). Fraser (2004) condemns the practice of presenting children with *Smarties* at the communion rail; an act he describes as patronising and one which trivialises the communion. He maintains that children can enhance the worshipping community with more conviction in the taking of bread and wine than the many adults who display a casual approach to communion. Jackson (2004) suggests that children will not accept the discrimination of exclusion from communion and sees such actions as one reason why young people leave the Church before they are old enough for confirmation. It is most unlikely that the reason young people leave the Church is this simple, as Kay and Francis (1996) point out. Even so, it would seem that this was a line of thinking inherent within the Ely Report (1971).

Against this developing backcloth, the Church of England felt it necessary to issue guidelines on communion before confirmation (Church of England, 1997). These guidelines made it clear that, since communion before confirmation is a departure from the inherited norm, it requires special permission and that, after consultation, every diocesan bishop would have the discretion to make a general policy whether or not to entertain new applications for communion before confirmation.

In November 2000, the Church of England General Synod debated a motion from the Diocese of Bristol requesting the House of Bishops to initiate change in Canon Law so that Synod could decide whether communion before confirmation should be the nationally agreed common practice, rather than leaving the decision to individual dioceses and parishes. The motion was amended to read:

> That this Synod request the House of Bishops to continue to monitor the implementation in dioceses of its 1997 guidelines on communion before confirmation and *to report back to Synod by 2005*, with a recommendation as to whether any changes in canon law are required as a result of developing practice and understanding in the Church. (Church of England, 2001)

The delay in the House of Bishops being required to report back to Synod prompted the introduction of the Church of England, *Common Worship Initiation Services: rites on the way and reconciliation and restoration*

(Church of England, 2004), which Delap (2006) describes as owing much to the *Roman Catholic Rite of Christian Initiation of Adults*. It includes a rite of *Admission of the Baptised to Communion* (pp. 44–48), together with the reminder that the rite is intended for use in the circumstances covered by the guidelines agreed by the House of Bishops on the *Admission of Baptised Persons to the Holy Communion before Confirmation* (Church of England, 1997). It should be noted, however, that these guidelines were determined as being intended for use with children in families regular in worship, while the 2004 rite clearly states that "Individual parishes must seek the agreement of the diocesan bishop before introducing communion before confirmation" (Church of England, 2004, note 1: 44). The report to Synod in 2005 (Church of England, 2005a) indicated that 1,650 churches, roughly 10% of all Church of England churches, are admitting the non-confirmed to communion. The report goes on to recommend that children who have been baptised but who are not yet confirmed and who are not yet ready or desirous to be confirmed, as required by paragraph 1(a) of Canon B15A, may be admitted to holy communion, subject to regulations which essentially require the approval of the diocesan bishop. The Board of Education, at its meeting in May 2005, considered the draft regulations prepared by the Legal Office on the basis of the Board's discussion and agreed that they should be laid before Synod for general discussion. At its meeting in July 2005, Synod took note of the report with a view to its return to Synod for final approval in 2006 (Church of England, 2005b). However, when Synod met again in November 2005, the Right Reverend Stephen Venner, Bishop of Dover, moved that the *Admission of Children to Holy Communion Regulations* be considered and after debate the proposal was given overwhelming support (Church of England, 2005c).

In February 2006 the *Regulations* were duly approved under paragraph 1(c) of Canon B15A (Church of England, 2006). Under these regulations, children who have been baptised but who have not yet been confirmed and who are not yet ready and desirous to be confirmed, as required by paragraph 1(a) of Canon B15A, may be admitted to holy communion but only provided that the conditions set out in the regulations are satisfied. These conditions place severe and important restriction on the concept of open access to holy communion by children. First, application to grant access to holy communion by baptised but non-confirmed children must be made to the diocesan bishop by an incumbent and, before granting permission, the diocesan bishop must satisfy himself that the proposal is supported by the Parochial Church Council, that adequate provision is in place in the parish to prepare children for communion, that provision is in place to continue to nurture them in the Christian life and most significantly that children are encouraged to be confirmed at the appropriate time. Second, an incumbent shall not admit a child to holy communion unless he or she is satisfied that not only are they baptised but also that the person having parental responsibility for the child is content that the child be so admitted. These regulations came into force in June 2006.

Reiss (1998) has identified the problems that can arise when a child who is admitted to communion in one parish visits a second parish which has a different practice. Such difficulties are likely to continue across Church of England parishes. This is even more the case when children admitted to communion in a Church of England parish visit a Church in Wales' parish, where the regulations regarding admitting children to communion remain dependent on the *Book of Common Prayer* (Church in Wales, 1984).

The Church in Wales *Book of Common Prayer* stipulates that the service of baptism of infants requires the parents and godparents to see that the child is taught the creed, the Lord's Prayer, and the Ten Commandments and is instructed in the catechism. Also, it is emphasised that it is the duty of parents and godparents to ensure that the child is brought to the bishop to be confirmed. At the point of confirmation, the bishop seeks the assurance that such instruction has been carried out. Furthermore, the regulations clearly state that, except with the permission of the bishop, no one shall receive holy communion until such time as he or she is confirmed or ready and desirous to be confirmed. Even so, it is evident that a considerable number of experimental schemes for non-confirmed children to receive communion are approved by Church in Wales diocesan bishops. For 2003, for the first time, the Representative Body of the Church in Wales began to collect details from each of the dioceses concerning numbers of pre-confirmation communicants, for two key categories, having previously commenced the collection of simple totals of pre-confirmation communicants for 2001 and 2002. Since 2003, details are published showing the number of under eighteen-year-old pre-confirmation communicants and the number of eighteen-year-old and over pre-confirmation communicants for each diocese of the Church in Wales. In five of the six dioceses of the Church in Wales the total number of non-confirmed communicants increased notably in each year from 2001 to 2003, while in the remaining diocese the increase was less notable. Littler (2006) notes that almost a quarter (22%) of Church in Wales parishes claimed to be admitting children to communion before confirmation in 2003, with the permission of the diocesan bishop. Clearly, access to communion by non-confirmed children is widespread and it is hardly surprising that Johnson (1999) comments that confusion reigns with regard to confirmation and access to communion.

The position is not made any clearer by the introduction within the Church in Wales of an *Additional Order for the Holy Eucharist* (Church in Wales, 2004). The *Additional Order for the Holy Eucharist* is incorporated into the existing *Book of Common Prayer* and includes in its introduction, *Guidelines for the Celebration of the Eucharist with Children*. When the 'Bill' was presented to the Church in Wales Governing Body for approval in April 2004, an additional guideline was included stating that, "while it is of the greatest importance that all communicants should prepare themselves properly before receiving communion, special care should be devoted to children in this respect".

This reference to children in relation to the eucharist represents a significant theological departure from the instructions concerning the preparation of young people for communion through confirmation and contained in the same *Book of Common Prayer*. A not dissimilar situation results from the Church in Wales' decision to incorporate into the *Book of Common Prayer, Additional Orders of Service for Christian Initiation*. The relevant Bill (Church in Wales, 2006a) was passed by the Governing Body of the Church in Wales in September 2006 and, while this marks an important development in the Church's approach to Christian initiation, it does not depart from the *Book of Common Prayer* but rather is incorporated into it. Indeed, the resulting new *Services for Christian Initiation* (Church in Wales, 2006b) claims "to provide an addition to the *Book of Common Prayer* and not a substituted resource". It is noteworthy that, while the *Order for the Public Baptism of Infants* (contained within the new *Services for Christian Initiation*) places no specific requirement on parents and godparents to teach the child the creed, the Lord's Prayer and the Ten Commandments, it does require that "Every effort should be made to enable baptised children to become active members of the worshipping community, to receive appropriate instruction in the Christian faith and in due course be confirmed by the bishop" (Church in Wales, 2006b, note 1: 4).

It would seem that the *Ely Report's* key conviction that all the blessings of initiation necessary for access to communion are received at baptism in a single sacramental moment falls a long way short of recognition within the Church in Wales, thirty-five years on.

Littler, Francis and Thomas (2002) conclude their analysis of the data collected in 1993 by claiming that the views expressed by Church in Wales clergy at that time would seem to demand serious consideration of the revision of the Church's baptism promises and rules for confirmation. In the light of subsequent developments in the position of the Anglican Church in both England and Wales, regarding access to communion by children, it is relevant to ask clergy how far these changing perspectives are being mediated at the local level and to what extent clergy are influenced by personal beliefs and attitudes in their implementation.

METHOD

Sample

Two surveys of stipendiary parochial male clergy within the Church in Wales, administered in 1993 and 2003, resulted in a combined total of 542 completed questionnaires. In 1993, 375 questionnaires were delivered and a response rate of 64% resulted in 242 completed questionnaires (of which 222 were from male clergy). In 2003, 593 copies of the same questionnaire were delivered and a response rate of 66% resulted in 391 completed questionnaires (of which 320 were from male clergy). Given the change in the status of clergywomen between 1993 and 2003 resulting from the ordination of women clerics as priests (Church in Wales, 1996), and in order that the samples might be combined, the views of clergywomen are omitted. While this reduces the sample size and excludes an important group of clerics, Littler (2007) has shown that on matters relating to initiation into the Church in Wales the views of clergywomen and clergymen differ significantly in very few instances.

Instrument

As part of a larger survey concerned with Christian initiation, two sets of questions were included in the questionnaire relevant to the admission of children to communion. The first set proposed nine questions

374   KEITH LITTLER

on the criteria for admitting children to communion. The second set proposed seven questions on the criteria for withholding communion from children. The questions are listed in tables one and two and in tables three and four. Each question was assessed on a five-point Likert scale requesting a response of: agree strongly, agree, not certain, disagree, or disagree strongly. Churchmanship was assessed by inviting the respondents to locate themselves within a seven-point semantic space anchored by the two descriptors: Catholic and Evangelical (Randall, 2005).

Analysis

The following analyses propose to examine the responses of clergymen to these two sets of questions by both age group and churchmanship. For this purpose the five-point Likert scales are collapsed into dichotomous categories by combining the agree strongly and agree responses and by combining the disagree strongly, disagree and not certain responses. The relevance of age was examined by comparing the views of those under the age of 50 (N = 208) with the views of those aged 55 and over (N = 246). To create some separation between the groups those aged between 50 and 54 (N = 88) were omitted from the analysis. The relevance of churchmanship was examined by comparing the views of those who located themselves on the two points closest to the Catholic pole of the seven-point semantic space (N = 206) with the views of those who located themselves on the three points closest to the Evangelical pole (N = 124). To create some space between the two wings of the Anglican Church those who opted for the other two points on the seven-point scale (N = 212) were omitted from the analysis. Littler (2006) has demonstrated that there were approximately 9% more clergy aged over 50 years in 2003 compared with 1993. He argues that this is due, at least in part, to older men and women being ordained during the period and maintains that it is unlikely that these developments significantly influence the results of combining the two samples. Comparison of the data provided by Littler (2006) and Thomas (1995) shows that, in many cases, the differing viewpoints of Catholics and Evangelicals intensified during the decade from 1993 to 2003 but did not change in respect of the areas of disagreement.

Discussion

The relevance of age of clergymen

Table 16.1 shows the responses of clergymen to the nine questions on criteria for admitting children to communion cross-tabulated by the age group of respondents. It is immediately apparent that the older group of clergymen adopt a more 'traditional prayer book' stance on admitting children to communion and are less inclined than their younger colleagues to embrace a practice of admitting baptised but unconfirmed children to communion. The data demonstrate that clergymen in the over 55 years age group significantly disagree with their colleagues in the under 50 years age group regarding five of the nine criteria concerning children being admitted to communion. Less than half (49%) of clergymen in the older age group believe that children should be admitted to communion because it is a meal for the whole family, while 59% of clergymen in the younger age group support this viewpoint. Although almost two-thirds (65%) of the older group of clergymen believe that children should be admitted to communion because it is a means of grace, a significantly greater percentage of the younger group of clergymen (75%) feel this way.

These two significant differences are of interest because they show the extent to which clergymen who are under the age of 50 years tend to place importance on quite different criteria for admitting children to communion compared with their older colleagues. The younger clergymen are apparently more influenced by broader issues of inclusiveness: offering an open communion table, inviting and welcoming young people to share in the communion without being first required to pass a test. That the older clergy show less support for such a stance would imply that they place greater importance on maintaining traditional patterns of worship with which they and their congregations feel comfortable and at ease. It may be added that Table 16.1 also shows that a greater percentage of the younger clergymen (42%) support baptised infants being welcomed to communion compared with the older clergymen (35%), although in this instance the difference is not significant.

Table 16.1 shows that there is also disagreement between the two age groups of clergymen when it comes to the practicality of stipulating an acceptable age when unconfirmed but baptised churchgoing children might be admitted to communion. The data demonstrate that

KEITH LITTLER

Table 16.1: Criteria for admitting children to communion—
age of clergy

	Under 50 agree %	55 plus agree %	χ^2	p<
Children cannot take full part in communion services unless they receive communion	50	45	1.1	ns
Children should be admitted to communion because it is a meal for the whole family	59	49	4.5	.05
Children should be admitted to communion because it is a means of grace	75	65	4.9	.05
Infants who have been baptised should be welcomed to receive communion	42	35	2.3	ns
Churchgoing seven-year-olds who have been baptised should be welcome to receive communion before confirmation	59	43	11.6	.001
Churchgoing nine-year-olds who have been baptised should be welcome to receive communion before confirmation	62	46	11.6	.001
Churchgoing eleven-year-olds who have been baptised should be welcome to receive communion before confirmation	64	52	6.0	.05
There should be a service of admission to first communion	58	57	0.0	ns
Churches which admit children to communion should also encourage them to attend nurture groups	76	70	2.1	ns

the age of seven years would be acceptable to 59% of clergymen in the under 50 age group, but to significantly fewer (43%) in the over 55 age group. The age of nine years would be acceptable to 62% of clergymen in the younger age group, but to significantly fewer (46%) in the older age group of clergymen. The age of eleven years would be acceptable to 64% of clergymen in the younger age group, but to significantly fewer (52%) in the older age group of clergymen. The percentage of clergymen under 50 and the percentage of clergymen over 55 who support baptised but unconfirmed children receiving communion marginally increase with the age of the child. While the two age groups of clergymen remain significantly different in viewpoint, over half of the older clergymen (52%) support the notion of eleven-year-olds who have been baptised being welcome to receive communion before confirmation. It would seem that the view of Holeton (1981)

A CHURCH DIVIDED BY THEOLOGY AND PRACTICE   377

that admission to communion in the Anglican Church has tended to be associated with the process of growing up, still holds good. However, it should be emphasised that the questions put to the clergymen relate specifically to *churchgoing* children: a prescription generally retained in the revised eucharistic services in both the Church of England (2006) and the Church in Wales (2006b).

Table 16.2 shows the responses of clergymen to the seven questions on criteria for withholding communion from children, cross-tabulated by the age group of the respondent. The data generally demonstrate the greater commitment of the older group of clergymen to the relevant regulations of the *Book of Common Prayer* (Church in Wales, 1984) and show them to be more inclined than their younger colleagues to withhold communion from children in accordance with these regulations. Thus, 39% of clergymen in the over 55 year age group believe communion should be withheld from children until they have been confirmed, while significantly fewer (22%) clergymen in the under 50 year age group see this as a necessary requirement. Over half (53%) of clergymen in the older age group believe communion should be withheld from children until they understand what participation in the eucharist involves, and this presumably implies that teaching and preparation has taken place before a young person comes to the communion. By contrast, only 35% of clergymen in the younger age group feel that access to communion by children should be delayed in this way. Even so, a majority of clergymen in both age groups agree that some form of preparation is necessary: 74% of older clergymen feel this way as do 65% of younger clergymen, although the difference is not statistically significant.

A minority of clergymen in both age groups feel that it remains necessary for children to know the catechism before being made welcome to receive communion, and therefore only a minority deem that a lack of such knowledge is a sound reason for withholding communion from them. However, a significantly greater proportion of the older clergy (22%) believe this requirement of the *Book of Common Prayer* should be maintained. Only one-tenth (10%) of the younger clergy feel that the teaching of the catechism is necessary, while the remaining 90% presumably recognise that recently approved confirmation services no longer place this requirement on clergy (Church in Wales, 1989).

The distinctiveness of the views of clergymen within different age groups is confirmed in the above responses. While clergymen over 55 years of age display greater resistance to change, clergy under 50 years

378 KEITH LITTLER

Table 16.2: Criteria for withholding communion from children—
age of clergy

	under 50 agree %	55 plus agree %	χ^2	p<
Churches should not give communion to children until they have been confirmed	22	39	16.6	.001
Churches should not give communion to children until they are desirous of being confirmed	32	39	2.0	ns
Churches should not give communion to children until they are old enough to understand what is happening	35	53	15.0	.001
Churches should not give communion to children until they have committed themselves to the Lord Jesus	34	33	0.1	ns
Churches should not give communion to children until they know the catechism	10	22	12.2	.001
Churches should not give communion to children until they have attended a preparation programme	65	74	4.0	ns
Churches should not give communion to children until they are part of a Christian nurture group	26	32	2.1	ns

of age demonstrate greater support for a model much closer in practice
and ethos to the Ely Report of 1971.

The relevance of churchmanship

Table 16.3 shows the responses of clergymen to the nine questions
on criteria for admitting children to communion cross-tabulated by
the churchmanship of the respondents (self-designated as 'Catholic'
or 'Evangelical' in their approach to ministry). The data demonstrate
two significant points of difference between Catholic clergymen and
Evangelical clergymen in respect of their views on criteria for admitting
children to communion. First, Catholic clergymen clearly feel that it is
not acceptable for children to present themselves for communion without
the *rite of passage* being marked in a formal way. While fewer than half
(46%) of the Evangelical clergymen believe there should be a service
of admission to first communion, almost two-thirds (65%) of Catholic
clergymen deem this to be important. Second, Catholic clergymen and

A CHURCH DIVIDED BY THEOLOGY AND PRACTICE 379

Table 16.3: Criteria for admitting children to communion—
Evangelicals and Catholics

	Evangelical agree %	Catholic agree %	χ^2	p<
Children cannot take full part in communion services unless they receive communion	48	40	2.1	ns
Children should be admitted to communion because it is a meal for the whole family	62	48	6.1	.05
Children should be admitted to communion because it is a means of grace	66	75	3.2	ns
Infants who have been baptised should be welcomed to receive communion	40	35	0.7	ns
Churchgoing seven-year-olds who have been baptised should be welcome to receive communion before confirmation	52	49	0.2	ns
Churchgoing nine-year-olds who have been baptised should be welcome to receive communion before confirmation	55	51	0.5	ns
Churchgoing eleven-year-olds who have been baptised should be welcome to receive communion before confirmation	59	54	0.8	ns
There should be a service of admission to first communion	46	65	11.6	.001
Churches which admit children to communion should also encourage them to attend nurture groups	78	74	0.7	ns

Evangelical clergymen take up contrasting stances about children being admitted to communion simply on the basis of family membership. While 62% of Evangelical clergymen believe that children should be admitted to communion because it is a meal for the whole family, less than half (48%) of Catholic clergymen feel this way.

These results demonstrate two fundamental theological differences in the viewpoints of Evangelical and Catholic clergymen. First, it seems that Evangelical clergymen support the notion of children accompanying their parents at the 'family communion', apparently agreeing with Fowler (1984) and Meyers (1995) that the churchgoing family environment is a sound and proper place within which the faith of the child may be nurtured and encouraged to develop. Catholic clergymen, by contrast, are less likely to take this stance. Second, by demonstrating significantly less regard for a service of admission to first communion,

Evangelical clergy, by implication, show less regard than do their Catholic colleagues for any service that implies that something needs adding to the service of baptism. If this is the case then it is a point of fundamental theological importance. It would appear that the long standing debate concerning the relative positions of Mason (1893) and Lampe (1967) is still very much alive among Church in Wales clergymen and warrants further research.

Table 16.4 shows the responses of clergymen to the seven questions on criteria for withholding communion from children, cross-tabulated by the churchmanship of the respondents (self-designated as 'Catholic' or 'Evangelical' in their approach to ministry). The data demonstrate three significant points of difference between Catholics and Evangelicals. First, a fundamental difference is displayed regarding their respective understandings of the way in which individuals approach their worship. This is evidenced from the way in which Catholic clergymen and Evangelical clergymen respond to the suggestion that communion should be withheld from children until they have committed themselves to the Lord Jesus. As many as 58% of Evangelical clergymen feel that, if this aspect of religious commitment and faith is absent, then communion should be withheld from a child. By contrast, only 27% of Catholic clergymen base importance on this as a criterion for withholding communion from a child and apparently seek evidence of 'readiness' through other criteria, such as knowledge of the Lord's Prayer, the ten commandments, the Apostle's Creed and other preparatory requirements prescribed by the *Book of Common Prayer* (Church in Wales, 1984).

Second, the extent to which Catholic clergymen are more likely than Evangelical clergymen to deem failure to observe the requirements of the *Book of Common Prayer* as criteria for withholding communion from children, is born out by other data from Table 16.4. Almost a fifth (19%) of Catholic clergymen continue to place importance on children knowing the catechism and would consider failure in this respect to be good reason for withholding communion from children. While this is a minority of Catholic clergymen it is a significantly larger minority than Evangelical clergymen expressing this point of view (11%).

Third, the fact that 52% of Evangelical clergymen believe communion should be withheld from children until they are old enough to understand what is happening, while significantly fewer (39%) of Catholic clergymen agree, is at first sight surprising and demands explanation. It is most likely that this implies that while more than

A CHURCH DIVIDED BY THEOLOGY AND PRACTICE

Table 16.4: Criteria for withholding communion from children—
Evangelicals and Catholics

	Evangelical agree %	Catholic agree %	χ^2	p<
Churches should not give communion to children until they have been confirmed	26	33	1.6	ns
Churches should not give communion to children until they are desirous of being confirmed	35	36	0.1	ns
Churches should not give communion to children until they are old enough to understand what is happening	52	39	5.4	.05
Churches should not give communion to children until they have committed themselves to the Lord Jesus	58	27	31.1	.001
Churches should not give communion to children until they know the catechism	11	19	4.6	.05
Churches should not give communion to children until they have attended a preparation programme	69	72	0.3	ns
Churches should not give communion to children until they are part of a Christian nurture group	32	30	0.2	ns

half (52%) of Evangelical clergy are of the view that if confirmation is to be supported it should involve older candidates, they also hold the view that children can understand and appreciate the significance of the communion bread and wine from a very young age. Certainly Maxwell E. Johnson maintains this position and describes in some detail the tender age at which communion was administered to his own daughter (Johnson, 1999: 375). It is unlikely that the data imply that only a minority (39%) of Catholic clergymen believe communion should be withheld until some degree of maturity is arrived at when young people can 'confirm' their baptism promises. It is more likely that Catholic clergymen generally hold the view that age and understanding are not such strong criteria for granting access to communion as are other more prescribed theological rules and regulations. Certainly the responses of Catholic and Evangelical clergy to the 2001 *Church Times Survey* show that Catholic clergy within the Church of England place significantly greater importance on the development of faith in their

382 KEITH LITTLER

own lives through traditional forms of worship than do their Evangelical colleagues (Francis, Robbins and Astley, 2005: 169, table 7.4).

CONCLUSION

Recent amendments to the regulations for granting children access to the Anglican communion (Church in Wales, 2006b; Church of England, 2006) go some way toward meeting the criticism of those who feel that change is long overdue. It remains, however, that Anglican teaching on this matter continues to be mediated at the local level through the personal beliefs and attitudes of local parochial stipendiary clergy, albeit sometimes restricted by the views of churchwardens, as Howells and Littler (2007) have demonstrated. There is a very real sense in which Anglican theologies relating to those rites which grant access by children to communion not only continue to be deeply debated but are further subjected to the vagaries of pastoral whim.

This study shows that key aspects of the beliefs of Church in Wales parochial stipendiary clergymen are influenced by both age and churchmanship. With regard to age, older clergymen show a greater reluctance than younger clergymen to embrace changes to the regulations provided by the *1984 Book of Common Prayer*. With regard to churchmanship, Catholics and Evangelicals hold significantly different views both in respect of fundamental theological reasons for withholding communion from children and in respect of the practical aspects of admitting children to communion. It would seem that with regard to both age and churchmanship, Church in Wales clergymen are divided by theology and practice in respect of their views on the access of children to communion. There is a real sense in which the above data suggest that Evangelical clergymen and clergymen under 50 years of age share a common desire to implement the broad aims and principles of the Ely Report (1971). At the same time the data suggest that Catholic clergymen and clergymen over 55 years of age are more inclined to support the classic locus of Anglican teaching on the admission of children to communion.

It may be that such diversity within the Church in Wales is to be welcomed. The Church in Wales, in common with the Anglican Church generally, claims to be a 'broad' church characterised by diversity in churchmanship. In this context Shakespeare and Rayment-Pickard (2006) present a persuasive case for approaching the eucharist, whether

A CHURCH DIVIDED BY THEOLOGY AND PRACTICE

for children or adults, with a new sense of belonging which can grow more freely "when we have jettisoned the baggage of authoritarianism, sectarianism and fear" (p. 98). Crockett (2005) contributes to the point in the following manner:

> Many of us are convinced that the God in whom Anglicans believe is not a static God, nor a narrow God. The people of God, therefore, are not called to be static or narrow either. Movement and breadth, however, are often troublesome and problematic qualities with which to live. I should like to think that the enduring strength of the Anglican Church is not that of a stone edifice, but, rather, that of the tall eucalyptus tree in my garden which bends and turns in the breeze, but which continues to thrive. (Crockett, 2005: viii)

He goes on to say that the flexibility and diversity that are the mark of Anglicanism may also, paradoxically, be its Achilles' heel. Time will tell whether the rich diversity confirmed by the above data will prove to be an expression of the enduring strength of a multifaceted and inclusive church, or whether it will ultimately further demonstrate the presence of yet another fault-line which could tear the church apart (Francis, Robbins and Astley, 2005).

What the above data show, however, is that support for a break with tradition and for baptised children to be granted access to communion, as the *Ely Report* recommended over 30 years ago, comes from those Church in Wales clergymen who are under 50 years of age, as opposed to those Church in Wales clergymen who are over 55 years of age, and from Evangelical clergymen as opposed to Catholic clergymen. So long as the younger group of clergymen retain these same views as they age, and if the proportion of Evangelical clergymen increases as Brierley (2006) projects, it is likely that the demands by clergy for change will exceed the contributions of recent developments in Church in Wales services relating to children and the eucharist (Church in Wales, 2006b). On the basis of the evidence provided by the above data it may well be that pressure will mount for the recommendations of the Ely Report (1971) to be implemented by the Church in Wales.

References

Avery, O. (1992), A Lutheran examines James W. Fowler, in J. Astley and L.J. Francis (eds.), *Christian Perspectives on Faith Development*, pp. 122–134, Leominster, Gracewing.
Binfield, C. (1994), The purley way for children, in D. Woods (ed.), *The Church and Childhood*, pp. 461–476, Studies in Church History 31, Oxford, Blackwell.

384   KEITH LITTLER

Brierley, P. (ed.) (2006), *Religious Trends 6*, London, Christian Research.

Church in Wales (1971), *Church Initiation: a report of the doctrinal commission of the Church in Wales*, Cardiff, Church in Wales Publications.

—— (1984), *Book of Common Prayer*, Cardiff, Church in Wales Publications.

—— (1989), *Children and Holy Communion*, Cardiff, Church in Wales Publications.

—— (1996), *To Enable Women to be Ordained as Priests: Canon 23 promulgated on 19 September*, Cardiff, Church in Wales Publications.

—— (2004), *An Order for the Holy Eucharist*, Cardiff, Church in Wales Publications.

—— (2006a), *Bill to Incorporate into the Book of Common Prayer Additional Orders of Service for Christian Initiation*, A report of the Select Committee, Cardiff, Church in Wales Publications.

—— (2006b), *Services for Christian Initiation*, Cardiff, Church in Wales Publications.

Church of England (1971), *On the Way: towards an integrated approach to Christian initiation*, A working party report to the Church of England House of Bishops, London, Church House Publishing.

—— (1997), *Admission of Baptised Persons to Holy Communion Before Confirmation, GS488*, London, General Synod of the Church of England.

—— (2001), *Report of Proceedings of General Synod, Vol. 31, No. 3, motion by the diocese of Bristol to change Canon Law B15A relating to communion before confirmation*, London, Church House Publishing.

—— (2004), *Common Worship Initiation Services: rites on the way and reconciliation and restoration, GS1546*, Report of the Liturgical Commission, London, General Synod of the Church of England.

—— (2005a), *Children and Holy Communion: a review, GS1576*, London, General Synod of the Church of England.

—— (2005b), *Resourcing Mission of the Church of England: interim report, GS1580B*, London, General Synod of the Church of England.

—— (2005c), *Admission of Baptised Children to Holy Communion, GS1596*, London, General Synod of the Church of England.

—— (2006), *Admission of Baptised Children to Holy Communion Regulations, GS1596Y/A*, London, General Synod of the Church of England.

Craven, D. (2005), It's the adults who don't understand objections to children's receiving communion say more about adults' than childrens' questions of faith, *Church Times*, No. 7426, p. 10, col. 3–5.

Crockett, A. (2005), Foreword, in L.J. Francis, M. Robbins and J. Astley, *Fragmented Faith? Exposing the fault-lines in the Church of England*, pp. vii–viii, Milton Keynes, Paternoster Press.

Delap, D. (2006), Rites on the way, in P. Bradshaw (ed.), *A Companion to Common Worship*, vol. 2, pp. 128–141, London, SPCK.

Ely Report (1971), *Christian Initiation: birth and growth in Christian society*, London, Church Information Office.

Fisher, J.D.C. and Yarnold E.J. (1989), The west from about AD500 to the Reformation, in C. Jones, G. Wainwright and E.J. Yarnold (eds.), *The Study of the Liturgy*, pp. 110–117, London, SPCK.

——. (2005), *Christian Initiation: confirmation then and now*, Chicago, Illinois, Hillenbrand.

Fowler, J.W. (1984), *Becoming Adult, Becoming Christian: adult development and Christian faith*, San Francisco, California, Harper and Row.

Francis, L.J., Robbins, M. and Astley J. (2005), *Fragmented Faith? Exposing the fault-lines in the Church of England*, Milton Keynes, Paternoster Press.

Fraser, G. (2004), Safe in the hands of children: give children real communion not jelly babies, *Church Times*, No. 7391, p. 10, col. 1.

Harden, R. (2004), Lichfield lifts ban on children, *Church Times*, No. 7392, p. 7, col. 2–5.

A CHURCH DIVIDED BY THEOLOGY AND PRACTICE 385

Holeton, D.R. (1981), *Infant Communion: then and now*, Nottingham, Grove.

———. (1991), *Christian Initiation in the Anglican Communion*, Nottingham, Grove.

———. (1998), Initiation, in S. Sykes and J. Booty (eds.), *The Study of Anglicanism*, pp. 261–272, London, SPCK.

Howells, A. and Littler, K. (2007), Children and communion: listening to churchwardens in rural and urban Wales, *Rural Theology*, 3, 13–22.

Jackson, H. (2004), Children at the font and altar, *Church Times*, No. 7394, p. 10, col. 4.

Johnson, M.E. (1999), *The Rites of Christian Initiation: their evolution and interpretation*, Collegeville, Minnesota, Pueblo Liturgical Press.

Kay, W.K. and Francis, L.J. (1996), *Drift from the Churches: attitude toward Christianity during childhood and adolescence*, Cardiff, University of Wales Press.

Lampe, G.W.H. (1967), *The Seal of the Spirit* (second edition), London, SPCK.

Littler, K. (2006), The views of Church in Wales clergy on initiation: 1993–2003, unpublished DMin dissertation, University of Wales, Bangor.

———. (2007), The ordination of women and inclusivity within the Church in Wales: theological and psychological considerations, *Archiv fur Religionspsychologie*, 29, 319–324.

Littler, K., Francis, L.J. and Thomas, T.H. (2002), The admission of children to communion: a survey among Church in Wales clerics, *Contact: international journal of pastoral studies*, 139, 24–38.

Lowther Clarke, W.K. (1932), Confirmation, in W.K. Lowther Clarke assisted by C. Harris (eds.), *Liturgy and Worship*, pp. 443–457, London, SPCK.

Mason, A.J. (1893), *The Relation of Confirmation to Baptism*, New York, Macmillan.

Meyers, R. (1995), *Children at the Table: the communion of all baptized in Anglicanism today*, New York, Church Hymnal Corp.

Randall, K. (2005), *Evangelicals Etcetera: conflict and conviction in the Church of England's parties*, Aldershot, Ashgate.

Reiss, P. (1998), *Children and Communion: a practical guide for interested churches*, Cambridge, Grove.

Shakespeare, S. and Rayment-Pichard, H. (2006), *The Inclusive God: reclaiming theology for an inclusive church*, Norwich, Canterbury Press.

Strange, W.A. (1996), *Children in the Early Church: children in the ancient world, the New Testament and the early church*, Carlisle, Paternoster Press.

Thomas, H. (1995), Christian Initiation within the Church in Wales, Unpublished MPhil dissertation, Trinity College, Carmarthen.

Whitaker, E.C. (1970), *Documents of the Baptismal Liturgy*, London, SPCK.

LIST OF CONTRIBUTORS

Tania ap Siôn is Executive Director of the St Mary's Centre for Religious Education at St Deiniol's Library and Research Fellow in the Warwick Religions and Education Research Unit, Institute of Education, University of Warwick. Her recent publications include, 'Distinguishing between intention, reference, and objective in an analysis of prayer requests for health and well-being: eavesdropping from the rural vestry', in *Mental Health, Religion, and Culture* (2008) and 'Experiencing education in the new Christian schools in the UK: listening to the male graduates', in *Journal of Beliefs and Values* (2007) with L.J. Francis and S. Baker.

The Revd Professor Jeff Astley is Director of the North of England Institute for Christian Education (NEICE) and Honorary Professorial Fellow in Practical Theology and Christian Education, University of Durham, UK. His recent publications include *Ordinary Theology: looking, listening and learning in theology* (2002) and *Christ of the Everyday* (2007).

Sylvia Baker originally trained and worked as a research biologist and then became a teacher. In 1978 she co-founded one of the new Christian schools. Her current role involves research into the outcomes of Christian schooling. Her recent publications include *The Love of God in the Classroom: the story of the new Christian schools* (2005) with D. Freeman and 'Experiencing education in the new Christian schools in the United Kingdom: listening to the male graduates', in *Journal of Beliefs and Values* (2007) with T. ap Siôn and L.J. Francis.

The Revd Dr Mark J. Cartledge is Senior Lecturer in Pentecostal and Charismatic Theology at the Department of Theology and Religion, University of Birmingham. His recent publications include *Speaking in Tongues: multi-disciplinary perspectives* (2006), and *Encountering the Spirit: the charismatic tradition* (2006).

Dr Ann Christie is Senior Lecturer in Theology and Ministry at York St John University, UK, and Consultant on Ordinary Theology to the North of England Institute for Christian Education (NEICE).

388 LIST OF CONTRIBUTORS

Her recent publications include 'Who Do You Say I Am? Answers from the Pews', in *Journal of Adult Theological Education* (2007).

Dr Jaco S. Dreyer is Associate Professor in the Department of Practical Theology of the University of South Africa. He is a co-author of *Is there a God of Human Rights? The Complex Relationship between Human Rights and Religion: a South African case* (2004).

The Revd Canon Professor Leslie J. Francis is Professor of Religions and Education in the Warwick Religions and Education Research Unit, Institute of Education, University of Warwick. His recent publications include *British Methodism Today: what circuit ministers really think* (2006) with J. Haley and *Gone for Good? Church-leaving and returning in the 21st century* (2007) with P. Richter.

Professor Dr R. Ruard Ganzevoort teaches practical theology at Kampen Theological University, the VU University Amsterdam, and Windesheim University of Applied Sciences, Zwolle, The Netherlands. His recent publications include 'Scars and stigmata: trauma, identity and theology', in *Practical Theology* (2008) and 'Coping with tragedy and malice', in N. Van Doorn-Harder and L. Minnema (eds.), *Coping with Evil in Religion and Culture* (2008).

Sabine Zehnder Grob is psychologist and doctoral student integrated in a National Research Program (NRP58) of the Swiss National Science Foundation with a project called Value Orientation and Religiousness—relevance for the formation of identity and mental health of adolescents. Furthermore she is attending a post-graduate course in behavioral-cognitive therapy (CBT) for children and adolescents and in this context is particularly interested in child-oriented psychology of religion.

Professor Dr Chris A.M. Hermans is Professor of Empirical Practical Theology at Radboud University Nijmegen, The Netherlands. His recent publications include 'Primary school students' metacognitive beliefs about religious education', in *Educational Research Evaluation* (2006) with T. van der Zee and C. Aarnoutse, and 'Expressing otherness in interreligious classroom communication: empirical research into dialogical communication in religiously pluriform learning situations in

LIST OF CONTRIBUTORS 389

Catholic primary schools', in *Journal of Empirical Theology* (2008) with S. van Eersel and P. Sleegers.

Professor Dr Stefan Huber is Adj. Professor at the Center for Religious Studies (CERES), University of Bochum (Germany). His recent publications include 'Centrality and content: a new multidimensional model for the measurement of religiosity', in *The International Journal for the Psychology of Religion* (2008) and *What the World Believes. Analysis and Commentary on the Religion Monitor* (2008).

Professor Dr Christoph Käppler is psychologist, psychotherapist for children, adolescents and families, and master of children's rights. He is Professor for the promotion of social and emotional development and Dean of the faculty for special education at the University of Education Ludwigsburg, Germany. His recent publications include 'Trans-cultural adaptation and psychometric properties of the Sense of Coherence Scale in mothers of preschool children', *Interamerican Journal of Psychology* (in press) with K. Bonanato, D. Barbabela, J.P.T. Mota, M.L. Ramos-Jorge, S.M. Paiva and I.A. Pordeus and 'Psychische Gesundheit und Zugang zu professioneller Hilfe—Was denken Kinder, Jugendliche und ihre Eltern darüber?' in Schweizerischer Nationalfonds, Themenheft des NFP52 (Hrsg.), *Antisoziales Verhalten bei Kindern, psychosoziale Risiken von Jugendlichen: Was bringt Prävention und Beratung?* (2006).

Dr William K. Kay is Reader in Practical Theology and Director of the Centre for Pentecostal and Charismatic Studies, University of Bangor. His recent publications include 'Apostolic Networks in Britain: an analytic overview', in *Transformation* (2008) and 'Pentecostals and angels', in P.G. Riddell and B.S. Riddell (eds.), *Angels and Demons* (2007).

Dr Constantin Klein is Doctoral Fellow at the Institute for Psychology II, University of Leipzig, Germany. His recent publications include 'Is football Religion? Theoretical perspectives and research findings' (2006) and 'Religiousness and mental health: an overview about findings, conclusions and consequences for clinical practice' (2007).

The Revd Dr Keith Littler is part-time lecturer at Bangor University and Honorary Research Fellow, St Mary's Centre at St Deiniol's Library. Recent publications include 'The ordination of women and inclusivity within the Church in Wales: theological and psychological considerations', in *Archiv für Religionspsychologie* (2007) and 'Who says grandparents matter?' in *Journal of Beliefs and Values* (2008).

Professor Dr Dr Christoph Morgenthaler is Professor for Pastoral Care and Pastoral Psychology at the University of Bern, Switzerland. His recent publications include 'Tapes and Tables: mixed methods research on family religion', in *Journal of Empirical Theology* (2007) and 'Qualitative, Quantitative and Phenomenological Approaches to Experience—Complementary and Contrary. Empirical-Theological Soundings from a research Project on Family Rituals', in H.-G. Heimbrock and C.P. Scholz (eds.), *Religion: Immediate Experience and the Mediacy of Research* (2007).

Professor Dr Ulrich Riegel is Professor of Practical Theology and Religious Education at the University of Siegen. His recent publications include *Europe: secular or postsecular?* (2008) with H.-G. Ziebertz and 'Religious Education and Values', in *Journal of Empirical Theology* (2007) with H.-G. Ziebertz.

Dr Mandy Robbins is Senior Research Fellow in the Warwick Religions and Education Research Unit, Institute of Education, University of Warwick. Her recent publications include 'Psychological type and prayer preferences: a study among Anglican clergy in the United Kingdom', in *Mental Health Religion and Culture* (2008) with L.J. Francis, and *Clergywomen in the Church of England: a psychological study* (2008).

Professor Dr Hans Schilderman is a full professor at Radboud University Nijmegen and holds the chair of Religion and Care at the Faculty of Religious Studies. Hans Schilderman publishes on spiritual care, religious ritual and methodical issues in pastoral theology. His recent publications include *Religion as a Profession* (2005) and *Discourse in Ritual Studies* (2007).

Professor Friedrich Schweitzer is Chair of Practical Theology and Religious Education, University of Tübingen, Germany. His recent publications include *Religious Education Between Modernization and Globalization* (2003), with R.R. Osmer and *Religionspädagogik* (2006).

LIST OF CONTRIBUTORS 391

Dr Thijs Tromp is junior researcher at Kampen Theological University and staff member of Reliëf, Christian Association of Health Care Institutions.

Professor Dr Johannes (Hans) van der Ven is Professor in Comparative Empirical Science of Religion, especially Religion and Human Rights, Faculty of Religious Studies, Center of Ethics, Radboud University Nijmegen, The Netherlands. His recent publications include *Normativity and Empirical Research in Theology* (2004) with M. Scherer-Rath and *Is There a God of Human Rights?* (2004), with J.S. Dreyer and H.J.C. Pieterse.

Professor Dr Hans-Georg Ziebertz is Professor of Practical Theology and Religious Education at Würzburg University, Germany. His recent publications include *Religious Education in a Plural Western Society* (2008) and *Dreaming the Land: theologies of resistance and hope* (2007) with F. Schweitzer.

NAME INDEX

Abelard, P., 183, 195
Acock, A.C., 312, 318
Adorno, T.W., 24, 28, 39, 344, 363
Ady, G., 24
Aldridge, A., 274, 289
Allport, G.W., 135, 148
Andresen, J., 98
Anthony, F.-V., 45, 66–68, 91, 97
ap Siôn, T., xv
Archer, J., 144, 148
Arendt, H., 97
Argyle, M., 136, 140, 142, 146, 148, 151, 292, 318
Asad, T., 56, 68
Astley, J., xv, 178–179, 185, 195, 221, 243, 363, 382–384
Audi, R., 74, 97
Aurelius Augustinus, 265

Bailey, E.I., 209, 212–213
Bainbridge, W.S., 73, 82, 99
Baker, S., xv, 220–222, 224–225, 243
Barclay, C.R., 201, 203, 213
Barnes, J., 68
Barret, J.L., 97–98
Barrett, P., 146, 149
Batson, C.D., 135, 148
Bechtel, W., 69
Becker, G.E., 363
Beinert, W., 95, 97
Beit-Hallahmi, B., 136, 142, 146, 148, 292, 318
Bell, C., 110, 124
Bell, S., 325
Bem, S.L., 143–144, 146–148, 152
Bengston, V.L., 296, 312, 319
Bennett, G.A., 138, 149
Berg, D.N., 25
Berger, P., 270, 272–274, 276, 289
Berkowitz, S., 116, 124
Bertilson, M., 75–76, 86, 91–92, 97
Bhanot, S., 67–69, 138, 150
Bien, J., 7, 24
Biesinger, A., 159, 176, 319
Bigelow, J., 103, 124
Bittlinger, A., 323, 336
Bjarnason, T., 296, 318
Blamey, K., 25, 40

Blando, J.A., 203, 214
Blood, M., 250, 265
Bloom, H., 190, 195
Blumer, H., 84, 97
Blumtritt, J., 341, 363
Boersema, D., 92, 97
Bogdahn, M., 254, 265
Bohlmeijer, E., 198, 212–214
Boltanski, L., 53, 68
Booty, J., 385
Bosch, D., 56, 68
Boschki, R., 158, 173, 176
Bourdieu, P., 3, 5, 10, 12, 13, 20–24
Bourke, R., 138, 148
Bowman, P.J., 203, 215
Boyer, P., 50, 68, 86, 97
Bradshaw, P., 384
Branaman, A., 124
Braun, W., 98
Brierley, P., 278, 289, 328, 336, 383–384
Brown, C.G., 148
Brown, D., 98, 277, 289
Brown, L.B., 138, 150, 296, 303–304, 319, 328, 336
Bruce, S., 82, 98
Brugman, G., 201, 203, 213
Bruner, J.S., 201, 213
Bryman, A., 19, 24
Buber, M., 54, 157, 175
Buchholz, R., 250, 265
Budgen, V., 324, 336
Burgess, H.J., 219, 243
Burks, A.W., 99
Burleigh, M., 57, 68
Butler, A., 321, 336

Cady, L.E., 98
Cairns, J.M., 218, 244
Campbell, W.S., 149, 152
Campiche, R.J., 292, 318
Campo-Arias, A., 133, 148
Carter, C., 116, 124
Carter, M., 136–138, 147–148, 150, 321, 327, 337
Cartledge, M.J., xv, 276–277, 279–280, 284–286, 288–289
Cassirer, E., 43, 68
Cavalli-Sforza, L.L., 294, 304, 318

NAME INDEX

Chadwick, P., 217, 244
Chalke, S., 187, 195
Chamboredon, J.-C., 12, 24
Chan, R., 140, 149
Charbonnier, L., 266
Chen, K.-H., 294, 304, 318
Chesnik, C., 95–96, 98
Chia, E., 56, 68
Choo, P.F., 144, 152
Christie, A., xv, 178, 195
Cinnirella, M., 142, 151
Clark, C.A., 195, 318
Clarke, E., 211, 213
Clark-King, E., 179, 195
Claudy, T., 251, 265
Cloninger, C.R., 77, 98
Coates, G., 323
Coburn-Staege, U., 363
Coenders, M., 69
Cogollo, Z., 133, 148
Coleman, P., 212
Coleman, S., 363
Collins, P., 363
Conrad, J., 159, 176
Coombs, B., 323
Corbin, J., 84–85, 99
Coskun, D., 46, 68
Cox, E., 218, 244
Craig, C.L., 321, 336
Craven, D., 368, 384
Crockett, A., 383–384
Crossland, J., 140, 148
Cruickshank, M., 217, 244

D'Aquili, E., 107, 124
Danser, D.B., 296, 318
Danziger, K., 275, 289
Darwin, C., 32, 39
Davies, D.J., 185, 195
Davis, S.T., 290
de Graaf, N.D., 65, 70
de Groot, A.D., 36, 39, 82, 98
de Hart, J., 291, 296, 303, 312, 317, 318
de Pater, W., 93, 98
de Vries, B., 208, 214
de Vries, H., 54, 68
Deakin, R., 220, 244
Delap, D., 370, 384
den Boer, J., 48, 68
Dent, H.J., 218, 244
Denzinger, H., 255, 265
Dettloff, W., 254, 265
DeVellis, R.F., 280, 289

Dewey, J., 60, 68
Diduca, D., 133, 138, 152
Doedens, F., 156, 175
Dornbusch, S.N., 294, 304, 318
Doyal, L., 116, 124
Draper, J.W., 32, 39
Drecoll, V.H., 254, 265
Dreyer, J.S., xiv, 4, 6, 13–15, 18, 24–25, 27, 29, 31, 35, 37, 45, 71
Dtaz, C.F., 133, 148
Dubach, A., 292, 318
Dudley, M.G., 294, 304, 319
Dudley, R.L., 294, 304, 319
Dunbar, R., 55, 68
Dunham, C.C., 296, 312, 319
Dupuis, J., 63, 68
Durham, W., 46, 68
Durkheim, E., 103, 109, 111, 113, 124, 348
Dye, C., 323
Dyer, A.E., 323, 330, 337

Ebeling, G., 254, 265
Ebertz, M.N., 292, 319
Edelbrock, A., 176
Eek, J., 133, 149
Eichhorn, R., 250, 265
Eisinga, R., 65, 69
Elsenbast, V., 156, 176
Emmons, R.A., 77, 98
Engelhardt, K., 170, 175
Enger, T., 133, 149
Erdheim, M., 343, 363
Erickson, J.A., 296, 319
Evans, T.E., 133, 149
Eysenck S.B.G., 135–137, 139, 149
Eysenck, H.J., 136–139, 141, 146, 149
Eysenck, M.W., 135, 149

Failing, W.-E., 209, 212, 214
Fairweather, E.R., 195
Farley, E., 177–178, 195
Fay, B., 11, 24
Fearn, M., 137, 149
Feldman, M.W., 294, 304, 318
Felling, A., 49, 69, 101, 125
Ferguson, C., 116, 124
Ferreira, A.V., 133, 149
Feyerabend, P., 75–76
Fisher, J.D.C., 366–367, 384
Flew. A., 256, 265
Flick, U., 162, 175
Flor, D.L., 296, 319
Forgas, J.P., 148

NAME INDEX

Foster, R., 323
Fowler, J.W., 107, 124, 368, 379, 383–384
Francis, L.J., xiv–xv, 47, 67, 69–70, 132–134, 136–141, 143–152, 218–219, 223–225, 244, 289, 296, 303–304, 319, 321–322, 326–328, 336–337, 363, 369, 373, 382–385
Fraser, G., 369, 384
Fraser, N., 52, 69
Freeman D., 220–222
Freeman, M., 204, 214
French, S., 140, 151
Frenkel-Brunswick, E., 344, 363
Freud, S., 135, 151, 271
Frisby, D., 4, 24
Fry, P.S., 198, 214
Fuchs, B., 292, 318
Fuchs-Heinritz, W., 173, 175
Fulcher, J., 270–272, 289
Funder, D.C., 327, 337
Furniss, G., 272–275, 289

Gadamer, H.-G., 8, 10, 24
Ganzevoort, R.R., xv, 199, 209–210, 212, 214
Garcia, P.G., 5, 25
Gardner, H., 106, 124
Garrett, J.B., 250, 267
Garrod, A., 69
Gaskin, J.C.A., 256, 265–266
Geertz, C., 108, 113, 119, 124
Gibbs, D., 137, 152
Gibson, H.M., 304, 319
Gieryn, T.F., 32, 39
Gijsberts, M., 70, 340, 363
Gill, R., 223, 244
Givón, T., 56, 69
Glaser, B., 84, 90, 98
Glass, J., 296, 312, 319
Glock, C.Y., 48–49, 69–70, 252, 266–267, 297–298, 319–320
Godelier, M., 104, 124
Goetz, J.P., 12, 24
Goffman, E., 108–109, 113, 124, 270–271, 289
Goldstein, B., 250, 265
Goodale, J., 250, 267
Gorsuch, R., 292, 304, 317, 319
Gothoni, R., 98
Gottwald, E., 157, 175
Gough, I., 124
Gräb, W., 266
Graham, G., 69

Granqvist, P., 296, 319
Grimes, R.L., 96, 98, 108–110, 117, 124
Grob, S.Z., xv
Grom, B., 291, 304, 319
Gronover, M., 159, 176
Gross, R.M., 92, 98
Grotenhuis, M.K., 69
Guest, M., 290
Guha, A.-A., 341–342, 363
Gutmann, A., 70
Guttandin, F., 250, 265

Habermas, J., 8, 10, 13, 24, 31, 53, 157, 175
Hagekull, B., 296, 319
Hahn, L.E., 24
Haight, B.K., 198, 212, 214–215
Haight, R., 194–195
Halstead, J.M., 244
Hammond, P., 250, 266
Hansebo, G., 211, 214
Hanson, E., 211, 213
Hanson, N.R., 73–74, 77–81, 87
Harden, R., 368, 384
Harkness, J., 67, 69
Harper, M., 323, 337
Harris, C., 385
Hartshorne, C., 99
Hasselmann, C., 56, 69
Healy, J.M., 214
Heimbrock, H.-G., 209, 212, 214
Heinisch, R., 144, 152
Heitmeyer, W., 360, 363
Hello, E., 70
Hendrix, S., 198, 214
Herbert, D., 84, 270, 275, 348, 363
Hermans, C.A.M., xiv, 66–69, 91, 97, 133, 149, 214
Hermans, D., 214
Hermans, H., 44, 69, 201, 214
Hermans-Jansen, E., 201, 214
Herms, E., 254, 266
Heron, J., 4, 24
Hervieu-Léger, D., 64, 69
Herzbrun, N.B., 296, 319
Hick, J., 63, 69
Hihlgren, M., 211, 214
Hill, B.V., 222, 223, 244
Hills, P., 140, 151
Hirschman, A., 44, 69
Ho, R., 250, 266
Hocken, P.D., 323, 337
Hoffman, M.L., 69

NAME INDEX

Hoffmann, J.P., 54, 146, 152
Hoge, D.R., 294, 296, 303–304, 312, 319–320
Holeton, D.R., 366–368, 376, 385
Honneth, A., 52, 69
Hood, R.W. Jr., 292, 304, 317, 319
Hoorn, J.F., 122, 124
Hopkins, J., 189, 192, 195
Horn, L., 198, 215
Hornsby-Smith, M.P., 219, 244
Houtepen, A., 97–98
Howells, A., 382, 385
Huber, S., xv, 249, 252, 258–259, 266, 293, 297, 319
Huberman, A.M., 82, 98
Hubert, H., 104, 124, 201
Hütte, S., 169, 175
Huizing, W., 211–212, 214
Hume, D., 71, 75, 256, 266
Hunsberger, B., 292, 304, 317, 319

Ihde, D., 6, 24
Inbody, T.L., 189–190, 196
Innes, J.M., 148
Israel, J., 46, 69

Jackson, C., 146, 149
Jackson, H., 369, 385
Jackson, R., 155–156, 170, 175
Jacoby, M., 52, 69
Janoff-Bulman, R., 201, 203–204, 209– 210, 214
Jenkins, R., 12, 24
Johnson, E.A., 189, 196
Johnson, M.E., 368, 385, 381
Jones, B., 323
Jones, C., 384
Jones, S.H., 139–140, 149, 321, 327, 336–337
Jorm, A.F., 136, 151
Joseph, S., 133, 138, 140, 149, 151–152
Jüngel, E., 255, 266
Jung, C.G., 69, 135, 151

Kant, I., 47, 69, 256, 266–267
Käppler, Ch., xv
Katz, Y.J., 67, 69, 134, 138, 141, 147, 150
Kay, W.K., xv, 136–138, 147–152, 170, 176, 321–323, 327–328, 330, 333–335, 337, 352, 360, 363, 369, 385
Kendal, D., 290
Kerner, H.-J., 319

Kerr, S., 138, 150
Kieren, D.K., 317, 319
Kim, J., 61, 69
Kitcher, P., 74, 98
Klaghofer, R., 295, 299, 312, 319
Klein, C., xv
Klein, K., 201, 203, 214
Klein, S., 201, 214
Kliss, O., 176
Klöcker, M., 267
Klosinski, G., 319, 343, 363
Knapp, N., 296, 319
Knauth, T., 157, 175
Knipscheer, C.P.M., 198, 215
Koenig, H.G., 135, 151
Kohlberg, L., 107, 124
Konijn, E.A., 122, 124
Konrad, L., 296, 319
Konstant, D., 219, 244
Krais, B., 24
Krüger, J.S., 11, 24
Kühn, U., 254, 266
Kuhn, T.S., 74–77, 98
Kuitert, H.M., 190, 196
Kunneman, H., 11–12, 24
Kunz, J.A., 211, 215
Kwiran, M., 137, 150

Lampe, G.W.H., 367, 380, 385
Lankshear, D.W., 137, 150, 244
Larson, D.B., 12, 24
Latham, R., 287, 290
Laughlin, C., 107, 124
Lavinson, D.J., 363
Lawson, E.T., 50, 69, 73, 80, 82–83, 86, 91, 97–98, 107, 124
LeCompte, M.D., 12, 24
Lemert, C., 124
Lenski, G.E., 143, 151
Lester, D., 138, 140, 150, 152
Leuener, H., 266
Leung, K., 66–67, 70, 99
Lévi-Strauss, C., 106, 112–113, 124
Lewis, C.A., 132–133, 138, 141, 148, 150–151
Lewis, J.M., 138, 150
Lewis, M., 203, 215
Lichtblau, K., 267
Littler, K., xv, 372–374, 382, 385
Lloyd-Jones, D.M., 324, 337
Lloyd-Jones, M., 324–325, 337
Loewenich, H.v., 170, 175
Loewenthal, K.M., 142, 151

NAME INDEX

397

Lord, K., 212, 214
Lötzsch, F., 256, 266
Lowther Clarke, W.K., 366, 385
Luckman, T., 143, 151, 276
Luther, M., 254–255, 265–266

MacKenzie, P., 220, 245
MacLeod, A.K., 142. 151
Maes, J., 250, 267
Malinowski, B., 103–105, 113, 116, 124
Malley, B., 98
Maltby, J., 138, 151
Mann, A., 187, 195
Margalit, A., 52, 69
Marshall, D.G., 24
Martin, L.H., 96, 98
Martin, M., 140, 148
Martin, R., 70
Mason, A.J., 367, 380, 385
Mauss, M., 103–104, 124
Mayer, P., 270, 290
Mayring, P., 163, 175
Maznah, I.R., 144, 152
McAdams, D.P., 201, 203–204, 207, 215
McCarthy, T., 24
McCauley, R.N., 50, 69, 73, 80, 82–83, 86, 91, 98, 107, 124
McCullough, M.E., 135, 151
McCutcheon, R.T., 58, 69, 98
McGrath, A.E., 181, 196, 254, 267
McGuire, M.B., 272–273, 276, 290
McManus, J., 107, 124
Mead, G.H., 103, 270–271, 275, 290
Medin, D., 64, 69
Mendelsohn, L., 31, 39
Mentzel, M., 57, 70
Merton, R.K., 32–33, 39
Mette, N., 169, 175
Meyers, R., 368, 379, 385
Miedema, S., 155, 175
Mies, L., 214
Miles, B.M., 82, 98
Miller, A.S., 146, 152
Mirels, H.L., 250, 267
Moberg, D.O., 143, 152
Mohler, P.P., 67, 69
Mol, H., 142, 152
Montgomery, A., 137, 150
Moore, M.E., 214
Moosbrugger, H., 266, 319
Morgenthaler, Ch., xv, 295, 319
Morton, T., 323
Mouton, J., 3–4, 24

Mueller, C., 61, 69
Müller, G., 254, 267
Mumford, J., 323
Münchmeier, R., 346–347, 360, 363
Munayer, S.J., 132, 152
Munro, B., 317, 319
Murphy, J., 217, 244
Murray, I.H., 325, 337

Nelson, H.M., 294, 304, 320
Neto. F., 133, 149
Newcomb, T.M., 304, 320
Ng, P., 132, 138, 150
Nice, R., 24
Nieuwesteeg, J.J., 198, 215
Nipkow, K.E., 157, 175
Noble, J., 323
Nurmi, J.-E., 350, 363

O'Collins, G., 290
O'Grady, P., 40
O'Keeffe, B., 223–224
Ogden, C.K., 105, 124
Oomens, S., 69
Oser, F., 295, 299, 312, 319
Oste, J.P., 198, 215
Oviedo, H.C., 133, 148
Ozer, D., 214

Packer, M.J., 214
Pals, D., 49, 70
Pamuk, O., 41, 70
Pargement, K.I., 77, 98
Parker, K.A., 92, 98
Passeron, J.-C., 12, 24
Patten, L., 203
Patten, A.H., 215
Payne, V.J., 321, 337
Pearson, P.R., 136–137,147, 150, 304, 319, 321, 327, 337
Peirce, C.S., 74, 77–79, 85, 89, 91–94, 97–99
Perkins, M., 348, 363
Pesch, O.H., 254, 266, 267
Peters, A., 254, 267
Peters, J., 49, 69
Peters, V., 99
Petrillo, G.H., 294, 296, 303–304, 312, 319
Philipchalk, R., 138, 150, 328, 336
Piaget, J., 106–107, 445, 124
Pieterse, H.J.C., 14, 25, 45, 71
Pleijter, A., 61, 70

NAME INDEX

Pollard, G., 155, 176
Poloma, M.M., 334, 337
Popper, K., 28, 33–34, 39–40, 73–76, 82, 99
Posel, D., 3, 25
Potter, H., 251
Potter, V.G., 93, 99
Potvin, R.H., 304, 320
Poyntz, C., 220, 244
Pyysiäinen, I., 99

Ragin, Ch., 60, 66, 70, 73–74, 82–85, 87–91, 99
Rahner, K., 255, 267
Randall, K., 322, 337, 374, 385
Rappaport, R.A., 80, 99
Rawls, J., 44, 70
Ray, J., 250, 267
Rayment-Pichard, H., 382, 385
Reagan, C.E., 6, 25
Rehm, J., 254, 267
Reinharz, S., 13, 25
Reiss, P., 371, 385
Revelle, W., 137, 152
Reviere, R., 116, 124
Reynolds, J., 203, 207, 215
Rich, E.E., 217, 244
Richard, M., 259, 266
Richards, A.I., 274, 290
Richards, I.A., 105, 124
Rickers, F., 157, 175
Ricoeur, P., 6–8, 10–11, 17, 21, 24–25, 29–32, 34, 40, 43–44, 48, 51–53, 70
Riedl, A., 340, 345, 363
Riegel, U., xv, 352, 363
Rigby, P., 40
Rippl, S., 344, 363
Robbins, M., 67, 69, 134, 137–138, 140–141, 150, 152, 323, 327, 337, 363, 382–384
Robinson, G.D., 31, 40
Rocklin, T., 137, 152
Roman, R.E., 138, 152
Ross, H., 211, 213
Rubin, D.C., 213
Ruiter, S., 65, 70
Rydgren, J., 340–341, 363

Sagberg, S., 155, 176
Sahin, A., 67, 70, 147, 152
Saludadez, J.A., 5, 25
Sanford, R.N., 344, 363
Santosh, R., 67–69, 138, 150

Satlow, M., 59, 70
Sayer, A., 11, 25
Schechner, R., 108–110, 125
Scheepers, P., 70, 312, 320
Scheepers, P.L.H., 69, 340, 363
Scheidler, M., 176
Schenk, J., 144, 152
Scherer-Rath, M., 24, 71
Schilderman, H., xiv, xv, 62, 70, 101, 113, 117, 125
Schillebeeckx, E., 50, 70, 98
Schlenker, C., 176
Schmidt, C., 163, 175
Schmitt, M., 250, 267
Schoenrade, P., 135, 148
Schoonenberg, P., 50, 70
Schreiner, P., 155–156, 176
Schreuder, O., 49, 69
Schroots, J.J.F., 198, 201, 215
Schüssler Fiorenza, F., 97, 99
Schütz, A., 104, 125
Schütze, F., 201, 203, 215
Schwartz, S., 31, 40
Schweitzer, F., xv, 156–160, 171–174, 176, 319
Scott, J., 270–272, 289
Segers, J., 88, 99
Seyfarth, C., 250, 267
Shakespeare, S., 382, 385
Shapiro, J.J., 24
Shuster, M., 287, 290
Shuter-Dyson, R., 138, 152
Sieg, U., 156, 176
Smith, C.M., 191, 196
Smith, E.I., 296, 304, 319
Smith, J., 54, 56, 70
Smith, K.K., 25
Smith, M.M., 86, 99
Smith, P., 250, 267
Sonnberger, K.I., 63, 70
Spilka, B., 292, 304, 317, 319
Sprondel, W.M., 250, 267
Staal, F., 102, 125
Stanton, N., 323
Stark, R., 48, 70, 73, 82, 99, 142, 145–146, 152, 252, 267, 297, 320
Steinacker, P., 170, 175
Steinke, I., 162, 175
Sterkens, C., 66–68, 91, 97
Stewart, A.J., 214
Strange, W.A., 365–366, 385
Strauss, A., 84–85, 90, 98–99, 290
Streib, H., 125, 266

NAME INDEX

Svehla,G., 304, 320
Swiggers, P., 93, 98
Sykes, S.W., 185–187, 191, 196, 385

Tappan, M.B., 214
Taylor, C., 52, 70, 179, 196
ten Have, P., 89, 99
ter Hark, M., 34, 40
Terwey, M., 253, 267
Thangaraj, M., 56, 70
Thatcher, A., 218, 244
Theunissen, M., 54, 70
Thévenot, L., 53, 68
Thomas, D.L., 296, 320,
Thomas, H., 374, 385
Thomas, T.H., 373, 385
Thompson, E.H., 143–144, 152
Thompson, J., 277, 290
Thompson, J.B., 25, 40
Thönissen, W., 255, 267
Towler, R., 184–185, 196
Tramitz, C., 341, 363
Tromp, T., xv, 211–212, 214
Tronto, J., 212, 215
Tugwell, S., 323, 337
Turner, V., 108–110, 125
Tusting, K., 290
Tworuschka, U., 267
Tyrell, H., 250, 267

Ultee, W.C., 38, 40, 65–66, 70
Urquart, C., 323

Valdés, M., 40
Valkenberg, P., 45, 63, 70
van de Vijver, F., 66–67, 69–70, 99
van der Vyver, J., 68
van den Berg, J., 52, 70
van den Hengel, J., 40
van den Hoonaard, W.C., 84, 89, 99
van der Slik, F., 312, 320
van der Ven, J.A., xiii–xiv, 4, 14, 24–25,
    28, 40, 42, 45, 55, 60, 71, 214, 252,
    267, 271, 275–276, 290, 348 363
van Dongen, L., 198, 201, 215
van Heijst, A., 212, 215
Vascovics, L.A., 212, 214
Ventis, W.L., 135, 148
Verschuren, D., 88, 99
Verweij, J., 61, 71
Vial, Th., 50, 71
Vij, S., 134, 150
Vine, I., 135, 152

Virgo, T., 323, 325, 337
Visser, J., 199, 214
von Kardorff, E., 162, 175

Wacquant, L.J.D., 5, 13, 20, 22, 24
Wagner, H., 256, 267
Wagner-Friedrich, J., 254, 267
Wahl, K., 341, 363
Wainwright, G., 384
Wakeman, H., 193, 196
Walford, G., 220, 244
Walker, A., 323, 337
Walker, L.D., 203, 214
Wallis, A., 324–325, 337
Wallis, J., 324, 337
Walsh, W.H., 256, 267
Ward, F., 274, 290
Watson, B., 244
Watson, K., 245, 220
Watt, L.M., 201, 215
Waxman, S., 64, 69
Weber, M., 28, 32, 44, 47, 63, 71, 102,
    125, 250–251, 267
Webster, J.D., 214–215
Weigert, A.J., 296, 320
Weinsheimer, J., 24
Weiss, P., 99
Weisse, W., 156–157, 175–176
Wester, F., 99
Westerhof, G., 214
Whitaker, E.C., 367, 385
White, A., 140, 150
White, A.D., 32, 40
White, G., 270, 273, 275, 290
Whitehouse, H., 86, 99
Wilcox, C., 137, 139–140, 144, 146,
    149, 151–152
Willaime, J.-P., 156, 175
Willi, J., 294, 320
Williams, E., 137, 152
Williams, R., 250, 266
Wilson, G., 146, 149
Wilting, J., 250, 267
Winnicott, D.W., 343, 363
Winter, M., 192, 196
Witte, J., 68, 70
Wolf, C., 253, 267
Wollack, S., 250, 267
Wong, P.T.P., 198, 201, 215
Wood, A.W., 256, 267
Woodhead, L., 290
Worthington, E.L., 296, 318
Wössner, J., 292, 320

NAME INDEX

Wraight, H., 278, 289
Wulff, D., 49, 71

Yablon, Y., 138, 141, 150
Yarnold, E.J., 366, 384
Youtika, A., 133, 138, 152

Zahl, P.F.M., 187, 196
Ziebertz, H.-G., xv, 4, 25, 28, 40, 71,
133, 141, 151, 170, 176, 348, 352,
360, 363
Zwingmann, C., 266, 319

SUBJECT INDEX

abduction, 73–74, 78–79, 81–83, 85–87, 92–93
academy, xi, xiii–xiv, 69–70, 177, 221
adolescents, xv, 133, 144, 155–176, 231, 237, 284, 312, 341, 343
  pre-adolescents, 295, 316–318, 338–363, 367 *see also* children
adults, 173, 179, 198–199, 241, 272, 296, 367, 369
Adventists, xv, 269, 278, 282–283, 285–286
affiliation, religious, 129–131, 140, 160, 249–265, 322, 346, 348
agency, 13–15, 80, 212, 275, 289
alterity, 41, 51, 68
Anglicans, xv, 63, 131, 177, 180, 217–219, 274, 277, 322, 326, 336–337, 365, 367–368, 373–374, 377, 382–383
Apostolic Networks, xv, 321–323, 325–327, 331, 334–337
atonement, 181–195
autonomy, 7–8, 29, 41, 44, 116, 205, 208, 210, 296
awareness, 75, 88, 133, 163, 231
  self-, xiii, 85

baptism, 50, 329–333, 365–385
Baptists, 131, 322, 326
belief, xv, 30, 33, 35, 37, 39, 48, 55, 58, 78, 82, 85, 95, 98, 102–103, 106, 109, 113, 118–120, 123, 129–131, 139, 146, 148, 152, 165, 168, 179–180, 184–186, 193, 196, 209–210, 221, 224, 232, 238, 243, 249, 251–257, 259–261, 263–266, 269–270, 272–274, 281, 283–284, 286–287, 289, 293, 296, 302, 304, 318, 322–323, 328, 336, 347–348, 350–351, 355–357, 368, 373, 382
  personal, xv, 249, 252, 365, 373, 382
  religious, 98, 129, 131, 148, 249, 252, 254, 256, 264–266, 296, 318, 347, 355–357

Calvinists, 47, 63, 250, 323
capitalism, 33, 47, 250

Catholics, 49–50, 62–63, 95, 101, 131, 150, 155–156, 158–160, 163–169, 171, 196, 217–220, 244, 249, 253–265, 278, 297, 332–333, 346, 352–353, 365–366, 368, 370, 374, 378–383
children, xv, 45, 52–55, 64–65, 106, 133, 143, 156–158, 160, 166–167, 173–174, 179, 190, 217–245, 270–272, 291–320, 341, 343–344, 365–385
Christology, 46, 97, 180, 199, 277, 280, 328
Church in Wales, xv, 365, 368, 371–373, 377, 380, 382–385
Church of England, 219–220, 244, 278, 337, 368–371, 377, 381–382, 384–385
churchmanship, 321–322, 365, 374, 378, 380, 382
classification, 12, 23, 48, 61–63, 83, 89–90, 111, 205, 225, 310, 321–322, 326–327, 329, 335
clergy, xv, 46, 177, 288, 321–322, 324, 327, 329, 337, 365, 368, 373–383, 385
  -men, 365, 373–388
  -women, 365, 373
cognitive, 30, 37–38, 40, 44, 49, 51, 69, 71, 86, 96–98, 106–107, 111, 121–123, 129, 186, 214, 251, 258, 272, 298, 312
communication, 7, 11, 14–16, 24, 31, 38, 50, 69–70, 113, 157, 173, 178, 185, 193, 221, 229, 239, 271, 275, 305, 317, 352
  see also dialogue/dialogical
communicative action, theory of, 157
communion, xv, 204, 365–385
  see also eucharist
comparative research, xv, 39, 41–71, 88, 90–91, 95–96, 127–152
culture, 7, 10–11, 13–15, 21, 24, 28–29, 34, 39, 42–48, 52–53, 57, 59–60, 65–70, 80, 86–87, 97–99, 102–113, 116–117, 124, 131, 140, 150–152, 157, 169, 214, 219, 222–223, 241, 243, 251, 270, 272, 285, 318, 321,

SUBJECT INDEX

339–346, 348, 350–352, 354–356, 363
crosscultural, 59, 96
intercultural, 21, 352
multicultural, 11, 70, 156, 171, 240, 339
pluralism, 344, 355
sociocultural, 31, 35, 37–39, 110–113, 116, 122, 350, 352

data, xiii–xv, 11–12, 16, 60–62, 65, 73–75, 78, 81–89, 92–93, 138, 141, 144–145, 155, 158, 161, 170–172, 174, 177, 183, 188, 190–191, 193–194, 198, 220, 223–225, 241–242, 252–253, 256, 264, 281, 284, 291, 297, 302–306, 309, 312, 317–318, 327, 334, 340, 352, 362, 365, 374–375, 377–378, 380–399
analysis, 14–15, 19, 70, 91, 98–99, 300, 373
collection, 14, 28, 61, 277, 299, 306
description, 61
display, 20
narrative, 200
numerical, 59
verbal, 59
see also empirical; comparative research; qualitative; quantitative
denominations/denominational, xv, 46, 51, 63, 66, 101, 127, 131, 155–161, 163–169, 171–174, 217–218, 223–224, 233, 249–250, 253–255, 257–258, 260–261, 263–265, 286, 297, 321–326, 328, 330–333, 335, 353
dialogue/dialogical, 8, 29, 34, 56, 64, 68, 70, 85, 135, 139, 142, 155–161, 167–173, 175–176, 266–267, 276, 352, 357–358, 360, 362
ecumenical, 254
learning, 155, 157, 173
religious education, xv, 155, 157–161, 167–173
self, 276
distanciation, xiv, 3–4, 6–13, 15–23
distancing, 7, 8, 27–30, 32, 36, 39–40
self-, 8–9

ecumenical, xv, 155, 157, 254, 269, 278, 282–283, 286, 333, 335
education, 15, 24, 70, 140, 156, 180, 206, 213, 217–227, 229–231,

233, 239–241, 243–245, 269–270, 278–279, 281–287, 293–294, 319, 340, 343–345, 349, 354, 356, 360, 362–363, 370
Christian schools, xv, 233–245
religious education, xi, xiii, xv, 69, 149–150, 152, 155–161, 167–176, 218, 224, 231, 244, 254, 298–299, 307–314
theological education, 177–179, 195, 278
empirical, 40, 51, 71, 144, 179, 244, 287, 289, 319, 349, 363
ascertainment, 85
analysis, 31, 144, 264
characteristic, 102
concepts, 340
content, 211
cycle, 36–37
data, 28, 170, 224, 347, 356, 358
evidence, 128–129, 174, 190, 197, 212, 250, 253
example, 130
facts, 34, 8
grounds/basis, 142, 170
indicators, 140, 222
inference, 75
inquiry/explanation, 61, 74, 81, 113, 339, 348
insight, 39
literature, 135, 139
measures, 196
methodology, 4, 27
models, 286
operationalism, 258
phenomena, 35–36, 105
psychology, 96, 127
reality, 33, 36, 92
reports, 106
research, xi, xiii–xv, 3, 5–6, 10–11, 20, 23–25, 27, 30, 35–38, 47–48, 71, 73–74, 76, 82–84, 87–88, 90–91, 102–103, 127, 130, 132–134, 148–149, 155, 170–171, 174, 190, 214, 222–223, 250, 269, 276, 291, 304, 321, 363;
see also comparative research; qualitative; quantitative
researcher, 13
results, 175
science, 73–75
study/studies, 48, 53, 63, 77, 101, 103, 125, 139, 170, 176, 254, 256, 265, 289, 296–297, 304, 312, 363

SUBJECT INDEX

task, 132
testing, 86, 91, 95, 122, 300, 305
theology, xiii, 3–6, 10–11, 17, 20, 23,
   27–28, 37, 39, 68, 87, 127–128,
   152, 195, 197, 214, 223, 241,
   252–253, 289, 319, 337
value, 130
work, 123, 170–171, 190, 299
world, 60
empirical-theological
literature, 276
models, 269, 272, 277, 283, 287, 289
study, 289
epistemology/epistemic, xv, 4–6, 13,
   17, 19, 21–24, 27–28, 30–33, 35–37,
   39, 69, 73–76, 81, 86–87, 97, 101,
   121–123
   see also empirical; experience;
   justification; knowledge; objectivity;
   perception; postmodernism/
   postmodernity
evangelicals/evangelicalism, xv, 177,
   180–181, 187–191, 217, 220–222,
   244–245, 269, 278, 282–283, 286,
   323–326, 328, 336–337, 365, 374,
   378–383, 385
eucharist, 49–50, 55, 83, 95, 164–165,
   365–368, 372, 377, 382
   see also communion
experience, xv, 11, 20–21, 29, 41, 44,
   47–48, 50–51, 53, 55, 64–65, 74,
   80, 85–86, 95–96, 98, 104, 108–109,
   112–116, 119–120, 122–124, 136,
   140, 142–143, 146, 148, 155,
   159–160, 166–169, 172, 179, 182,
   186, 189, 191–192, 194, 197–198,
   202–203, 205, 208, 211, 219–222,
   224, 226, 228–229, 231–232,
   234–243, 252, 259, 263, 271,
   275, 291, 295, 298–299, 301, 303,
   307–308, 312, 318, 326, 329, 333,
   336–337, 339–346, 351, 354, 360,
   362, 368
religious, 74, 81, 84–85, 89, 95–96,
   138, 151
extraversion, 128, 136–138, 149–150,
   152, 321, 327, 330–331, 333–335, 337

family, xv, 45, 52, 64, 131, 143, 206,
   208, 232, 237, 243, 270–271,
   291–320
Free Church, 63, 217–218
functionalism, 103–104, 107–108, 111,
   113–115, 118, 124, 270

gender, 10, 14, 18, 21, 52, 142–145,
   147–152, 269, 280, 283–284, 300,
   317, 320, 328, 330–331, 336–337,
   339, 347
trans-, 269, 277, 280, 283–287

habitus, 3, 11, 13, 20–23, 360
hermeneutics, 3, 6–11, 13, 16–18,
   23–25, 27, 29–34, 36, 38–40, 42–43,
   57, 64, 68, 163, 200, 214, 251

idea(s), xv, 3–7, 9, 12–13, 16, 19–20,
   22, 28–30, 37, 56, 60, 63, 67, 73–75,
   77, 81–88, 90–93, 103, 106–108,
   137, 181, 185–188, 191–192, 195,
   219, 232, 250–251, 254, 259,
   274, 301, 337, 340, 342, 347,
   361
-complexes 185
identity, xiii, 10, 33, 41–45, 48–49,
   51–53, 57–59, 61, 63–64, 68,
   101–102, 104, 113, 117–119, 122,
   129, 152, 158, 196, 198–199, 207,
   211, 215, 220, 243, 245, 258, 263,
   274–276, 322, 326, 348, 361, 363
cultural, 43–44, 68, 102, 348
denominational, 158, 258, 263
personal, 33, 117, 199, 207
religious, xiv, 41–45, 47–49, 53,
   56–59, 63–64, 68
social, 44, 57–58, 104
individual differences, 127–152
information, 11, 37, 84, 94, 129, 204,
   206, 207, 211, 229, 250, 267, 313,
   328, 351, 365, 384
interactionism, 103, 107–109, 112–113,
   117
symbolic, 270
introversion, 128, 136, 327, 334

justification, 68, 75, 179, 195, 199, 209,
   222, 249–251, 253–257, 259–261,
   263–264, 267, 345

knowledge, 7–8, 12, 14–15, 17–18, 22,
   24, 27–37, 40, 48, 73–74, 85, 92,
   94–95, 97, 111–112, 169, 177–179,
   195, 212, 220, 237, 239, 242, 289,
   377, 380
absolute, 7, 34, 94
objectifying, 7
personal, 178
total, 7
truthful, 3–4, 17, 23

404 SUBJECT INDEX

language, 11, 14, 16, 25, 30, 51–52,
76, 96, 104–105, 107, 112, 124, 130,
132–133, 180, 184–186, 190–191,
193, 204, 209, 251, 275, 277, 280,
285, 368
linguistic, 29–30, 40, 67, 105–106,
110–111, 127, 132, 202–203, 205,
208
equivalence, 60, 66
Lutherans, 63, 249, 253–257, 260–262,
346, 353, 383

mass, *see* eucharist
meaning, 5–7, 9, 11–12, 27, 29–39,
41, 51, 62, 84–85, 87, 89–90,
95, 102–103, 105–114, 117–121,
124–125, 131, 159, 164–165,
180–181, 185–186, 192–193,
197–203, 209–214, 271–273, 275,
284, 287, 292, 299, 317, 340, 342,
352
mental health, 134–139
Methodists, 278, 322

narrative, xv, 5, 20, 49, 56, 106, 110,
119, 139, 185, 197–206, 209–215,
222, 348, 369
analysis, 197, 213
autobiographical, xv, 197–198, 200
autonomy, 205
coherence, 44
competence, 197–198, 202, 205–206,
208, 212–213
construction, 197, 200, 209, 214
data, 200
identity, 198
method, 197, 199
organisation, 199
quality, 203
self-, 201, 214
structure, 177
narrator, 199–203, 206–209
neuroticism, 136, 138–139, 150–151,
321, 327, 330–331, 333–334,
337
New Churches, 274, 322, 326, 328

objectivity, xiii, 4–6, 9, 12–13, 21, 28,
31, 34, 39–40, 92, 96, 98, 181, 197,
221–222, 241, 243, 306, 309, 343
objective truth, 92, 96
ontological, 4, 7, 10, 13, 121, 188, 277
ordinary theology, xv, 177–180, 185,
195, 243

participation, xiv, 3–11, 13–23, 27–36,
39, 45, 51, 64, 66, 96–97, 101, 119,
123, 140, 143, 149, 165, 319, 345,
366, 377
Pentecostals, xv, 84–85, 269, 276,
278, 282–283, 285–288, 321–323,
326–328, 334–335, 337
perception, 12, 34, 110, 122, 173, 211,
239, 306, 310–11, 315–317, 360
self-, 289, 295, 339, 347, 349–351,
357, 360
personality, xv, 77, 98, 122, 128,
135–136, 138, 141, 143–152, 201,
204, 215, 235, 237, 252, 258, 265,
267, 272, 319, 321–323, 326–331,
333–337, 339, 342, 344–345, 363
theory, xv, 77, 321–322, 326–327,
335–336
see also extraversion; introversion;
neuroticism; psychoticism
phenomena, xv, 10–11, 28, 30, 31, 35,
36, 44–45, 58, 63, 64, 81, 83, 85–86,
88–90, 97, 101, 103, 105, 107, 128,
178, 202–203, 252, 317, 343, 350, 352
phenomenology, 10, 54, 86
pluralism, *see* religious pluralism
positivism, 4, 13, 23–24, 33, 39
postmodernism/postmodernity, 3–5,
20–21, 24, 54, 176
poststructuralism, 4
preaching, 196, 249, 252, 283, 287,
289–290, 324
Presbyterians, *see* Calvinists
Protestants, 33, 63, 131, 155–156,
158–160, 163–169, 249–250,
253–254, 256–267, 297, 323–324,
346, 352, 366
psychoticism, 136–138, 146, 149–151,
165–167, 321, 327, 330, 333–334,
336–337

qualitative
assessment, 197
data, 65, 98
design, 24
dualism, 17
material, 155, 162–163
method/methodology, xi, 4, 28, 30,
41, 59–60, 62, 64–68, 70–71, 84,
90, 99, 155, 175, 180
perspectives, xv, 154–245
research, 3–10, 12, 15–20, 23, 25, 27,
29, 35, 41, 59, 61–62, 73–74, 82,
88–91, 99, 162, 175, 180, 213

SUBJECT INDEX

researcher, 5, 15, 19, 35, 60, 90
studies/investigation, 67, 170, 195, 276
quantitative
  data, 91, 213, 269, 276
  dualism, 17
  instrument, 288
  measures, 197
  method/methodology, xi, 4, 28, 30, 41, 59–60, 62, 64–68, 155
  perspectives, xv, 247–385
  research, xiv, 3–10, 12–15, 17–20, 23, 25, 27–29, 35, 59, 61–62, 73–74, 82, 88–91, 151
  researcher, 5, 19, 35, 60, 90
  results, 163
  strategies, 70
  studies/surveys, 28, 62, 67, 162, 174
  technique, 66

reflexivity, 3, 13, 20–24
religiosity, 67, 70, 77, 99, 127–129, 131, 133, 136, 138, 141–147, 149–152, 176, 249, 252, 257–266, 291–293, 297–298, 300, 302–303, 305–307, 309–311, 313–317, 320, 336–337, 358, 360, 363
  inter-, 357, 359
  mono-, 357, 359
  multi-, 350, 357, 359
  see also belief, religious; experience, religious; identity, religious; individual differences; ritual
religious pluralism, xv, 68, 97, 339, 346–347, 349–351, 353, 359–362
reminiscence, 198–199, 203, 206–207, 211–212
retroduction, 73–75, 78–79, 82, 85, 93
ritual, xv, 42, 44–51, 56, 58, 61, 64, 69, 73, 80–88, 91, 96–99, 101–125, 186, 252, 258, 275, 291, 298, 301–308, 368

sample/sampling, 12, 14, 137, 140–141, 144–145, 152, 160, 162, 171, 173, 180–181, 183–188, 190–191, 193–194, 201, 252, 256–258, 263–264, 269–272, 277–279, 286, 297, 301, 329–330, 339, 351–353, 358, 373
schools, see education
social sciences, xiv, 5–7, 24–25, 28, 77, 87, 95–96, 99, 102, 106, 115, 123–124, 127–130, 135, 139, 142, 147, 150, 197, 200, 223, 288, 300

social scientist, xiv, 96, 124, 129–130
socialization, xv, 20, 142–143, 145, 173, 188, 269, 277, 279–287, 291–296, 305, 311, 313, 317, 319, 341, 344, 362
  factors in, xv, 47, 173, 179, 269–270, 281–286, 295–296
  religious, xv, 169, 291–296, 299, 309–310, 312, 316–317, 319
  theory, 142–143, 276
soteriology, xv, 180, 185–186
  confused/difficulties over, 190–193
  evangelical, 187, 189
  exemplarist, 181–183
  ordinary, 177, 180, 186, 194
  traditionalist, 184, 189
  see also atonement
stimulus, 13, 64
structuralism, 103, 105–108, 111–113, 117, 122, 124, 270
  post- 4
subjective/subjectivity, 4, 6–9, 13, 21, 28–29, 31, 38, 92, 149, 181–183, 198–200, 306, 349, 351

theologians, xi, xiii–xiv, 95–96, 129–130, 134, 142, 147, 187, 191, 193, 219, 223, 250, 254–255, 277
theology/theological, xi, xiii–xv, 14, 25–25, 40, 63, 68–71, 98–99, 125, 128–130, 133–135, 138–139, 147, 149–150, 158, 164, 176–178, 180–198, 200, 204, 212, 214, 217, 219–225, 241–244, 249–269, 276, 278–281, 284–287, 289, 302, 319, 322–324, 326, 335–337, 365, 367–378, 379–382, 385
  academic, xiii–xiv, 175, 178–180, 185, 191, 195, 221
  data, xiii–xiv
  discipline, 101
  education, 131, 177–179, 195, 278
  empirical, see empirical; empirical-theological
  exemplarist, 181
  listening, 179
  liturgical, 186
  materials, xiii
  models, 97, 141, 157, 269, 276–277, 281, 283
  moral, 135, 139
  notions, xiii
  ordinary, xv, 177–180, 185, 195, 243
  questions/problems, xiv, 39, 102

SUBJECT INDEX

reflection, 201, 209, 218–219
research, 71, 73, 269
sediment, 249, 252–257, 261,
    263–264
student, xv, 269, 272, 277–278, 285,
    287, 289
systematic, 102, 188, 196
theory, 95
see also atonement; Christology;
    soteriology; Trinity/Trinitarian
theory, xiv–xv, 157, 182–184, 186–188,
    223, 250, 270–271, 273, 276,
    341–342
theoretical perspectives, xiv–xv, 1–152
see also personality theory
traditionalism, 184
transcendence, xiii, 41, 44, 61, 69, 74,
    77, 80, 82, 84, 94–95, 97, 122, 274

Trinity/Trinitarian, xv, 46, 269,
    272–273, 276–278, 280–290, 385
truth/truthful, xiv, 3–10, 17–20, 22–25,
    27–30, 33–36, 46, 68–69, 73–75, 86,
    92–94, 96, 168, 172, 188, 337, 344,
    348, 351–352, 357, 363

United Reformed Church, 278

well-being, 77, 103, 128, 134, 139–141,
    197–215

xenophobia, xv, 339–351, 353–363

youth, *see* adolescents

EMPIRICAL STUDIES IN THEOLOGY

1. VEN, VAN DER, J.A. *God Reinvented?* A Theological Search in Texts and Tables. 1998. ISBN 978 90 04 11330 5
2. VIAU, M. *Practical Theology.* A New Approach. 1999. ISBN 978 90 04 11440 1
3. VERMEER, P. *Learning Theodicy.* The Problem of Evil and the Praxis of Religious Education. 1999. ISBN 978 90 04 11650 4
4. ZUIDBERG, G. *The God of the Pastor.* The Spirituality of Roman Catholic Pastors in the Netherlands. 2001. ISBN 978 90 04 11700 6
5. PIETERSE, H.J.C. (ed.) *Desmond Tutu's Message.* A Qualitative Analysis. 2001. ISBN 978 90 04 12050 1
6. ZUIDGEESt, P. *The Absence of God.* Exploring the Christian Tradition in a Situation of Mourning. 2001. ISBN 978 90 04 12057 0
7. HERMANS, C.A.M. ET AL., (eds.) *Social Constructionism and Theology.* 2002. ISBN 978 90 04 12318 2
8. STERKENS, C. *Interreligious* Learning. The Problem of Interreligious Dialogue in Primary Education. 2001. ISBN 978 90 04 12380 9
9. HERMANS, C.A.M. Participatory Learning. *Religious Education in a Globalizing Society.* 2003. ISBN 978 90 04 13001 2
10. VEN, VAN DER, J.A. & M. SCHERER-RATH (eds.) *Normativity and Empirical Research in Theology.* 2004. ISBN 978 90 04 12663 3
11. HERMANS, C.A.M. & M.E. MOORE (eds.) *Hermeneutics and Empirical Research in Practical Theology.* The Contribution of Empirical Theology by Johannes A. van der Ven. 2004. ISBN 978 90 04 14208 4
12. SCHILDERMAN, H. *Religion as a Profession.* 2005. ISBN 978 90 04 14452 1
13. SMEETS, W. *Spiritual Care in a Hospital Setting.* An Empirical-theological Exploration. 2006. ISBN 978 90 04 15189 5
14. SCHILDERMAN, H. (ed.) *Discourse in Ritual Studies.* 2006. ISBN 978 90 04 15800 9
15. STREIB, H. (ed.) *Religion inside and outside Traditional Institutions.* 2007. ISBN 978 90 04 15792 7
16. SAKWA, M.M. *Bible and Poverty in Kenya.* An Empirical Exploration. 2008. ISBN 978 90 04 16462 8
17. FRANCIS, L.J., M. ROBBINS & J. ASTLEY (eds.) *Empirical Theology in Texts and Tables.* Qualitative, Quantitative and Comparative Perspectives. 2009. ISBN 978 90 04 16888 6